D0850406

REVIEW of PERSONALITY
and SOCIAL PSYCHOLOGY:1

REVIEW OF
PERSONALITY AND SOCIAL PSYCHOLOGY

Editor: LADD WHEELER, *University of Rochester*

Associate Editors:
Henry Alker, *Humanistic Psychology Institute, San Francisco*
Clyde Hendrick, *University of Miami*
Lawrence S. Wrightsman, *University of Kansas*

Editorial Board

WITHDRAWN
REVIEW
of
PERSONALITY
and
SOCIAL
PSYCHOLOGY

———————1———————

Edited by
LADD WHEELER

Published in cooperation with the SOCIETY FOR PERSONALITY AND
SOCIAL PSYCHOLOGY (Division 8, American Psychological Association)

 SAGE PUBLICATIONS   Beverly Hills   London

Copyright © 1980 by Sage Publications, Inc.

For information address:

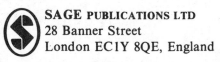

SAGE PUBLICATIONS, INC.
275 South Beverly Drive
Beverly Hills, California 90212

SAGE PUBLICATIONS LTD
28 Banner Street
London EC1Y 8QE, England

Printed in the United States of America

International Standard Book Number 0-8039-1457-1 (hardcover)
0-8039-1458-X (softcover)

International Standard Serial Number 0270-1987

FIRST PRINTING

CONTENTS

Editor's Introduction

T his new annual series was originated by the Society for Personality and Social Psychology (Division 8 of the American Psychological Association) as a special means of international communication. A current problem in our field is that personality and social psychologists do not know one another's work. It is true that they read some of the same journals, but each group also has its more specialized journals and book series, and the information overload can be impossible. As a social psychologist, I am not likely to find the time to read many long and detailed empirical studies in personality. But I *do* want to know what is happening in that closely allied field, and I want my students to know. For example, in this first volume, I learned more about personality measurement from McClelland's chapter than I would have believed possible from such a small investment of time. And my view of personality theory was drastically changed by Wiggins's chapter. I believe a similar benefit will be gained by readers who are primarily steeped in the literature of personality—and who are likely to find valuable insights from social psychologists in the pages that follow.

A second problem is that we North Americans aren't very much aware of advances made in other places. Only a handful of American psychologists are aware of Gudman Smith's 20-year research program on perceptgenesis (described in this volume). By having a distinguished international Editorial Board, we hope to help reduce this type of provincialism.

In a letter to me after I was named Editor, Irwin Altman wrote: "I feel that the *Review* should not only be a summary and integration of established areas of personality and social psychology, but I would very much like to see it receptive to emerging areas that have a sufficient base of empirical and theoretical work. In this respect, the *Review* can serve as *the* main evolutionary vehicle of the field . . . ." I agreed with Irv then, I agree now—let us try to achieve these goals. In our endeavor, we welcome the suggestions of our readers and colleagues in the areas of personality and social psychology for topics and authors (both in North America and abroad).

The *Review* will not be limited to any particular type of article, and—as you will see—there are many types in this first volume. We will always try, however, to focus on the frontiers of theory and method. We have tried to select articles of fascination to any serious graduate student or professional, and the articles have been written without the assumption of extensive background in the area. The decision of the Society to publish the *Review* in both soft- and hardcover editions is consistent with our belief that it should be read, marked, and carried around by a lot of people (not just the well-heeled).

No idea is the product of a single individual—and the concepts which led to the *Review's* debut grew out of the thoughts of a number of individuals, including Harry Triandis, Jerry Clore, James H. Davis, Ross Parke, Bibb Latané, Seymour Rosenberg, Irwin Altman, and Clyde Hendrick. I have profited from their suggestions. Another set of intellectual debts is certainly owed to the Fellows of the Society (who were generous with both their suggestions for articles, and for possible Editorial Board members); to the Editorial Board; and to the following individuals who assisted in the article review process: John Brigham, Robert C. Carson, Kenneth Craik, Germaine de Montmollin, Robert S. Feldman, G. P. Ginsburg, Irving Janis, Eric Klinger, Walter Mischel, Reidar Ommundson, Harry Reis, William McKinley Runyan, and Edward Sampson. The Associate Editors were more than helpful . . . they were wonderful! And I (as well as the Publishers) am indebted to Barbara Fox for assistance with the cover design.

This volume is the first of a series. As such, it is the first step in building a tradition. We have tried to select original essays of interest and continuing value . . . rather than to attempt a review of the published work of the previous year. The 10 to 12 articles selected for this and each of our subsequent volumes are designed to build an open-ended reference library for those who are serious about personality and social psychology. Like Bacon, I feel that some are meant to be tasted, some to be chewed, and many (if not most) to be digested over time. As the series grows, it will reflect where we are going—even more than where we have been; and, with the publication of each volume, I trust you will agree that we will share a greater insight into where we now are.

—Ladd Wheeler
Rochester, New York

Motive Dispositions

THE MERITS OF OPERANT
AND RESPONDENT MEASURES

DAVID C. McCLELLAND

David C. McClelland is Professor of Psychology at Harvard University. His research interests are in human motivation and particularly power motivation. He is the author of *Power: The Inner Experience* (Irvington).

$\mathbf{S}$o-called projective tests have been attacked as scientifically value-less ever since psychologists first began using them. The case against them usually runs as follows: Their split-half and test-retest reliabilities are low. Therefore they provide unreliable measures. If the measures are unreliable, they cannot be valid. Therefore, validity coefficients some-times obtained with them must be due to chance or some other variables. In any case, the validity coefficients often are not obtained again when they study is repeated which is only to be expected if the measures are unreliable. This is especially true when projective measures are cor-related with school performance, which is the type of performance most easily and most often obtained by psychologists to ascertain the validity of any psychological characteristic. These arguments have not gone unanswered (McClelland, 1951, 1958, 1966, 1971a, 1972; Atkinson, 1960; deCharms et al., 1955; deCharms and Muir, 1978), but the charges

AUTHOR'S NOTE: I am very grateful for comments on an earlier draft of this article by J. W. Atkinson, Richard deCharms, Heinz Heckhausen, Julius Kuhl, Dan McAdams, Bernard Weiner, and David Winter.

have been reiterated in recent years with increasing vigor (Klinger, 1966; Scott & Johnson, 1972; Entwisle, 1972). To such authors it is a matter of amazement that psychologists continue to use projective test measures when the case against them is so obvious and watertight. Entwisle (1972, p. 390) quotes with approval Jensen's statement that "A satisfactory explanation of the whole amazing phenomenon is a task for future historians of psychology and will probably have to wait upon greater knowledge of the psychology of credulity than we now possess."

These authors usually also endorse personality measures obtained from structured personality questionnaires because they are internally consistent and have high test-retest reliability. Furthermore, some scores from so-called objective tests regularly correlate with school performance, the ultimate test of validity to many psychometricians. To be sure, Mischel (1968) has complained that very reliable objective personality measures do not seem to do a very good job of predicting what people will do, but the defenders of scientific virtue simply nod their heads and admit that maybe we do not have and never will have a very good science of personality anyway.

Is it as bad as all that? Is it possible that I and others continuing to use projective tests are as credulous as Jensen makes us out to be? In view of their arguments, how can I go on working with measures like *n* Achievement or *n* power (McClelland, 1975)? I thought for years that the case for the use of a measure like *n* Achievement had been so carefully and painstakingly made that psychologists generally would understand it in time and see that the attacks made on it often contained elementary errors. But I have decided that most psychologists are busy and do not have the time to follow an argument that is a little more subtle than the one on which the attacks are based. All they know is that there have been attacks and they sound reasonable. And the more often they are repeated, the more people believe there must be something to them. So it has seemed desirable to state the case once again as carefully as possible for the so-called projective measures and, in the process of doing so, to compare their merits with those of questionnaire measures of personality.

CONSTRUCT VALIDITY

Let us begin by straightening out our terminology. I came to the study of personality as an experimental psychologist interested in a general theory of behavior. This had important consequences as we shall see in a moment for what validity meant to me. It also explains why internal consistency or test-retest correlations did not interest me much. They simply are not reported in the *Journal of Experimental Psychology* and, not being trained as a psychometrician, I had not been indoctrinated in the belief that a measure has to show high reliability before it can be used. It also led me to seek a more general term than "projective test" to describe the measures we were obtaining. For "projective" refers to a theory that people are projecting their wishes into fantasy. The fact is that we were obtaining a sample of a person's behavior or thoughts in a standardized situation. I favor referring to these thought samples as operant because in Skinner's sense it is not possible to identify the exact stimulus that elicits them. More generally speaking they are responses that the subject generates spontaneously. Not the stimulus or the response or the instructional set is strictly controlled by the experimenter.

By way of contrast, *respondent* measures often specify the stimulus, the response, and the instructional set. In a typical personality test, subjects are presented with a specific stimulus (e.g., a statement like "I work like a slave . . ."); they are limited to agreeing or disagreeing with it to a greater or lesser degree; and they are set to give an overall evaluation of their behavior in a specified area. In the Thematic Aptitude test (TAT) on the other hand, the stimulus is vague, the subject can write about anything at all, and typically does not know exactly what the experimenter is getting at. That is, subjects are not being asked to conceptualize or make judgments about their behavior. There are all sorts of gradations between these two extremes, which I have discussed more fully elsewhere (McClelland, 1951). For example, some degree of stimulus control is exercised in the TAT by varying the cue characteristics of pictures. And questionnaires can ask for factual reports of behaviors, such as whether the subject jogs regularly, which can be considered operant and which do not call for the set of self-evaluation. But for the sake of simplicity I will use the terms *operant* and *respondent* from here on to refer to extreme differences in the degree of control the experimenter exercises in obtaining responses from a subject, as illustrated by the contrast between a TAT and a self-evaluative questionnaire.

What impressed me as long ago as 1951 is that operant and respondent measures generally do not correlate with each other and therefore should provide independent estimates of different aspects of personality—even when they purport to be related to the same theme.

To put it as simply as possible, the n Achievement measure obtained by coding operant thoughts does not correlate with what I prefer to call v (for value) Achievement (deCharms et al., 1955; Atkinson & Litwin, 1960) obtained from respondent questionnaires like the Edwards (1957) Personal Preference Schedule or the Jackson (1966) Personality Research Form or the Mehrabian (1969) measure of achieving tendency. This lack of correlation bothers a lot of people and they have used it as an argument that therefore, since the v Achievement measures are more reliable, this proves that the n Achievement is not valid. To me, it demonstrated that these measures get at different aspects of personality—n Achievement at operant trends I called motives and v Achievement at values which I called schemas (McClelland, 1951). Both types of variables are necessary to predict behavior (McClelland, 1979) and nothing but confusion results from insisting these two kinds of measures are assaying the same motive disposition and therefore should correlate highly.

There are many types of operants which I would classify as stylistic traits (McClelland, 1951). In a time when critics are wondering if there is anything consistent about personality (Mischel, 1968), it is worth recalling that some of them—like verbal productivity in writing stories (Entwisle, 1972), length of speech bursts (Takala, 1977), and expressive movements (Allport and Vernon, 1931)—are quite consistent. They deserve a lot more attention in personality study, but to discuss them here would be to expand this review out of shape. So let us focus on motive measures obtained from operant thoughts, although not all measures obtained from operant thoughts reflect motives (see Loevinger, 1966; Stewart, Note 1).

How do you decide that something is a measure of a motive? The answer is clear in terms of the general theory of behavior. Ever since Melton's (1952) synthesis of earlier work, it has been generally agreed that motives drive, direct, and select behavior. Hunger in a rat (or any other animal) makes it more active *(drives)*, focuses its attention on some stimuli more than others *(directs)*, and facilitates learning a maze to get food. That is, if there is food reward, its satisfaction of the hunger drive *selects* out responses that lead to the food reward. Early work with the n Achievement score, and later work with the other motive scores, was aimed at demonstrating that the scores were measures of a motive because people who scored high in fact behaved in these three ways as if they were more motivated. Table 1, reproduced from an earlier publication (McClelland, 1971a), illustrates how the n Achievement

TABLE 1
Validity of Fantasy and Self-Report Measures
of *n* Achievement in Predicting Behavior

Motive Function

	Fantasy Measure	*Self-Report Measure*
A. Directing	Percentage taking moderate risks in a ring toss game	
Hign n Ach	61%	36%
Low n Ach	36	62
	p = .04	p = .02
B. Driving	Percentage persisting longer than average in a final examination	
High n Ach	60	42
Low n Ach	32	55
	p = .03	n.s.
C. Selecting	Percentage above average in final examination grade	
High n Ach	64	58
Low n Ach	32	46
	p = .02	n.s.

SOURCE: After Atkinson and Litwin 1960.

measure satisfies these three criteria of whether a motive is operating. Subjects scoring high in *n* Achievement persist longer, focus on moderate, challenging goals, and demonstrate that they have learned more in the course. These findings have been chosen for presentation because they make the main points of the argument in the context of a single experiment, not because they are the only or the best evidence of the functional characteristics of the achievement motive. For example, the *directing* function of *n* Achievement has been demonstrated in tachistoscopic recognition of achievement-related words (McClelland & Liberman, 1949), its *driving* function in the larger number of entrepreneurial acts it engenders (Warner et al., cited in McClelland & Winter, 1969), and its *selecting* function in the faster learning it promotes of moderately difficult materials (McClelland et al., 1953).

Table 1 also shows the results for another purported measure of *n* Achievement derived from a respondent questionnaire instrument, the Edwards Personal Preference Inventory. The *v* Achievement measure fails all three tests for the presence of a motive and therefore, if the logic of general behavior theory is correct, it cannot be considered a measure of a motive. In my terminology it is a measure of something else—the conscious value placed on achievement—a part of the self-picture. Years ago deCharms et al. (1955) demonstrated that v Achievement has different behavior correlates than n Achievement. For example, people high in v Achievement are more influenced by expert opinion than those low in v Achievement, whereas expert opinion makes no difference to people high and low in n Achievement. Why has it been so difficult to get psychologists to acknowledge that these are two different and generally *uncorrelated* measures of different aspects of personality though they often bear the same name? For that matter, why do psychometricians so preoccupied with the issue of the reliability of their measures repeatedly fail to take the elementary step of demonstrating that the respondent measures are in fact measures of *motives* rather than attitudes or values?

For obvious reasons psychologists do not like coding stories written to pictures; it is expensive, time-consuming, and difficult to train scorers to high coding reliability.[1] Therefore, many attempts have been made, including several in my laboratory, to find an objectively scorable instrument which will correlate highly enough with the n Achievement measure to qualify as a substitute for it. So far as I know, all of these efforts have failed, for the very good reason, I tend to believe, that operant and respondent measures generally tap theoretically distinct aspects of personality.

The finding shown in Table 1 of a relation between n Achievement and course grades will certainly not go unchallenged by the critics of operant thought measures. They have gone to great lengths to assemble published and unpublished data on the relationships between n Achievement and performance both at molar and task levels (Klinger, 1966; Entwisle, 1972). Their conclusion is that while there are some positive relationships, there are at least an equal number of nonsignificant relationships, which is what one would expect according to Entwisle, if the n Achievement measure is unreliable. "Recent studies, carefully done and more extensive in scope than earlier studies, yield few positive relationships between need achievement and other variables" (Entwisle, 1972). The examples she gives to back up this statement are drawn largely from studies of classroom performance and behavior, the favorite proving ground for validity among psychometricians. So is it not a biased selection of the facts to suggest, as Table 1 does, that n Achievement leads to superior performance in the classroom?

Yes it is, and I included the information on examination performance in Table 1 partly for simplicity of exposition but chiefly to make a point about the relation of n Achievement to performance in the most dramatic way possible. For the fact is that both friends and foes of the n Achievement measure have repeatedly made a basic theoretical error in assuming that there should be a direct simple relationship between n Achievement and performance—in all kinds of situations. Ever since the publication of *The achievement motive* (McClelland et al., 1953), it has been known that n Achievement has a very variable and probably over-all insignificant relationship to school performance. It amazes me that so much energy has gone into proving this point over and over again. And ever since the publication of Atkinson's (1957) ground-breaking theoretical contribution on risk-taking, we have known the reason why. What his theory states in a nutshell is that moderate risk-taking (or challenge in the performance situation) is the chief incentive for people high in n Achievement. They will work harder than other people when the probability of success is moderate *but not if the probability of success is very high or very low.*

In other words, the incentive that people high in n Achievement are concerned about (moderate probability of doing better) has to be present in the situation in order for them to perform better than those low in n Achievement. Some findings reported by French (1955) a gen-eration ago illustrate the point in another way. She observed how hard people high and low in n Achievement worked when the incentives provided in the situation differed. For one group the incentive was "to perform as well as possible," for another the incentive was to help the experimenter, and for a third group the incentive was to be excused from work. She found that *only* under the first incentive condition (doing better) did those high in n Achievement perform significantly better than those low in n Achievement. And when the incentive was time off from work, those with low n Achievement actually performed some-what better. An elementary principle of general behavior theory is that an incentive or reward must be appropriate to the drive if the drive is to facilitate the acquisition of responses relative to satisfying it. A hungry rat will not learn to run a maze faster unless food is provided as the reward. If Entwisle and Jensen are incredulous over my simple-mindedness, may I confess to a similar incredulity over their apparent ignorance of so elementary a principle?

So it is impossible to determine whether there should be a relation between n Achievement and performance in most of the instances which Klinger (1966) and Entwisle (1972) have laboriously collected because we do not know what the incentive conditions were. We do know that many classroom teachers do not provide the moderate challenge incentive necessary to engage the motivation of subjects high in *n* Achievement (deCharms, 1976). And we know that the incentives provided by teachers if they match the dominant motive levels of the students facilitate their performance (McKeachie, 1961). So we might expect a large number of nonsignificant relationships between *n* Achievement and school performance with occasional exceptions like the one reported in Table 1 which comes from Atkinson's own class taught, one might assume, with the principle of moderate challenge very much in the mind.

Fortunately, Weinstein (1969) and Korman (1974) appear to have understood this point. Weinstein (1969) examined studies in which *n* Achievement was related to the moderate risk incentive. He reports 15 studies showing a significant positive relationship and 2 instances of no relationship. Not bad as psychological research goes, when there are so many contaminating variables—such as extraneous incentives—that can distort results. And there are at least two other studies confirming this relationship (McClelland and Watson, 1973; Horner, 1968). Unfortunately despite this impressive evidence of construct validity, Korman then goes on to conclude that the *n* Achievement variable is not valid because it does not pass the multitrait, multimethod criterion of validity, proposed by Campbell and Fiske (1959). In short, as we have already seen, it does not correlate with *v* Achievement measures higher than with outside variables. But the Campbell and Fiske proposal deals with how to determine whether you have a measure of something when you do not have any clear theoretical criteria for deciding whether you have a measure of something. In this case we do: the *n* Achievement measure passes the "drive, direct, and select" criteria for determining whether something is a motive measure and the *v* Achievement measure does not. To throw out the *n* Achievement on the ground that it does not correlate with a *v* Achievement measure would be like throwing away thermometers because they do not agree very well with subjective estimates of how hot it is in a humid environment.

PREDICTIVE VALIDITY: LIFE OUTCOME STUDIES

One may counter the above line of argument by saying: Who cares about all those theoretical fine points? If you have to determine just what incentives a classroom teacher is providing before you know whether there is to be a relationship with school performance, does not the whole enterprise become impractical? What we should be interested in predicting is school performance regardless of circumstances. What we should be doing is predicting real-life outcomes.

Indeed we should, but there are many important life outcomes besides school performance. In fact, there is surprising little evidence that how well one does in school is related to any other life outcomes of importance (McClelland et al., 1958; McClelland, 1971b).

Occupational Success

What about real-life outcomes? Do operant thought variables predict them? Consider first success as a Commanding or Executive Officer (CO/XO) in the Navy. This provides an example of a good operant measure of a life outcome of some practical importance. What are the personality characteristics of the man who works his way to the top in the Navy, when performance is rated by superior officers? Winter (1979) has summarized the contribution of various tests to predicting this criterion. As expected on theoretical grounds (McClelland, 1975), the "leadership motive pattern" as coded in operant thought contributes significantly in a multiple regression equation to determining who is more likely to be considered an outstanding Commanding or Executive Officer. The leadership motive pattern had been previously defined (McClelland, 1975) as consisting of average or above n Power which is greater than n Affiliation, plus high Activity Inhibition (i.e., the number of times the word *not* appears in a protocol, usually signifying inhibition of action). In common sense terms men who are interested in exercising influence, who are well controlled, but are not concerned with being liked should make better leaders or managers. This turned out to be true not only for more successful senior Naval Officers but also for better senior managers in large businesses (McClelland & Burnham, 1976). It is worth noting also that other successful types of officers lower down in over-all responsibility—for example, petty officers—did not show this pattern. So no claim is being made that this motive pattern will lead to greater success in all types of management positions.

The Strong-Campbell Vocational Interest Blank (Strong and Campbell, 1969) was also administered to the CO/XO group and despite the fact that it provided some 29 *reliable* scores, including a scale designed specifically to get at military interests, only one of them contributed significantly to predicting the successful CO/XO criterion. Since the one significant correlation was not predicted and had not been obtained in other similar circumstances, it is possible that it represents one of the significant relationships to be expected by chance among so many correlations. This is not to say that no respondent measures predicted this criterion or success in other officer roles, but those that did were usually reports of perceptions of the situation (representing schema variables) or reports of frequent actions taken (trait variables). Together motive, trait, and schema variables produced a multiple r of .68 with the criterion of success as CO/XO, a very respectable showing in psychological research of this type (McClelland, 1980). In my view the showing is more respectable than usual because it consciously acknowledged that at least three types of independent variables (motives, traits, and schemas) are necessary to account for variations in behavior. From this point of view one of the most pointless activities in contemporary psychological science is the attempt to reduce these variables to a single trait variable by correlating them with each other—usually with nonsignificant results.

However, strictly speaking, concurrent not predictive validity is involved here. The men were tested after they were in place and the operant thought findings might be the result of superior or inferior performance in their jobs. Fortunately predictive data are also available. The 1956-1960 management trainees for the American Telephone and Telegraph Company were given a version of the TAT (Bray et al., 1974). Their careers were followed and the management level they attained was determined after 8 and after 16 years with the company. The TATs were retrieved, scored blind for the three social motives and Activity Inhibition, and the scores corrected for correlations with protocol length.[2] The prediction of future success as a manager in the company after 16 years (an operant life outcome measure) from the leadership motive pattern at entry is quite striking. Only 40 of the men showed this pattern at the outset but 80% of them had reached levels 3 or higher 16 years later as compared with only 55% of those with other motive patterns, $X^2(1) = 6.82$, $p < .01$. The data for n Achievement are also interesting. On theoretical grounds, n Achievement should promote success as an "individual contributor" or small business entrepreneur (see McClelland and Winter, 1969) but not as a manager of other people, because people high in n Achievement are interested in assuming personal responsibility, want concrete feedback on how well *they* (not others) are doing, and in general want the satisfaction from doing better themselves. Managers, on the other hand, must be interested in helping or influencing others to perform well. The findings for the relation of n Achievement to promotion in AT&T are consistent with this interpretation. The need for achievement leads to more rapid promotion at lower levels when the performance of the person himself, rather than those under him, is the basis for promotion, but not at higher levels of responsibility when the management of others is involved (McClelland & Boyatzis. Note 2).

So the operant thought measures proved quite useful in predicting real-life operant outcomes. What about respondent personality measures? Bray et al. (1974) also administered in 1956-1960 the Edwards Personal Preference Schedule and the Guilford-Martin (1948) Inventory of Factors, GAMIN. None of the 20 highly reliable measures obtained from these self-report questionnaires predicted significantly level of management attained later in AT&T. Small wonder that people like Mischel (1968) are discouraged about the possibility of developing a science of personality so long as they depend on questionnaire measures of this type.

School Success and Life Success

To make the point even more clearly, let us take a look at what predicts success in school (predominantly a respondent measure) and success in later life (predominantly an operant measure). Intelligence or achievement tests (respondent measures) represent the one successful measure of individual differences according to the traditional standards of psychometricians. They are highly reliable and they are valid in the sense that they predict grades in school. On the other hand, operant thought measures like n Achievement, as Entwisle (1972) correctly points out, have a very uneven and questionable record of predicting grades in school. I have explained previously why this is so: One simply cannot predict performance from motive levels without knowing what the incentives in the situation are. But the fact remains that, in this instance, respondent measures are generally valid and operant measures generally are not. The reason lies in the nature of the criterion: Grades for the most part represent performance under standardized conditions, often in response to test questions not unlike those they answered in getting an achievement or intelligence test score. These answers in turn do not usually reflect what the person gravitates toward doing over time. It is for this reason, as I have argued elsewhere (McClelland, 1971b), that grades in school (respondent behaviors) show such low correlations with life outcomes (operant behaviors). If this general line of reasoning is correct, operant thought measures (e.g., motive scores) ought to do a better job of predicting life outcomes because the latter generally represent operant trends in behavior. In a reanalysis of some data presented by Skolnick (1966), I showed that at least among males operant thought measures relate more often to operant than respondent life outcome measures (McClelland, 1966).

What has been needed to check this hypothesis is some measure of "life success," which is at least roughly comparable to "school success." Recently such a measure has been designed for a study of the long-term effects of going to a liberal arts college (Winter et al., in press). Information was gathered by questionnaire from graduates of a college after they had been out in life for 10 years. A very general index of "life success" was devised consisting of a combination of income earned, occupational success, participation and leadership in community organizations, and subjective satisfaction with one's career and life in general. Early occupational success was determined according to objective criteria used in the field. For example, teachers were categorized as more or less successful in terms of the prestige of the institution at which they were teaching, professional rank attained (including whether they had achieved tenure), and publications. Information on each of the several variables was standard scored across subjects and an individual's standard score on each variable summed to give an overall "life success" index in which each component was equally weighted. Obviously there can be dispute as to just what should enter into such an index, just as there can be dispute as to whether physical education grades should enter into grade point average, but an effort was made to get as broad an index as possible representing the various components that make up "success in life."

Table 2 displays the correlations between a TAT measure of maturity of adaptation (McClelland, 1975; Stewart, Note 1) and the Scholastic Aptitude Test (SAT) score with measures of success in college and in later life. As expected, SAT scores correlate significantly with a measure of academic success (even in this institution which is highly selective), and the TAT measure does not. In this instance I have chosen a more general characteristic scored from the TAT in preference to the motive scores because the motive scores should predict particular kinds of life outcomes not overall success in adapting to life. But for what it is worth, neither the n Achievement score nor any of the other motive scores predicts academic honors, confirming what Entwisle (1972) has argued.

The TAT and SAT measures were both obtained in freshman year so that the predictions to life outcomes cover a 14-year span. Their utility in predicting life outcomes is dramatically different. The SAT combined

TABLE 2

Correlations Between Operant and Respondent Thought Measures
with School (Respondent) and Life (Operant) Outcomes for Males

Thought measures	N	in school (respondent): graduated with honors	N	in life (operant): composite adult attainment[a]
Operant (TAT stage of adaptation score)[b]	181	−.11	49	.26*
Respondent (SAT verbal + math score)	299	.26***	54	−.26*

*p < .08; ***p < .001

a. Sum of standard scores for income, early success in law, business, teaching, and medicine, career satisfaction, membership and office holding in voluntary organizations, high happiness and low unhappiness now. See Winter et al., in press.
b. Modal stage score (Stages 1-4) after each stage score has been standardized across subjects. See Winter et al., in press.

Math and Verbal score tends to be *negatively* related to overall success in life. And also grades in school (graduating with honors) has no significant relationship to success in life (r = −.16). One cannot even take consolation in the fact that perhaps the measure of life success is too broad (including such subjective variables as happiness) to capture the advantage that academic intelligence should give one in life. For the fact is that combined SAT scores are also negatively correlated (r = −.25) with early success in law, medicine, teaching, and business. And even more specifically SAT Math score is negatively correlated with early success in the natural sciences (r = −.24, N = 53). These negative relationships, while surprising in view of the great faith college admissions officers, professors, and the public put in SAT scores, should not be taken as characteristic of the relationships over the whole range of scores, for the students in this sample were drawn heavily from the upper ranges of SAT scores. However, the results emphasize once again that whenever test scores are correlated with life as opposed to school outcomes, the relationships tend to be very low or nonexistent (McClelland, 1971b). The most reasonable interpretation of the results is that certain minimum levels of academic intelligence are necessary for certain occupations, but that success within those occupations—or in life in general—is much more apt to be the result of making certain operant responses which should be better predicted by operant thought measures.

At least in this instance that appears to be true. The TAT estimate of level of maturity at the operant thought level in freshman year is positively and near significantly related to general success in life 14 years later. And there are numbers of other significant correlations between TAT measures and operant life outcomes. To mention only the one which we have discussed previously, the leadership motive pattern (average or above n Power$>n$ Affiliation, high Activity Inhibition) is significantly associated (r = .23, N = 95, p$<$.05) with office holding in voluntary organizations 14 years later (Winter et al., in press). The SAT score on the other hand is correlated –.10 with this outcome. These are not high correlations, but there are important reasons why we should not expect them to be high. On the one hand we know these characteristics change by senior year as a result of liberal arts education, and we are attempting to predict from precollege characteristics. On the other hand as Winter et al. (in press) show, there are many other predictive and situational variables (such as being married and having a child) which moderate the relationships between personality variables and life outcomes. But hopefully Table 2 makes the main theoretical point clear: In general, respondents predict respondents and operants predict operants.

Child-rearing Antecedents of Operant and Respondent Measures of Motives

Longitudinal data exist over an even longer period of time suggesting that operant TAT measures reflect stable and meaningful personality characteristics. McClelland and Pilon (Note 3) have recently reported a study of the relationship between early child-rearing practices and adult motive scores. The ratings of parent behavior were made in 1951 by a team of observers working from recorded interviews with mothers (Sears et al., 1957) who had a five-year-old child at the time. Of these children, 78 were given the TAT and other tests 26 to 27 years later when they were to 31 to 32 years old. Correlations were run between ratings on 69 child-rearing practices (plus 14 factor or composite scores) and adult motive levels as determined from the TAT. Since a number of significant correlations would occur by chance, it was further required that any relationship found had to be significant not only in the total sample but also in separate white and blue collar samples and in the subsamples of men and women. By this strict criterion 2 early child-rearing practices (scheduling feeding and severe toilet training) were found to be positively related to adult n Achievement and 2 positively to adult n

Power (permissiveness about sex and aggression). It is difficult to see how these correlations have been obtained if the motive measures are as unreliable and full of random error as Entwisle (1972) makes them out to be. It seems reasonable to infer that some early learning experiences produced individual differences in motive levels in early childhood which remained stable enough over time so that the differences could still be detected more than 25 years later.

On the other hand, inconsistent correlations were found between child-rearing practices and a respondent measure of motivation—the need for approval score developed by Marlowe and Crowne (1964) despite its high internal consistency and high test-retest reliability. The same result was obtained for an adjective check list measure of achievement, dominance, and affiliation orientations (Gough and Heilbrun, 1965). These self-report measures not only did not correlate with operant thought measures of n Achievement, n Power, and n Affiliation but they also showed inconsistent patterns of correlation with early child-rearing variables. Such a result fits the hypothesis that self-reports, as the most restricted type of respondent measure, are more shaped by current stimulus conditions (e.g., what it seems socially desirable to report about oneself) than operants and hence show less evidence of longitudinal stability.

Predicting Susceptibility to High Blood Pressure

Let us consider another recent longitudinal study in which operant thought measures of motives were able to predict blood pressure 20 years later (McClelland, 1979). The theory involved goes back to some careful clinical analyses by Saul (1939) and Alexander (1939). They found that hypertensives were characterized more often than other patients by "suppressed rage," that is, by an urge to be assertively angry which was inhibited from direct expression. A somewhat similar description (designated Type A behavior) has been more recently applied to individuals who are prone ;to cardiovascular disease or heart attacks (Friedman and Rosenman, 1974). From a study of these descriptions it was hypothesized that these individuals as compared with others would be more often high in n Power (Winter, 1973) and high in Activity Inhibition, both operant measures as defined and used previously in other studies (McClelland, 1975). It was reasoned further that n Affiliation should not be higher than n Power, as in the management studies (since that might modulate assertiveness) and that individuals with this motive syndrome, especially if subjected to stress, would tend to develop high blood pressure over time possibly because of chronic activation of the sympathetic nervous system. This turned out to be the case. It was possible to find and score TATs which a group of male graduates of a prestigious college had provided in their early 30s and to contrast the blood pressures of the high n Power, high inhibition (HH) group with the blood pressure of the rest of the subjects both 12 years earlier in college and 20 years later when they were in their early 50s. Of the HH subjects, 61% had definite signs of high blood pressure in their early 50s as compared with 23% of the remaining subjects, $X^2_{(1)} = 7.88$, $p < .01$. This difference remained significant even when small differences in blood pressure in college were controlled for. It was assumed that the relationship was this strong because as a group these men mostly were involved in prestigious high-stress occupations.

But has it not proven possible with simpler and cheaper questionnaire measures of similar types of behavior to predict who is likely to have cardiovascular problems? Perhaps, but the record is not so clear. Caplan et al. (1975), for example, report correlations of a Type A questionnaire measure with systolic blood pressure of .00 and with diastolic blood pressure of –.01 in a sample of 390 white and blue collar workers. On the other hand, several studies have shown that people who have cardio-vascular disease or who have had a myocardial infarction give significantly more Type A answers to questions than other individuals (Dembroski et al., 1978). That is, they describe themselves as more driven, concerned about time, irritable, and so on. But usually the questionnaires have been administered after they have heart trouble and it could be that their responses are conditioned by that fact. So in one study (Friedman et al., 1974) a serious attempt was made to see if answers to personality type questions given *before* the person had a myocardial infarction (MI) would differentiate those who later had a heart attack from those who did not. They found some item responses that significantly differentiated the MI group from the control groups but they were not Type A items, as predicted, and for the most part they were items referring to health problems that might have been precursors of MI like agreeing that in the past year they had often found that poor health had made them miserable most of the time. As the investigators sum it up, "Items representing 'emotional drain' and 'somatization' proved to be associated with MI, but these relationships were no longer apparent when persons with coronary symptoms and diagnoses at the time of testing were removed from the study group" (Friedman et al., 1974).

Since the high inhibited n Power syndrome results in behavior very like that described clinically as Type A behavior, it looks as if the investigators, misled by the presumed higher reliability of the questionnaire method and its greater ease of application, settled on a less adequate method of identifying Type A persons. Once again it looks as if an obstensibly unreliable operant thought measure does a better job of *predicting* an operant life outcome criterion (blood pressure) than supposedly more reliable direct questionnaire measures.

THE VALIDITY OF RESPONDENT MEASURES

One might well wonder, in view of the evidence reviewed so far, why psychologists continue to use respondent measure of motives, since they do not seem to relate to life outcomes. Evidence for their validity comes chiefly from three sources: correlations with judgments of others, with the behaviors covered in the questionnaire, and with scores on other tests (Scott and Johnson, 1972). All these types of evidence contain important opportunities for contamination between the two variables which are correlated. Such contamination can lead to spuriously high estimates of validity.

Consider the validity of self-report measures of Type A behavior in predicting cardiovascular disease. Two types of contamination between predictor and criterion can easily occur. First, people may report that they feel hurried, driven, irritable, and so on as a result of having had a heart attack. If they have had the heart attack already, their feelings of distress may be the result of wanting to do something but fearing that it may bring on further heart attacks. In this case the psychological condition is the result of what it is trying to predict. Second, even when psychological items predict later heart attacks, they may reflect earlier criterion-related behavior—to being in poor health prior to having a heart attack. It is difficult to see how one can speak of "predictive" or even "concurrent" validity when people are simply reporting on symptoms which are part of the criterion in the first place.

To some extent validity is established by correlating something with itself. Nowhere is this clearer than in research on the relation of anxiety to school performance. Typically an anxiety questionnaire is developed containing a number of items like "Nervousness while taking an exam or test hinders me from doing well"; "The more important the examination, the less well I seem to do"; and so on (Alpert and Haber, 1960). Is it surprising that agreement with items like these is highly negatively related to grade point average (r = −.50)? In what sense can one speak of the "validity" of such a test when subjects who know they are doing poorly in their courses are simply saying that they do poorly? If subjects were asked in one question how well they did in exams and in the next how well they did in courses, would a correlation between the two be evidence of validity? Would it not be more proper to conceive of such a correlation as evidence of internal consistency or reliability?

This kind of contamination between self-report scales and the criteria they are validated against is common, often because researchers do not examine carefully the items in the self-report scales that are being validated. Recently a researcher announced to me that she thought I would be happy to know that she had discovered that women who were achievers had a high "need to achieve." I asked her how she had found that out. And she answered that the women who had objectively achieved more score higher on the "need Achievement" scale of the Jackson (1966) Personality Research Form (PRF). I pointed out to her (1) that so far as I knew there was no evidence to indicate the PRF scale measured a motive by the ordinary criteria of general behavior theory and (2) that I did not find it very impressive that women who knew they were achievers said they were—that is, said they worked hard, chose work over play, and so on—in a self-report questionnaire. This did not seem to me to be evidence of the validity of the PRF scale but of contamination between test answers and the criterion. She went away unconvinced and in this respect she is like many other personality researchers who continue to get satisfaction from correlating something with itself, phrased in a slightly different way. This type of error is particularly blatant when someone reports as evidence of validity the fact that two test measures intercorrelate when there is item overlap in the two measures—for example, in the Edwards and Jackson PRF measures of v Achievement.

The same problem arises in a subtler form when self-reports on questionnaires are validated against the judgments of others. As I have pointed out previously (McClelland, 1972), often this means no more than that a person (e.g., a friend or a teacher) has listened to what a person says about himself and faithfully reflects that in his or her judgments about the person. If some children in a classroom ask for extra work and say they like to study, chances are that they will say in a self-report questionnaire that they work hard, like to study, and so on and that the teacher will say about them that they work hard, like to study, and so on. Is that evidence of validity or are both observers responding to the same information? It is a fact that what people say about themselves will be correlated with what other people say about them (Scott and Johnson, 1972) but that is evidence that the two judgments are not independent rather than evidence of validity of the test.

It is worth noting that when judges are asked not to rate other people's n Achievement but to identify those who show the behavioral characteristics of people with high n Achievement, their choices correlate significantly with the n Achievement measure, and not with the Edwards v Achievement measure (Marlowe, 1959).

Such criticisms of respondent, self-report measures of motives are meant to create caution in constructing and interpreting them, not to condemn them. It is obviously important in predicting behavior to know the characteristics of such schemata or cognitive maps as those covering achievement or power strivings. Our knowledge of achievement behavior has been greatly advanced by studies of the cognitive aspects of how choices in the achievement area are made (cf. Weiner, 1974; Heckhausen, 1980). This line of research developed logically out of a consideration of the cognitive elements that were implicit in stating that subjects high in n Achievement were concerned with doing well. For such a concern implies that a person must know when he or she has produced an outcome, must react positively or negatively to success or failure, must have standards as to what "doing well" means, must be able to distinguish between effort and task difficulty, and so on. So why is not a study of such cognitive elements a study of the achievement motive? Why *should* n Achievement and v Achievement (which refers to these cognitive elements in achievement schemata) turn out to be so unrelated? The answer lies in the fact that causal or achievement schemata apparently develop somewhat independently of the achievement motive as a function of the conceptualization of personal experiences and social norms. In typical experiments young children are tested to find out in some way if they can distinguish between a task which is easy or hard, an outcome which they did or did not produce, and so on. What it is important to remember is that children display affect over self-produced outcomes long before these achievement schemata develop fully (Heckhausen, 1980). A child of 10 months can show marked pleasure in crawling back and forth over a raised threshold between two rooms (a moderately difficult task) long before he or she has developed any reportable cognitive schemata as to what is going on. In fact, as mentioned earlier, the key experiences for developing *n* Achievement (as opposed to *v* Achievement) may occur as early as the first months of life (from scheduling of feeding) and certainly by 12 to 18 months when toilet training begins (McClelland and Pilon, Note 3). Thus one has to conceive of early achievement-related experiences shaping an affective motive disposition which relates only very imperfectly to conscious attributions and judgments formed through later more conceptual learning.

Both types of learning should influence achievement behaviors, the earlier learning (for *n* Achievement) being more important for determining operant behaviors when external determinants are less salient, and the later learning (for *v* Achievement) being more important for determining choices when external factors are more salient. Unfortunately, too little research using *both* need and value measures has been carried out. One example will have to suffice to illustrate its virtues. French and Lesser (1964) compared the performance of women high and low in *n* Achievement on two types of tasks. One was the intellectual task (scrambled words) commonly used in research of this type. Another was a social skills task in which the women were asked, for example, to list as many different ways as they could in which they would go about making friends in a strange town. They also sorted the women according to their values—whether they were oriented around a career or traditional women's roles values. The values the women subscribed to influenced which task the women high in *n* Achievement performed better on. Women high in *n* Achievement who were career oriented did better on the intellectual task when it was linked to career development, while those high in *n* Achievement who were tradition oriented did better on the social skills task (when it was linked to success as a wife and mother). Let us hope that the decade of the 1980s will see more studies of this multivariate type rather than endless squabbles over what the achievement motive is related to (e.g., Meyer et al., 1976) dictated by the fact that it is not recognized that *n* Achievement and *v* Achievement are two different relatively independent aspects of personality.

RELIABILITY

Finally we come to the issue which in the minds of many is decisive in determining that respondent measures of personality ought and operant measures ought not to be used. Scales derived from self-report questionnaires are usually internally consistent and have high test-retest reliability coefficients. Therefore, the argument runs, they are measuring something. Operant measures, based on thought samples, are not highly internally consistent and do not usually have high test-retest reliability coefficients. Therefore, they are not measuring anything consistently enough to claim the attention of a serious scientist.

Let us examine a little more closely why people give consistent or inconsistent responses. In general, people are consistent if they think they are supposed to be and inconsistent if they think they are supposed to be. A personality self-report measure sets them to be consistent in the following ways:

(1) By saying or implying that the subject should give honest answers, should state how he or she really feels about something. Suppose the question is, "Do you daydream frequently?" The subject answers "Yes." Then he or she is given the questionnaire again at a later date and again confronts the same question. Is the answer now likely to be "No?" Obviously not, because if the answer is changed, the implication is either that the person did not give an honest opinion the first time or did not know his or her own mind. Subjects know they are supposed to answer the same question in the same way when it is asked again and avoid varying the response because it might make them look inconsistent or confused in the eyes of others or themselves.

(2) By tapping generalized response sets which lead subjects to give consistently negative or positive or socially desirable answers regardless of the content of the items (Edwards, 1957; Couch and Keniston, 1960).

(3) By asking the same question in many different ways. The test anxiety questionnaire referred to earlier is typical. It asks whether they are nervous in taking an exam, whether they get upset, block in understanding a question, fear getting a bad grade, and so on. Once again subjects are set to be consistent. Who would answer that they get upset but are not afraid? But more than that, as D'Andrade (1965) has demonstrated, there is so much semantic overlap among the adjectives used in different descriptions that the subjects cannot really discriminate what is being asked. They are answering the same question, semantically speaking, over and over again and it is the psychologist who is fooled into thinking that he has established response consistency, when the subject cannot tell one stimulus from another.

(4) By asking questions about the past, the answers to which cannot properly vary. If a subject reports that he was sent to the principal's office for cutting up in school, technically his answer to that question ought never to vary no matter how his personality has changed in the meantime. About 30% of the items on the Pd scale of the Minnesota

Multiphasic Personality Inventory refer to the past in this way; for example, one such item reads: "During one period when I was a youngster I engaged in petty thievery" (Dahlstrom et al., 1972). High test-retest reliability for such scales is practically guaranteed by including items referring to the past, the answers to which should not change if the person is truthful. What is clearly incorrect is to infer from such test-retest correlations on the Minnesota Multiphasic Personality Inventory that a personality characteristic such as psychopathy is consistent over time. What is consistent is the tendency to give truthful answers about the past. The person might have changed totally and be an honest, law-abiding citizen, but might still tend to score high on the Pd scale if he continued to answer truthfully questions about his youthful misbehaviors.

Looked at in this light the high measured reliabilities of self-report questionnaires seem spurious or inflated by response sets that make it impossible to be sure just what the real consistency of the characteristic would be if the sets could be removed. These considerations also make it a little clearer why measures obtained in this way have little predictive validity for life outcomes. For reliability is obtained at the cost of sensitivity to real changes in people. They will continue judging themselves in the same way, even though they have changed, because of the strain toward self-consistency.

The most reasonable inference to be made from these facts is that *the true reliability of characteristics measured in the usual type of personality questionnaires (with consistency response sets removed) is unknown.* Obtained reliability coefficients should certainly not be taken at their face value.

But what are we to make of the unreliability of operant measures? Again an analysis of the situation people are in when making an operant response readily explains their inconsistency. On a TAT, subjects are told to be creative and original. If they are presented with the same picture again, they are unlikely to think that telling the same story again (which would make them appear consistent) is an example of being creative or original. Or even if they are confronted with a different picture it is unlikely they will tell the same story that they just told because that, too, is not being original. So alternate forms do not solve this problem. The so-called sawtooth effect in the achievement content of successive stories has been known ever since Atkinson's (1950) doctoral thesis. It means simply that subjects are trying not to repeat themselves according to instructions. The very word *imaginative* implies thinking something different just as words like "be honest, tell how you really feel" imply being truthful and therefore consistent.

Winter and Stewart (1977) have demonstrated that obtained test-retest correlations are much higher if the set to be different is broken by instructions on the second TAT administration as follows: "Do not worry about whether your stories are similar or different from the stories you wrote before. Write whatever stories you wish." Under this set the test-retest correlation for *n* Power rose to the more respectable level of around .60.

Actually however, the difficulty is not completely resolved in this way so far as motive scores are concerned for two reasons. In the first place it has been known for nearly 50 years (Telford, 1931) that something then called "associative refractory phase" exists. There is a built-in tendency to avoid repeating operant responses. It is so well-known in clinical psychology that if a subject repeats a response in a free association test, it is considered a sign of abnormality. The adaptive value of varying operant responses in learning is well-known and treated under the heading of alternation behavior in general behavior theory (Walker, 1964). I am doubtful that a simple instruction to the effect that one does not have to vary a response is sufficient to override altogether such a powerful determinant of operant behavior.

In the second place, motivation stakes its claim to consideration as an important concept in general behavior theory in large part on the fact that it explains *inconsistencies* in behavior just as habits explain consistencies. When a hungry dog is trying to get out of a cage to get to food, it will try a wide variety of *different* responses. Why would we expect it to provide internally consistent responses? If it is whining, it may not be scratching; if it is trying to push through the slats, it is not pawing at the latch. One would not expect high correlations among these responses any more than one would expect signs of achievement motivation in different stories to be highly correlated. In clinical terminology, motivation is conceived in terms of an alternative manifestations model. If a motive expresses itself one way, there is no need for it to express itself in another way. Hence the alternative manifestations are not highly intercorrelated as the consistency hypothesis assumes they should be. For example, subjects high in *n* Power may express their motivation by power-oriented reading, by feelings of controlled anger, by expressing anger toward people, or by joining organizations to feel more powerful, depending on their level of maturity (McClelland, 1975, p. 45). The sum of these action tendencies among men is not as highly correlated with *n* Power as the maximum expression of any one of the four—a direct confirmation of the alternative manifestations model.

Atkinson and Birch (1978) have argued that the assumptions of traditional psychometric theory do not correspond with the most reasonable assumptions of a general theory of behavior and have demonstrated using computer simulation that incorporates the latter assumptions, that construct validity of operant measures does not require internal consistency as measured by Cronbach's alpha. That is, if the measure of validity is correct assignment of a person to thirds of the *n* Achievement distribution on the basis of total time spent thinking about achievement, then the percentage of persons correctly assigned remains high even though internal consistency is low, zero, or even negative. Without going into details of their model, its essential point is that response tendencies rise and fall, alternate with and influence each other so that it is incorrect, as in traditional psychometric theory, to treat each story as an independent assay of a characteristic which ought to correlate highly with every other independent assay of the characteristic.

Kuhl (1978) has also called attention to the fact that more sophisticated methods of dealing with latent person parameters reveal more consistency than is obtained by traditional measurement methods. It is a hopeful sign that these recent developments toward a better understanding of the consistency problem may at long last serve to bring psychometric theory into line with general behavior theory.

So what are we to conclude about the reliability of operant measures? What all of these arguments add up to is that test-retest and internal reliability coefficients cannot adequately measure the true reliability of operant characteristics. Just as we concluded that reliability coefficients overestimate true reliability of respondent measures, we must also conclude that they underestimate the true stability of operant measures. Practically speaking, what does this mean? One can feel somewhat reassured by the Winter and Stewart (1977) finding that certain instructions improve measured test-retest reliabilities of operant measures to a respectable level. Bt the main argument for the stability of operant motive measures has to come from the validity studies reported above. For the proof that validity cannot be higher than reliability also works the other way: Reliability must be at least as high as validity. And the validity coefficients for the operant motive measures measured over periods of 15 to 25 years are substantial. To take just one example, the high inhibited n Power motive pattern predicts the proportion of subjects with high blood pressure 20 years later with a chi square of 7.88. This in turn converts to a phi coefficient and from that to an estimated validity correlation coefficient of .51 (Wert et al., 1954, p. 302). A similar prediction from the same variable to management success in AT&T after 16 years yields an estimated r of .33. So the reliability of the power motive syndrome measured in the TAT must be substantial for such validity coefficients to be obtained over such long time periods. For what it is worth, my opinion based on these studies and others is that true stability coefficients for TAT motive measures over short periods of time are in the .55 to .65 range with lower values being obtained for students than for adults in stable life situations (see Andrews, 1967). Over longer periods of time such as 10 to 25 years, the stability coefficients appear to be in the .30 to .50 range. Such results would also fit theory because there is significant evidence that special learning experiences in adulthood can alter motive levels (McClelland and Winter, 1969).

SENSITIVITY OF OPERANT AND RESPONDENT MEASURES

Elsewhere I have argued (McClelland, 1971a) that another criterion of the validity of a measure is whether it responds sensitively to known variations in the characteristic it is supposed to be measuring. A thermometer is sensitive if it responds in a linear fashion as a lighted match is moved closer to it. The TAT motive measures have this type of validity since they were derived from comparing the thoughts of people in a state of motive arousal with the thoughts of people not in a state of arousal. Respondent measures that attempt to measure traits do not have this characteristic. Years ago I attempted to validate the anxiety or neuroticism scale of a well-known personality test by posting false grades after an exam, which I thought should create at least some increase in anxiety in students who performed generally well. However, to my chagrin, there was no significant increase in the personality anxiety test scores associated with the presumed increase in experimentally aroused anxiety.

The reason of course is clear: Trait test questions ask about the past or how you generally feel. That insures high internal consistency and high test-retest reliability but it also insures insensitivity. People will tend to get the same scores no matter how much they have changed or no matter what the conditions are under which they take the test.

But there is a serious problem involved in this differential sensitivity of the two types of measures that often goes unrecognized by those trained in the psychometric tradition. It is very simply that operant measures are much more likely to be influenced by the conditions of test administration than respondent measures are. This means much more care must be taken when operant measures are used to insure that testing conditions are standardized, neutral with regard to arousing cues, and the same for all subjects tested. It is surprising how often the most elementary precautions on these matters are ignored. For example, some years ago, a large-scale testing program was carried out on high school students in which it was decided to obtain some TAT measures, rather against the better judgment of the psychometricians running the study. They wanted to test a large number of students at once, to save time, and discovered that the only way they could do this was to administer the tests during the lunch hour (when large numbers of students were free) in the school cafeteria (the only room with tables to write on which was large enough to accommodate the sample). Even the most elementary knowledge of the effects of hunger on operant thoughts (McClelland and Atkinson, 1948) should have warned the testers that the stories they obtained under these conditions would scarcely be typical of the way the students generally thought about achievement or power or affiliation. Yet they went ahead anyway, doubtless misled by the fact that the other measures they were using were unlikely to be influenced by testing conditions, and later reported, not surprisingly, that the the motive measures obtained were not related to any of their other measures (most of which were respondent anyway).

Or consider another more recent example. Some psychologists wanted to test the findings and the theory presented by McClelland et al. (1972) to the effect that heavy drinkers tend to score higher on n Power and lower on Activity Inhibition (in operant thought) than do light drinkers. So they rounded up a group of alcohol abusers attending a clinic where they administered the TAT and a group of control subjects who took the same TAT in a university setting. They found that while the two groups differed in n Power in operant thought, as expected, they did not differ as predicted in the Activity Inhibition score. The alcoholics scored just as high in Activity Inhibition as the controls. Unfortunately it is really not possible to know whether this represents a true finding or the result of the difference in testing conditions, for it is entirely likely that alcoholics would be influenced by the fact that they took the test in a setting in which there was pressure to control their drinking. At the very least both groups of subjects should have been tested under the same conditions when the pressure for self-control was not too strong, if one was interested in observing differences in this dimension between the two groups. Even this precaution of course does not remove the selection bias involved in testing only alcohol abusers who had come in for help.

Unfortunately, operant measures are quite easily influenced by conditions of test administration. This does not mean research cannot be done with them, but it does mean that researchers must be careful in controlling for situational influences and that many of the studies using operant measures reported in the literature have been marred by carelessness in conditions of test administration.

Summary

It is premature to dismiss operant thought measures as mere "fantasies" as Entwisle (1972) urges. For when they are administered under neutral conditions, coded in standard fashion with high coder reliability, they have proven to have high validity in predicting operant behaviors over long periods of time, and other types of behavior in theoretically appropriate contexts. Therefore they must represent motive characteristics of greater stability than is suggested by the relatively low coefficients of internal and test-retest reliability usually reported.

A close examination of the testing conditions involved in computing reliability coefficients suggests that such coefficients will be high when subjects are set to give a consistent generalized account of themselves and low when they are set to be creative or original. Thus, personality questionnaires generally give spuriously high estimates of reliability due to consistency and social desirability sets, and projective tests yield spuriously low estimates of reliability due to a variability set.

The consistency and desirability sets also make questionnaire measures less sensitive to real changes in the person, which helps explain why self-report measures (of motives at least) have generally poor predictive validity. Another reason for the predictive validity of self-reports of motives for life outcomes is that they measure responses to specific stimuli rather than the general trends in initiating responses that characterize both operant thought measures and operant life outcomes. On the other hand, respondent measures are useful for getting at schemata, values, or attitudes which influence choices among alternatives.

Reports of failure to obtain results when using operant thought measures to detect individual differences in motive strengths are often due to one or more of the following reasons: (1) The experimenters have administered the TAT under conditions which preclude getting representative samples of the way in which subjects think under "neutral" or normal conditions. (2) The authors have attempted to correlate the operant motive measures with respondent measures which are strongly influenced by the controls set upon them—on the stimulus (a question), the response (agree-disagree), and on the instructional set (to be consistent, to present oneself in a desirable fashion). Under these conditions, motives can play less of a role in determining responses and therefore motive measures seldom correlate with respondent measures. (3) The experimenters have failed to understand how the theory of motivation applies to behaviors expected in a particular situation. The most common failure is in not specifying the incentives present in the situation, for general motivation theory predicts that a given motive will drive, direct, and select only that behavior which is relevant to the incentive or reward that satisfies the motive.

If due caution is exercised, operant thought measures of differences in motive strength have great value for understanding general trends in operant behavior. Questionnaires or respondent measures have less utility for this purpose but as measures of values and attitudes are important for predicting responses to particular situations. The best type of personality study will employ operant measures of motives, respondent measures of schemata, and measures of habitual responses (traits) to predict behavior.

NOTES

1. Entwisle (1972) is under the impression that somebody has confused coding reliability with test score reliability, but so far as I can determine, she is the only person to have done so.

2. It has been routine practice for years in all research I have had anything to do with to correct motive scores in this way, although Entwisle (1972) does not seem to realize it in arguing that some of the correlations of the motive variables with outside measures may be due to an ability factor associated with verbal productivity.

REFERENCE NOTES

1. Stewart, A. J. *Scoring manual for stages of psychological adaptation.* Boston, Mass.: Boston University, Department of Psychology, 1977.
2. McClelland, D. C. and Boyatzis, R. *Motivational predictors of promotion in the American Telephone and Telegraph Company: a longitudinal study.* Presented at the meeting of the American Psychological Association, New York, August 1979.
3. McClelland, D. C. and Pilon, D. A. Sources of adult motives in patterns of parent behavior in early childhood. Cambridge, Mass.: Unpublished report, Department of Psychology and Social Relations, Harvard University, 1979.

REFERENCES

Alexander, F. Emotional factors in essential hypertension. *Psychosomatic Medicine,* 1939, 1, 175-179.
Allport, G. W. and Vernon, P. E. *A study of values.* Boston: Houghton Mifflin, 1931.
Alpert, R. and Haber, R. N. Anxiety in academic achievement situations. *Journal of Abnormal and Social Psychology,* 1960, 61, 207-215.
Andrews, J.D.W. The achievement motive and advancement in two types of organizations. *Journal of Personality and Social Psychology,* 1967, 6, 163-168.
Atkinson, J. W. Studies in projective measurement of achievement motivation. Unpublished doctoral dissertation, University of Michigan, 1950.
Atkinson, J. W. Motivational determinants of risk-taking behavior. *Psychological Review,* 1957, 64, 358-372.
Atkinson, J. W. Towards experimental analysis of human motivation in terms of motives, expectancies, and incentives. In J. W. Atkinson (ed.), *Motives in fantasy, action and society.* Princeton, N.J.: Van Nostrand, 1958.
Atkinson, J. W. Personality dynamics. *Annual Review of Psychology,* 1960, 11, 255-290.
Atkinson, J. W. & Birch, D. *Introduction to motivation.* New York: Van Nostrand, 1978.
Atkinson, J. W. & Litwin, G. H. Achievement motive and test anxiety conceived as motive to approach success and motive to avoid failure. *Journal of Abnormal and Social Psychology,* 1960, 60, 52-63.
Bray, D. W., Campbell, R. J., & Grant, D. L. *Formative years in business: a long-term study of managerial lives.* New York: Wiley, 1974.
Campbell, D. T. and Fiske, D. Convergent and discriminant validation by the multitrait-multimethod matrix. *Psychological Bulletin,* 1959, 56, 81-105.
Caplan, R. D., Cobb, S., French, J.R.P., Jr., Van Harrison, R., & Pinneau, E. R. *Job demands and worker health,* Ann Arbor, Mich.: Institute for Social Research, 1975.

Couch, A. S. & Keniston, K. Yea-sayers and nay-sayers: agreeing response set as personality variable. *Journal of Abnormal and Social Psychology*, 1960, 60, 151-174.

Dahlstrom, W. G., Welsh, G. S. & Dahlstrom, L. E. *An MMPI handbook*. Minneapolis: University of Minnesota, 1972.

D'Andrade, R. G. Trait psychology and componential analysis. *American Anthropologist*, 1965, 67, 215-228.

deCharms, R. *Enhancing motivation: Change in the classroom*. New York: Irvington-Halstead-Wiley, 1976.

deCharms, R., Morrison, H. W., Reitman, W., & McClelland, D. C. Behavioral correlates of directly and indirectly measured achievement motivation. In D. C. McClelland (ed.), *Studies in motivation*. Englewood Cliffs, N.J.: Prentice-Hall, 1955.

deCharms, R. & Muir, M. S. Motivation: social approaches. *Annual Review of Psychology*, 1978, 29, 91-113.

Dembroski, T. M., Weiss, S. M., Shields, J. L. Haynes, S. G., & Feinleib, M. *Coronary prone behavior*. New York: Springer, 1978.

Edwards, A. L. *The social desirability variable in personality assessment and research*. New York: Dryden, 1957.

Entwisle, D. R. To dispel fantasies about fantasy-based measures of achievement motivation. *Psychological Bulletin*, 1972, 77, 377-391.

French, E. G. Some characteristics of achievement motivation. *Journal of Experimental Psychology*, 1955, 50, 232-236.

French, E. G. & Lesser, G. S. Some characteristics of the achievement motive in women. *Journal of Abnormal and Social Psychology*, 1964, 68, 119-128.

Friedman, G. D., Vry, H. K., Klatsky, A. L., & Siegelantz, A. B. A psychological questionnaire predictive of myocardial infarction: results from the Kaiser-Permanente epidemiologic study of myocardial infarction. *Psychosomatic Medicine*, 1974, 36, 327-343.

Friedman, M. & Rosenman, R. H. *Type A behavior and your heart*. New York: Fawcett, 1974.

Gough, H. G. & Heilbrun, A. B., Jr. *The adjective check list manual*. Palo Alto, Calif.: Consulting Psychologists Press, 1965.

Guilford, J. P. & Martin, H. G. *Guilford-Martin inventory of factors: manual*. Beverly Hills, Calif.: Sheridan Supply, 1948.

Heckhausen, H. *Motivation Und Handeln*. New York: Springer Verlag, 1980.

Horner, M. S. Sex differences in achievement motivation and performance in competitive and noncompetitive situations. Unpublished doctoral dissertation, University of Michigan, 1968.

Jackson, D. N. A modern strategy for personality assessment: the personality research form. *Research Bulletin No. 33c*. London, Canada: University of Western Ontario, Department of Psychology, 1966.

Klinger, E. Fantasy need achievement as a motivational construct. *Psychological Bulletin*, 1966, 66, 291-308.

Korman, A. K. *The psychology of motivation*. Englewood Cliffs, N.J.: Prentice-Hall, 1974.

Kuhl, J. Situations-, reaktions- und personbezogene Konsistenz des Leistungsmotivs bei der Messung mittels des Heckhausen-TAT. *Archiv fuer Psychologie*, 1978, 130, 37-52.

Loevinger, J. The measuring and measurement of ego development. *American Psychologist*, 1966, 21, 195-206.

Marlowe, D. Relationships among direct and indirect measures of the achievement motive and overt behavior. *Journal of Consulting Psychology,* 1959, 23, 329-341.

Marlowe, D. & Crowne, D. P. *The approval motive: studies in evaluative dependence.* New York: Wiley, 1964.

McClelland, D. C. *Personality.* New York: Sloane-Dryden-Holt, 1951.

McClelland, D. C. Methods of measuring human motivation. In J. W. Atkinson (Ed.), *Motives in fantasy, action and society.* New York: Van Nostrand, 1958.

McClelland, D. C. Longitudinal trends in the relation of thought to action. *Journal of Consulting Psychology,* 1966, 30, 479-483.

McClelland, D. C. *Assessing human motivation.* Morristown, N.J.: General Learning Press, 1971. (a)

McClelland, D. C. Testing for competence rather than for "intelligence." *American Psychologist,* 1971, 28, 1-14. (b)

McClelland, D. C. Opinions predict opinions: so what else is new? *Journal of Consulting and Clinical Psychology,* 1972, 38, 325-326.

McClelland, D. C. *Power: the inner experience.* New York: Irvington-Wiley, 1975.

McClelland, D. C. Inhibited power motivation and high blood pressure in men. *Journal of Abnormal Psychology,* 1979, 88, 182-190.

McClelland, D. C. Is personality consistent? In A. I. Rabin (ed.), *Symposium in honor of Henry A. Murray.* New York: Wiley, 1980.

McClelland, D. C. & Atkinson, J. W. The effect of different intensities of the hunger drive on thematic apperception. *Journal of Experimental Psychology,* 1948, 38, 643-658.

McClelland, D. C., Atkinson, J. W., Clark, R. A., & Lowell, E. L. *The achievement motive.* Englewood Cliffs, N.J.: Prentice-Hall, 1953.

McClelland, D. C. & Burnham, D. Power is the great motivator. *Harvard Business Review,* March-April 1976, 25, 159-166.

McClelland, D. C., Baldwin, A. L., Bronfenbrenner, U., & Strodtbeck, F. L. *Talent and society.* New York: Van Nostrand, 1958.

McClelland, D. C, Davis, W. B., Kalin, R., & Wanner, E. *The drinking man: alcohol and human motivation.* New York: Macmillan, 1972.

McClelland, D. C. & Liberman, A. M. The effect of need for achievement on recognition of need-related words. *Journal of Personality,* 1949, 18, 236-251.

McClelland, D. C. & Watson, R. I., Jr. Power motivation and risk-taking behavior. *Journal of Personality,* 1973, 41, 121-139.

McClelland, D. C. & Winter, D. G. *Motivating economic achievement.* New York: Macmillan, 1969.

McKeachie, W. J. Motivation, teaching methods, and college learning. *Nebraska symposium on motivation,* 1961, 9, 111-142.

Mehrabian, A. Measures of achieving tendency. *Educational and Psychological Measurement,* 1969, 29, 445-451.

Melton, A. W. Motivation and learning. In W. S. Monroe (ed.), *Encyclopedia of educational research.* New York: Macmillan, 1952.

Meyer, W., Folkes, V., & Weiner, B. The perceived informational value and affective consequences of choice behavior and intermediate difficulty task selection. *Journal of Research in Personality,* 1976, 10, 410-423.

Mischel, W. *Personality and assessment.* New York: Wiley, 1968.

Saul, L. Hostility in cases of essential hypertension. *Psychosomatic Medicine,* 1939, 1, 153-161.

Scott, W. A. & Johnson, R. C. Comparative validities of direct and indirect personality tests. *Journal of Consulting and Clinical Psychology,* 1972, 38, 301-318.

Sears, R. R., Maccoby, E. E., & Levin, H. *Patterns of child rearing.* New York: Harper & Row, 1957.

Skolnick, A. Motivational imagery and behavior over twenty years. *Journal of Consulting Psychology,* 1966, 30, 463-478.

Strong, E. K., Jr. & Campbell, D. P. *Strong Vocational Interest Blank for Men.* Stanford, Calif.: Stanford University Press, 1969.

Takala, M. Consistencies and perception of consistencies in psychomotor behavior. In D. Magnusson and N. S. Endler (eds.), *Personality at the crossroads: current issues in interactional psychology.* Hillsdale, N.J.: Erlbaum, 1977.

Telford, C. W. The refractory phase of voluntary and associative processes. *Journal of Experimental Psychology,* 1931, 14, 1-36.

Walker, E. Psychological complexity as a basis for a theory of motivation and choice. *Nebraska symposium on motivation,* 1964, 12, 47-97.

Weiner, B. *Achievement motivation and attribution theory.* Morristown, N.J.: General Learning Press, 1974.

Weinstein, M. S. Achievement motivation and risk preference. *Journal of Personality and Social Psychology,* 1969, 13, 153-172.

Wert, J. E., Neidt, C. O., & Ahmann, J. S. *Statistical methods in educational and psychological research.* Englewood Cliffs, N.J.: Prentice-Hall, 1954.

Winter, D. G. *The power motive.* New York: Macmillan, 1973.

Winter, D. G. *Navy leadership and management competencies: convergence among tests, interviews, and performance ratings.* Boston, Mass.: McBer and Co., 1979.

Winter, D. G., McClelland, D. C., & Stewart, A. J. *Competence in college: evaluating the liberal university.* San Francisco, Calif.: Jossey-Bass, in press.

Winter, D. G. & Stewart, A. J. Power motive reliability as a function of retest instructions. *Journal of Consulting and Clinical Psychology.* 1977, 45, 436-440.

Childhood Attachment Experience and Adult Loneliness

2

PHILLIP SHAVER
CARIN RUBENSTEIN

Phillip Shaver was Associate Professor of Psychology and head of the Doctoral Program in Personality and Social Psychology at New York University. He is now at the University of Denver. Besides loneliness, his research interests include self-awareness, sex roles, and social motivation. He is coauthor of *Measures of Social Psychological Attitudes.*
Carin Rubenstein is Associate Editor of *Psychology Today* magazine. She is the coauthor, with Phillip Shaver, of *What It Means To Be Lonely* (Delacorte, forthcoming). She is most interested in disseminating information about psychological research to the public.

L oneliness is similar in many ways to hunger. Both terms, loneliness and hunger, can be used to designate either feelings or drive states. Both lead to restlessness, distraction, and frustration if their aims are not attained. Both, by calling attention to painful deficits, identify needs for important and perhaps vital provisions (chemical in the one case, social and emotional in the other). Both ultimately require explanations based in evolutionary biology.

Given these marked similarities, one would expect social psychologists to have focused attention on loneliness to the same extent that experimental psychologists have focused on hunger. But this is far from the case. In fact, until recently "loneliness" did not appear in *Psychological Abstracts* or *Sociological Abstracts* or in social psychology textbooks. Although considerable space has customarily been devoted to such related topics as interpersonal attraction (Byrne, 1971) and the

AUTHORS' NOTE: We would like to thank Tracey Revenson for assisting with the literature review and discussing the contents of this article with us, and thank Hill Goldsmith, Gail Goodman, William Runyan, Dan Stokols, and Harry Triandis for commenting on earlier drafts. Our research has been supported by a Challenge Fund Grant from New York University.

effect of fear on the choice to affiliate (Schachter, 1959), loneliness—the deep longing for intimacy and community—has usually been ignored.[1]

There are reasons for this. As Weiss (1973) and Gordon (1976) point out, loneliness is an embarrassment in this culture, a sign of personal failure; even to study it is to risk being tainted. At the end of his pioneering book, Weiss confesses: "I am aware of how uncomfortable I feel about having assumed the role of advisor to the lonely. There is something undignified, indeed faintly comic, about the role: Dear Abby, Miss Lonelyhearts. . . . This discomfort must be among the reasons for the paucity of serious attention to loneliness" (1973, p. 236). Another reason is that until recently most social psychologists selected research topics which could be illuminated by brief laboratory experiments. Attraction to a stranger, or choosing to affiliate for a few minutes with fearful strangers, is amenable to laboratory study, whereas most aspects of sexual relationships, marital conflict, divorce, long-term friendship, and attachments between children and parents are not.

Today research priorities are changing—possibly reflecting the needs of American society—and loneliness is beginning to receive its due. Peplau et al. (1978) have published an extensive bibliography on the topic, measures of loneliness have been designed and validated (e.g., Rubenstein & Shaver, 1980; Russell et al., 1978), and at least two anthologies have been assembled (Hartog & Audy, 1980; Peplau & Perlman, in press). So far, however, little attention has been paid to childhood antecedents of loneliness or to ways in which these antecedents might be incorporated into emerging theoretical frameworks. We hope, by concentrating on possible antecedents of loneliness and conceptualizing them in cognitive terms, to facilitate research and suggest promising links between currently distinct research areas and theoretical paradigms.

In the remainder of this article we will: (1) briefly consider conceptual and operational definitions of loneliness; (2) outline two theoretical approaches to adult loneliness; (3) show how these relate to evidence and theory concerning possible childhood antecedents of adult loneliness, especially parental divorce; and (4) suggest avenues for future research.

CONCEPTUAL AND OPERATIONAL DEFINITIONS

Loneliness, like all affective states, is difficult to define precisely because the referent is subjective. Nevertheless, there is considerable overlap among recent definitions: (1) "being without a companion; feeling deserted, desolate; being alone and regretting it" *(Scribner-Bantam English Dictionary,* 1979); (2) "Loneliness appears always to be a response to the absence of some particular type of relationship or, more accurately, a response to the absence of some particular relational provision" (Weiss, 1973, p. 17); and (3) "Loneliness exists to the extent that a person's network of social relationships is smaller or less satisfying than the person desires" (Perlman & Peplau, in press). The psychologists (Weiss, Peplau, and Perlman) are more sensitive than the editors of the dictionary to the fact that loneliness does not necessarily imply being alone (Shaver & Rubenstein, 1979), but the dictionary is probably wiser than the psychologists in emphasizing feelings ("deserted, desolate, regretting it") as well as causes.

Psychologists have become increasingly aware of the danger of reifying traits and feelings (Bowlby, 1973; Mischel, 1976; Schafer, 1976)—that is, treating them as if they were things—especially in cases where the construct in question has been devised and named by psychologists (e.g., ego strength). However, in a forthcoming article, Weiss (in press) warns of the opposite problem in studies of loneliness, that is, of neglecting the fact that for most people loneliness is a distinct and highly identifiable state. In constructing the 20-item UCLA Loneliness Scale, Russell et al. (1978) completely avoided the term *loneliness,* concentrating instead on statements that might reveal a discrepancy between desired and actual social relationships; for example, "I lack companionship." In discussing this strategy, Weiss (in press) says: "A discrepancy between the desired and realized may, perhaps, explain the development of loneliness. But this is a hypothesis. I think we should not prevent ourselves from testing our hypotheses by making them true by definition."

In our work (Rubenstein & Shaver, 1980, in press) we have used a more straightforward eight-item scale, each item of which contains the word *lonely.* The items, minus their scaled answer alternatives, are as follows: (1) When I am completely alone, I feel lonely. (2) How often do you feel lonely? (3) When you feel lonely, how lonely do you feel? (4) Compared with people your age, how lonely do you think you are? (5) I am a lonely person. (6) I always was a lonely person. (7) I always will be a lonely person. (8) Other people think of me as a lonely person. The scale has yielded internal consistency reliabilities (coefficient alpha) around .90 in several large survey studies of adult Americans.

In reporting our results, and in examining other studies, we will mean by "loneliness" a self-reported, self-labelled affective state. The causes of the state are thus left open for empirical inquiry.[2]

TABLE 2
Factor Analysis of Feelings When Lonely

Factor 1: Desperation	Factor 2: Depression	Factor 3: Impatient Boredom	Factor 4: Self-Deprecation
Desperate	Sad	Impatient	Unattractive
Panicked	Depressed	Bored	Down on self
Helpless	Empty	Desire to be elsewhere	Stupid
Afraid	Isolated	Uneasy	Ashamed
Without hope	Sorry for self	Angry	Insecure
Abandoned	Melancholy	Unable to concentrate	
Vulnerable	Alienated		
	Longing to be with one special person		

This suggestion gains plausibility when one examines the list of feelings that form Factor 1 in Table 2: helpless, afraid, abandoned, vulnerable—the term *abandoned* being the one Weiss himself used. Similarly, Factor 3 in Table 2 overlaps remarkably well with Weiss's description of childhood social isolation; he uses the terms *boredom, marginality,* and *exclusion;* and we find "bored" and "desire to be elsewhere." Our conceptually and empirically related Alienation factor (in Table 1) contains the phrases "not being needed" and "having no close friends."

Thus we have good reason to take Weiss's distinction seriously and to pursue his suggestion that the prototypes (and perhaps antecedents) of adult emotional and social isolation are experienced in childhood. Exploring this theme will be the main task of the second half of this article.

An Attribution Theory of Loneliness

Peplau and her colleagues (Perlman & Peplau, in press; Peplau et al., 1979) have adapted Weiner's (1974) attribution theory of achievement motivation to the study of loneliness. Their strategy makes good sense if one accepts the assumption (advanced by Gordon, 1976) that loneliness is often perceived, at least in our culture, as a personal failure. Weiner (1974) showed that the four most common explanations for success and failure in the achievement realm—ability, effort, task difficulty, and luck—can be arrayed in a two-by-two table (see Table 3), one dimension

TABLE 3

Weiner's (1974) Causal Attribution Model Applied to

Explanations of Loneliness

	Locus of Control	
Stability	Internal	External
Stable	I am lonely because I'm unlovable; I'll never really be worth loving. It's depressing; I feel empty. I sit around at night alone, getting stoned, eating, and diverting myself with TV. (Weiner's ABILITY cell.)	The people around here are cold and impersonal; none of them share my interests or live up to my expectations. I'm sick of this place and don't intend to stay here much longer. (Weiner's TASK DIFFICULTY cell)
Unstable	I'm lonely now, but won't be for long. I'll stop devoting so much time to work and go out and meet some new people. I'll start by calling the man I met at Ken's party. (Weiner's EFFORT cell)	My lover and I have split up. That's the way relationships go these days; some of them work and some of them don't. Next time, maybe I'll be more fortunate. (Weiner's LUCK cell)

NOTE: The comments in the cells are hypothetical and meant only for illustration. They are, however, quite similar to comments we have recorded in interviews with lonely people (Rubenstein & Shaver, in press).

being internal versus external locus of control and the other, temporal stability (stable versus unstable).[6]

The importance of these causal categories for research on feelings such as loneliness (Weiner et al., 1978) is that affective reactions to success and failure, and subsequent task-oriented behavior, are influenced by attribution processes. Internal attributions following success, for example, enhance pride and encourage future effort; the attribution of failure to low ability results in shame and withdrawal from the task.

Loneliness can be conceptualized in an analogous way. A person who is experiencing emotional or social isolation often asks him- or herself *why,* and a variety of answers are possible: "I am unlovable." "I am surrounded by snobs who do not appreciate my good qualities." "I have not exerted enough effort to meet people in my new neighborhood." The affective consequences of different attributions are predictable; for example, "perceiving that loneliness is due to stable causes should lead a person to anticipate prolonged loneliness [an unpleasant state of affairs]; unstable causes should lead to greater optimism about improving one's social life" (Perlman & Peplau, in press). Low self-esteem and, in severe cases, depression are likely to accompany internal, stable attributions for loneliness ("I am lonely because I am uninteresting, unattractive, lacking in all social graces").[7]

Results of a factor analysis of 21 reactions to loneliness (Rubenstein & Shaver, 1980) are shown in Table 4. The first factor, Sad Passivity, accounts for 46.4% of the common variance and seems to be a concomitant of prolonged loneliness. The factor correlates $r = .42$ ($p < .001$) with our loneliness scale, and .49 and .46, respectively, with the Depression and Self-Deprecation factors shown in Table 2. Elsewhere (Rubenstein & Shaver, 1980) we have described a vicious cycle in which some lonely people attribute their loneliness to internal, stable factors; these self-blaming attributes then lead to depression and sad passivity, which in turn militate against the formation of new or more rewarding social ties.

The other factors shown in Table 4 represent reactions to loneliness which characterize people who are seldom lonely. This is especially true for Factor 4, Social Contact; people who react to loneliness by contacting others are obviously making an effort, in Peplau and Weiner's terms, and although we do not have direct evidence regarding their attributions, it seems likely that they view loneliness as a temporary (unstable) state which can be dispelled by effort.

Peplau and her colleagues have not examined the attribution patterns of children or looked for childhood antecedents of particular attributional proclivities (such as self-blame). Nevertheless, their theoretical framework is eminently suitable for this research task. Dweck and Goetz (1978), among others, have shown that Weiner's (1974) theory of motivation applies to young children and that attributional retraining of test-anxious children is effective in altering their behavior. A major goal of the present article is to suggest that a similar approach be taken to the study and treatment of loneliness.

ATTACHMENT AND SEPARATION IN CHILDHOOD

Bowlby's Theory

For our purposes the best account of attachment and separation during childhood is the one Bowlby (1969, 1973, 1980) presents in his three-volume study *Attachment and Loss*. This account has several

TABLE 4
Factor Analysis of Responses to Loneliness

Factor 1: Sad Passivity	Factor 2: Active Solitude	Factor 3: Spending Money	Factor 4: Social Contact
Cry	Study or work	Spend money	Call a friend
Sleep	Write	Go shopping	Visit someone
Sit and think	Listen to music		
Do nothing	Exercise		
Overeat	Walk		
Take tranquilizers	Work on a hobby		
Watch television	Go to a movie		
Drink or get "stoned"	Read		
	Play music		

virtues: (1) it examines the research literature on both humans and nonhuman primates and considers the "environment of evolutionary adaptedness" in which attachment behavior arose; (2) it conceptualizes the residue of early separation experiences in terms of "models" of self and the social world, and these models can easily be reconceptualized in terms compatible with current cognitive approaches to clinical and social psychology; and (3) it reviews evidence for the long-term effects of early separations and losses. We do not have space to recapitulate Bowlby's careful and well-documented argument in detail or to cite all of the evidence in its favor (for recent and largely supportive reviews see Ainsworth et al., 1978; Rajecki et al., 1978; Rutter, 1979; Sroufe & Waters, 1977). For the moment we accept the main features of the argument and consider its possible implications for adult loneliness.

Bowlby began with clinical observations of young children who were separated from their mothers. ("Mother" is generally used to designate the child's caretaker, whether or not this is actually the child's biological mother.) Typically such children went through three identifiable stages. The first was *protest,* a mixture of anger and crying, which lasted for a variable number of hours. Eventually, if the mother failed to return, *despair* set in; the child became quiet, listless, and noticeably sad. Finally, the child showed what Bowlby calls *detachment;* if the mother returned late in this phase, the child showed no interest in her, whereas if she returned before this phase the child showed intense emotion and clinging behavior.

Examination of ethnological data and laboratory experiments involving nonhuman primates convinced Bowlby that the attachment of human infants to their mothers is based in instinctive processes. Both primate and human infants are born with certain reflexes (e.g., grasping) and needs (e.g., for contact comfort; Harlow & Mears, 1979) which make it likely that they will remain in close proximity to their mother. Research by Harlow and others (summarized by Bowlby, 1969, 1973; Harlow & Mears, 1979; Rajecki et al., 1978) called into question the once common secondary drive explanation of such proximity-maintaining behavior.[8] Physical contact with the mother appears to be more important for attachment than is simple receipt of food from her. Bowlby also noted the importance of eye contact, crying, smiling, reaching, and clinging in maintaining close contact between mother and infant.

The usual pattern of attachment in both humans and nonhuman primates is: (1) establishment of a strong primary attachment relationship (which in humans appears to occur during the second half of the first year of life) and (2) gradual physical separation from the primary attachment figure in favor of exploration of the environment and establishment of additional social ties (which in humans is evident during the second year of life and after). When voluntary separation occurs, especially at first, the infant requires frequent visits back to mother and regular visual and auditory contact with her. In Bowlby's terms, the infant uses the mother as a secure base of operations. (For a much more detailed examination of the "separation-individuation" process, see Mahler, 1971, and Mahler et al., 1975.) Gradually, beyond the second year of life, the child can tolerate longer periods of separation, especially if the meaning and extent of these are negotiated between child and mother. (Of course such negotiation is impossible before the child develops the requisite cognitive and linguistic skills.)

At all phases of development, the child is more likely to show attachment behaviors (crying for help, clinging to a parent) when it is tired, ill, in pain, or frightened.[9] Thus, even an older and apparently quite independent child may become "clingy" at times. Bowlby argues that fear is instinctively triggered by certain cues—unfamiliar surroundings, pain, darkness, sudden noise, looming objects, and being alone—and that the fear is especially intense when two or more such cues are combined. This makes sense from an evolutionary standpoint, since one function of attachment behavior seems to be protection of the infant from danger, including predators. Danger, in our "environment of evolutionary adaptedness" and probably in our current environment as well, is often associated with these natural cues. (A child alone is much more likely than an accompanied child to be hit by a car in a modern city, for example.) If the child is not comforted by an attachment figure, its fears are magnified.

The ideal parent, according to Bowlby, is regularly available to the child during the first few years of life, continually affectionate and supportive, and able gently to urge separation and exploration when the child begins to chose these. Anything less than this ideal behavior is likely to result in "anxious attachment," a pattern of emotions and behavior which includes clinging, undue anxiety upon separation, and lack of confidence in self and others. As mentioned earlier, prolonged separation experiences may result in another nonoptimal outcome: detachment and consequent inability to form satisfying attachments.

With this background in mind, Bolwby's theory can be summarized in three propositions:

> The first is that when an individual is confident that an attachment figure will be available to him whenever he desires it, that person will be much less prone to either intense or chronic fear than will an individual who for any reason has no such confidence. The second proposition concerns the sensitive period during which such confidence develops. It postulates that confidence in the availability of attachment figures, or a lack of it, is built up slowly during the years of immaturity—infancy, childhood, and adolescence—and that whatever expectations are developed during those years tend to persist relatively unchanged throughout the rest of life. The third proposition concerns the role of actual experience. It postulates that the varied expectations of the accessibility and responsiveness of attachment figures that different individuals develop during the years of immaturity are tolerably accurate reflections of the experiences those individuals have actually had [1973, p. 235].

In the early years of life the actual presence of an attachment figure is a major determinant of "whether a person is or is not alarmed by any potentially alarming situation" (Bowlby, 1973, p. 273). But beginning in the second year and continuing thereafter, the requirement of actual presence is gradually eased as the child gains confidence that an attachment figure not actually present will be available, "accessible and responsive," should this become desirable. "After the third birthday *forecasts* of availability or unavailability become of increasing importance, and after puberty they are likely in turn to become the dominant variable" determining feelings of personal security (Bowlby, 1973, p. 273).

In our studies (Rubenstein & Shaver, 1980) and in earlier research by others (e.g., Rosenberg, 1965), loneliness and pessimism about relations with others were inversely correlated with self-esteem. (Our subjects were adults, Rosenberg's were adolescents.) Bowlby's analysis suggests a reason for this reliable pattern of correlations:

> Confidence that an attachment figure is, apart from being accessible, likely to be responsive can be seen to turn on at least two variables: (a) whether or not the attachment figure is judged to be the sort of person who in general responds to calls for support and protection; (b) whether or not the self is judged to be the sort of person towards whom anyone, and the attachment figure in particular, is likely to respond in a helpful way. Logically these variables are independent. In practice they are apt to be confounded. As a result, the model of the attachment figure and the model of the self are likely to develop so as to be complementary and mutually confirming. Thus an unwanted child is likely not only to feel unwanted by his parents but to believe that he is essentially unwantable, namely unwanted by anyone. . . . Though logically indefensible, these crude over-generalizations are . . . the rule. Once adopted, moreover, and woven into the fabric of the working models, they are apt . . . never to be seriously questioned [1973, p. 238].

Bowlby cites evidence for several quite different parental behaviors or behavioral styles which can promote anxious or insecure attachments; these "include both refusing to respond to a child's approaches, for example by sulking, and threatening to leave home or to send the child away" (1973, p. 243). Bowlby claims that such threats are quite common among frustrated parents and much more damaging than parents realize: "Because they deliberately cast doubt on whether the attachment figure will be available when needed, such threats can greatly increase a person's fear that he will be abandoned, and thereby greatly increase also his susceptibility to respond to other sanctions fearfully" (1973, p. 243).

The hypothesis that insecure attachment produces chronic anxiety led Bowlby to hypothesize that adolescents and adults who had attachment problems during childhood would exhibit more stress symptoms. Evidence in support of the hypothesis has been reported by Rosenberg (1965) and others and discussed extensively by Bowlby (1973, 1980). In our survey studies of adult loneliness (Rubenstein & Shaver, 1980), we have consistently included a list of 19 psychological problems and psychosomatic symptoms. The correlation between a factor-analytically derived index of stress symptoms and scores on our loneliness scale has been around .60 ($p < .001$) in every sample we have investigated. Moreover, as we discuss in a later section of this article, adult respondents whose parents were divorced while the respondents were growing up had significantly higher scores on the index of stress symptoms.

In summary, there is good reason to believe that psychological attachment of children to their caretakers is a universal and in part innately determined process which originally functioned and still functions to protect human infants from danger. When frightened, infants and children are especially likely to show intense attachment behavior, which makes good sense in terms of evolution. If children are not allowed to develop secure attachments, or if their attachments are threatened by separation from parents, the children may develop models of self and the social world which are detrimental to later self-esteem, health, and interpersonal relations.

Case Examples: Short-Term Effects of Separation, Real and Threatened

So far, because of space limitations, we have written at a very abstract level. Since we want to suggest that childhood experiences are emotionally powerful enough to form lasting cognitive impressions, it may be worthwhile to present two brief concrete examples exerpted by Bowlby from a study of 700 four-year-old children in Nottingham, England, conducted by Newson and Newson (1968).

A miner's wife commented as follows when asked whether her daughter ever wanted to be held and cuddled:

> Ever since I left her that time I had to go into hospital (two periods, 17 days each, child aged 2 years), she doesn't trust me any more. I can't go anywhere—over to the neighbors or in the shops—I've always got to take her. She wouldn't leave me. She went down to the school gates at dinner time today. She ran like mad home. She said, "Oh, Mum I thought you was gone!" She can't forget it. She's still round me all the time.

This example involves real separation from a parent; Newson and Newson (1968) also found that *threats* of abandonment, used as a discipline technique by more than a quarter of the parents interviewed, can be quite damaging. Another miner's wife described a fairly typical threat incident as follows:

> I once did—and upset her so much that I've never said it any more. [What did you say?] Well, she was having an argument with me, and she says to

me "You don't live here! Hop it!" So I says, "Oh, well, I can do that! Where's my coat? I'm moving!" So I got my coat from the back and I was gone. I just stood outside the door, and she cried so bitter, she did. As soon as I came in, she got hold of my leg and wouldn't let go. . . . I'll *never* say it no more.

Intense Loneliness as a Component of Borderline Psychopathology

In recent years psychoanalytic psychotherapists have devoted increased attention to the "borderline patient," the patient whose form and degree of pathology place him or her somewhere on a continuum between neurotic and psychotic (Grinker et al., 1968; Kernberg, 1967; Kohut, 1971). Clinicians who work with borderline patients disagree on the proper way to characterize their fundamental problems, but most agree that abandonment and loneliness are common themes. Adler and Buie (1979), for example, "have observed a core experiential state of intensely painful aloneness" (p. 83).

> When we view borderline patients on a spectrum extending from psychotic to more nearly neurotic experience, we find that those closer to psychosis experience this aloneness more frequently and intensely. . . . A or total inability to maintain positive fantasies or images of sustaining people in his past or present life. At these times the patient often states that he has no fantasies at all; at other times he has fantasies, but they consist of unsustaining or disruptive negative memories and images of the people who are important to him [p. 83].

Adler and Buie (1979), using concepts proposed by Piaget (1954), Fraiberg (1969), and Mahler (1968, 1971; Mahler et al., 1975), attempt to account for the intense loneliness of the borderline patient in terms of mother-infant interactions during the second year of life. At this time, cognitive immaturity and separation or rejection experiences can combine to disrupt normal formation of positive, sustaining images of a trustworthy caretaker. (Similar but less elaborated ideas were propounded earlier by Erikson, 1950, who spoke of the development of basic trust or mistrust.) Much more information must be gathered before the loneliness of the borderline patient can be fully understood, but current evidence is sufficient to add to the claim that vulnerability to loneliness in adulthood can often be traced back to childhood experiences.[10]

Short- and Long-Term Effects of Parental Divorce on Children

No part of the picture we are attempting to sketch has been adequately researched as yet, but one source of childhood separation experiences—parental divorce—has been examined with a variety of research techniques (behavioral observation, interviews, large-scale surveys) and the results are quite informative, even if still subject to some debate. Studies in this area can be usefully divided into two rough categories, retrospective and immediate. In the first kind of study, adolescents or adults are questioned years after the divorce experience; in the second, children are observed and questioned at the time of the divorce or shortly thereafter. Results from each kind of study will be reviewed briefly, with an eye toward possible reasons for the relationship we obtained (Rubenstein et al., 1979) between parental divorce and later loneliness. We should also mention that we obtained a clear effect of age of respondent at the time of the parents' divorce: Respondents who underwent the divorce process at an earlier age were lonelier as adults, lower in self-esteem, and suffered from more stress symptoms. No such effects were found for respondents who had lost a parent by death.[11]

Retrospective studies. Rosenberg (1965), in a study mentioned earlier, classified respondents' families according to whether the natural parents were living together, divorced, separated voluntarily, or separated by death. A series of analyses revealed that parental divorce and separation, but not death, were associated with lower self-esteem and increased pyschosomatic symptomatology. (Results for loneliness were not broken down by family type, but we know that loneliness was correlated with low self-esteem and high symptom scores in this study, as in our own.) Respondents who were younger at the time of the divorce showed greater deficits.

In a more recent publication, Wilson et al. (1975) reanalyzed data from a 1973 study of a random sample of American adults, comparing offspring of stepfather families with offspring of families in which both natural parents were present. Respondents who had lived with a stepfather (i.e., had been separated from their natural father) were not as likely as the comparison group to feel that "most people are fair" or "helpful"; and they were not as happy as the comparison group with their own current marital life. Notice that the belief differences obtained are quite compatible with Bowlby's ideas.

Schooler (1972), examining data from a 1964 survey of adult males, found that men whose parents divorced or separated before they (the respondents) were 16 years old exhibited greater anxiety and expressed greater distrust of others—again in line with Bowlby's predictions. (As in Rosenberg's study and in our own, men who had, during childhood, lost a parent by death were not similarly anxious or distrustful of others, so separation is not the whole story, a point we will take up later.)

In the most recent analysis of adult data, Kulka and Weingarten (1979) compared the results of a 1957 nationwide survey (discussed by Gurin et al., 1960, in *Americans View Their Mental Health*) and a 1976 replication of that survey (currently being prepared for publication). Kulka and Weingarten also compared adult offspring from "intact" homes with those from homes "disrupted by divorce or marital separation." Respondents from disrupted homes often said that childhood and adolescence were the most unhappy periods in their lives and were more likely to have "felt an impending nervous breakdown." They were also more likely to expect "bad things" to happen to them, "find things hard to handle when bad things happen" (men only), report more current anxiety (again men only), and (for respondents between 21 and 34 years old) report more disease symptoms. The "disrupted" group was more likely to report having experienced marital problems (which goes along with findings of other studies indicating "intergenerational transmission of marital instability"; Pope & Mueller, 1976; Rutter, 1979).

It should be noted that the term *intact* is somewhat misleading. Nye (1957), in a study of 780 high school students, compared those from "broken homes" (which he treated as a single category) with those from "unhappy unbroken" homes, homes in which parents quarreled often and were both perceived by their child to be less than satisfied with the marriage. Summarizing the results, Nye wrote: "Stated positively . . . adolescents in broken homes show less psychosomatic illness, less delinquent behavior, and better adjustment than do children in unhappy unbroken homes" (p. 358). This is compatible with the argument we are developing here, if one is willing to assume that relations between parents and children are often very poor when the parents are at odds with each other (Landis, 1960; Lynn, 1974). (Bowlby, 1973, mentions that in such situations real and imagined threats of abandonment are common.)

Summarizing the adult studies: Living through the divorce of one's parents especially when very young, seems to predispose a person to later loneliness and to low self-esteem, distrust of others, health problems, and doubts about one's own marriage. Not every child of divorce develops these symptoms, of course (Wallerstein & Kelly, 1980), but their repeated appearance in several studies suggests that they are common consequences of divorce. Taken together, the set of problems and symptoms are just what one would expect on the basis of Bowlby's theory: loneliness, anxiety and stress, and pessimistic models of oneself and one's social world.

Studies conducted immediately after the divorce. Adjustment to parental divorce, when studied immediately after the event, appears to be age-related—age serving as a rough indicator of cognitive and social maturity. Children construct their own interpretations of the complex divorce situation, and these interpretations vary with age. The most detailed examinations of postdivorce reactions in children and adolescents have been conducted by Hetherington et al. (1976, 1977) and Wallerstein and Kelly (1974, 1975, 1976, 1980; Kelly & Wallerstein, 1976). For the following summaries we rely heavily on their work and on a speculative article by Longfellow (1979) which proposes a cognitive-developmental conceptualization of the impact of divorce on children.

Preschool years. Wallerstein and Kelly (1975) studied 34 preschool children, aged 3 to 6, shortly after the parents' separation and again 12 to 18 months later. Immediate effects of the divorce included increased neediness, unhappiness, helplessness, and diminished self-esteem. One year after the separation, the intensity of these reactions had subsided in a little over half (56%) of the cases, but there remained a pervasive neediness in relationships, evidenced by clinging and desperation for physical contact. The most vulnerable preschoolers came from families where a high degree of family disruption persisted. In many of these cases the (custodial) mothers appeared emotionally overwhelmed by the divorce and unable to provide sufficient love and warmth to their children.

Hetherington et al. (1977) compared 48 preschool children from divorced homes with a matched control sample and found that the children of divorced parents exhibited significantly more negative (e.g., socially disruptive) behaviors. Felner and his associates (Felner et al., 1975, in press) obtained similar results with preschool children of divorce and a matched sample on measures of school performance and acting-out behavior. The main findings, even for this young group, are in the area of self-esteem, anxiety, and style of interpersonal behavior, all issues which appeared prominently in studies of adult offspring of divorced parents.

The most interesting evidence, from the present point of view, concerns self-blame:

> One of the most pervasive reactions of the slightly older preschool child (3½-6) was that of self-blame—an attitude that was found to be "highly resistant to educational interventions by parents or by the clinical staff" (Wallerstein & Kelly, 1975, p. 605). . . . A social cognitive-developmental

interpretation of these findings would focus on the fact that preschoolers think largely in an egocentric way. . . . Their explanations are apt to center on themselves. Thus, they conceptualize the divorce as if it happened between *them* and their parents, or as a result of their own wrongdoing. The result is often self-blame, very likely for an illogical reason. For example, "Daddy left home because I was a bad boy—I didn't put away my toys" [Longfellow, 1979, p. 300].

We suggest, as a hypothesis for future research, that this early tendency toward self-blame, combined with the relatively primitive, powerful, and unprotected nature of the young child's attachment to parents, lays the foundation for later separation anxiety, vulnerability to stress, and proneness to use internal, stable attributions (Perlman & Peplau, in press) to explain feelings of loneliness.

Early latency. The 7- and 8-year-old children were not as likely to blame themselves for the divorce, but they felt rejected, deprived, and abandoned nevertheless (Kelly & Wallerstein, 1976). They were more adept than the preschoolers at expressing their feelings but had trouble acknowledging conflicting feelings toward a particular parent (e.g., both sadness and anger). Also, as Longfellow notes:

They do not appear to understand that mother and father are *mutually* unhappy in their marital relationship and that it is their *mutual* dissatisfaction which motivated the divorce. Instead, [they] believe that one of the parents got mad and either left or made the other one leave. They may reason that if they make mother similarly mad, they too will suffer these dire consequences [1979, p. 302].

Later latency. These children (aged 9 and 10) understood even better than the early latency children that the divorce was not their fault; they were also able to use coping strategies such as increased activity and seeking emotional support and defense mechanisms such as denial and avoidance (Wallerstein & Kelly, 1976). This age group more than any other explicitly referred to intense loneliness, indicating that they were able to reflect and articulate their feelings. (We believe that the younger children can safely be said to *be* lonely, but they do not use that word.) The older children could also infer their parents' feelings fairly accurately—an ability which sometimes augmented their loneliness when they noticed that "their parents were so embroiled in their own stuggles that they paid only peripheral attention to their children" (Longfellow, 1979, p. 303).

Adolescence. Wallerstein and Kelly (1974) studied 21 adolescents, aged 13 to 18, and found their most frequent reactions to divorce to be feelings of anger, sadness, loss, shame, embarrassment, helplessness, and a sense of betrayal by the parents. They typically used distancing and withdrawal from parents as defenses against these feelings, some remaining detached and distant, "verging on aloofness," a year after the marital separation. A critical issue for adolescents is sexual identity and their own sexual and marital future. Adolescents who experience parental separation often become concerned about the possibility of separation occurring later in their own lives. Many in Wallerstein and Kelly's sample claimed they would never marry, or made a decision to marry later than their parents and be more selective in their own choice of partner. (Similar results were obtained in earlier studies; for example, Landis, 1960. Kulka and Weingarten's, 1979, study indicates that children of divorce actually do wait longer to marry.)

In other words, adolescents—because of their relative cognitive maturity—are better able to see the divorce as mainly the parents' problem, with possible implications for the general nature of marriage. They are upset by parental divorce, to be sure, but not in the same way or to the same extent as the preschoolers. Thus, the direct studies of children and adolescents generate findings that are congruent with findings from retrospective studies of adults.

Parental Divorce as Compared with Parental Death

Several of the studies we have reviewed indicate that parental divorce is a more powerful determinant of later loneliness than is death of a parent. (See also the recent review articles by Rutter, 1979; Crook & Eliot, 1980). Careful consideration of this difference may reveal something important about the childhood antecedents of later loneliness. Obviously, loss of a parent is not the only important factor in the divorce experience.

Divorce is not usually a sudden occurrence. Prior to separation and divorce, many parents quarrel intensely, and in the process may neglect or upset their children. Moreover, children may attempt to intervene and feel helpless or disregarded when their attempts fail, as they almost certainly must. Death, on the other hand, especially the death of a young parent, usually comes suddenly, and although young children sometimes blame themselves for a parent's death, in time most of them come to understand that the loss was not their fault. Therefore, what Bowlby calls a "model of the social world" is likely to be very different for children of divorce as compared with children who experience the death of a parent.

Once divorce occurs, the parent who retains custody of the child— usually the mother—may disparage the absent parent and question his (or her) trustworthiness. This may create doubts in the child's mind about the value and sincerity of the absent parent's love and support. The noncustodial parent, while visiting the child, may sow similar seeds of doubt regarding the custodial parent. Furthermore, the custodial parent will most likely have moments of exasperation when the existence of the child (or children) is a burden—for example, a financial liability or a hindrance to new romance. During such moments the child may be told, or may infer, that his or her value and security is in question. (Similar frustrations occur in the lives of widows, of course, but the divorced parent often has a rougher time of it because of the continued existence, and sometimes nearby presence, of the disaffected partner.)

Once a parent dies, he or she never returns. Children sometimes deny this for a while (or fail to understand it), but most begin to accept the permanence and irreversibility of the parent's absence. After divorce, however, children typically continue to see or communicate with the noncustodial parent, and these encounters raise anew the possibility that the parent might be enticed or convinced to return home. In most instances, of course, all such efforts are in vain and the child repeatedly feels powerless. This is just the kind of experience that fosters internal, stable attributions for failure (Dweck & Goetz, 1978; Weiner, 1974) and may also lead to internal, stable attributions for loneliness.

COGNITIVE COMPONENTS OF LONELINESS

Loneliness, at least the kind that Weiss (1973) calls emotional isolation, seems to arise when a person's primary attachment figure is inaccessible or when the person has no primary attachment figure. For children, this attachment figure is usually a parent; for adults it is typically a spouse or lover (although the implied sexual component of adult attachment need not always be present). We agree with Weiss (1973, 1975) that the attachment process continues throughout life and that adult loneliness is similar in many ways to the feelings experienced by young children when they are separated from a parent. (See also Knudtson, 1976; Lerner and Ryff, 1978, and Troll and Smith, 1976, for preliminary outlines of a life-span perspective on human attachment processes.)

How do cognitive factors influence this feeling state? The evidence suggests that cognition enters at two different points in the temporal stream of feeling: (1) when social situations are appraised ("He's about to leave me; if I'm not 'good' he will abandon me")[12] and (2) when feelings of loneliness and separation anxiety are *explained to oneself* ("This confirms that I am inherently unlovable"). As we have seen, childhood experiences can influence these two kinds of cognitive processes in various ways.

For example, the appraisal of adult social situations is based on what Bowlby calls "models of social life" which are grounded in childhood experiences. Recent work by cognitively oriented clinicians (e.g., Beck, 1976; Meichenbaum, 1976; reviewed by Shaver, 1978) indicates that the overlearned assumptions, images, and expectations included in appraisals such as these are often unconscious, not because of repression or other Freudian defense mechanisms but because overlearning usually results in faster, more automatic, less attended-to thought processes. In most situations this "automatization" of thought is beneficial, because it allows attention and high-level cognitive processes to be devoted to novel or complex problems; in the case of undesirable thought and behavior patterns, however, automatization makes change difficult.

Systematic examination of what Beck (1976) calls "automatic thoughts" has been undertaken in the study and treatment of certain emotional disorders, but not yet in the study of loneliness. As mentioned earlier, Dweck and Goetz (1978), working in the area of achievement motivation and fear of failure (which is analogous to loneliness in certain respects), have shown how one might explore and alter the cognitive components of loneliness.

Our review of studies on the impact of divorce on children suggests ways in which attributional biases related to chronic or frequent loneliness, especially the bias toward self-blame, can be affected by childhood experiences and by a child's cognitive-developmental level when certain life events occur. Earlier we quoted Bowlby's claim that "the varied expectations of the accessibility and responsiveness of attachment figures [developed during childhood] are tolerably accurate reflections of the experiences [that] individuals have actually had." In light of research on cognitive development, especially on developmental factors affecting children's understanding of divorce, Bowlby's statement should be amended. Social expectations, although clearly based on real events, may be *in*tolerably *in*accurate when filtered through immature cognitive lenses.

Faulty, self-damaging cognitions do not exist in a behavioral vacuum, of course. In fact, they contribute powerfully to the course of behavior and may be altered by behavioral outcomes. A fruitful perspective on this matter has been developed by Wachtel (1977a, 1977b), who focuses on self-perpetuating interaction cycles. Wachtel describes a man who "frequently acts in an excessively and inappropriately meek, helpful, or cooperative manner." He "*suffers* from this pattern of behavior, either directly or indirectly (e.g., depression, low self-esteem, psychosomatic symptoms)." His behavior, says Wachtel, "leads to a variety of ways in which he gets taken advantage of , dismissed, deprived, and frustrated." This makes him angry, and because he has received unpleasant treatment in the past (e.g., physical punishment, parental rejection or threats of rejection) whenever he has exploded angrily, intense anger now increases his (partly unconscious, automatic) efforts to be "nice," meek, and helpful.

> Thus, although his defensive behavior may be understood as a response to conflict over angry impulses, the impulses themselves can be seen as a function of the defense against them: Were he not acting in such a way that he constantly stifled himself and invited others to do so, he would not be so full of rage. On the other hand, were he not so full of rage . . . he would not be so afraid of giving up the desperate defensive efforts. Impulse leads to defense, defense leads to impulse, and the cycle keeps maintaining itself [Wachtel, 1977b, p. 318].

Wachtel does not talk specifically about loneliness, but one can imagine ways in which his approach could be fruitfully applied to the study of loneliness. Our in-depth interviews with lonely adults (Rubenstein & Shaver, in press) and preliminary laboratory studies (e.g., Solano, 1979) suggest that many lonely people are either "clingy" in relationships (exhibiting behavior which, when seen in children, Bowlby calls anxious attachment) or aloof, closed, and distant (in children, Bowlby calls this detachment). The first kind of person discloses personal information too quickly, pushes for signs of affection and commitment too soon and too vigorously, and ultimately gets rejected. The second kind of person is reluctant to disclose personal information at all, feels too vulnerable to show signs of interest and commitment, and ultimately gets rejected or ignored. Both kinds of people fear rejection, have been rejected in the past, and hold certain (perhaps unconscious) assumptions about the rejection process. Both, in an attempt to avoid the pain of rejection, act in ways that make rejection likely.

There are also likely to be cross-cultural differences in the determination of loneliness (Triandis, personal communication). People probably develop a kind of "adaptation level" (Helson, 1968) for a certain frequency of interactions with others (or others of particular kinds). If so, deviations in either direction from this expected level might be experienced as unpleasant—and labelled "crowdednes" or "invasion of privacy," on the one hand, and loneliness on the other. Whether there are universal limits on the acceptable range of adaptation levels remains to be seen. In any case, a more complete analysis of cognitive factors in loneliness should take adaptation level into account.

Cognitive Reworking of Earlier Social Experience

We tried to make a preliminary case (based on Longfellow, 1979) for the importance of cognitive development as a mediator between attachment experiences and their cognitive and emotional residues. According to our line of reasoning, individual differences in response to adult social isolation, rejection, or loss are due in part to age differences (actually, cognitive-developmental differences) between people when certain key childhood events (e.g., parental divorce) occur in their lives.

Another possible source of individual differences, even between people who experience similar events at similar ages, is the extent to which cognitive, emotional, and behavioral residues of these experiences are reconceptualized at later stages of cognitive development. As Wachtel (1977a) has shown, traumatic social experiences in childhood do not remain frozen, like "wooly mammoths" (his term), in the unconscious, there periodically to melt and come back to life in their original form. The cognitive results of these experiences are dynamically related to behavior and are affected (albeit slowly in some cases) by new experiences and new conceptualizations. It seems likely that both social experience (new friendships, new love affairs, psychotherapy) and cognitive development push for continual or periodic reconsideration of assumptions and expectations about social relations. The processes by which these cognitive wooly mammoths are maintained or transformed over time are only beginning to receive research attention (Cantor & Mischel, 1979; Ross, 1979).

SUMMARY AND COMMENT

We have suggested a complex causal path, leading from experiences in infancy and childhood to a lasting vulnerability to adult loneliness. Evidence for the path is somewhat tenuous, since relevant longitudinal studies have yet to be conducted and retrospective studies have been sketchy to date. (In fact, most were done for other purposes.) In the research area where most is known at the moment—that having to do with the effects on children of parental divorce—our case holds up well; but even this area is controversial and full of unresolved questions.

Besides outlining possible causal connections, we have shown the relevance of cognitive-developmental theory to the study of loneliness and, admittedly in a very preliminary way, have pointed to the potential compatibility of various theoretical approaches: those of Weiss, Peplau, Bowlby, Beck, Wachtel, and several students of cognitive and social development. We hope we have made the point that a cognitive approach to loneliness suggests many fruitful avenues for research and clinical intervention.

At first sight, loneliness may seem to be mainly a practical problem and not a very significant one at that (hence Weiss's reference to Miss Lonelyhearts); loneliness might not seem to be a good focus for basic research in personality and social psychology. The impact of divorce on children might seem even more to be a practicial or "applied" matter. Closer examination reveals, however, not only that loneliness is theoretically central to social pyschology (in fact, occupying a position analogous to hunger in experimental psychology, as we said at the outset) but also that serious study of loneliness quickly brings one face to face with a host of fundamental theoretical problems. What is the relationship between social cognition and emotion? As a person develops cognitively and reworks past experiences, how are feelings and social behavior affected? What do certain kinds of social relationships (e.g., adolescent and adult love affairs) contribute to the reworking process? Can the negative effects of traumatic social experiences be minimized by social support from other children (e.g., siblings); and can adults other than parents reduce the negative effects of parental loss, rejection, and neglect? Can cognitive-therapeutic interventions, either during childhood or later, when adult emotional and social isolation manifest themselves, reduce the intensity, frequency, and recurrence of loneliness?

The major findings obtained so far in the study of loneliness are robust and highly replicable. We have obtained the same relationships between variables, usually within a few correlation points, in every city we have studied; and findings from different research teams fit together well (Peplau & Perlman, in press), despite the use of a wide variety of measures. Loneliness may thus provide an excellent topic area in which to tackle some of the field's most important and difficult theoretical questions.

NOTES

1. For a recent exception which may mark the beginning of a trend, see the second edition of Middlebrook's (1980) *Social Psychology and Modern Life.*

2. Our concern may prove unwarranted. Russell et al. (1978) obtained a correlation of $r = .79$ between the UCLA scale and a self-report question which asked specifically about loneliness, and we have obtained correlations above .60 between our scale and the UCLA scale. Still, it is wise in the early phases of research to remain aware of possible limitations of these initial measures.

3. For the analyses reported in this article we have randomly selected 2,000 cases from the New York sample and have used all 1,500 cases from the Worcester sample. Results from other cities (Charlotte, North Carolina; Fort Meyers, Florida; Wichita, Kansas; Billings, Montana) will be mentioned only in a general way (e.g., "our studies"), but every finding we report was essentially the same (and statistically significant) in every sample. In cities where market research information was available from newspaper editors, we checked the representativeness of our samples and found them to be surprisingly representative. Moreover, the distribution of loneliness scores was about the same from city to city—always close to a normal distribution.

4. The same factors emerge, in this and subsequent analyses, whether varimax or oblique rotation is employed. Also, the factor structure is quite similar for males and females, so we will discuss only the combined results for all respondents. For details of the factor analyses and a more complete description of our findings, see Rubenstein and Shaver (1980, in press).

5. Additional psychometric support for Weiss's (1973) typology has been obtained by Brennan and Auslander (1979), who were also not aware of that typology when their instruments were designed.

6. Recently Weiner and his coworkers have been exploring a third dimension, controllability, but it has yet to be well-integrated into the theory. We will ignore this dimension in the present article, although in the future it may become important to loneliness researchers.

7. Several studies supporting the validity of Peplau's model are summarized in a forthcoming review chapter by Perlman and Peplau (in press).

8. Bowlby (1973) argues persuasively that much of Freudian psychoanalytic theory is based on the questionable secondary drive notion. Examination of the most recent treatise on psychoanalytic ego psychology (Blanck & Blanck, 1979) reveals that secondary drive is still a central concept.

9. It would be interesting to reconsider the results of Schachter's (1959) well-known experimental studies of fear and affiliation from an evolutionary standpoint.

10. Support for a connection between childhood feelings of loneliness—or of social and emotional isolation—and adult psychopathology can be found in a study by Fleming and Ricks (1970): "Feelings of isolation and alienation differentiated the pre-schizo-

phrenics and control group more strikingly than any other area of emotional experience" (p. 248).

11. Similar findings have been obtained recently by Toni Falbo (personal communication) at the University of Texas, using the UCLA Loneliness Scale.

12. The term *appraisal* was used in Arnold's (1960) theory of emotion and has been taken up subsequently by many other emotion theorists.

13. Other researchers (e.g., Eysenck & Eysenck, 1969) have shown that introversion-extraversion is partly determined by genetic factors. More recent research (Hill Goldsmith, personal communication) indicates that introversion-extraversion is a multidimensional construct, only one component of which concerns sociability. Loneliness researchers investigating this issue may want to use measures that are more specific than the global measures of extraversion.

REFERENCES

Adler, G. & Buie, D. H., Jr. Aloneness and borderline psychopathology: The possible relevance of developmental issues. *International Journal of Psychoanalysis,* 1979, *60,* 83-96.

Ainsworth, M.D.S., Belhar, M. C., Waters, E., & Wall, S. *Patterns of attachment.* Hillsdale, N.J.: Erlbaum, 1978.

Arnold, M. *Emotion and personality, I.* New York: Columbia University Press, 1960.

Beck, A. T. *Cognitive therapy and the emotional disorders.* New York: New American Library, 1976.

Blanck, G. & Blanck, R. *Ego psychology II: Psychoanalytic developmental psychology.* New York: Columbia University Press, 1979.

Bowlby, J. *Attachment and loss,* Vol. I. *Attachment.* London: Hogarth Press, 1969. (Penguin edition, 1971)

Bowlby, J. *Attachment and loss,* Vol.II. *Separation: Anxiety and anger.* London: Hogarth Press, 1973. (Penguin edition, 1975).

Bowlby, J. *Attachment and loss.* Vol. III. *Loss: Sadness and depression.* London: Hogarth Press, 1980.

Brennan, T. & Auslander, N. *Adolescent loneliness* (Vol. 1) Boulder, Colo.: Behavioral Research Institute, 1979.

Buss, A. H. & Plomin, R. *A temperament theory of personality development.* New York: Wiley, 1975.

Byrne, D. *The attraction paradigm.* New York: Academic Press, 1971.

Cantor, N. & Mischel, W. Prototypes in person perception. In L. Berkowitz (ed.), *Advances in experimental social psychology* (Vol. 12). New York: Academic Press, 1979.

Crook, T. & Eliot, J. Parental death during childhood and adult depression: A critical review of the literature. *Psychological Bulletin,* 1980, *87,* 252-269.

Dweck, C. S. & Goetz, T. E. Attributions and learned helplessness. In J. H. Harvey et al. (eds.), *New directions in attribution research* (Vol. 2). Hillsdale, N.J.: Erlbaum, 1978.

Erikson, E. H. *Childhood and society.* New York: W. W. Norton, 1950.

Eysenck, H. J. & Eysenck, S.B.G. *Personality structure and measurement.* San Diego: Robert Knapp, 1969.

Felner, R. D., Ginter, M. A., Boike, M. F., & Cowen, E. L. Parental death or divorce and the school adjustment of young children. *American Journal of Community Psychology,* in press.

Felner, R. D., Stohlberg, A., & Cowen, E. L. Crisis events and school mental health referral patterns of young children. *Journal of Consulting and Clinical Psychology,* 1975, *43,* 305-310.

Fleming, P. & Ricks, D. Emotions of children before schizophrenia and before character disorder. In M. Roff & D. Ricks (eds.), *Life history research in psychopathology* (Vol. 1). Minneapolis: University of Minnesota Press, 1970.

Foot, H. C., Chapman, A. J., & Smith, J. R. (eds.) *Friendship and social relations in children.* New York: Wiley, 1980.

Fraiberg, S. Libidinal object constancy and mental representation. *The psychoanalytic study of the child,* 1969, 24, 9-47.

Gordon, S. *Lonely in America.* New York: Simon and Schuster, 1976.

Grinker, R. R., Sr., Werble, B., & Drye, R. C. *The borderline syndrome.* New York: Basic Books, 1968.

Gurin, G., Veroff, J., & Feld, S. *Americans view their mental health.* New York: Basic Books, 1960.

Harlow, H. F. & Mears, C. *The human model: Primate perspectives.* Washington, D.C.: V. H. Winston, 1979.

Hartog, J. & Audy, R. (eds.). *The anatomy of loneliness.* New York: International Universities Press, 1980.

Helson, H. *Adaptation-level theory.* New York: Harper & Row, 1968.

Hetherington, E. M., Cox, M., & Cox, R. Divorced fathers. *Family Coordinator,* 1976, *25,* 417-428.

Hetherington, E. M., Cox, M., & Cox, R. The aftermath of divorce. In J. H. Stevens & M. Mathews (eds.), *Mother-child, father-child relations.* Washington, D.C.: National Association for the Education of Young Children, 1977.

Kelly, J. P. & Wallerstein, J. S. The effects of parental divorce: Experiences of the child in early latency. *American Journal of Orthopsychiatry,* 1976, *46,* 20-32.

Kernberg, O. Borderline personality organization. *Journal of the American Psychoanalytic Association,* 1967, *15,* 641-685.

Knudtson, F. W. Life-span attachment: Complexities, questions, considerations. *Human Development,* 1976, *19,* 182-196.

Kohut, H. *The analysis of the self.* New York: International Universities Press, 1971.

Kulka, R. A. & Weingarten, H. The long-term effects of parental divorce in childhood on adult adjustment: A twenty year perspective. Presented at the Annual Meeting of the American Sociological Association, Boston, August 1979.

Landis, J. T. The trauma of children when parents divorce. *Marriage and Family Living,* 1960, *22,* 7-13.

Lerner, R. M. & Ryff, C. D. Implementation of the life-span view of human development: The sample case of attachment. In P. Baltes (ed.), *Life-span development and behavior* (Vol. 1). New York: Academic Press, 1978.

Longfellow, C. Divorce in context: Its impact on children. In G. Levinger & O. C. Moles (eds.), *Divorce and separation: Context, causes and consequences.* New York: Basic Books, 1979.

Lynne, D. B. *The father—his role in child development.* Belmont, Calif.: Wadsworth, 1974.

Mahler, M. S. *On human symbiosis and the vicissitudes of individuation.* New York: International Universities Press, 1968.

Mahler, M. S. A study of the separation-individuation process and its possible application to borderline phenomena in the psychoanalytic situation. *The Psychoanalytic Study of the Child,* 1971, *26,* 403-424.

Mahler, M. S., Pine, F., & Bergman, A. *The psychological birth of the human infant.* New York: Basic Books, 1975.

Meichenbaum, D. *Cognitive behavior modification.* New York: Plenum, 1976.

Middlebrook, P. *Social psychology and modern life.* New York: Random House, 1980.

Mischel, W. *Introduction to personality.* Englewood Cliffs, N.J.: Prentice-Hall, 1976.

Newson, J. & Newson, E. *Four years old in an urban community.* Chicago: AVC, 1968.

Nye, F. I. Child adjustment in broken and in unhappy unbroken homes. *Marriage and Family Living,* 1957, *19,* 356-360.

Peplau, L. A. & Perlman, D. (eds.). *Loneliness: A sourcebook of current theory, research, and therapy.* New York: Wiley, in press.

Peplau, L. A., Russell, D., & Heim, M. Loneliness: A bibliography of research and theory. *JSAS Catalog of Selected Documents in Psychology,* 1978, *8,* 38. (Ms. 1682)

Peplau, L. A., Russell, D., & Heim, M. An attributional theory of loneliness. In I. Frieze et al. (eds.), *Attribution theory: Applications to social problems.* San Francisco: Jossey-Bass, 1979.

Perlman, D. & Peplau, L. A. Toward a social psychology of loneliness In R. Gilmour & S. Duck (eds.), *Personal relationships in disorder.* London: Academic Press, in press.

Piaget, J. *The construction of reality in the child.* New York: Basic Books, 1954. (Orig. pub. in 1937)

Pilkonis, P. A. & Zimbardo, P. G. The personal and social dynamics of shyness. In C. E. Izard (ed.), *Emotions in personality and psychopathology.* New York: Plenum, 1979.

Pope, H. & Mueller, C. W. The interorganizational transmission of marital instability: Comparisons by race and sex. *Journal of Social Issues,* 1976, *32,* 49-66.

Rajecki, D. W., Lamb, M. E., & Obsmacher, P. Toward a general theory of infantile attachment: A comparative review of aspects of the social bond. *Behavior and Brain Sciences,* 1978, *1,* 417-436.

Rosenberg, M. S. *Society and the adolescent self-image.* Princeton, N.J.: Princeton University Press, 1965.

Ross, L. The intuitive psychologist and his short-comings. In L. Berkowitz (ed.), *Cognitive theories in social psychology.* New York: Academic Press, 1979.

Rubenstein, C. M. & Shaver, P. Loneliness in two northeastern cities. In J. Hartog & R. Audy (eds.), *The anatomy of loneliness.* New York: International Universities Press, 1980.

Rubenstein, C. M. & Shaver, P. The experience of loneliness. In L. A. Peplau & D. Perlman (eds.), *Loneliness: A sourcebook of current theory, research, and therapy.* New York: Wiley, in press.

Rubenstein, C. M., Shaver, P., & Peplau, L. A. Loneliness. *Human Nature,* 1979, *2,* 59-65.

Rubin, Z. *Children's friendships.* Cambridge, Mass.: Harvard University Press, 1980.

Russell, D., Peplau, L. A., & Ferguson, M. Developing a measure of loneliness. *Journal of Personality Assessment,* 1978, *42,* 290-294.

Rutter, M. Maternal deprivation, 1972-1978: New findings, new concepts, new approaches. *Child Development,* 1979, *50,* 283-305.

Schachter, S. *The psychology of affiliation.* Stanford, Calif.: Stanford University Press, 1959.

Schafer, R. *A new language for psychoanalysis.* New Haven, Conn.: Yale University Press, 1976.

Schaffer, H. R. & Emerson, P. E. Patterns of response to physical contact in early human development. *Journal of Child Psychology and Child Psychiatry,* 1964, *5,* 1-13.

Schooler, C. Childhood family structure and adult characteristics. *Sociometry,* 1972, *35,* 255-269.

Schribner-Bantam English dictionary. New York: Bantam Books, 1979.

Shaver, P. Integrative trends in psychotherapy. *Human Nature,* 1978, *1,* 21-24.

Shaver, P. & Rubenstein, C. M. Living alone, loneliness, and health. Presented to the 87th Annual Convention of the American Psychological Association, New York City, September 4, 1979.

Solano, C. Loneliness and self-disclosure. Presented to the 87th Annual Convention of the American Psychological Association, New York City, September 4, 1979.

Sroufe, L. A. & Waters, E. Attachment as an organizational construct. *Child Development,* 1977, *48,* 1184-1199.

Troll, L. & Smith, J. Attachment through the life-span: Some questions about dyadic bonds among adults. *Human Development,* 1976, *19,* 156-170.

Wachtel, P. *Psychoanalysis and behavior therapy: Toward an integration.* New York: Basic Books, 1977. (a)

Wachtel, P. Interaction cycles, unconscious processes, and the person-situation issue. In W. Magnusson & N. Endler (eds.), *Personality at the crossroads.* Hillsdale, N.J.: Erlbaum, 1977. (b)

Wallerstein, J. S. & Kelly, J. B. The effects of parental divorce: The adolescent experience. In E. J. Anthony & C. Koupernik (eds.), *The child in his family* (Vol. 3). New York: Wiley, 1974.

Wallerstein, J. S. & Kelly, J. B. The effects of parental divorce: Experiences of the pre-school child. *Journal of the American Academy of Child Psychiatry,* 1975, *14,* 600-616.

Wallerstein, J. S. & Kelly, J. B. The effects of parental divorce: Experiences of the child in later latency. *American Journal of Orthopsychiatry,* 1976, *46,* 256-269.

Wallerstein, J. S. & Kelly, J. B. *Surviving the break-up: How children actually cope with divorce.* New York: Basic Books, 1980.

Weiner, B. *Achievement motivation and attribution theory.* Morristown, N. J.: General Learning Press, 1974.

Weiner, B., Russell, D., & Lerman, D. Affective consequences of causal ascriptions. In J. H. Harvey et al. (eds.), *New directions in attribution research* (Vol. 2). Hillsdale, N. J.: Erlbaum, 1978.

Weiss, R. S. *Loneliness: The experience of emotional and social isolation.* Cambridge, Mass.: MIT Press, 1973.

Weiss, R. S. *Marital separation.* New York: Basic Books, 1975.

Weiss, R. S. Issues in the study of loneliness. In L. A. Peplau & D. Perlman (eds.), *Loneliness: A sourcebook of current theory, research, and therapy.* New York: Wiley, in press.

Wilson, K. L., Zurcher, L. A., McAdams, D. C., & Curtis, R. L. Stepfathers and stepchildren: An exploratory analysis from two national surveys. *Journal of Marriage and the Family,* 1975, *37,* 526-536.

Groupthink   3

A CRITIQUE
OF JANIS'S THEORY

JEANNE LONGLEY
DEAN G. PRUITT

Jeanne Longley is Organization Development Consultant with Cummins Engine Co., Charleston, South Carolina. Her research interest is in small group decision making. Her applied interests are in the issues of decentralization, communication processes, job redesign, and team concept in industrial settings.
Dean G. Pruitt is currently a Professor of Psychology at State University of New York at Buffalo. He specializes in the topics of social conflict, bargaining, and group decision making. He has published a monograph on *Problem Solving in the Department of State* and a book (with R. C. Snyder) on *Theory and Research on the Causes of War.* He has another book in press on *Negotiation Behavior.*

In *Victims of Groupthink,* Janis (1972) contends that certain common processes by which groups develop and maintain consensus can undermine the quality of group decision making. As evidence for this thesis, he cites six case studies of foreign policy decisions by the government of the United States, four of which resulted in poor decisions and two in good decisions. He also proposes a series of useful guidelines for groups to help them overcome the problems of "groupthink."

Though this book is quite stimulating and has considerable practical value, it has to our knowledge provoked only four pieces of statistical research (Courtwright, 1976; Flowers, 1977; Tetlock, 1979; and a study by Wong-McCarthy cited in Janis, 1979). This lack of empirical follow-up can probably be attributed to three deficiencies in the theory: an inadequate definition of "groupthink"; an oversimplified evaluation of groupthink resulting from lack of attention to the type of issue under

AUTHORS' NOTE: Preparation of this manuscript was supported by National Science Foundation Grant BNS76-10963A03.

group consideration; and many unclarities and gaps in statements about the relationships between variables.

The first part of this article will be devoted to efforts to remedy these deficiencies. Separate sections will deal with the definition of groupthink, evaluation of groupthink, and two areas of theoretical unclarity and confusion: one involving the processes of groupthink and the other involving the mechanisms by which the supposed antecedents of groupthink affect these processes. The emphasis in these latter two sections will be both on clarifying Janis's position and critiquing this position.

Having laid this groundwork, it will be possible in the latter part of the article to extend the theory of groupthink by relating it to several other bodies of theory and research on small groups. A number of testable hypotheses will be presented throughout the article.

DEFINITION OF GROUPTHINK

In his initial statement, Janis (1972) defined "groupthink" as "a mode of thinking that people engage in when they are deeply involved in a cohesive in-group, when the members' strivings for unanimity override their motivation to realistically appraise alternative courses of action" (p. 9). This definition has the defect of referring to variables at three points in the causal chain; that is, group cohesiveness is an antecedent of strivings for unanimity, which are an antecedent of the failure to realistically appraise alternative courses of action. With such a definition, it is hard to build causal propositions about the antecedents and consequents of groupthink, because the definition contains many of the essential theoretical points.

This definitional problem has been considerably alleviated in two recent statements of the theory (Janis & Mann, 1977; Janis, 1979) that employ a flow chart showing cause and effect. This chart is shown in Figure 1. (The entries in this chart are, with one exception, all discussed in Janis's original volume. What the chart adds is a clarification of the causal sequences in Janis's thinking.) In the left-hand box are five antecedent conditions that predispose a group to develop and maintain an inadequate consensus on the issue under consideration. In the second box is the concept "concurrence-seeking tendency," which is also sometimes called "pressures toward uniformity" (Janis, 1979). In the third box are eight "symptoms of groupthink," which are presumably manifested by groups that are seized by a concurrence-seeking tendency. These symptoms are of three types: consensus-producing activities (col-

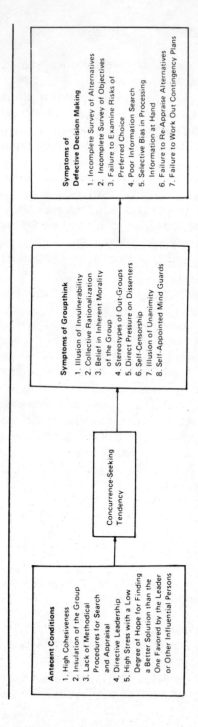

Antecent Conditions

1. High Cohesiveness
2. Insulation of the Group
3. Lack of Methodical Procedures for Search and Appraisal
4. Directive Leadership
5. High Stress with a Low Degree of Hope for Finding a Better Solution than the One Favored by the Leader or Other Influential Persons

Concurrence-Seeking Tendency

Symptoms of Groupthink

1. Illusion of Invulnerability
2. Collective Rationalization
3. Belief in Inherent Morality of the Group
4. Stereotypes of Out-Groups
5. Direct Pressure on Dissenters
6. Self-Censorship
7. Illusion of Unanimity
8. Self-Appointed Mind Guards

Symptoms of Defective Decision Making

1. Incomplete Survey of Alternatives
2. Incomplete Survey of Objectives
3. Failure to Examine Risks of Preferred Choice
4. Poor Information Search
5. Selective Bias in Processing Information at Hand
6. Failure to Re-Appraise Alternatives
7. Failure to Work Out Contingency Plans

Figure 1: Theoretical Analysis of Groupthink Based on Comparisons of High-Quality with Low-Quality Decisions by Policy-Making Groups.
Source: DECISION MAKING by Irving L. Janis and Leon Mann. (Copyright © 1977 by the Free Press, a Division of Macmillan Publishing Co., Inc.)

lective rationalization, direct pressure on dissenters, self-censorship, and mind guarding, which is behavior aimed at shielding the group from outside opinions that do not agree with its biases), perceptions of own group (illusion of invulnerability, belief in inherent morality of the group, and illusion of unanimity), and perceptions of adversary groups (stereotypes of out-groups). The fourth box contains eight faulty decision-making processes that presumably result from the activities and perceptions specified in the prior box. By the logic of Janis's position, a fifth box might have been added at the end of the sequence containing the words "likelihood of a poor outcome."

In the context of this flowchart, Janis (1979) redefines "groupthink" as "concurrence-seeking," a term that appears in the second box in the flowchart.[1] This new definition refers to a process at only one point in the causal chain and hence should contribute to clearer thinking and more active research in this area. This is not to say that the flowchart shown in Figure 1 is without problems—a number of difficulties will be discussed below—but only that the new definition of groupthink is more cogent than the old one.

EVALUATION OF GROUPTHINK

A negative evaluation of groupthink pervades all of Janis's writings about the topic. Such an evaluation is actually incorporated in the initial definition of the phenomenon by use of the value-laden term *realistically* in the section that speaks of failure to "realistically appraise alternative courses of action." The later definition as "concurrence-seeking" is not evaluative per se, but the flowchart shown in Figure 1 clearly specifies that concurrence seeking leads to defective decision making.

However, is this accurate? Is concurrence seeking always counterproductive of good decision making? Janis's position on this matter seems to ignore the need groups always have in the long run to reach agreement on an issue, stop discussing it, and move on to other matters. Such symptoms of groupthink as self-censorship, urging dissenters to curtail their remarks, avoiding the influx of outside opinions, and even collective rationalization are *eventually* necessary in many decision-making sequences.

A distinction between "differentiation" and "integration" developed by Lawrence and Lorsch (1969) is useful for sharpening this point. These authors are concerned with organizational decision making, but their concepts can be extended to groups as follows: "differentiation" can be

defined as proliferation of ideas and debate and "integration" as efforts
to achieve unity. Groupthink can be thought of as a decision process
that involves too much integration and too little differentiation. But
both processes are needed for effective decision making.

How would Janis respond to this criticism? Clues about his probable
answer can be seen in a discussion of individual decision making by
Janis and Mann (1977). These authors argue that individuals tend to
bolster (i.e., develop rationalizations for) their decisions at the point
where they "lose hope of finding a more satisfactory solution" and that
this process has the virtue of freeing the decision maker from worry and
thus making him or her ready for action. Hence it seems probable that
what Janis was actually condemning in *Victims of Groupthink* was *early*
concurrence seeking, efforts to reach agreement before the group has
had a chance to inventory alternatives and gather evidence relevant to
them. However, even this enlightened position seems to ignore the
importance of the *type of decision task* under consideration. When
decisions are simple or routine, early consensus seeking may well be
desirable, especially if there are time pressures.

Katz and Kahn (1978) distinguish between two types of decision task:
problems and dilemmas. Problems "can be solved in the frame of
reference suggested by (their) nature, by past precedents for dealing with
(them), or by the application of existing policy" (p. 489). Dilemmas are
novel and their solutions are not straightforward. Dilemmas require
"reformulation" and "innovation" and hence a thorough inventory and
appraisal of existing alternatives. By contrast, such an appraisal may
actually be counterproductive for dealing with simple, routine problems, introducing unnecessary costs, complexities, and delays in their
solution. This suggests that, while early concurrence seeking should be
avoided when dealing with dilemmas, it may actually be *tailor-made for
success* when dealing with problems.

This discussion implies that if we want to evaluate groupthink negatively, we must define it as *premature* concurrence seeking or, in the
terminology used by Lawrence and Lorsch (1969), as premature integration associated with inadequate differentiation. Such a definition would
be hard to operationalize in the present day since we lack detailed theory
about the information-processing requirements of different sorts of
tasks. Hence, for the time being, research in this area should probably
deal mainly with groups that are trying to solve novel, complex tasks of
the type we are calling dilemmas. In such settings, decisions are likely to
be better the more time is spent on them, the greater the number of ideas

generated, and so on. Hence, unidirectional measures of groupthink can be employed, such as the number of possible solutions voiced during the group discussion. Such an approach was taken in the two experiments that have been inspired by Janis's writing (Courtwright, 1976; Flowers, 1977).

CLARIFYING THE PROCESSES OF GROUPTHINK

The arrow linking the second and third boxes of Figure 1 implies that the processes listed in the third box are manifestations of a concurrence-seeking tendency. Four of these processes—pressures on dissenters, self-censorship, mind guarding, and collective rationalization—can indeed be so regarded. Pressures on dissenters and self-censorship are tactics for achieving concurrence. Mind guarding is a method of protecting an emerging or actual consensus that seems likely to be questioned outside the group. Collective rationalization occurs after a decision has been made and is a way of maintaining the consensus. However, the other four processes seem to have a different character.

The illusion of invulnerability and the illusion of unanimity appear to be antecedents of premature concurrence rather than consequences of a desire for concurrence. When people have the illusion that their group is invulnerable, they become overly optimistic and are not motivated to examine carefully the "real losses that could arise if their luck does not hold" (Janis, 1972, p. 37). This is likely to lead to incomplete processing of the available evidence and abbreviated contingency planning, producing premature concurrence.

The illusion that the group is unanimous also has the impact of reducing information processing, but for another reason. If the group seems to have reached consensus, its members are likely to view it as useless to continue seeking new alternatives or information regarding old ones. This illusion also contributes to self-censorship because many people are afraid of being the only deviant in a group. Having such a status runs the risk of being labelled as an "odd ball" and being criticized or otherwise disciplined by the other group members (Allen, 1975). In essence, the illusion of unanimity is a self-fulfilling prophecy, producing concurrence because nobody cares or dares to challenge the group's apparent position.

The remaining two processes in box three—belief in the inherent morality of the group and stereotypes of outgroups—seem unrelated to concurrence seeking except that, *like all other issues,* they are topics on which concurrence can be achieved. These processes apparently got into the list because they were found in several of the case studies of inadequate decision making examined by Janis. But is this a proper reason to include them in a *theory* of groupthink? A theory should be a logical progression of ideas, not a grab-bag of phenomena that were correlated with each other in a sample of six cases.

Inclusion of these last two processes also limits the applicability of the theory to decisions about how to deal with another party where moral issues are at stake. All six cases in the original sample were of this type. But there are many other types of decision that may nevertheless manifest premature consensus and hence yield to an analysis employing the other terms in the theory. Hence this limitation seems unwise.

In fairness to Janis, it should be noted that he tries, in *Victims of Groupthink*, to explain how the eight "symptoms of groupthink" hang together. He argues that these symptoms represent different ways decision makers attempt to enhance their self-esteem when faced with perplexing choices that are beyond their level of competence or that tempt them to violate ethical standards. Agreement with other group members bolsters confidence in one's own views, hence the pressure on dissenters, self-censorship, and mind guarding that are often found in groups. In addition, "A shared illusion of invulnerability and shared rationalizations can counteract unnerving feelings of personal inadequacy and pessimism about finding an adequate solution during a crisis" (p. 203). Also a sense that the ingroup is moral and negative stereotypes of the outgroup serve to allay group members' doubts about their own ethical posture. Without the illusion of invulnerability, "the sense of group unity would be lost, gnawing doubts would start to grow, confidence in the group's problem-solving capacity would shrink and soon the full emotional impact of all the stresses generated by making a difficult decision would be aroused" (p. 205).

Unfortunately however, this explanation serves to add greater confusion of Janis's theory since (1) self-esteem is not mentioned elsewhere in the theory, being omitted from Figure 1, and (2) this explanation does not help to clarify the causal link postulated between the concurrence-seeking tendency and the symptoms of groupthink.

In summary, the eight "symptoms of groupthink" appear to be a loose bag of partially related ideas. Four of them can be seen as outgrowths of concurrence seeking. But two others appear to be antecedents of premature concurrence, while the remaining two seem entirely unrelated to concurrence. Janis's effort to explain the coherence among these symptoms relies on a further variable, the desire for self-esteem, that is not systematically related to the other terms in the theory. It is not surprising that a theory of this complexity and indefiniteness has seldom inspired research.

CLARIFYING THE ANTECEDENTS OF GROUPTHINK

Cohesiveness as the Key Antecedent

The antecedent of groupthink most prominently mentioned by Janis is high group cohesiveness. No definition of "cohesiveness" is provided, but one suspects that he is using it in the usual way to mean "the total field of forces which act on members to remain in the group" (Festinger, 1950) or, more simply, the degree to which the members find their group attractive.

Janis (1972) argues that cohesiveness is a necessary but not a sufficient condition for achieving groupthink. For a cohesive group to become a victim of groupthink, it must *also* be insulated from other groups, have directive leadership, and/or lack procedures for generating and appraising new options. In short, cohesiveness is assumed to interact with other variables to determine the likelihood of groupthink.

How can this interaction be explained? Janis does not spell out the answer to this question in so many words. But he seems to imply that insulation from other groups, directive leadership, and the absence of search and appraisal procedures encourage the premature impression among group members that a group norm[2] or party line has developed. Group members conclude early in the discussion that their group is trending in a particular direction and then, if the group is also cohesive, limit their statements of opposing views and criticize others for making such statements. This interpretation is most clearly acknowledged in the following quotation from Janis and Mann (1977), "When a directive leader announces his preference on a policy issue . . . the members of a cohesive group will tend to accept his choice somewhat uncritically as if it were equivalent to a *group norm*" (p. 131, italics added).

This formulation implies the importance for groupthink of any condition that produces an early impression of the existence of a group norm. For example, homogeneity of member background, early domination of the discussion by a particular faction, and initial straw votes among the group membership should all have this impact if the group is sufficiently cohesive for its members to rally around an emerging group norm. Janis mentions two of these conditions in *Victims of Groupthink* but does not systematically link them to cohesiveness or the early impression that there is a party line.

The importance for groupthink of the prior existence of a norm can be seen in two of the historical cases that Janis (1972) views as illustrating groupthink. In both cases, a single alternative appears to have emerged at an early stage in the deliberations and to have been resolutely defended thereafter by the processes of groupthink. In the decision to launch the Bay of Pigs invasion, this norm apparently resulted from *early endorsement by high-status group members*. These were two representatives from the Central Intelligence Agency, who were given an especially privileged position in the discussion by President Kennedy, and by the President himself after a period of time. In the decision not to fly reconnaissance missions north of Hawaii just before the Japanese attack on Pearl Harbor, the norm resulted from *generally shared preconceptions* about the strength of the American Navy and the weakness of the Japanese military capability which were brought into the meetings on this issue. The process by which the initial decision was made is not so clear in the other two cases illustrating groupthink, the decision to invade North Korea during the Korean War and the decision to bomb North Vietnam during the Vietnam War. But it is clear that, in typical groupthink fashion, these decisions were defended after they were made by collective rationalization and avoidance of adverse evidence. Once a group norm had been established, it tended to be defended.

A point Janis made about the sources of cohesiveness needs to be underscored at this time. "Concurrence-seeking tendencies probably are stronger when high cohesiveness is based primarily on the rewards of being in a pleasant 'clubby' atmosphere or of gaining prestige from being a member of an elite than when it is based primarily on the opportunity to function competently on work tasks with effective co-workers. In a cohesive policy-making group of the latter type, careful appraisal of policy alternatives is likely to become a group norm to which the members conscientiously adhere; this helps to counteract groupthink" (p. 201). Evidence favoring this point can be derived from a study of dyads by Back (1951). When cohesiveness was based on member attraction to the task, there was more debate before reaching consensus than when it was based on attraction to the other group members or on group prestige.

Studies of Cohesiveness and Groupthink

Cohesiveness was an independent variable in both of the experiments that have been done on groupthink. In Courtwright's (1976) study, high

cohesiveness was produced by telling the group members that questionnaire results showed that they were compatible and by having them
interact for 10 minutes prior to the discussion; low cohesiveness, by
telling them that there was no reason to believe that they would be
compatible and by not letting them interact. In Flowers's (1977) study,
members of high-cohesive group were friends and members of low-
cohesive groups were strangers. In both studies, the groups tried to
develop a solution to a novel and complex problem. The following
measures of group process were employed to operationalize groupthink:
number of solutions proposed (both studies), number of agreements and
disagreements with other group members (Courtwright), and number of
facts introduced into the discussion (Flowers).

Manipulation checks for cohesiveness were successful, but this variable was not significantly related to any of these measures of groupthink.
This negative result can be understood in the Courtwright study because
no effort was made to encourage the development of an early impression
of the existence of a group norm. This mistake was not made in the
Flowers study, which manipulated the directiveness of group leadership
in a 2 × 2 design with cohesiveness. Janis's hypothesis that high cohesiveness produces symptoms of groupthink when the leader makes efforts to
steer the group in a particular direction was not supported. But flaws in
the procedure make us hesitate to reach conclusions about the adequacy
of Janis's hypothesis. It is not clear that the appointed leaders in this
study were capable of steering the group in one direction or the other. In
the words of the author, "Janis's groups had powerful leaders who could
exercise reward and punishment as well as legitimate, expert, and
perhaps referent power . . . over their members, whereas the leaders in
this experiment held only certain legitimate power" (p. 895).

There was one significant finding in the Flowers study—directive
leadership produced fewer proposed solutions and fewer facts introduced in the discussion than nondirective leadership. This is not surprising since directive leaders were encourgaed to curtail the discussion as
well as to state their own opinions at the beginning of the discussion.
Hence this is a questionable test of Janis's hypothesis about the importance of directive leadership as an antecedent of groupthink.

In summary, the evidence from these two studies suggests that group
cohesiveness per se is not capable of producing groupthink. The studies
do not adequately deal with the more refined hypothesis that a cohesive
group will exhibit symptoms of groupthink when other conditions cause
the group to seem committed to a particular solution at an early point in
the deliberations.

How Cohesiveness Works

Several explanations for how cohesiveness contributes to groupthink are provided at different points in Janis's writings. One explanation is that cohesiveness encourages euphoria about the group and hence an illusion of invulnerability that curtails examination of the possible negative consequences of an emerging consensus (Janis, 1972, pp. 36-37). A second explanation is that members of cohesive groups are motivated to "maintain esprit de corps" (pp. 35-36) and to "preserve the unity of the group" (p. 201), leading to self-censorship of doubts once the group seems to be moving in a particular direction. A reasonable point that Janis does not make is that such an effect is particularly likely to be found when the unity of a cohesive group is in some sort of danger, as when the members of a close family develop differing views on a political issue. A third explanation for the impact of cohesiveness is given by Janis and Mann (1977). They argue that each member of a cohesive group is "dependent on the group and displays (a) readiness to adhere to the group's norms" (p. 131). The meaning of this point is not altogether clear; but the word *dependence* is presumably that employed by Janis (1972) in the following statement, "When a member is dependent on the group for bolstering his feelings of self-confidence, he tends to exercise self-censorship over his misgivings" (p. 205). In other words, the members of a cohesive group come to rely on that group for their self-esteem.

A fourth explanation is that more cohesive groups put greater pressure on dissenters to alter (or keep quiet about) their views (p. 41), a conclusion that is supported by some of Schachter's (1951) findings. The nature of such pressure can range from "urging the dissident member to remain silent" (p. 41) to the treatment that was accorded Secretary of Defense McNamara after he began to question American commitment to the Vietnam War. "With each passing month McNamara was gradually eased out of his powerful position, finding himself less and less welcome at the White House, until finally he was removed from his high office in 'a fast shuffle' by the President" (p. 124).

This last explanation makes cohesive groups seem rather harsh toward deviants. We know also that members of cohesive groups are especially motivated to retain their membership. Hence it would not be surprising if members of cohesive groups were especially fearful of opposing an emerging group norm. Yet on this point Janis (1972) reaches precisely the opposite conclusion, arguing that "the more cohesive a group becomes, the *less* the members will deliberately censor what they say because of fear of being socially punished for antagonizing the leader or any of their fellow group members" (pp. 200-201, italics added). This latter conclusion is based on the assumption that member security is a "central feature of increased group cohesiveness" (p. 199). But this is not a reasonable stance, because one can easily imagine groups that consist of people who value their membership but do not feel secure with one another. An example would be many male/female dyads in the early stages of courtship, a topic to which we shall return in a later section. It seems more cogent to treat cohesiveness and member security as separate variables that interact in their impact on the groupthink phenomena. The 2 × 2 matrix shown in Figure 2 will be useful for examining this interaction.

It seems reasonable to suppose that the extent of self-censorship (i.e., conformity to the apparent group norm) is a joint function of cohesiveness and member security, such that it is especially high in groups with *high cohesiveness and low member security* (type B in Figure 2). This is because individuals should only be concerned about other members' impressions of them to the extent that they value group membership *and* feel insecure about this membership. This hypothesis has two testable implications for the theory of groupthink: (1) self-censorship will be a function of member insecurity in high-cohesive but not in low-cohesive groups [(B - A)>(D - C)] and (2) self-censorship will be a function of group cohesiveness in groups involving low member security but not in groups involving high member security [(B - D)>(A - C)].

Stress

We have discussed four of the five antecedents of groupthink given in the first box of Figure 1. The fifth antecedent, "high stress with a low degree of hope for finding a better solution than the one proposed by the leader or other influential persons," was added to the theory after publication of *Victims of Groupthink*. It is an outgrowth of Janis and Mann's (1977) analysis of the sources of defensive avoidance in individual decision making. As far as we can see, there is little solid evidence linking stress to the incidence of groupthink. Among Janis's (1972) six cases, the one apparently involving the least stress (in the sense that an important problem was seen as urgently in need of solution) is the failure of the Navy to anticipate the Japanese attack on Pearl Harbor. Though worried about what the Japanese were going to do next, the members of the decision-making group appear to have mainly been going about their business as usual. Yet processes of groupthink were apparently at

	High Cohesiveness	Low Cohesiveness
High Member Security	A	C
Low Member Security	B	D

Figure 2: Two × Two Matrix Showing the Independent Variation of Group Cohesiveness and Member Security

work in their failure to attend to available information about Japanese intentions. Conversely, the case that apparently involved the most stress, the Cuban Missile Crisis, showed little evidence of groupthink. Janis (1979) cites a study by Wong-McCarthy showing that Nixon and his advisors employed more "supportive statements" in a period of high than of low stress, suggesting that they were failing to argue with one another. However these data are quite fragmentary, being based on a sample of only two time periods which could have differed in many other ways besides the stress on the decision makers. Hence it is hard to take them very seriously.

EXTENSIONS TO OTHER BODIES OF THEORY

Having clarified and critiqued Janis's theory of groupthink, it is now possible to sketch relationships to several other bodies of theory and thus extend this theory.

Stages of Group Development

A number of writers have observed that groups go through standard stages of development in the same way that individuals move from lesser to greater maturity. As these stages are usually described, it would appear that groupthink is more likely to be encountered in earlier than later stages. In presenting group stage theory, we shall lean on the writings of Cohen and Smith (1976), Fisher (1974), and Tuckman (1965), which synthesize the work of numerous other writers. These authors are concerned with the behavior of problem-solving or therapy groups. While somewhat different accounts are given by each author, three basic stages are seen in all three treatments. These can be called dependent integration, counterdependent differentiation, and interdependent integration.

The early dependent integration stage can be described as a period of "false cohesiveness," in which most members do not feel secure enough to initiate conflict. Group members are uncertain about their roles and status and thus are concerned about the possibility of being made a scapegoat or even excluded from the group. Hence they are likely to avoid expressing opinions that are different from those proposed by the leader or other powerful persons in the group, to avoid conflict by failing to criticize one another's ideas, and even to agree overtly with other people's suggestions while disagreeing covertly. Such actions sound very much like symptoms of groupthink. In the second, counter-dependent differentiation stage, conflict is very much in evidence. Members feel free to proliferate differing ideas, criticize one another, and challenge the leader. Groupthink is clearly not a problem at this stage, but there is likely to be another difficulty, in Lawrence and Lorsch's (1969) terms, that of insufficient integration. Too much time is spent in controversy and not enough attention is given to developing solutions that are generally agreeable to the group members. The third, interdependent integration, stage occurs when a group becomes able to both differentiate (propose a variety of ideas and critically appraise them) and integrate (reach a consensus that synthesizes the best ideas and has the commitment of the entire group). In this stage, the members are secure enough about their roles and status to challenge one another but also have ways of reaching agreement.

The notion that groups go through such stages may help interpret two of the cases described in *Victims of Groupthink*. Both involved the same cohesive decision-making group, Kennedy's foreign policy advisors. Symptoms of groupthink were evident in the Bay of Pigs Crisis, which came early in the Kennedy presidency. Janis notes that in these discussions, there was a "shared illusion of unanimity," "suppression of personal doubts," and social pressure on members who expressed deviant viewpoints. As a result, ideas put forward by the Central Intelligence Agency were adopted without the critical appraisal that would have uncovered blatant errors in the plan. Decision making in the later Cuban Missile Crisis did not show symptoms of groupthink. Though the group was still cohesive, conflict was faced openly. The discussion can be characterized by Cohen and Smith's (1976) term *integrated autonomy*. Each member was an independent thinker, yet there was a feeling of equality and cooperation that allowed the group to reach agreement on a complicated plan of action. We are suggesting in this comparison that the Kennedy group was in the first stage of group development during the Bay of Pigs Crisis and had advanced to the third stage by the time of the Cuban Missile Crisis. If so, the critical difference would be that the members had come to feel much more secure about their status in the group by the time of the second crisis. The early sense of false cohesiveness had been replaced by a sense of confidence and security.

Integrative Bargaining

One manifestation of groupthink is that the differing perspectives that sometimes exist within a group are not fully aired and hence are not well-synthesized in the final decision. Instead, one dominant perspective drowns out all the others. This phenomenon has its parallel in the integrative bargaining literature (Pruitt & Lewis, 1975, 1977; Pruitt & Carnevale, 1980), where the failure of group members to *maintain high aspirations* is believed to encourage a decision that provides low joint benefit to the membership as a whole. For high joint benefit to ensue, group members must maintain a problem-solving orientation *but also* be stubborn about their aspirations so long as there is any chance of achieving their goals and values.[3] It follows that conditions which diminish joint profit by reducing level of aspiration are likely to be antecedents of groupthink.

One such condition is high time pressure. In studies of negotiation, Pruitt and Drews (1969) have shown that time pressure erodes level of aspiration and Yukl et al. (1976) have shown that it is an antecedent of low joint profit. This suggests that time pressure encourages groupthink.

Joint profits have also been found to be low in the early stages of male/female courtship. In an experiment on negotiation, Fry et al. (1979) showed that undergraduate dating couples achieved lower joint profit than cross-sex stranger couples. Evidence that this effect was due to reduced aspirations can be seen in the fact that the dating couples typically terminated bargaining as soon as either party had mentioned an alternative that satisfied both parties' minimal aspirations, while the stranger couples ordinarily went on bargaining beyond this point. This finding supports the hypothesis mentioned in the previous section that the earliest stage of group development typically involves a condition of false cohesiveness in which group members find one another attractive but are distrustful of each others' feelings. This presumably causes them to be fearful of conflict and to avoid pressing their own viewpoints or interests when these seem opposed to those of other group members.[4] This finding suggests, as hypothesized earlier, that groups will show more signs of groupthink in the earlier stages of their development.

Deviancy

One of Janis's (1972) guidelines for avoiding groupthink is that "at every meeting devoted to evaluating policy alternatives, at least one member should be assigned the role of devil's advocate" (p. 215). His or her job should be to develop arguments against any emerging consensus.

A sizable segment of the research effort in social psychology has been devoted to the impact of a deviant on group behavior. Hence this prescription can potentially be enriched by bringing it in closer contact with the research literature.

There are two mechanisms by which a devil's advocate can counteract groupthink. One is by presenting ideas that stimulate other group members to think more deeply. The other is by encouraging other potential deviants to speak out. The latter function is supported by Asch's (1956) classic experiment in which conformity to an obviously incorrect group norm dropped from 33% to 5% of the responses when one group member other than the subject deviated from this norm.

There are three potential problems with the recommendation to appoint a devil's advocate. One is that the devil's advocate will have *too much* influence, contributing to a kind of reverse groupthink. This can happen if he or she becomes a substitute directive leader or discourages others from stating their opinions for fear of being "shot down." A second danger is that the devil's advocate will have *too little* influence. This can occur if the role becomes ritualized, a strong possibility whenever the devil's advocate is appointed rather than emergent. A third problem is that the role of devil's advocate is an uncomfortable one and hence group members may refuse to take this role or to enact it as vigorously as is needed to persuade group members to scrutinize an emerging consensus.

A solution to the first two problems is suggested by Hollander's (1960) finding that a deviant's influence is a function of his or her status in the group. This suggests that a person with very high status is inappropriate for the role of devil's advocate because of the danger of overwhelming the group *and* that a person with low status may not be sufficiently influential to have an impact over the group. Hence it would appear that the most effective devil's advocate is one with moderate to moderately high status.

Where the devil's advocate is in danger of having too little influence, some of Moscovici and Nemeth's (1974) recommendations can also be followed. These authors present evidence that a deviant gains influence by taking a consistent position in a confident manner. Recent results

(Longley, 1980) cast some doubt on the importance of consistency but provide further evidence for the importance of looking confident in the eyes of the other group members.

The latter point suggests an additional defect in Janis's recommendation that the devil's advocate should be appointed. Group members know that an appointed devil's advocate is playing a role. Hence he or she is not likely to be seen as confident in his or her statements. This is likely to impair his or her influence over the group. The solution to this problem is to have the devil's advocate an emergent rather than an appointed position. Groups need to establish the norm that the individual who, on the basis of the discussion, sees himself or herself as most in disagreement with the emerging consensus should speak up vigorously against this consensus.

The third problem of risking nonacceptance or unpopularity with the group can be solved by establishing a norm for the emergence of two deviants instead of one. This follows from Asch's finding that people are much more likely to deviate when they see themselves as having an ally than when they feel alone in their opposition to the rest of the group.

In summary, we hypothesize that the most effective devil's advocate should be of moderately high status, behave in a consistent and confident manner, emerge from the group rather than being appointed, and receive support from another group member.

CONCLUSIONS

Three deficiencies of Janis's theory of groupthink have been examined in an effort to interpret the fact that this theory has inspired so little research. These deficiencies are in the areas of the definition of groupthink, the evaluation of this phenomenon, and the logic regarding processes and causal sequences.

Until recently the definition of "groupthink" was so complicated that it was difficult to think about it theoretically or to find an appropriate operationalization for it. However, Janis's (1979) most recent definition as "concurrence-seeking" should largely resolve this problem.

The categorically negative evaluation of groupthink that is found in all writings on this topic would seem to ignore the type of decision task a group is facing. In more routine problem-solving situations, early concurrence seeking, in the sense of rapid integration of ideas into a solution, is probably quite appropriate. This suggests that if groupthink is to retain a purely negative connotation, it needs to be defined as "premature concurrence seeking."

Among the processes Janis described are the eight "symptoms of groupthink" seen in Figure 1. Two of these symptoms are logically unrelated to consensus formation and should probably be dropped from the theory in the interest of tightening its logic. These are "belief in the inherent morality of the group" and "stereotypes of out-groups." The remaining six symptoms relate to consensus formation in several different ways, suggesting that groupthink should be viewed as a set of phenomena rather than a single phenomenon.

The antecedent of groupthink Janis mentioned most is group cohesiveness. Yet the logic of Janis's position and recent research evidence suggest that this position needs to be qualified. We argue that cohesiveness is only likely to lead to groupthink when group members feel insecure and there is an emerging or actual group norm in the direction of a particular solution. Indeed, where groups have norms encouraging methodical procedures for search and appraisal, cohesiveness may work in the opposite direction and discourage groupthink. Research by Back (1951) suggests that such norms are particularly likely to develop when cohesiveness is based on member attraction to the tasks undertaken by the group.

Three of the other antecedents Janis suggested—directive leadership, insulation of the group, and lack of methodical procedures for search and appraisal—appear to have their impact by encouraging the early development of a group norm in the direction of a particular solution. Hence these can be seen as having a joint impact with cohesiveness on the likelihood that symptoms of groupthink will develop.

Finally, there is little evidence in Janis's case studies or elsewhere linking his fifth antecedent, "high stress with a low degree of hope for finding a better solution than the one proposed by the leader or other influential persons," to groupthink.

Clarification and systematization of groupthink theory make it possible to link this theory to several other traditions in social psychology. For example, it can be argued that groupthink is most likely to occur in an early stage of group development involving "false cohesiveness." In this stage, group members are most likely to avoid expressing differences of opinion out of uncertainty about roles and status. This speculation is bolstered by research in the tradition of integrative bargaining showing that courting couples are particularly likely to avoid conflict by lowering their aspirations and thus end up with low joint benefit. This line of research also suggests that time pressures are likely to induce groupthink.

Finally, it is proposed that a devil's advocate will be useful in combatting groupthink to the extent that he or she is of moderately high status, behaves in a consistent and confident manner, emerges rather than being appointed, and is supported by another group member.

NOTES

1. The notion that "concurrence-seeking" or the "concurrence-seeking tendency" produces the symptoms of groupthink is mentioned in *Victims of Groupthink,* but groupthink is not defined as concurrence seeking in that volume.

2. We recognize that the term *norm* is being used somewhat unconventionally in the sense of a standard or group choice.

3. There is a parallel between this formulation and the Lawrence and Lorsch (1969) theory of effective decision making in complex environments. Maintenance of aspirations can be thought of as contributing to differentiation, while a problem-solving orientation (a desire to find a solution that is acceptable to all parties) can be seen as contributing to integration of the group members' various views.

4. This is the only carefully controlled study we know that tests the hypothesis that conflict avoidance characterizes the earliest phase in the development of a cohesive group.

REFERENCES

Allen, V. L. Social support for nonconformity. In L. Berkowitz (ed.), *Advances in Experimental Social Psychology* (Vol. 9). New York: Academic Press, 1975.

Asch, S. E. Studies of independence and conformity: I. A minority of one against a unanimous majority. *Psychological Monographs,* 1956, *70*(9) (Whole No. 416).

Back, K. W. Influence through social communication. *Journal of Abnormal and Social Psychology,* 1951, *46,* 9-23.

Cohen, A. M. & Smith, R. D. *The Critical Incident in Growth Groups: Theory and Technique.* La Jolla, Calif.: University Associates, 1976.

Courtright, J. A. *Groupthink and Communication Processes: An Initial Investigation.* Unpublished doctoral dissertation, University of Iowa, 1976.

Festinger, L. Informal social communication. *Psychological Review,* 1950, *57,* 271-282.

Fisher, B. *Small Group Decision Making.* New York: McGraw-Hill, 1974.

Flowers, M. L. A laboratory test of some implications of Janis's groupthink hypothesis. *Journal of Personality and Social Psychology,* 1977, *35,* 888-896.

Fry, W. R., Firestone, I. J., & Williams, D. Bargaining process in mixed-singles dyads: Loving and losing. Presented at the annual meeting of the Eastern Psychological Association, Philadelphia, 1979.

Hollander, E. P. Competence and conformity in the acceptance of influence. *Journal of Abnormal and Social Psychology,* 1960, *61,* 361-365.

Janis, I. L. *Victims of Groupthink.* Boston: Houghton-Mifflin, 1972.

Janis, I. L. Preventing groupthink in policy-planning groups: Theory and research perspectives. Presented at the second annual meeting of the International Society of Political Psychology, Washington, D.C., 1979.

Janis, I. L. & Mann, L. *Decision Making.* New York: Free Press, 1977.

Katz, D. & Kahn, R. L. *The Social Psychology of Organizations.* New York: Wiley, 1978.

Lawrence, P. R. & Lorsch, J. W. *Organization and Environment: Managing Differentiation and Integration.* Homewood, Ill.: Irwin, 1969.

Longley, J. *A Test of Two Theoretical Approaches to Minority Influence: Hollander Versus Moscovici and Nemeth.* Unpublished doctoral dissertation, State University of New York at Buffalo, 1980.

Moscovici, S. & Nemeth, C. Social influence II: Minority influence. Chapter 5 in C. Nemeth (ed.), *Social Psychology: Classic and Contemporary Integrations.* Skokie, Ill.: Rand McNally, 1974.

Pruitt, D. G. & Carnevale, P.J.D. The development of integrative agreements in social conflict. In V. J. Derlega and J. Grzelak (eds.), *Living with Other People.* New York: Academic Press, 1980.

Pruitt, D. G. & Drews, J. L. The effect of time pressure, time elapsed, and the opponent's concession rate on behavior in negotiation. *Journal of Social Psychology,* 1969, *5,* 43-60.

Pruitt, D. G. & Lewis, S. A. The development of integrative solutions in bilateral negotiation. *Journal of Personality and Social Psychology,* 1975, *31,* 621-633.

Pruitt, D. G. & Lewis, S. A. The psychology of integrative bargaining. In D. Druckman (ed.), *Negotiations: A Social-Psychological Perspective.* Beverly Hills, Calif.: Sage, 1977.

Schachter, S. Deviation, rejection and communication. *Journal of Abnormal and Social Psychology,* 1951, *46,* 190-207.

Tetlock, P. E. Identifying victims of groupthink from public statements of decision makers. *Journal of of Personality and Social Psychology,* 1979, *37,* 1314-1324.

Tuckman, B. W. Developmental sequence in small groups. *Psychological Bulletin,* 1965, *63,* 384-399.

Yukl, G. A., Malone, M. P., Hayslip, B., & Pamin, T. A. The effects of time pressure and issue settlement order on integrative bargaining. *Sociometry,* 1976, *39,* 277-281.

Perceptgenesis 4

A PROCESS PERSPECTIVE
ON PERCEPTION-PERSONALITY

GUDMUND J.W. SMITH
BERT WESTERLUNDH

Gudmund J.W. Smith is Professor of Psychology, Lund University. He is the coeditor
(with W. Froehlich, J. G. Draguns, and U. Hentschel) of *Psychological Processes in
Cognition and Personality* (Hemisphere, in press) based on the first international conference on microgenesis.
Bert Westerlundh, a pupil of Smith and U. Kragh, has worked in the fields of perceptgenesis, imagery research, the theory of personality, and psychological biography. He
has published three books. He holds a research position at the Lund University Department of Psychology. His current interests include the experimental analysis of personality and developing micro- and perceptgenetic techniques into fruitful tools for a general
phenomenological theory of perception and its interrelationships to personality functioning.

Perceptgenesis (called PG for short in the following text) is a topic
known to comparatively few American psychologists. Some well-read
people may vaguely associate to Heinz Werner's microgenesis or even to
the German term *Aktualgenese*. These associations are only partly correct. PG is indeed related to microgenesis but also represents a development beyond it. The reason why PG is not better known in the United
States, in spite of a stream of publications over nearly three decades
presenting theory as well as a number of efficient personality tests, may
be threefold: (1) it is of Swedish origin, often published in Scandinavian
periodicals or university monographs; (2) PG approaches personality
with laboratory techniques generally used in studies of perception, at
first sight this may seem strange both to clinicians and experimentalists;
and (3) the theory is based on a number of assumptions which seem
either incomprehensible or offensive to the traditional psychologist.
This third point is probably the most important one because PG seems
to turn psychology upside-down. First of all, PG regarded "processes"
as the central concern of psychology long before that started to become
fashionable, at least in certain quarters; even such American psycholo-

gists as George S. Klein and his associates with their orientation toward similar perception-personality issues as PG were not explicitly process-oriented. Second, stimuli are not primarily considered as the instigators of psychological processes, as in the stimulus-response tradition, but are treated as their ultimate points of reference. In other words, the experience of reality is supposed to be the outcome of processes originating in the perceiver (processes which only gradually divest themselves of their subjective contents) or, to touch the most controversial assumption, processes reflecting the life experience of the individual in a systematic manner, early experiences impressing early parts of a process and later experiences subsequent parts. Closely involved in all this has been another of the great controversies— subliminal perception.

HISTORICAL ROOTS

The historical roots of PG will not be covered in detail here. Instead, we refer to the excellent review by Flavell and Draguns (1957) and to a later article by Draguns (1961). The idea of a genesis "secretly" preceding everyday perception seems to have occurred to Sander (1927) in Germany and Gemelli (1928) in Italy at about the same time, and independently. Schilder's (1928) and Werner's (1927) early formulations are also worth considering in the historical context. The genetic approach to perception became widely known through the German term *Aktualgenese* and inspired a number of research endeavors, even after World War II (Linschoten, 1959; Graumann, 1959; Drösler & Kuhn, 1960; Draguns, 1961, 1963; Fröhlich, 1964). More recent work in this tradition is presented in Fröhlich et al. (in press). The original framework of this research was a general psychology concerned with the structural properties of percepts, and the methodological approach was mainly descriptive-phenomenological, at least in Sander's laboratory.

The Anglo-Saxon public became acquainted with this "genetic" perspective through Heinz Werner's (1956) microgenesis. Werner's term was meant to be an approximation of *Aktualgenese* but his approach came to differ from the original German one in many ways. There was more emphasis on the similarity between the principles governing the micro-processes behind perception, on the one hand, and on those intrinsic to the macro-development from infancy to adulthood, on the other. Early stages in a micro-process as well as in ontogeny were thus supposed to be characterized by a high degree of fusion between feeling and perception (physiognomic perception) and at the same time by lacking integration of different functions; later stages by increasing differentiation, articulation, and integration.

The *central assumption* in Sander's *Aktualgenese* as well as in Werner's micro-genesis was thus that percepts do not come about instantaneously but are the end products of processes which extend over time. Because these processes are generally very brief—they may be completed in fractions of a second—percepts appear to come about as soon as the perceiver confronts the outside stimulation. This quasi-instantaneity may be regarded as a functional illusion because the individual's attention is directed toward the Concluding *C-phase*, not the Prepatory *P-phases*. When, through repetition, the micro-process becomes more and more abbreviated and automatized, the instantaneity, naturally, becomes less illusory.

This process model would seem rather trivial if it did not include the additional assumption that percepts do not come about as the result of a series of quantitative increments of process intensity, resulting from repeated fixations of one and the same stimulus, but via a succession of qualitative changes. As formulated by Kragh and Smith (1970, p. 25): The micro-process cannot be conceived as "a cumulative reinforcement of an initially weak but correctly transcribed pattern of excitation." The end-stage of perceptual development "appears to be related to the prestages, not as a sum to its parts but as a differentiated and specific part-component to the complex component pattern from which it has gradually evolved. With reference to the stimulus motif, the perceptual process would be subtractive (eliminative) rather than additive as it proceeds from composite to more unambiguous meanings, from global formations to less 'syncretic' and more isolated ones."

Special techniques were invented to lay bare these processes which only rarely, or only indirectly, came to the perceiver's own attention. These techniques should prevent the final C-phase from appearing quasi-momentarily and thus prolong the preparatory sections of the genesis and make them accessible to inspection. Among commonly exploited early techniques were tachistoscopic fragmentation and systematic reduction of brightness and clarity. The first presentation of a stimulus was thus so brief or faint or blurred that the perceiver could just barely sense its existence. Only after a series of prolonged (or more intense or less blurred) exposures was he supposed to give a correct report (reach the C-phase). The succession of reports from the first presentation to the final correct one was treated as a reflection of the perceptual process. The credibility of such an assumption will be dealt with later in the text.

PERCEPTGENESIS: INTRODUCTORY DEFINITION

The term *microgenesis* is very general and therefore easily becomes misleading. The Lund University group, on which the major part of this essay is going to be focused, adopted the more concrete term *perceptgenesis*, instead. PG particularly refers to the analysis of percepts and perceptual processes. The PG model is defined by the methodology employed in this analysis. The operational or, rather, operativistic mode of theorizing (cf. below) implied by the explicit reference to methodology is not, however, the only difference between the PG perspective and the *Aktualgenese* tradition, and is not even the major difference. The hallmark of the PG model is its association with problems of personality.

The early study of *Aktualgenese* with its ultimate roots in Wundtian psychology had no interest in personality, not even in differential psychology. Heinz Werner, to be sure, made room for individual differences within his developmental psychology and sensory-tonic field theory but he showed no intention of letting such concepts as personality or "self" become points of crystallization in his theorizing. His observations of similarities between micro- and macro-perspectives of development concerned general, not individual characteristics. Studies in the Werner (1956) tradition by Stein (1949), Phillips and Framo (1954), and others made use of group data, for example, the similarities between the microgenesis of Rorschach responses in a group of adults, on the one hand, and the typical change from early to adult age of Rorschach response preferences, on the other.

In Lund, students of PG tried particularly to exploit the process perspective for a description of personality organization and functioning. Perceptual processes as laid bare by means of various PG methods were thus supposed to represent personality in its historical-hierarchical dimensions. Early sections of a "full-fledged" PG were, in this view, more closely related to deep-seated, archaic levels of functioning than middle or late sections which, in their turn, reflected more advanced levels. At the threshold of the C-phase, finally, the individual again attained his present or manifest level of adaptation. Simultaneously, the personal life history of the individual was unfolded in his PG, early experiences in early P-phases and later experiences in subsequent ones. This direct before-after parallelism between various aspects of the PG (the aspect to be emphasized partly depending on the choice of stimulus motif), on the one hand, and life history, on the other, has been most explicitly advocated by Kragh (1955, 1960a, 1962b, 1980;

Kragh & Smith, 1970). C-phase contents usually dominate the focus of attention, but P-phase contents may nonetheless remain as an aura around the focus giving the perceptual world a personal touch of emotion and early reminiscences.

Since a PG is supposed to proceed from preparatory to fully prepared stages, the issue of subliminal perception must be central (cf. also below). The well-established fact that it is possible to correctly interpret messages sent via subliminal channels could mean either of two things, most probably both: (1) That awareness is not a necessary condition for a perceptual process to be correctly recognized. Much evidence from research in subliminal perception supports this conclusion (Dixon, 1971). (2) That a correct interpretation is somehow embedded already in early P-phases. As a matter of fact, subliminal stimulation can be effective far below the recognition threshold. However, this "directional force" of the stimulus probably could not make itself felt in competition with other, more subjective themes until the PG had gotten well under way.

BASIC METHODS

Many of these general assumptions have been supported by empirical studies. In order to make the studies and their results more comprehensible, however, we will have to review some basic methods.

1. *The tachistoscopic techniques* belong to the classical tools for prolonging the PG. They generally imply that a stimulus is first presented very briefly, just below the threshold of the subject's recognizing that anything at all is being shown, and thereafter at successively prolonged exposure times until the consensus meaning of the stimulus has been reported. The presentation series is usually geometric. The brightness of the stimulus should be kept so low as to ensure that the PG reaches the C-phase after about 10 to 20 presentations. The subject reports after each exposure what he has seen or glimpsed. He may also be asked to make schematic drawings.

1.1 *The Defense Mechanism Test (DMT)* uses (for individual testing) a special slide-contrivance into which the subject looks through an aperture. The stimulus (there are several versions) depicts a central person (the hero) and a peripherally placed person constituting a threat to the former. If a threat initiates an anxiety reaction (which remains submanifest because the threat is not directed at the subject himself but at the projection of his self, the hero), the subject may either (1) display this anxiety in reports of black or otherwise threatening qualities in what he has seen or (2) meet the anxiety with defensive reactions. These take the form of transformations of the content of the picture (the hero, the threat, or the relation between them) in a nonthreatening direction. The distortions are quite stable phenomena, with forms known from the psychoanalytic theory of defense. The regularity of their form and appearance has allowed—as is the case with other qualitative PG techniques—the construction of a formalized scoring scheme.

The DMT is thus supposed to lay bare the typical defensive activities in a subject. One distortion might be to see a lifeless face, a mask, a statue, or an object instead of the threatening face, a reaction called repression because it implies decathecting the threat by making it less human, less involved with one's self, and is particularly common in hysterics. Immobility is a central characteristic of this defense mechanism, in the DMT as in psychoanalysis (cf. Fenichel, 1946, p. 150). More obvious structural similarities between a defensive transformation in DMT and a psychoanalytic defense mechanism are illustrated by the case of isolation—where the subject may "isolate" the hero and the threat from each other by means of a barrier, or cover the threat with a white, innocuous spot—and by identification with the agressor where the hero is doing the threatening, not vice versa as intended in the picture. Other transformations correspond to such defensive operations as turning against the self, reaction-formation, introjection, projection, and so on. For a detailed description, see Kragh (1959, 1960b, 1969), Kragh and Smith (1970), or Westerlundh (1976).

1.2 *The Meta-Contrast Technique (MCT)* is related to DMT but was originally based on techniques derived from experiments with subliminal perception (Smith & Henriksson, 1956). Two stimuli, A and B, are presented on a screen in front of the subject. Stimulus A may be incongruent with B or imply a threat directed at the person depicted in B. The subject is first acquainted with B alone which, throughout the remaining test, is presented at an exposure time making correct identification possible. Without the subject knowing it, A is then introduced immediately before B, first at brief exposure times which are gradually prolonged. The presentation series is terminated when the perception of A, developing within the established frame of B, has reached its C-phase. In case A is threatening, perception of it is often distorted in a similar way as in a DMT protocol. However, perception of B may also change under the influence of the subliminal perception of A. In some cases B might start to change slightly (sensitive reactions), in other cases grossly (paranoid reactions). The conflict between the established B and the surfacing A may lead to the disappearance of all ordered perceiving (zero phases). In cases of depression, A cannot really "break through" but is reported as a meaningless structure over several phases (stereotypy). Since the perceiver can easily be observed by the experimenter, notations of nonverbal reactions are recommended, especially in experiments with children. Descriptions of the MCT are given in Smith and Nyman (1961), Kragh and Smith (1970), Smith and Danielsson (1979a), and Hentschel and Smith (1980).

1.3 *Tachistoscopic presentations ad modum DMT* have been tried with other thematic stimuli: a stimulus depicting a middle-aged man and a youngish man (Kragh & Kroon, 1966; Johnson, 1966); a stimulus with a mother spoon-feeding a baby (Smith, Almgren, Andersson, Englesson, Smith, & Uddenberg, 1978); neutral interactions (father-son, peers, male-female), where the genesis has been the dependent variable in different experiments on personality (Sjöbäck & Westerlundh, 1975, 1977; Westerlundh, 1976); a mother turning away from and leaving a baby, a baby on the verge of falling (Magnusson, Nilsson, & Henriksson, 1977), and so on. Even the MCT technique has been exploited with new picture motifs (e.g., Friedman & Andersson, 1967). All these various stimuli were applied, not primarily to map the individual's defensive armor as with the DMT and MCT stimuli, but to analyze, like the TAT, deep-seated reactions to important human constellations. Still, the PG technique differs from the traditional projective techniques in that it presents the subject's reactions in systematic order from stimulus-distal to stimulus-proximal phases. Another difference, which also implies a practical advantage, is that in a PG test the subject does not have to interpret the picture or make up a story about it but just to describe it as it looked to him. It may be added that interrater reliabilities for all tachistoscopic techniques mentioned are very high for well-trained raters.

2. *The aftereffect techniques* are new and unique to the Lund University group. A first version of an afterimage test was tried by Smith (1949) in a twin study and a modified version by Kragh (1955). A more definite serial afterimage method was put to clinical use by Smith and Kragh (1967). Aftereffects are useful as PG tools because they are unknown to most subjects who need time—or a series of repeated confrontations—to adapt these elusive and yet observable phenomena to the outside physical world. The subject is thus confronted with the aftereffect again and again—in a series of 10 to 20 massed trials—until it has become stabilized. Various aspects of the aftereffect are reported or measured.

2.1 *The Serial Afterimage Test* utilizes afterimages (AIs) of a red schematic face (with a sad expression, particularly effective to bring about interindividual variation, Fries & Smith, 1970). The fixation distance is 40 cm, the fixation time 20 sec, and the projection distance 60 cm, the number of presentations 16 with adults, 10 with children. The AI size is measured, its intensity judged, and its color named. Immature children are likely to get positive and size-constant AIs, adults negative AIs which grow in size proportionally to the increasing projection distance (Ruuth & Smith, 1969; Ruuth, 1970; Ruuth & Andersson, 1971; Smith & Danielsson, 1978a). Among the most striking characteristics in AI serials are the dark and large AIs typical of anxiety states, the successively diminishing AIs reflecting depressive constriction, the intermittent regressions to immature AIs in schizophrenics, and the stimulus-incongruent AI changes in sensitive subjects (Smith, Ruuth, Franzén, & Sjöholm, 1972; Andersson, Fries, & Smith, 1970; Smith, Fries, Andersson, & Ried, 1971; Smith, Sjöholm, & Andersson, 1971; Smith, Sjöholm, & Nielzén, 1974, 1975, 1976; Smith & Nordström, 1975; Smith & Danielsson, 1979a).

2.2 *The Spiral Aftereffect Technique (SAE)*, employed by Andersson and coworkers (Andersson, 1967, 1969, 1971; Andersson, Franzén, & Ruuth, 1971; Andersson, Johansson, Karlsson, & Olsson, 1969; Andersson & Ruuth, 1971; Andersson & Weikert, 1974; Lindén, 1977), rests on the aftereffect caused by a rotating 2 1/2 turns Archimede's spiral when, after a fixation of 45 sec, the subject looks at a stationary circle or, if the subject is a preschool child, a schematic face. At least 10 massed trials are included in a test with school children or adults. The basic measure is the duration of the SAE. The subject is obviously faced with two extreme possibilities: to rely on the subjective impression and report a long SAE or to rely on the reality of the stationary circle and deny the SAE as soon as possible. Between the extreme reliance on intraceptive factors, on the one hand, and extraceptive factors, on the other, are the more common intermediary cases. It is not only important to know the final, more or less stabilized SAE duration of the last trials but also how the duration changes from the initial trial to the last one. SAE duration alternates in a dialectical way during ontogeny (Andersson, Ruuth, & Ageberg, 1977) and can best be understood within a developmental frame of reference (Andersson, in press). Subjects with tendencies to negate self-related experiences (e.g., primitive or conversion hysterics) are likely to show a short final SAE duration preceded by a successive decrease over trials. Those who increase their duration over trials toward a long final SAE tend instead to negate the nonself pole of experience and be dominated by anxieties and depressive moods. Subjects who prefer a final SAE of intermediate duration are likely to have a more marked differentiation between self and nonself.

   2.3 *The Oculogyral Illusion (OGI)*, that is, the effect on a person's perception of a stationary light in darkness by foregoing body rotation, has been exploited by Nilsson (1972a, 1972b; Nilsson & Henriksson, 1967a, 1967b; Nilsson & Tibbling, 1972). Many of the results obtained with this technique are analogous to those found with the SAE.

   3. *Serial methods* involving the study of how individuals adapt to a new, often conflicting situation must be considered more marginal to the PG theme. The process perspective is still central, but here, the prestages of perception are not directly studied. Instead, interest is centered on how the subject manages to acquire certain skills, such as drawing when viewing the performance in a mirror or naming the printing-colors of color-words representing other colors. The serial color-word test (CWT), based on Thurstone's (1944) version of Stroop's test, has been widely used (Smith & Klein, 1953; Smith & Nyman, 1959; Nyman & Smith, 1959, 1961; Hentschel, in press; Hentschel & Schubö, 1976). The formal properties of the method have been analyzed in detail (Sjöberg, 1974; Smith & Nyman, 1974; Hentschel & Schubö, 1976; Schubö & Hentschel, 1978) and parallel versions have been constructed (Hentschel, 1973; cf. Smith & Borg, 1964). The mirror-drawing test was one of the very first attempts to exploit the process perspective (Smith, 1952). Much of the theorizing around these tests was inspired by the "cognitive control" tradition.

   4. *There are other alternatives.* The study of serial changes in perceptual meaning, especially the use of tachistoscopic procedures allowing asssessment of defensive operations, are unique to PG. The superiority of the tachistoscope over other information-reduction techniques (in terms of stimulus equivalence between different presentations and such) has been well-demonstrated by Kragh (1955). However, the question arises if the PG operationalizations of defense are limited to tachistoscopic perceptual reports.

   Sjöbäck and Westerlundh (1975, 1977) resurrected the old microgenetic technique of presenting a stimulus (in this case, a mother-child scene), at first at very weak and then at successively increased intensities. Analogous to "tachistoscopic," this could be called the "amauroscopic" technique. It was found that the resulting geneses were not phenomenologically different from tachistoscopic ones. The same types of perceptual transformations were found and could be scored using the ordinary PG scoring scheme. Correlating these results with results obtained on the same subjects using the tachistoscope demonstrated that amauroscopic transformations had the same defensive significance as tachistoscope ones.

Westerlundh (1980) presented the DMT pictures using a technique originally proposed by F. Sander and later used (with geometrical figures) by Butzmann (1940). It consists of presenting the stimulus monocularly, at first peripherally and later to increasingly central parts of the retina. The classical *Aktualgenese* description of the process (1. no differentiation of figure and ground; 2. primitive Gestalt; 3. ambiguously complex Vorgestalt; 4. correct recognition) was substantiated, but it was also found that the perceptual reports contained a wealth of transformations of the same order as those seen in tachistoscopic geneses. The results from the peripheral genesis were surprisingly well-related to the personality classifications of the serial CWT, which strengthens the idea that their significance is the same as that for tachistoscopic results. PG operationalizations of defensive processes are valid also for other perceptual process techniques.

5. *There is the inverted PG method.* In a number of studies, Smith and Danielsson (1978b, 1979b) have combined a conventional straight PG series with an inverted one, that is, after the straight series has reached its C-phase, the experimenter has reversed the procedure and presented the stimulus at gradually decreasing exposure times. Once confronted with the "correct" meaning of the stimulus, would the subject now stick to that meaning and at most "subtract" from it in his reporting while the visibility diminished; or would he again make contact with qualitatively different subjective meanings, perhaps the very meanings he reported early in his straight PG? If creativity is defined as an individual's inclination to transgress the confines of an established perceptual context, creative individuals would be able to recover many subjective themes. In a group of researchers and a group of artistically inclined students, the richness of their straight PGs correlated with their emotional involvement in research or artistic work, and the richness of their inverted PGs correlated with their ability to generate original ideas, in the group of researchers, or their urge to create, in the artistic group. A subliminal, threatening stimulus administered before the onset of the inverted PG in the latter group tended to increase the number of subjective themes recovered or, to express it more drastically, to wake a dormant urge to create. A rich inverted PG also correlated with closeness to early childhood reminiscences and appreciation of dreams. The project is still in progress.

EMPIRICAL STUDIES

Some results of the application of PG methods have already been mentioned. We will try to summarize the main findings here insofar as they bear upon the central theme of the present review, the credibility and usefulness of the basic PG assumptions.

1. Many of the empirical studies concern correlations between PG characteristics and independent criteria. Particular care has been taken to define the criteria. Personality inventories have generally been shunned as either superficial or misleading instruments. Findings of independent authors support each other to a high degree. Many of the most important correlations have been cross-validated several times. The correlational level is often above .50.

1.1 *Clinical studies* have demonstrated the diagnostic efficiency of nearly all methods mentioned above. Repression in the sense of DMT and MCT has thus been established as a central defense strategy in hysterics, and isolation in compulsives. Discontinuities in MCT have proved to be grave psychotic signs, like regressions in the AI test and so on. An important part of the analysis concerns the difference between late and early signs in the test which, on the whole, corresponds to the difference between manifest and latent tendencies in real life.[1] An example from a study of AI serials in depressives may suffice (Smith, Kragh, Eberhard, & Johnson, 1970). Depressives with strong signs of manifest anxiety had corresponding AI signs late in the series; but where retardation had relegated the anxiety symptoms to the role of latent trigger mechanisms, the AI signs appeared early and were soon suppressed by diminishing AI size. In endogenous depressives, with no apparent early history of anxiety, there were no anxiety signs at all in the AI serials. Other studies (with MCT) have shown how defensive strategies change during ontogeny in a sequence consistent with most clinical observations. Children first show open fear which they try to counter by means of such overt actions as flight. Later, both affect and the defensive operations against it are freed from the immediate tie to the stimulus and work on an intrapsychic level. Among the classical defenses as mapped by the test, denial is early, repression is delayed to the oedipal or post-oedipal age, and isolation is a strategy most typical of late latency or prepuberty (Smith & Danielsson, 1979a; cf. Lindbom, 1968). Many of the clinical studies have appeared in three books (Kragh & Smith, 1970; Andersson, Nilsson, Ruuth, & Smith, 1972; Hentschel & Smith, 1980; cf. Nilsson & Almgren, 1970; Almgren, 1971; Eberhard,

Johnson, Nilsson, & Smith, 1965; Smith, Sjöholm, & Nielzén, 1975; Hagberg, 1973).

1.2 PG techniques are used for the *selection of personnel who risk meeting extreme stress* in their work. The DMT was originally constructed for selection of aircraft pilots. The tachistoscopic presentation of the threatening picture is a stress situation which gives rise to anxiety and defense against anxiety in predisposed persons. Intense use of defense mechanisms limits the amount of energy available for reality adaptation. This is especially perilous when aspects of the work situation itself function as chronic anxiety inductors. In military flying, accidents, loss of aircraft, and death are such aspects. Further, defense mechanisms are based on deep-seated cognitive and motor action tendencies. Under acute stress, persons with strong defenses will tend to react inadequately—with tragic results in the flying situation.

The test evidently taps factors of this order, since a great number of investigations have proved its effectiveness in military pilot selection (i.e., Kragh, 1960b; Neuman, 1978). The criteria here have been pass/fail in basic flight training and suitability/unsuitability in service performance from 6 to 12 years. Predictive validity with present evaluation of the test (Neuman, 1978) is around .50, giving a common variance of the test and pilot ability of .25. Since this is in a group which has already been highly preselected, using conventional techniques, and the contribution of the test is unique—its correlations with all other selection instruments being near zero—it gives a most effective contribution to the selection process. It is now in regular use in Sweden, Denmark, and Norway.

The DMT also correlates highly with ability as a front soldier (Johnson, 1966, 1967) and as an attack diver (Kragh, 1962c). For instance, in Johnson's (1967) study, the DMT strongly discriminates between decorated and nondecorated Finnish World War II fighters.

Andersson, Nilsson, and Henriksson (1970) employed, among other tests, the SAE, the CWT, and the MCT in an attempt to differentiate accident-loaded and accident-free car drivers. They found that the accident-loaded drivers differed from other drivers by their decreasing and short SAE durations, indicating extreme dependence on external factors (with bad internal control), high variability in CWT reading time, and iterated cleavage of the B picture in the MCT. All these characteristics of the accident-loaded group suggest a primitive-hysterical type of social-emotional adjustment.

1.3 Studies of *parallelisms between PGs and life history* started in the middle 1950s with Kragh's (1955; revised in Kragh & Smith, 1970) ambitious project on young men who had lost their fathers. Using a father-son stimulus, Kragh found that in the PGs of these subjects the father figure often vanished (after having been correctly spotted) and gave way to a female person (the mother serving as the father substitute). Kragh has made several case studies on this theme (Kragh, 1960a, 1962b, 1980). All these works seem to support the parallelism hypothesis, but it is very difficult to make waterproof tests.

Support is also coming from other sources. Smith and Nordström (1975), for instance, could show how the narcissistic defenses, which appeared close to the C-phase in young school children (where they should be manifest), were gradually shoved toward the middle or beginning of the PGs in older age groups (where they should belong to the past). The tendency for these defenses to become more sparsely represented at the same time could be ascribed to increasing condensation in the early sections of a PG as subjects grow older. Finally, Neuman (1978) regarded his data as indirect support of the micro-macro parallelism: When he weighted his defensive signs according to where they appeared in a PG, giving more weight to an early than to a late placement of a primitive sign and vice versa for a more mature one, the predictive efficiency of the DMT increased considerably.

2. In all projects where more than one PG technique has been employed, the correlations between them have been computed. There are significant correlations between, for instance, MCT and CWT (Eberhard, Johnson, Nilsson, & Smith, 1965; Almgren, 1971), MCT and the AI test (Smith & Danielsson, 1979a), DMT and SAE (Andersson & Weikert, 1974), CWT, SAE, and OGI (Andersson, 1967a; Nilsson & Henriksson, 1967b), and so on but the correlations are sometimes only moderate. Even DMT and MCT do not correlate very highly if the same scoring scheme is used for both tests (Palmqvist, 1974). Different techniques actualize different aspects of a patient's life history and functional system.

3. The qualitative PG techniques are highly sensitive instruments in *experimental personality research*. Even the best-conducted experimental research on psychoanalytic propositions has often been hampered by the crude nature of the dependent variables used. These have generally been gross indices of disturbance ("pathological ideation" and so on). PG techniques go beyond such measures and allow us, in a sense, to actually see the component parts of mental conflict in the perceptual reports, processes which the subject can hardly articulate in any other way.

Let us repeat that the PG techniques referred to here assess the individual's defense organization, as it manifests itself at a perceptual level. Psychoanalysis conceives of this organization as a complex hierarchical structure of strategies, differentially called into play, depending on the intensity and cognitive character of the eliciting anxiety. Some defenses, such as those drawn into neurotic conflict, are more or less structuralized, forever fighting forbidden drives. Others are latent potentialities, called upon only when outer or inner taractic stimulation activates anxiety. Defenses thus have more of a "trait" or more of a "state" character. The stable part of the defense organization—generally the one drawn into pathogenic conflict—is tapped by instruments such as the DMT and the MCT. On the other hand, it is possible to activate defenses normally held in abeyance by introducing anxiety-evoking experimental operations conceived from the psychoanalytic theory of conflict and defense. These elicited processes can be registered in a PG, used as a dependent variable.

PG researchers early saw the empirical and theoretical possibilities of experimentation. Thus, Kragh postulated that the subliminal threat in the DMT picture corresponds to the first part of Freud's (1926) threat-anxiety-defense conceptualization of the causation of defensive operations. Kragh (1962a) tested this by comparing reports to a DMT picture and those to a structurally equivalent one, where the threat was exchanged for a similar, but benign and smiling face. The threatening picture universally led to more reports of defensive transformations. Bokander and Lindbom (1967) used the MCT in an attempt to study the effects of aggressive films on minors. Among their main results they found that an MCT administered just after such a film contained more scorable indices of defense than a similar test given before the film. Andersson, Fries, and Smith (1970) introduced a threatening subliminal face in the middle of a serial afterimage experiment. This operation led to an increased frequency of reports of very big and very dark afterimages. Thus, they were able to validate experimentally the character of these reports as indicative of anxiety.

These experiments still use a generally anxiety-arousing operation to activate anxiety and defensive processes. However, within limits it is possible to create specific operations, relating to different conflicts and activating different parts of the defensive spectrum. Generally, many anxiety-evoking themes are condensed in a single representation, which leads to a multiplicity of reactions. On the other hand, this confluence can be greater or smaller, and the different themes can to some degree be purified. Thus, inner or outer stimuli activating genital sexual impulses will be met primarily by repression, whereas those that activate aggressive impulses are met by other defenses, especially isolation and reaction formation (Fenichel, 1946, p. 149).

Two group experiments (Westerlundh, 1979) can serve as illustrations. Both use young males as subjects and a before-after design, with the operation affecting the second PG. In both, the crucial response variable is reports to neutral Father-Son presentations. Father-Son PGs have often been used in experiments. Relating as they do to the resolution of the Oedipus complex, they allow for representation of material referring to both sexual, aggressive, and superego conflicts.

One experiment aims at activating conflict around genital sexuality. Between the two PGs, subjects have to copy a picture of a nude women as a "personality test." The other experiment uses subliminal stimulation. During the first PG a meaningless pattern in grey with two red spots is shown on the screen. This is structurally similar to the picture shown during the second PG: a pair of threatening, terrifying eyes with red pupils. Results are much in accordance with predictions (Fenichel, 1946; Peto, 1969). In the "sex" experiment, indices of repression and anxiety show significant increase in the second PG. In the "super-ego forerunner" experiment, indices of isolation, schizoid isolation, fear, and introaggression show such increase.

The two experiments, using the same stimulus material and the same basic set-up, give quite different results as a consequence of the differing experimental operations. The sensitivity of the PG technique seems well-demonstrated here.

The more ambitious attempts to test psychoanalytic propositions using PG techniques (Sjöbäck & Westerlundh, 1975, 1977; Westerlundh, 1976) have recently been reviewed (Westerlundh, in press). Independent PG instruments serve to identify subjects sensitive to the experimental operations. The DMT and a Mother-Child PG describe the individual's basic defense organization. Aspects of the latter are related to sensitivity to the experimental operations. There is thus a differential psychological perspective to consider in experiments on psychoanalytic propositions. Experimental operations will be effective on a certain subgroup of unselected subjects, those whose personality organization makes them predisposed to react with anxiety and defense in the conflict area evoked. Previous PG experiments with unselected groups yielded positive results mainly because they studied very prevalent conflicts. However, attempts to experimentally investigate many of the etiological hypotheses of psychoanalysis must of necessity use selected groups of subjects.

4. Some studies using PG methods have yielded *negative findings*. However, most of them are very difficult to evaluate because of suspected flaws in design and definition of criterion groups. Most of these studies have not been formally published.

The studies summarized here, only too briefly, have, naturally, established the practical usefulness of the PG methods. The tests can be employed for prediction of success and failure in stressing situations, for diagnosing the functional background of clinical symptoms, for exploring specific themes such as mother-child or father-son relations, and so on. The assessment theme is not central in this context but helps to highlight the methodological fruitfulness of the process perspective. It is quite clear that PGs reveal some lasting, under-the-surface characteristics of the perceiver. So do most projective tests, to be sure, even if their validity has often been questioned. However, data show that these characteristics are presented in a systematic and hierarchical order in PGs. Early signs are primitive, whereas late signs are more manifest and closer to present functioning and awareness.

THE PG MODEL

As stated, PG sees the perceptual act as a process moving from subjective prestages to the final intersubjective meaning of the stimulus. In optimal cases, the series of reports to iterated tachistoscopic presentations will reflect the "historical personality," the psychic structure formation during the individual's ontogenesis. The degree of condensation of personal meaning is bound to be high in the beginning of a PG, and the influence of intersubjective meaning tends to dominate at the end. This means that the clearest relationship between a PG and life history will be found in the middle part of the series of reports. As the PG proceeds toward the C-phase, the principles of visual organization become less archaic, less dreamlike and condensed, and more adapted to ordinary space-time categories.

Levels of meaning. A number of levels of meaning are involved in PG analysis. They are illustrated in the following example from Kragh and Smith (1970, see Figure 1). As explained by Kragh and Smith (1970, p. 27):

> The concept of *organization* will denote the visual form reported by the subject verbally and/or in the form of a drawing. The *meanings* are also given by the subject: in the report ("primary meanings"), in terms of associations to the organization ("secondary meaning"), and as recollections ("tertiary meanings"). The tertiary meanings may be amplified from other sources than the subject himself, e.g. from parents' reports. *Structure,* finally, is a construct; its contents are derived from information given in organization and meanings. It refers to the concept of personality and its definition will agree closely with the one used in psychoanalysis (cf. Munroe, 1955).

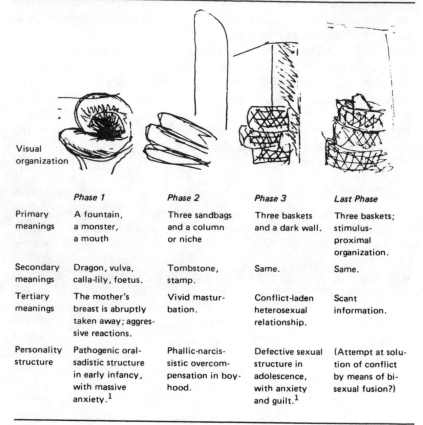

	Phase 1	Phase 2	Phase 3	Last Phase
Primary meanings	A fountain, a monster, a mouth	Three sandbags and a column or niche	Three baskets and a dark wall.	Three baskets; stimulus-proximal organization.
Secondary meanings	Dragon, vulva, calla-lily, foetus.	Tombstone, stamp.	Same.	Same.
Tertiary meanings	The mother's breast is abruptly taken away; aggressive reactions.	Vivid masturbation.	Conflict-laden heterosexual relationship.	Scant information.
Personality structure	Pathogenic oral-sadistic structure in early infancy, with massive anxiety.[1]	Phallic-narcissistic overcompensation in boyhood.	Defective sexual structure in adolescence, with anxiety and guilt.[1]	(Attempt at solution of conflict by means of bisexual fusion?)

Figure 1: **Transformation of organization, meanings and structure during the development of perception-personality: a concrete example.**

1. Anxiety would refer to the dark parts of the visual organization.

Types of analysis. There are two types of PG analysis of such material. In the more ambitious sequential-dynamic type, all levels of meaning are used by the psychologist. Here, he really tries to study the historical personality by relating several PGs from one person to each other in order to find "key phases" (isomorphic manifestations as regards content and place in different PGs). A full analysis of this type will show the individual development of personality structure. The other type of analysis is the formal type. Here, only the levels of organization, primary meaning, and structure are involved. Scoring a PG for indices of defense is an analysis of this order. The aim here is much more limited; no attempt is made to trace personality organization and development in full.

Transformations. The three basic ways of transformation of contents in a PG are elimination, cumulation, and emergence. *Elimination* refers to disappearance of contents which do not further influence the PG, *cumulation* to successive determination with continuance of contents, and *emergence* to cases where content continuity between reports seems negligible. These transformations exist on all levels of meaning. The constructs on the structural level are, however, designed to explain the transformations.

The PG model and psychological theory. This raises the question of the relationship between the PG model and theoretical constructs. Up to the level of structure, PG analysis is descriptive, representing continuity and change in perception-personality. The explanatory constructs are found at the structural level. PG has not developed unique constructs of this type. Instead, PG results have been interpreted in terms of general personality and cognitive theory. However, the basic PG assumptions about the micro-processes of perception and their relation to personality and life history clearly articulate the nature of those theories which can be used to explain PG results. Roughly, we can differentiate between mechanistic and dynamic theories. Mechanistic theories see personality or cognitive structure as an agglomeration of variables (traits, habits), whereas dynamic theories see it as a system, a dynamic organization. Mechanistic theories regard development as a quantitative increase or decrease, such as simple change in performance with age, an addition or subtraction of qualitatively uniform parts (e.g., habits). Dynamic theories claim that the development of structure over time is characterized by qualitative changes, according to principles that change and complicate during development. PG is compatible with dynamic theories, such as psychoanalysis and the cognitive genetic structuralism of Piaget. It is incompatible with mechanistic theories, such as various behavioristic ones.

The explanatory background of the PG system can only be offered by the individual's developmental history. This is one reason why it seems tempting to use psychoanalysis in combination with the PG approach. But psychoanalysis seems natural not only because of its developmental perspective but also for many other reasons. The hierarchical point of view of psychoanalysis, one aspect of which is that mental processes exist on different levels of a primary-secondary process continuum, is paralleled in PG by development from subjective to intersubjective contents in the series of reports. Further, PG has developed working operationalizations of concepts derived from the psychoanalytic theory of defense.

However, the relation to psychoanalysis, or any other theoretical system used in combination with the PG approach, must be dialectical. Psychoanalysis must first serve as a hypothetical frame of reference—to be accepted only when it has proved useful in empirical work. PG should also be used to revise this system, if possible to modernize it. Since PG work is concerned with the dynamic use of memory systems, a natural expansion would be in the direction of modern theories of learning and cognition.

Construction and reconstruction. The direction from the subjective prestages to a stimulus-proximal perception is called "construction in the direction of the objects" in PG. What happens here has psychologically a double aspect: The stimulus is interpreted in terms of meaning, and this meaning is related to successive layers of the life-historical meaning system. Early prestages carry a great amount of diffuse and condensed subjective meaning. Later stages are primarily characterized by an elimination of subjective contents and a preponderance of the consensus C-phase meaning.

However, for a conscious percept to come into being, a further psychological activity is necessary. The individual must grasp the significance of the constructed contents outgoing from his present cognitive and motivational level of functioning. This is called reconstruction. From a formal point of view, the direction of reconstruction is opposite to that of construction. Especially in the early phases of a PG, the individual must make contact with his own subjective levels of functioning. For certain minds, this is threatening. Many compulsives will exclude all subjective material from consciousness and only report in a PG when they have grasped the interpersonal meaning of the stimulus.

The concept of reconstruction thus comprises a number of determinants of perception of a primarily cognitive order. Two such important groups are set and defense mechanisms. Sets will influence reconstruction in certain directions. An "objectivistic" setting will easily induce a set only to report veridical information, with exclusion of prephases as a consequence. Defense mechanisms are activated by anxiety signals and lead to the specific transformations described earlier.

The relationship of construction to reconstruction is as follows: during our lives, we will consciously experience more and more (reconstruction). This successive experiencing is incorporated in the life-historical meaning system and is thus activated in later acts of construction. In terms of the historical personality, the act of construction implies an activation of the individual's earlier reconstructions.

The PG conceptualization of the processes just discussed can be summarized in a diagram (see Figure 2). The technique of fractioning is represented vertically as the successive presentations of the stimulus. The directions of construction and reconstruction are shown as arrows. The activation of a defensive operation is illustrated.

Method and data. Iterated tachistoscopic presentations of a stimulus give as data a series of perceptual reports. Can the contents studied here be said to be comparable to those in everyday perception? There are two issues involved: protraction of the perceptual act and fractioning of the stimulus presentation.

Ordinarily, perceiving serves immediate adaptive ends. Perceptual acts in an expectable environment are abbreviated in the service of adaptation (cf. below). However, given comparable conditions, the time intervals involved in uninterrupted and tachistoscopic vision are not incommensurate. If a subject is presented an object, not too familiar, not too simple, and with rather weak intensity, the time needed by the subject to reach correct recognition may well be protracted.

Equivalents of fractioning are found in everyday perception. Fractioning implies an intermittent repetition of stimulus presentation. Now, as is well-known, percepts come about as the results of discrete series of fixations. Eye movements are necessary for maintaining the percept. Prolonged fixation leads to the breakdown of the perceived and its return in a more primitive form (e.g., Pritchard, Heron, & Hebb, 1960).

In the PG situation, prestages of perception which normally do not reach phenomenological representation are apprehended and verbalized. Further, this reporting is reiterated. Will this affect the contents of the process? Will it, for instance, lead to a tendency to consolidate material once reported? Possibly, some such factors work in the PG situation. "Since any scientific measurement is likely to interfere with its object, a fact accepted long ago in physics, we have to be content with giving as faithful a reflection of perception as possible within the framework of a well-defined analysis" (Kragh & Smith, 1970, p. 22).

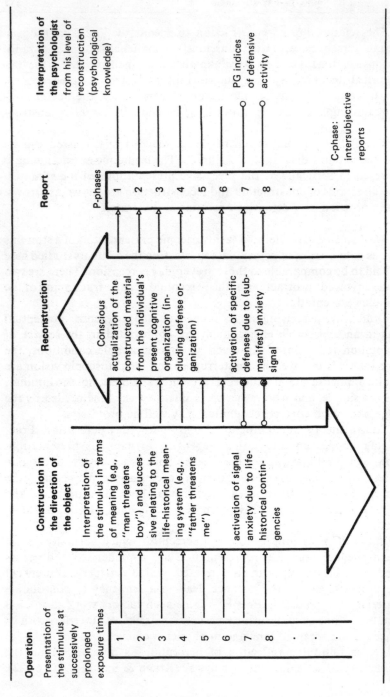

Operation

Presentation of
the stimulus at
successively
prolonged
exposure times

1
2
3
4
5
6
7
8
.
.
.

**Construction in
the direction of
the object**

Interpretation of
the stimulus in terms
of meaning (e.g.,
"man threatens
boy") and succes-
sive relating to the
life-historical mean-
ing system (e.g.,
"father threatens
me")

activation of signal
anxiety due to life-
historical contin-
gencies

Reconstruction

Conscious

actualization of the
constructed material
from the individual's
present cognitive
organization (in-
cluding defense or-
ganization)

activation of specific
defenses due to (sub-
manifest) anxiety
signal

Report

P-phases

1
2
3
4
5
6
7
8
.
.
.

C-phase:
intersubjective
reports

**Interpretation of
the psychologist**
from his level of
reconstruction
(psychological
knowledge)

PG indices
of defensive
activity

Figure 2: Schematic representation of the PG model of perception-personality.

However, there are a number of facts which indicate that such error factors are not too important. The end stages of fractioned perception do not differ, in a phenomenological sense, from ordinary perception. Moreover, error factors of the type discussed ought to lead to equivalent results in different subjects, whereas PGs show great individual personality-related variation. Finally, as stated above, the organization and character of the prephases of perception have been shown to be the same for a number of dissimilar information-reduction techniques, showing the stability and generality of these prephases. In all, PG seems to open a channel where normally covert signals, and not noise, predominate.

Operationism and perceptualism. PG researchers have tried to anchor their concepts firmly in empirical operations. The model has been called "operation-intrinsic" in a laudatory sense by its proponents and in a derogatory one by critical workers in the same tradition (e.g., Neuman, 1978). However, the "operationism" of PG researchers has limited itself to careful description of empirical parameters and their relations to constructs used. It has not inhibited their use of theoretical constructs, for example, from psychoanalysis. Further, these constructs are not thought of as specified in meaning by the empirical operations in the sense of operational definitions. It is not claimed that "defenses are what the DMT measures" and that their meaning is thereby specified. Instead, it is stated that responses to the DMT pictures contain indices of defense, which term here has much the same meaning as in psychoanalytic theory. The interest of PG workers to link operations to central constructs of personality theory could perhaps better be denoted by the term *operativism* than by the old term *operationism*.

The PG model is specifically concerned with percepts and perceptual processes. Some questions as regards this issue have been raised by Nilsson (in press), in an attempt to combine the developmental psychologies of psychoanalysis and Piaget. He observes that PG techniques differ as to character. In the qualitative PG techniques, such as the DMT and the MCT, data are meaningful perceptual contents as reported by the subject. Other techniques, such as the AI, the SAE or the CWT, give data about formal aspects of perception or even of performance. However, no serious attempt has been made to analyze the differences in functional level between various PG techniques and the significance of these differences for the understanding of empirical PG data. Nilsson prefers to designate the qualitative techniques the PG techniques proper. These techniques give information on a purely perceptual level of functioning, as distinct from a sensory-motor or a conceptual level. However, functioning on these different levels has not yet been studied in terms of a more comprehensive psychology of development within PG. Nilsson claims that only such an analysis can answer certain basic questions, such as how defensive functioning can appear in perceptual processes and why defenses take the special form they do there.

The basic ideas of Nilsson's theorizing seem reasonable enough, and it is certainly possible to place PG in a wider theoretical context. However, his arguments are not directed at the empirical results of PG.

PG and other process models of perception. As we have seen, PG is a phenomenologically oriented process model of perception-personality. There exist other such models of perception. A simple classification would be in physiological, formal-cognitive, and phenomenological process models. The physiological ones try to describe and explain the complicated processes in the nervous system that take place during the perceptual act. Refined electrophysiological methods provide opportunities for empirical study and control. A common process model in contemporary cognitive psychology is the formal-cognitive one. The act of perception is here generally represented in a flow diagram, showing the processing and storage of information. The main source of data comes from cognitive laboratory experiments.

The three types of models have different frames of reference and different fields of inquiry, but there is no basic incompatibility between them. Certain physiological and formal models have affinities to microgenetic/perceptgenetic ones. These related models have been summarized by Draguns (in press). The relationship of the PG model to formal models is rather that of content to form. While formal models postulate the mere existence of a number of memory systems in the perceptual process, PG articulates the contents that intensive investigation on this level of operation will yield. Emphasis on the subjective and affective nature of the early part of the perceptual process is a distinctive PG characteristic.

SOME ADDITIONAL ISSUES

How stable are the PG characteristics, the defensive structures in a DMT protocol, or the stylistic qualities in an aftereffect serial? Since these characteristics have been shown to correlate with independently established criteria of various kinds, they cannot very well be transient. Sizable test-retest correlations have been reported for DMT (Kragh &

Smith, 1970; Neuman, 1978) and for SAE (Andersson, 1969; cf. Nilsson & Henriksson, 1967a; Smith, Fries, & Andersson, 1969). Such high correlations, of course, imply that subjects remain virtually unchanged. Smith and Johnson (1962) employed two parallel versions of the MCT in a clinical sample undergoing psychiatric therapy. While change as a result of therapy was accompanied by change from the first to the second test occasion, little or no change, that is, high stability, was registered in a control group without intervening therapy. The non-randomness of serial AI trends was demonstrated by the administration of extraneous auditory stimulation which caused a repetition of trends preceding the signal (Smith, Sjöholm, & Andersson, 1971).

The perceptual world becomes more definite, less ambiguous not only as the child grows up but during the short span of a PG. We may call this a progressive stabilization of percepts. Since the C-phase of a young person is likely to be less definite than that of an adult, it is also less clearly set off from previous phases. On the whole, children's PGs are often characterized by incomplete elimination. In tachistoscopic tests one will often find that, instead of disqualifying one meaning when a new interpretation occurs to them, they hold on to the old meaning and thus entertain several meanings simultaneously, often close to or at the level of the C-phase (Smith & Nordström, 1975). The connection between C-phase and P-phase levels remains unbroken and self-evident, sometimes as late as the early teens.

Here we touch upon the important problem of conservation and renewal. The principle of conservation, of adherence to long-range developmental trends, is represented by cumulation in the PG process, and renewal or change by emergence. Emergence is more often observed in young people than in adults and exists even close to the C-phase. With mounting age it is shoved more and more toward the early P-phases, if it does not altogether disappear. As pointed out by Kragh and Smith (1974; Smith & Kragh, 1975), adults cannot always rely on emergence for their creative endeavors but have to use reconstruction of once-discarded P-phase meanings in order to break dominant C-phase conceptions and start anew. The more cut off the C-phase is from the P-phase part of the PG—or the more crucial but anxiety-provoking P-phases are blocked by defenses—the more difficult this reconstruction becomes.

Stimulus repetition leads to PG automatization. Even when retesting with parallel but not identical stimuli, experimenters will find that PGs are generally abbreviated. Early P-phases are the first to become extinct. Automatization thus means "that originally separate preparatory stages are shoved into each other and eventually disappear . . . (As a result of this the reflection of ontogenesis in perceptgenesis becomes) increasingly more fragmentary. In other words, the microgenesis gradually loses its personal flavor. At this stage the classical S-R paradigm may reign undisputed" (Smith, in press; cf. Smith & Borg, 1964). The successive automatization of the PG processes is, naturally, the key to effective energy economy.

SUMMARY AND CONCLUSIONS

Perceptgenesis has been described here as it developed from the continental *Aktualgenese* (microgenesis) to its present concern with problems of perception-personality. The perceptual processes laid bare by means of the PG methods are supposed to reflect personality in its hierarchical-historical dimensions: Starting at levels stamped by archaic principles of functioning and meanings related to early stages of life, these processes eventually free themselves from subjective dominance and reach the level of intersubjectively correct perception. A number of empirical studies attest to these basic assumptions. PG methodology has been widely and successfully exploited for diagnostic purposes, for the description of the course of psychotherapy, the selection of personnel applying for dangerous jobs, the experimental testing of psychoanalytic propositions, and so on. The studies conducted so far form a tight network to support PG as a group of effective methodologies for personality assessment and research.

PG is first of all a way of describing mental processes, that is, to break the stasis of "fossilized" (Vygotsky) psychology and focus on processes instead of states, on adaptation and growth. Its explanatory basis is the life history of the individual. The presuppositions of the PG model—representing a unification of ideas from developmental, cognitive, and personality psychology—are compatible with a number of theoretical conceptualizations in these areas. The empirical orientation of PG has created a data base which ought to assure its interest to workers in these fields of inquiry.

NOTE

1. The correspondence between a late sign and a manifest tendency does not, generally, mean that the subject becomes aware of this tendency in the test situation.

Exceptions are small children and severely disturbed patients where, for instance, manifest anxiety reactions are often displayed during testing.

REFERENCES

Almgren, P.-E. Relations between perceptual defenses defined by the Meta-Contrast Technique and adaptive patterns in two serial behavior test. *Psychological Research Bulletin (Lund)*, 1971, *11*, No. 3.

Andersson, A. L. Adaptive visual aftereffect processes as related to patterns of color-word interference serials. *Perceptual and Motor Skills*, 1967, *25*, 437-453.

Andersson, A. L. Adaptive regulation of visual aftereffect duration and social-emotional adjustment. *Acta Psychologica*, 1969, *29*, 1-34.

Andersson, A. L. Personality as reflected in adaptive regulation of visual aftereffect perception: a review of concepts and empirical findings. *Psychological Research Bulletin (Lund)*, 1971, *11*, No. 1.

Andersson, A. L. Toward a dialectical conception of the percept-genetic approach to perception-personality. In W. Fröhlich et al. (eds.), *Psychological processes in cognition and personality*. New York: Hemisphere, in press.

Andersson, A. L., Franzén, G., & Ruuth, E. Discontinuity of spiral aftereffect duration trends in acute schizophrenia. *Psychological Research Bulletin (Lund)*, 1971, *11*, No. 14.

Andersson, A. L., Fries, I., & Smith, G.J.W. Change in afterimage and spiral aftereffect serials due to anxiety caused by subliminal threat. *Scandinavian Journal of Psychology*, 1970, *11*, 7-16.

Andersson, A. L., Johansson, A., Karlsson, B., & Ohlsson, M. On self-nonself interaction in early childhood as revealed by the spiral aftereffect duration. *Psychological Research Bulletin (Lund)*, 1969, *9*, No. 11.

Andersson, A. L., Nilsson, A., & Henriksson, N.-G. Personality differences between accident-loaded and accident-free young car drivers. *British Journal of Psychology*, 1970, *61*, 409-421.

Andersson, A. L., Nilsson, A., Ruuth, E., & Smith, G.J.W. (eds). *Visual aftereffects and the individual as an adaptive system*. Lund, Sweden: Gleerup, 1972.

Andersson, A. L. & Ruuth, E. Relation between spiral aftereffect duration and rod-and-frame performance in early childhood. *Perceptual and Motor Skills*, 1971, *32*, 843-849.

Andersson, A. L., Ruuth, E., & Ageberg, G. Patterns of perceptual change in the ages 7 to 15 years: A cross-sectional study of the Rod-and-Frame Test and the spiral aftereffect technique. *Scandinavian Journal of Psychology*, 1977, *18*, 257-265.

Andersson, A. L. & Weikert, C. Adult defensive organization as related to adaptive regulation of spiral aftereffect duration. *Social Behavior and Personality*, 1974, *2*, 56-75.

Bokander, I. & Lindbom, K. The effects of aggressive films on minors. *Nordisk Psykologi*, 1967, *19*, 1-56.

Butzmann, K. Aktualgenese im indirekten Sehen. *Archiv für die gesamte Psychologie*, 1940, *106*, 137-193.

Dixon, N. F. *Subliminal perception. The nature of a controversy*. London: McGraw-Hill, 1971.

Draguns, J. G. Investment of meaning in schizophrenics and in children. Studies of one aspect of microgenesis. *Psychological Research Bulletin (Lund)*, 1961, *1*, No. 5.

Draguns, J. G. Responses to cognitive and perceptual ambiguity in chronic and acute schizophrenia. *Journal of Abnormal and Social Psychology*, 1963, *66*, 24-30.

Draguns, J. G. Microgenesis by any other name. . . . In W. Fröhlich et al. (eds.), *Psychological processes in cognition and personality*. New York: Hemisphere, in press.

Drösler, J. & Kuhn, W. F. Ein experimenteller Vergleich der visuellen Wahrnehmung von Kindern, Schizophrenen und Alkoholikern mit der tachistoskopischen Wahrnehmung normaler Erwachsener. *XVIth International Congress of Psychology, Individual papers*. Goettingen: German psychological society, *Congress report*, 1960, *1*, 1-2.

Ebernard, G., Johnson, G., Nilsson, L., & Smith, G.J.W. Clinical and experimental approaches to the description of depression and anti-depressive therapy. *Acta Psychiatrica Scandinavica*, 1965, *41* Supplement 186.

Fenichel, O. *The psychoanalytic theory of neuroses*. London: Routledge & Kegan Paul, 1946.

Flavell, J. H. & Draguns, J. G. A microgenetic approach to perception and thought. *Psychological Bulletin*, 1957, *54*, 197-217.

Freud, S. Inhibitions, symptoms and anxiety, 1926. *Standard Edition, 20*, 77-175. London: Hogarth, 1959.

Friedman, M. H. & Andersson, J. Body-image variability in peptic ulcer. A perceptual experiment with identical twins. *Archives of General Psychiatry*, 1967, *16*, 334-343.

Fries, I. & Smith, G.J.W. Influence of physiognomic stimulus properties on afterimage adaptation. *Perceptual and Motor Skills*, 1970, *31*, 267-271.

Fröhlich, W. *Unstimmigkeit, Erwartung und Kompromiss*. Habilitationsschrift, Universität Bonn, 1964.

Fröhlich, W., Smith, G.J.W., Draguns, J. G., & Hentschel, U. (eds.). *Psychological processes in cognition and personality*. New York: Hemisphere, in press.

Gemelli, A. Contributo allo studio della percezione, IV. *Contributi del Laboratorio di psicologia e biologia, università cattolica del Sacro Cuore*, Milano, 1928, *3*, 385-436.

Graumann, C. F. Aktualgenese. *Zeitschrift für experimentelle und angewandte Psychologie*, 1959, *6*, 410-448.

Hagberg, B. A prospective study of patients in chronic hemodialysis. *Journal of Psychosomatic Research*, 1973, *18*, 151-160.

Hentschel, U. Two new interference tests compared to the Stroop Color-Word Test. *Psychological Research Bulletin (Lund)*, 1973, *13*, No. 6.

Hentschel, U. Kognitive Kontrollprinzipien und Neuroseformen. In U. Hentschel & G.J.W. Smith (eds.), *Experimentelle Persönlichkeitspsychologie*. Wiesbaden, Federal Republic of Germany: Akademische Verlagsgesellschaft, 1980.

Hentschel, U. & Schubö, W. Serially Scored Color-, Picture-, and Figure-Word Test, their intercorrelations and interpretation. *Psychological Research Bulletin (Lund)*, 1976, *16*, No. 6.

Hentschel, U. & Smith, G.J.W.[eds.]. *Experimentelle Persönlichkeitspsychologie*. Wiesbaden, Federal Republic of Germany: Akademische Verlagsgesellschaft, 1980.

Johnson, M. Vad konstituerar en god soldat. *MPI-Rapport 44*, Stockholm, 1966.

Johnson, M. Psychological stress tolerance and experimental measurement of defense mechanisms. *Försvarsmedicin*, 1967, *3*, 2, 64-66.

Kragh, U. *The actual-genetic model of perception-personality*. Lund, Sweden: Gleerup, 1955.

Kragh, U. Types of precognitive defensive organization in a tachistoscopic experiment. *Journal of Projective Techniques*, 1959, *23*, 315-322.

Kragh, U. Pathogenesis in dipsomania. *Acta psychiatrica Scandinavica*, 1960, *35*, 207-222, 261-288, 480-497. (a)

Kragh, U. The defense mechanism test: a new method for diagnosis and personnel selection. *Journal of Applied Psychology*, 1960, *44*, 303-309. (b)

Kragh, U. Precognitive defensive organization with threatening and non-threatening peripheral stimuli. *Scandinavian Journal of Psychology*, 1962, *3*, 65-68. (a)

Kragh, U. A case of infantile animal phobia in adult precognitive organization. *Vita Humana*, 1962, *5*, 111-124. (b)

Kragh, U. Predictions of success of Danish attack divers by the Defense Mechanism Test (DMT). *Perceptual and Motor Skills*, 1962, *15*, 103-106. (c)

Kragh, U. *DMT—defense mechanism test*. Stockholm, Sweden: Skandinaviska Testförlaget, 1969.

Kragh, U. Rekonstruktion verschiedener Aspekte einer Persönlichkeitsentwicklung mit dem Defense Mechanism Test. Eine Fallbeschreibung. In U. Hentschel & G.J.W. Smith (eds.), *Experimentelle Persönlichkeitpsychologie*. Wiesbaden, Federal Republic of Germany: Akademische Verlagsgesellschaft, 1980, 107-131.

Kragh, U. & Kroon, T. An analysis of aggression and identification in young offenders by the study of perceptual development. *Scandinavian Journal of Psychology*, 1966, *5*, 80-90.

Kragh, U. & Smith, G.J.W. (eds.). *Percept-genetic analysis*. Lund, Sweden: Gleerup, 1970.

Kragh, U. & Smith, G.J.W. Forming new patterns of experience: A classical problem viewed within a percept-genetic model. *Psychological Research Bulletin (Lund)*, 1974, *14*, No. 6.

Lindbom K. Perceptual defense mechanisms registered by the Meta-Contrast Technique in normal and pathologic children. *Scandinavian Journal of Psychology*, 1968, *9*, 109-116.

Lindén, J. Children's understanding of the spiral aftereffect phenomenon as related to aftereffect duration and coordination of perspectives. *Psychological Research Bulletin (Lund)*, 1977, *17*, No. 1.

Linschoten, J. Aktualgenese und heuristisches Prinzip. *Zeitschrift für experimentelle und angewandte Psychologie*, 1959, *6*, 449-473.

Magnusson, P.-Å., Nilsson, A., & Henriksson, N.-G. Psychogenic vertigo within an anxiety frame of reference: an experimental study. *British Journal of Medical Psychology*, 1977, *50*, 187-201.

Munroe, R. L. *Schools of psychoanalytic thought*. New York: Holt, Rinehart & Winston, 1955.

Neuman, T. Dimensionering och validering av perceptgenesens försvarsmekanismer. En hierarkisk analys mot pilotens stressbeteende. *FOA rapport*, C 55020-H6, Stockholm, Sweden: Försvarets Forskningsanstalt, 5, 1978.

Nilsson, A. Comparisons between oculogyral illusion, turning sensation and nystagmus within a process frame of reference. *Psychological Research Bulletin (Lund)*, 1972, *12*, No. 3. (a)

Nilsson, A. The Influence of acoustic stimulation on the process regulation of nystagmus and oculogyral illusion. *Psychological Research Bulletin (Lund)*, 1972, *12*, No. 4. (b)

Nilsson, A. Intrapsychic defense within a genetic-hierarchical frame of reference. In Press.

Nilsson, Å. & Henriksson, N.-G. The oculogyral illusion—a form of rotation aftereffect—and its relation to the spiral aftereffect in repeated trials. *Psychological Research Bulletin (Lund),* 1967, *7,* No. 5. (a)

Nilsson, Å. & Henriksson, N.-G. Adaptive patterns in the oculogyral illusion and their relation to the serial color-word test. *Psychological Research Bulletin (Lund),* 1967, *7,* No. 6. (b)

Nilsson, Å. & Tibbling, L. Personality correlates of smokers with differing consumption of cigarettes. *Psychological Research Bulletin (Lund),* 1972, *12,* No. 1.

Nilsson, Å. & Almgren, P.-E. Para-natal emotional adjustment. *Acta Psychiatrica Scandinavica,* 1970 Supplement 220, 63-141.

Nyman, G. E. & Smith, G.J.W. A contribution to the definition of psychopathic personality. *Lunds Universitets Årsskrift, N.F., Series 2, 55,* No. 10. Lund, Sweden: Gleerup, 1959.

Nyman, G. E. & Smith, G.J.W. Experimental differentiation of clinical syndroms within a sample of young neurotics. *Acta Psychiatrica Scandinavica,* 1961, *37,* 14-31.

Palmqvist, A. Jämförelser av DMT och MCT baserade på fyra kliniska grupper. Lund, Sweden: Department of Psychology, 1974. (mimeo)

Peto, A. Terrifying eyes—a visual superego forerunner. *Psychoanalytic Study of the Child,* 1969, *24,* 197-212.

Phillips, L. & Framo, J. Developmental theory applied to normal and psychopathological perception. *Journal of Personality,* 1954, *22,* 464-474.

Pritchard, R. M., Heron, W., & Hebb, D. O. Visual perception approached by the method of stabilized images. *Canadian Journal of Psychology,* 1960, *14,* 67-77.

Ruuth, E. Afterimage perception and size-distance judgment in preschool children. *Psychological Research Bulletin (Lund),* 1970, *10,* No. 14.

Ruuth, E. & Andersson, A. L. Emmert's law reconsidered: a developmental study of visual afterimages. *Psychological Research Bulletin (Lund),* 1971, *11,* No. 8.

Ruuth, E. & Smith, G.J.W. Projected afterimages and cognitive maturity. *Scandinavian Journal of Psychology.* 1969, *10,* 209-214.

Sander, F. Experimentelle Ergebnisse der Gestaltpsychologie. *Berichte X Kongress für experimentelle Psychologie in Bonn 1927* (1928). Pp. 23-28.

Schilder, P. Uber Gedankenentwicklung. *Zeitschrift für Neurologie und Psychiatrie,* 1928, *59,* 250-263.

Schubö, W. & Hentschel, U. Improved reliability estimates for the serial Color-Word Test. *Scandinavian Journal of Psychology,* 1978, *19,* 91-95.

Sjöbäck, H. & Westerlundh, B. Amauroskopisk subliminal varseblivning. I. Person-interaktioner: effekter på ljuströskel och perceptgenes. Lund, Sweden: Department of Psychology, 1975. (mimeo)

Sjöbäck, H. & Westerlundh, B. Amauroskopisk subliminal varseblivning. II. Person-interaktioner: effekter på tidsskattning och perceptgenes. Lund, Sweden: Department of Psychology, 1977. (mimeo)

Sjöberg, L. Psychometric properties of the serial Colour-Word Test. *Scandinavian Journal of Psychology,* 1974, *15,* 15-20.

Smith, G.J.W. *Psychological studies in twin differences.* Lund, Sweden: Gleerup, 1949.

Smith, G.J.W. *Interpretations of behavior sequences.* Lund, Sweden: Gleerup, 1952.

Smith, G.J.W. Stabilization and automatization of perceptual activity over time. In W. Fröhlich et al. (eds.), *Psychological processes in cognition and personality.* New York: Hemisphere, in press.

Smith, G.J.W., Almgren, P.-E, Andersson, A. L., Englesson, I., Smith, M., & Uddenberg, G. The mother-child picture test. *Psychological Research Bulletin (Lund)*, 1978, *18*, No. 6.

Smith, G.J.W. & Borg, G. The problem of retesting in the serial Color-Word Test. *Psychological Research Bulletin (Lund)*, 1964, *4*, No. 6.

Smith, G.J.W. & Danielsson, A. Psychopathology in childhood and adolescence as reflected in projected afterimage serials. *Scandinavian Journal of Psychology*, 1978, *19*, 29-39. (a)

Smith, G.J.W. & Danielsson, A. Richness in ideas, ego-involvement and efficiency in a group of scientists and humanists. *Psychological Research Bulletin (Lund)*, 1978, *18*, No. 4-5. (b) [Also in Hentschel & Smith, 1980, 350-371.]

Smith, G.J.W. & Danielsson, A. Anxiety and defense against anxiety in childhood and adolescence. *Psychological Issues*, 1979, 512. (a)

Smith, G.J.W. & Danielsson, A. The influence of anxiety on the urge for aesthetic creation. *Psychological Research Bulletin (Lund)*, 1979, *19*, No. 3-4. (b)

Smith, G.J.W., Fries, I., Andersson, A. L., & Ried, J. Diagnostic exploitation of visual aftereffect measures in a moderately depressive patient group. *Scandinavian Journal of Psychology*, 1971, *12*, 67-79.

Smith, G.J.W. & Henriksson, M. Studies in the development of a percept within various contexts of perceived reality. *Acta Psychologica*, 1956, *12*, 263-281.

Smith, G.J.W. & Johnson, G. The influence of psychiatric treatment upon the process of reality construction. *Journal of Consulting Psychology*, 1962, *26*, 520-526.

Smith, G.J.W. & Klein, G. S. Cognitive controls in serial behavior patterns. *Journal of Personality*, 1953, *22*, 188-213.

Smith, G.J.W. & Kragh, U. A serial afterimage experiment in clinical diagnostics. *Scandinavian Journal of Psychology*, 1967, *8*, 52-64.

Smith, G.J.W. & Kragh, U. Creativity in mature and old age. *Psychological Research Bulletin (Lund)*, 1975, *15*, No. 7.

Smith, G.J.W., Kragh, U., Eberhard, G., & Johnson, G. Forms of depression as reflected in negative afterimage serials. *Acta Psychiatrica Scandinavica*, 1970, *46*, Supplement 219, 216-223.

Smith, G.J.W. & Nordstrom, M. Anxiety and defense against anxiety in childhood and adolescence. *Yearbook New Society of Letters at Lund*. Lund, Sweden: Gleerup, 1975. Pp. 67-102.

Smith, G.J.W. & Nyman, G. E. Psychopathologic behavior in a serial experiment. *Lunds Universitets Årsskrift, N.F., Series 2, 56*, No. 5. Lund, Sweden: Gleerup, 1959.

Smith, G.J.W. & Nyman, G. E. A serial tachistoscopic experiment and its clinical application. *Acta Psychologica*, 1961, *18*, 67-84.

Smith, G.J.W. & Nyman, G. E. The validity of the serial Color-Word Test. *Scandinavian Journal of Psychology*, 1974, *15*, 238-240.

Smith, G.J.W., Ruuth, E., Franzén, G., & Sjöholm, L. Intermittent regressions in a serial afterimage experiment as signs of schizophrenia. *Scandinavian Journal of Psychology*, 1972, *13*, 27-33.

Smith, G.J.W., Sjöholm, L., & Andersson, A. L. Effects of extraneous stimulation on afterimage adaptation. *Acta Psychologica*, 1971, *35*, 138-150.

Smith, G.J.W., Sjöholm, L., & Nielzén, S. Sensitive reactions and afterimage variegation. *Journal of Personality Assessment*, 1974, *38*, 41-47.

Smith, G.J.W., Sjöholm, L., & Nielzén, S. Individual factors affecting the improvement of anxiety during a therapeutic period of 1 1/2 to 2 years. *Acta Psychiatrica Scandinavica*, 1975, *52*, 7-22.

Smith, G.J.W., Sjöholm, L., & Nielzén, S. Anxiety and defense against anxiety as reflected in perceptgenetic formations. *Journal of Personality Assessment*, 1976, *40*, 151-161.

Stein, M. J. Personality factors involved in the temporal development of Rorschach responses. *Journal of Projective Techniques*, 1949, *13*, 355-414.

Thurstone, L. L. A factorial study of perception. *Psychometric Monographs*, 1944, *No. 4*.

Werner, H. Über die Ausprägung von Tongestalten. *Zeitschrift für Psychologie*, 1927, *101*, 181-195.

Werner, H. Microgenesis in aphasia. *Journal of Abnormal and Social Psychology*, 1956, *52*, 347-353.

Westerlundh, B. *Aggression, anxiety and defence*. Lund, Sweden: Gleerup, 1976.

Westerlundh, B. Conflict activation: Two experimental operations and their influence on perceptgenesis. *Psychological Research Bulletin (Lund)*, 1979, *19*, No. 8.

Westerlundh, B. Personal organization of the visual field. Presented at the second international conference on microgenesis and related issues. Lund, 1980.

Westerlundh, B. Percept-genesis and the experimental study of conflict and defence. In W. Fröhlich et al. (eds.), *Psychological processes in cognition and personality*. New York: Hemisphere, in press.

Detecting Deception

MODALITY EFFECTS

5

BELLA M. DePAULO
MIRON ZUCKERMAN
ROBERT ROSENTHAL

Bella M. DePaulo is an Assistant Professor of Psychology at the University of Virginia. Her interests are in nonverbal communication, help-seeking, and sociolinguistics.
Miron Zuckerman is currently Associate Professor at the University of Rochester. In addition to nonverbal communication, his research interests include attribution, judgment under uncertainty, and the psychology of control. He also likes to cook (when the company is deserving), watch movies (not necessarily Bergman's), and travel (when there is too much free time).
Robert Rosenthal is Professor of Social Psychology, Harvard University. Professor Rosenthal is the author of *Experimenter Effects in Behavioral Research* and the coauthor of *Pygmalion in the Classroom*.

Among verbal cues and various kinds of nonverbal cues, there is probably a pecking order. Verbal cues are ordinarily more informative about a wider variety of things than are purely nonverbal cues (cf. Schneider et al., 1978). Within the nonverbal domain, facial expressions are generally believed to be more informative than either body cues or tone of voice cues (cf. DePaulo & Rosenthal, 1979a). It should almost necessarily follow that combinations of channels will be more informative than any of the single channels that make up the combination; accordingly, DePaulo and Rosenthal (1978) have found, for eight different age levels, that people are better able to understand multiple-channel than single-channel nonverbal messages.

Although most studies relevant to the relative informativeness of different channels or cues have involved "pure" or nondeceptive communications, intuitions regarding deceptive messages are no less clear. When we asked 251 college students, "If you wanted to know whether someone was lying to you, do you think you could tell better by

AUTHORS' NOTE: Preparation of this paper was supported in part by the National Science Foundation.

communicating with them by telephone or in person, or could you tell about as well either way?" of the 251 students, 220 chose face-to-face (which would involve both visual and auditory cues) compared to only 7 who chose telephone communication. However, Ekman and Friesen's (1969) theory of nonverbal cues to leakage and deception challenges the intuitively compelling notion that access to greater amounts of information necessarily leads to greater understanding, and instead suggests that certain channels, which under ordinary circumstances are extremely informative, can be especially misleading under conditions of deception. In this article we review research and theory relevant to the relative transparency of different channels and modalities under conditions of deception. Our question, then, is, "What sources of verbal or nonverbal information are likely to be especially revealing when a person is deceiving?" We begin by briefly presenting Ekman and Friesen's formulation, plus other research and conceptualizations from outside the field of deception that might be relevant to the revealingness question; next, we review and summarize quantitatively the available studies on modality effects in the detection of deception; and finally, we propose a series of variables that we believe to serve as moderators of these modality effects.

THE EKMAN AND FRIESEN FORMULATION

According to Ekman and Friesen, a given channel will reveal that a person is lying (deception cues) and will reveal the person's true, rather than dissimulated, feelings (leakage cues) to the extent that a person is unable or unlikely to mask true affects or dissimulate feigned affects with that channel. A person's ability to deceive through a given channel is a function of that channel's sending capacity and the degree of internal feedback that a person receives from that channel. A greater sending capacity characterizes those channels which (1) can send a greater number of discriminable messages, (2) can send the messages more quickly, and (3) are highly visible or salient. Internal feedback is "our conscious awareness of what we are doing and our ability to recall, repeat, or specifically enact a planned sequence of motor behavior" (1969, p. 96). The likelihood that a person will try to decieve through a given channel is augmented to the extent that he or she receives a greater amount of external feedback about that channel, as when other people attend to it, comment on it, imitate it, react to it, or hold the person responsible or accountable for what he or she communicates through that channel.

On the basis of all of these criteria, Ekman and Friesen argue that the face, compared to the body, is especially well-equipped to lie effectively. The face is a highly visible channel, it can send an abundance of different messages and it can send them quite rapidly, it is a channel for which one receives fine-grained and highly differentiated internal feedback, and it is a channel that other people attend to, react to, and hold senders accountable for. Hence, senders should be ready and able to fool other people with their facial displays.[1] In contrast, the body is less controllable and hence more likely to give away both deception and leakage cues.

EXTENDING THE LEAKAGE HIERARCHY

Although Ekman and Friesen's theory was articulated only with respect to the face and the body (hands, legs, feet), it has subsequently been suggested that tone-of-voice cues, like body cues, may also reveal a person's true underlying affects. Attempting to extend Ekman and Friesen's formulation from the face and body to the tone of voice is necessarily a very tenuous enterprise. Although their model has markedly influenced research efforts in the field of deception, there have been few, if any, investigations of the postulates regarding sending capacity and internal and external feedback. In part, this is because certain aspects of these postulates would be extremely difficult to test. How, for example, would one determine the number of "discriminable stimulus patterns" that can be emitted by a given channel? Other constructs, however, such as accountability and internal feedback (as defined by the ability to recall or reenact a particular expression), should be much more amenable to an empirical test, with potentially fascinating results.

When we do attempt to apply the Ekman and Friesen criteria to vocal nonverbal cues, tone of voice seems to have more in common with the faking face than with the leaking body. For example, the voice can send many different kinds of messages, it is very salient (whereas one can ignore visual cues by simply looking away, it takes much more effort to avoid tone-of-voice cues), and people comment on it and react to it (e.g., "You sound tired" or "Don't talk to me in that tone of voice"). The internal feedback characteristics of the voice seem less immediately apparent, but Holzman and Rousey (1966), in their study of the reveal-ingness of the voice, note that "the larynx contains the highest ratio of nerve fibers to muscle fibers of any functional system, and it is therefore exquisitely responsive to intraorganismic changes" (p. 85). Further, awareness of one's own tone of voice is likely to be greater than aware-ness of one's own facial expressions for still another reason: Although people rarely see their own faces during social interactions, they cannot help hearing their own voices.

Although this analysis suggests that people should be quite ready and able to control their voices, the available evidence suggests otherwise. Even excluding studies of deception (which will be reviewed later), a series of investigations suggests that tone-of-voice cues can sometimes reveal true, underlying (though not always acknowledged) feelings about oneself and about other people.

Turning first to some of the impressionistic data, Scherer (1979) has noted that clinicians believe tone of voice to be an accurate index of patients' true emotional state and they frequently use it on an intuitive basis in making diagnoses. Holzman and Rousey (1966), in trying to explain people's negative reactions to tape-recordings of their own voices, suggest that "among the things subjects heard in their voices they heard something they had not wanted to hear, something expressed which they had not wanted to express but which nevertheless had been conveyed by voice qualities" (p. 85). Since most of us do not react negatively to our naturally occurring voice (as opposed to tape-recordings of our voice), it is possible that most of us do not really listen to the tone of voice in which we speak. Further, when we listen to our own voices, the tone is in fact different than it is on a tape-recording (because of differences in "bone-to-air conduction ratios"; Holzman & Rousey, 1966) and it is also different from the tone that others hear. Thus, the self-feedback provided by the vocal channel may be more illusory than real.

In another study of people's feelings about themselves, Bugental et al. (1976) showed that people with an external locus of control (i.e., people who feel that their outcomes are in the hands of fate, luck, or powerful other people) are very assertive verbally, but "leak" their true feelings of powerlessness and insecurity through their tone-of-voice qualities; internals, on the other hand, who believe that they are in control of their own outcomes, do not use very assertive words, but their true feelings of confidence are apparent to people who hear their voices. Finally, it has also been shown (Bugental & Love, 1975) that parents of children with emotional and behavioral problems, compared to parents of normal children, showed high verbal assertiveness but very low vocal assertiveness. Bugental and Love speculated that the parents' meek voices may have been revealing their lack of confidence in their ability to control their children.

Several other studies have suggested that tone of voice may reveal one's true, though unacknowledged, attitudes toward other people. In her formulation of a "repressed affect model," Weitz (1972) proposed that well-meaning college liberals may believe that they *should* have very positive attitudes toward blacks, even though they still harbor some hostility. In keeping with this conceptualization, Weitz demonstrated that whites who reported extremely favorable attitudes toward blacks, in contrast to those who reported more moderate attitudes, spoke to blacks in a cold and condescending way. The extremely positive attitudes that these whites tried to convey (on self-report scales) were belied by the sounds of their voices.

In a pair of studies by Milmoe and her associates, it was demonstrated that (1) doctors who had been successful in referring their alcoholic patients for further treatment spoke of their experiences with alcoholics in less angry voice tones (Milmoe et al., 1967) and (2) mothers whose voices sounded anxious and angry had more irritable children than mothers who sounded more calm and pleasant (Milmoe et al., 1974). Studies of interpersonal expectancy effects further suggest that tone of voice, either alone (Duncan & Rosenthal, 1968) or in combination with words (Adair & Epstein, 1968; Rosenthal, 1966, 1969; Snyder et al., 1977) may mediate subtle influence attempts.

From these studies, it seems reasonable to predict that tone of voice will be a source of leakage or deception cues: That is, tone-of-voice cues should betray a liar's true feelings, or at least reveal that deception is occurring. Because most tone-of-voice studies have compared vocal cues only to verbal cues, it is difficult to locate this channel very precisely in the pecking order. For example, should we expect tone-of-voice cues to be more revealing or less revealing than body cues? Some indirect evidence comes from a series of studies on sex differences in accommodation in nonverbal communication (Rosenthal & DePaulo, 1979a, 1979b). In those studies, it was hypothesized that as channels become more and more leaky, women would show less and less of their usual advantage over men at decoding nonverbal cues, as they politely refrained from reading those cues that senders were perhaps trying not to express. It was found that women were most superior to men at decoding face and least superior at judging voice, while their advantage was intermediate for the decoding of body cues. Although this evidence does not conclusively demonstrate that voice is leakier than body, it is consistent with that hypothesis.

Other kinds of cues or cue combinations have also been located within a leakage hierarchy. In the Rosenthal and DePaulo studies, for example, very briefly exposed face and body cues (perhaps comparable to what Ekman and Friesen have called "micromomentary displays") were hypothesized to be even more covert (leaky, uncontrollable) than voice cues, and discrepant nonverbal cues (e.g., a smiling face accompanying an angry voice) were postulated to be more covert still. Other kinds of cues are probably also relevant to the leakage construct. For instance, the physical distance and amount of eye contact that people maintain between themselves and another person probably reflect their true affect toward that other person (Argyle & Cook, 1976; Bell et al., 1978). Even verbal communications, probably the most overt and controllable of all the communications we have considered so far, probably have certain covert qualities. Even without adding tone-of-voice cues, there is probably a nearly infinite number of ways of verbally expressing any given idea or intention; these countless lexicalizations vary systematically in various affect-relevant ways (Wiener & Mehrabian, 1968).

We mention these other leakage channels only in passing since they have been almost entirely neglected in studies of human lie-detection. The channels or channel combinations most frequently investigated in studies of deception are face, body, tone of voice, verbal, audio (verbal plus tone of voice), and audiovisual (verbal plus tone of voice plus face and perhaps also body). As far as we know, no single study has examined all six of these modalities, and only one (DePaulo et al., Note 1) has included five of these modalities (all except body).

MODALITY EFFECTS IN DECEPTION RESEARCH: A QUANTITATIVE SUMMARY

In Tables 1 to 6 we describe all studies that we know of that report data relevant to skill at deception, separately by type of modality or modality combination. In the column labeled d we report the size of the deception-detection effects in standard deviation units (Cohen, 1977), whenever that statistic could be computed. A positive d indicates that deception was diagnosed at a better-than-chance level in that study, while a negative d indicates that the detection of deception was worse

(text continues on p. 146)

TABLE 1

Detecting Deception from Audiovisual Cues

Study	Senders (Liars)	Judges (Lie-Detectors)	Operation-alization of Modality	Type of Task	Judgments	d
DePaulo & Rosenthal (1979)	20 Ms 20 Fs	20 Ms 20 Fs	videotape	senders describe people they like and people they dislike; they also pretend to like the disliked person and pretend to dislike the liked person	ratings of liking, disliking, and deception (9-point scales)	1.64
DePaulo, Rosenthal, Green, & Rosenkrantz (Note 1)	20 Ms 20 Fs	8Ms 8 Fs	videotape	senders describe people they like and people they dislike; they also pretend to like the disliked person and pretend to dislike the liked person	ratings of liking, disliking, and deception (9-point scales)	.31
Geizer, Rarick, & Soldow (1977)	12 Ms	50 Ss	videotape	"To Tell the Truth" segments: one panelist tells the truth about his identity and the other two are imposters	judges allocate votes to panelists according to their apparent truthfulness	a
Harrison, Hwalek, Raney, & Fritz (1978)	36 Ms 36 Fs	36 Ms 36 Fs	face-to-face	senders answer 12 questions; questions concern factual information (e.g., demo-graphic data, personal preferences) and opinions	judges rate the answers as true or false	b

Table 1 (Continued)

Study	Senders (Liars)	Judges (Lie-Detectors)	Operationalization of Modality	Type of Task	Judgments	d
Krauss, Geller & Olson (Note 2) Study 1	Ms Fs	Ms Fs	face-to-face	senders described their opinions or future plans in response to 20 questions about politics, religion, personal future, and values	ratings of truthfulness (7-point scale)	c
Krauss, Geller, & Olson (Note 2) Study 2	Ms	Ms & Fs	videotape	senders described their opinions or future plans in response to 20 questions about politics, religion, personal future, and values (judges rated a subset of these responses)	ratings of truthfulness (7-point scale)	d
Kraut (1978)	5 Ms	12-18 judges per sender	videotape	senders role-play job applicants in a simulated interview for a dormitory advisor position	judges indicate via a swith whether at any given moment the sender was lying or telling the truth	.95
Littlepage & Pineault (1978)	3 Ms 3 Fs	23 Ms & Fs	videotape	"To Tell the Truth" segments: one panelist tells the truth about his/her identity and the other two are imposters	judges indicate which panelist is most likely to be telling the truth and which is least likely	.70

Table 1 (Continued)

Study	Senders (Liars)	Judges (Lie-Detectors)	Operation-alization of Modality	Type of Task	Judgments	d
Maier (1966)	88 Ms & Fs	88 Ms	face-to-face	role-play format in which a professor (the judge) tries to determine whether a student (the sender) cheated on an exam	professor's trust of the student (5-point scale) and grade assigned	.59
Maier & Janzen (1967)	4 Ms	47 Ms 10 Fs	judges observe (in person) role-played scenarios	senders role-play honest or dishonest students who try to convince a professor of their honesty	ratings of dishonesty (6-point scale)	1.02
Maier & Thurber (1968)	4 Ms	47 Ms 10 Fs	judges observe (in person) role-played scenarios	senders role-play honest or dishonest students who try to convince a professor of their honesty	ratings of dishonesty (6-point scale)	.33
Matarazzo, Wiens, Jackson, & Manaugh (1970)	80 Ms	2 Ms	one judge interacted face-to-face; the other observed from behind a one-way mirror	senders lied or told the truth about their living situation or their college major in a 30-minute interview	judges guess which condition (lie/truth) each sender was in	.36

a. An exact d and whether accuracy was better than chance could not be assessed.
b. Overall effect size for audiovideo plus audio-only was .48. Separate d's could not be computed for each condition alone, but deception-detection rates did not differ significantly between conditions.
c. An exact d could not be computed, but subjects communicating face-to-face were reported to be significantly less accurate at detecting lies than subjects communicating via an intercom.
d. An exact d could not be computed, but from the available graph, accuracy appears to be slightly below chance.

TABLE 2
Detecting Deception from Audio Cues

Study	Senders (Liars)	Judges (Lie-Detectors)	Operation-alization of Modality	Type of Task	Judgments	d
DePaulo, Rosenthal, Green, & Rosenkrantz (Note 1)	20 Ms 20 Fs	8 Ms 8 Fs	audiotape	senders describe people they like and people they dislike; they also pretend to like the disliked person and pretend to dislike the liked person	ratings of liking, disliking, and deception (9-point scales)	.57
Ekman, Friesen, & Scherer (1976)	16 Fs	15-36 Ss	audiotape	senders express a positive reaction to a positive and a negative film	ratings of outgoingness, expressiveness, sociability, dominance, honesty, sincerity, trustworthiness, calmness, relaxation, emotional stability, naturalness, felt pleasantness, and acted pleasantness	a
Fay & Middleton (1941)	3 Ms 3 Fs	23 Ms 24 Fs	public address system	senders answered 10 factual questions about themselves (e.g., height, handedness, attire)	judges rate each answer as truth or lie	1.40

Table 2 (Continued)

Study	Senders (Liars)	Judges (Lie-Detectors)	Operation-alization of Modality	Type of Task	Judgments	d
Harrison, Hwalek, Raney, & Fritz (1978)	36 Ms 36 Fs	36 Ms 36 Fs	sender and judge sat on either side of a table with a barrier (obstructing vision) between them	senders answer 12 questions; questions concern factual information (e.g., demo-graphic data, personal preferences) and opinions	judges rate the answers as true or false	b
Krauss, Geller, & Olson (Note 2) Study 1	Ms & Fs	Ms & Fs	intercom	senders described their opinions or future plans in response to 20 questions about politics, religion, person future, and values	ratings of truthful-ness (7-point scale)	c
Krauss, Geller, & Olson (Note 2) Study 2	Ms	Ms & Fs	audiotape	senders described their opinions or future plans in response to 20 questions about politics, religion, person future, and values (judges rated a subset of these responses)	ratings of truthful-ness (7-point scale)	d
Littlepage & Pineault (1978)	3 Ms 3 Fs	25 Ms & Fs	audiotape	"To Tell the Truth" seg-ments: one panelist tells the truth about his/her identity and the other two are imposters	judges indicate which panelist is most likely to be telling the truth and which is least likely	.68

135

Table 2 (Continued)

Study	Senders (Liars)	Judges (Lie-Detectors)	Operation-alization of Modality	Type of Task	Judgments	d
Maier & Thurber (1968)	4 Ms	47 Ms 51 Fs	audiotape	senders role-play honest or dishonest students who try to convince a professor of their honesty	ratings of dishonesty (6-point scale)	1.28
Streeter, Krauss, Geller, Olson, & Apple (1977)	32 Ms	15 Ms & Fs	audiotape	senders described their opinions or future plans in response to 20 questions about politics, religion, personal future, and values (judges rated a subset of these responses)	ratings of truthful-ness (7-point scale)	e

a. An exact d could not be computed since precise data were not reported. Judges' ratings of the honest clips did not differ significantly from their ratings of the deceptive clips.

b. Overall effect size for audiovideo plus audio-only was .48. Separate d's could not be computed for each condition alone, but deception-detection rates did not differ significantly between conditions.

c. An exact d could not be computed, but subjects communicating by intercom were reported to be significantly more accurate at detecting lies than subjects communicating face-to-face.

d. An exact d could not be computed, but from the available graph, accuracy appears to be at or below chance for face-to-face and above chance for intercom.

e. An exact d could not be computed, but the available data indicate that accuracy was slightly greater than chance. It is not clear whether these were the same data as in Krauss, Geller, and Olson (Note 2) or new data.

TABLE 3

Detecting Deception from Verbal Cues

Study	Senders (Liars)	Judges (Lie-Detectors)	Operation- alization of Modality	Type of Task	Judgments	d
DePaulo, Rosenthal, Green, & Rosenkrantz (Note 1)	20 Ms 20 Fs	8 Ms 8 Fs	transcript	senders describe people they like and people they dislike; they also pretend to like the disliked person and pretend to dislike the liked person	ratings of liking, disliking, and deception (9-point scales)	.27
Maier & Thurber (1968)	4 Ms	21 Ms 43 Fs	transcript	senders role-play honest or dishonest students who try to convince a professor of their honesty	ratings of dishonesty (6-point scale)	1.30

TABLE 4

Detecting Deception from Tone of Voice Cues

Study	Senders (Liars)	Judges (Lie-Detectors)	Operation-alization of Modality	Type of Task	Judgments	d
DePaulo, Rosenthal, Green, & Rosenkrantz (Note 1)	20 Ms 20 Fs	8 Ms 8 Fs	content-filtered audiotape	senders describe people they like and people they dislike; they also pretend to like the disliked person and pretend to dislike the liked person	ratings of liking, disliking, and deception (9-point scales)	−.13
Ekman, Friesen, & Scherer (1976)	16 Fs	15-36 Ss	content-filtered audiotape	senders express a positive reaction to a positive and a negative film	ratings of outgoingness, expressiveness, sociability, dominance, honesty, sincerity, trustworthiness, calmness, relaxation, emotional stability, naturalness, felt pleasantness and acted pleasantness	a
Streeter, Krauss, Geller, Olson, & Apple (1977)	32 Ms	15 Ms & Fs	content-filtered audiotape	senders describe their future plans in response to 20 questions about politics, religion, personal future, and values (judges rate a subset of these responses)	ratings of truthfulness (7-point scale)	b

Table 4 (Continued)

Study	Senders (Liars)	Judges (Lie-Detectors)	Operationalization of Modality	Type of Task	Judgments	d
Zuckerman, DeFrank, Hall, Larrance, & Rosenthal (1979)	30 Ms 30 Fs	77 Ss	content-filtered audiotape	senders lie or tell the truth about their attitudes toward marijuana, the foreign language requirement, minority admissions, and abortion	judges rate the answer as honest or deceptive (an additional 5 judges rated the voices on 9-point scales of assertiveness, pleasantness, dominance, honesty, and pitch)	.77

a. An exact d could not be computed since precise data were not reported. Judges' ratings of the honest clips did not differ significantly from their ratings of the deceptive clips.
b. An exact d could not be computed but the available data indicate that accuracy was slightly greater than chance.

TABLE 5

Detecting Deception from Face Cues

Study	Senders (Liars)	Judges (Lie-Detectors)	Operation- alization of Modality	Type of Task	Judgments	d
DePaulo, Rosenthal, Green, & Rosenkrantz (Note 1)[a]	20 Ms 20 Fs	8 Ms 8 Fs	videotape	senders describe people they like and people they dislike; they also pretend to like the disliked person and pretend to dislike the liked person	ratings of liking, disliking, and deception (9-point scales)	.04
Ekman & Friesen (1969)	2 Fs	76 Ss	film	psychiatric interviews; in two interviews, the patients feign well-being despite considerable disturbance; in a third interview, the patient is believed to be engaging in self-deception	Adjective Check List	b
Ekman & Friesen (1974)	16 Fs	113 Ss	videotape	senders express a positive reaction to a positive and a negative film	judges rate the behavior as honest or deceptive	−.16

Table 5 (Continued)

Study	Senders (Liars)	Judges (Lie-Detectors)	Operation-alization of Modality	Type of Task	Judgments	d
Ekman, Friesen, & Scherer (1976)	16 Fs	15-36 Ss	videotape	senders express a positive reaction to a positive and a negative film	ratings of outgoingness, expressiveness, soci-ability, dominance, honesty, sincerity, trustworthiness, calm-ness, relaxation, emo-tional stability, natural-ness, felt pleasantness, and acted pleasantness	c
Feldman (1976)	32 Fs	18-19 Fs	videotape	teachers (senders) praise a student who performed either well or poorly	judges rate how pleased the teacher was with her student (6-point scale)	1.82
Feldman (1979)[d]	13 Ms 15 Fs	23 Ss	videotape	senders express a positive reaction to a good or bad tasting drink	judges indicate how much the person really liked the drink (7-point scale)	−1.93
Feldman, Devin-Sheehan, & Allen (1978)[e]	8 Ms 8 Fs	28 Ms 27 Fs	videotape	teachers (senders) praise a student who performed either well or poorly	judges rate how happy the teacher was with his/her student	.73

141

Table 5 (Continued)

Study	Senders (Liars)	Judges (Lie-Detectors)	Operation-alization of Modality	Type of Task	Judgments	d
Feldman, Jenkins, & Popoola (1979)[f]	18 Ms 18 Fs	15 Ss	videotape	senders express a positive reaction to a good or bad tasting drink	judges indicate how much the person really liked the drink (7-point scale)	.93
Krauss, Geller, & Olson (Note 2)	Ms	Ms & Fs	videotape of senders who were communicating face-to-face or by intercom	senders described their opinions or future plans in response to 20 questions about politics, religion, personal future, and values (judges rated a subset of these responses)	ratings of truthfulness (7-point scale)	g
Littlepage & Pineault (1978)	3 Ms 3 Fs	16 Ms & Fs	videotape	"To Tell the Truth" segments: one panelist tells the truth about his/her identity and the other two are imposters	judges indicate which panelist is most likely to be telling the truth and which is least likely	-.21

Table 5 (Continued)

Study	Senders (Liars)	Judges (Lie-Detectors)	Operation- alization of Modality	Type of Task	Judgments	d
Littlepage & Pineault (1979)	2 Ms	22 Ms 10 Fs	videotape	senders lie and tell the truth about their first girlfriend and about the best thing that happened to them in the past week	judges indicate the extent of their belief or disbelief (6-point scale)	.25
Zuckerman, DeFrank, Hall, Larrance, & Rosenthal (1979)[h]	30 Ms 30 Fs	30 Ms 30 Fs	videotape	senders lie or tell the truth about their attitudes toward marijuana, the foreign language requirement, majority admissions, and abortion	judges rate the answers as honest or deceptive and they also rate the pleasantness of the sender's facial expression (9-point scale)	1.98

a. The upper part of the body was also visible.
b. An exact d could not be computed since data from only a subset of the adjectives were reported. The evidence presented is generally consistent with the suggestion that judges perceived the dissimulated rather than the true affects.
c. An exact d could not be computed since precise data were not reported. The authors note that "ratings made by observers exposed to the face became more positive from honest to deception (e.g., more sincere, more sociable, more relaxed) as compared to ratings made by observers exposed to the body which became more negative in deception (p. 24-25)." Hence, judges of the face perceived the dissimulated rather than the true affect.
d. Senders were Korean first-graders, seventh-graders, and college students; judges were Korean college students.
e. Senders and judges were third-graders.
f. Senders were first-graders, seventh-graders, and college students; judges were college students.
g. An exact d could not be computed, but from the available graph, accuracy appears to be at or below chance for face-to-face and substantially greater than chance for intercom.
h. Half of the subjects ("posed" condition) were told to try to make their lies readable.

TABLE 6

Detecting Deception from Body Cues

Study	Senders (Liars)	Judges (Lie-Detectors)	Operation-alization of Modality	Type of Task	Judgments	d
Ekman & Friesen (1969)	2 Fs	79 Ss	film	psychiatric interviews; in the two interviews the patients feign well-being despite considerable disturbance; in a third interview, the patient is believed to be engaging in self-deception	Adjective Check List	a
Ekman & Friesen (1974)	16 Fs	120 Ss	videotape	senders express a positive reaction to a positive and a negative film	judges rate the behavior as honest or deceptive	.15
Ekman, Friesen, & Scherer (1976)	16 Fs	15-36 Ss	videotape	senders express a positive reaction to a positive and a negative film	ratings of outgoingness, expressiveness, soci-ability, dominance, honesty, sincerity, trustworthiness, calm-ness, relaxation, emo-tional stability, natural-ness, felt pleasantness and expressed pleasantness	b

Table 6 (Continued)

Study	Senders (Liars)	Judges (Lie-Detectors)	Operation-alization of Modality	Type of Task	Judgments	d
Feldman (1976)	32 Fs	18-19 Fs	videotape	teachers (senders) praise a student who performed either well or poorly	judges rate how pleased the teacher was with her student (6-point scale)	-.22
Littlepage & Pineault (1979)	2 Ms	22 Ms 10 Fs	videotape	senders lie and tell the truth about their first girlfriend and about the best thing that happened to them in the past week	judges indicate the extent of their belief or disbelief (6-point scale)	2.51

a. An exact d could not be computed since data from only a subset of the adjectives were reported. The evidence presented is generally consistent with the suggestion that judges perceived the true rather than the dissimulated affects.
b. An exact d could not be computed since precise data were not reported. The authors suggest that the judges perceived the true rather than the dissimulated affect.

than chance. Whenever possible, the d's were based on judges' ratings of the degree of truthfulness or deceptiveness in a given message; when truthfulness ratings were not available, other relevant judgments were substituted (e.g., ratings of how much a person appeared to like a good-or bad-tasting drink). The tables also report the exact number and sex distribution of liars and lie-detectors for every study for which that information was available.

For each of the six modalities, the mean deception-detection effect was greater than zero; in fact, for three of the six modalities (all of those involving verbal cues), all of the effect sizes were greater than zero.

Most relevant to the Ekman and Friesen formulations are Tables 5 and 6, which summarize those studies relevant to the detectability of deception from the face and from the body. The mean detection effect across samples of judges who had access only to face cues does not differ significantly from the mean for the three studies that included a body-only condition. However, for four of the five studies which included both a face-only and a body-only condition, body was either computed to be (Ekman & Friesen, 1974; Littlepage & Pineault, 1979) or reported to be (Ekman & Friesen, 1969; Ekman et al., 1976) more revealing than the face. This latter trend is of course in keeping with the Ekman and Friesen suggestion that body cues will tip off the fact that deception is occurring more readily than will face cues.

A second way to look at the impact of face cues on the detection of deception is to ask whether the addition of face cues to other cues (as in comparing audio-only cues to audiovisual cues) actually impairs people's ability to detect lies. This is the result one would expect if observers actually are often fooled by the faking face. The mean detectability effects are in the predicted direction: People were more successful at detecting lies when they did not have access to facial cues (audio-only conditions) than when they did (audiovisual conditions). However, this difference is not statistically significant. Looking only at the investigations that included an audiovisual and an audio-only condition within the same study, the same trend emerges: In all of these studies, judges either performed about the same regardless of whether they had access only to audio cues or to audio cues and facial cues (Harrison et al., 1978; Littlepage & Pineault, 1978) or they did somewhat better at detecting deception when they did not have access to any facial cues (DePaulo et al., Note 1; Krauss et al., Note 2; Maier & Thurber, 1968).

In summary, the role of the face in perpetrating deception is still not entirely clear. There is some very tenuous evidence that it may in fact be more misleading than the body, as Ekman and Friesen suggested. What is clear, however, is that adding facial cues to verbal and vocal cues does *not* signficantly improve people's ability to detect lies (and in fact may even impede it). This finding is in stark contrast to findings reported in the nonverbal literature on the role of the face in the perception of *non*deceptive messages: People are markedly more successful at understanding nonverbal messages when facial cues are added to other cues (e.g., body and tone-of-voice cues) than when nonfacial nonverbal cues are presented alone (e.g., Rosenthal et al., 1979).

Because some of the most intriguing of the modalities studies outside of the field of deception (reviewed above) involved tone-of-voice cues, it is especially disappointing that tone-of-voice effect sizes could be estimated for only two studies—certainly not enough to draw confident conclusions about the role of the tone of voice in telling lies. One could alternatively investigate the impact of vocal nonverbal variables by examining the difference in detectability between audio messages (involving words plus tone) and purely verbal messages (words only). However, for this comparison, too, the data are inadequate, since only two studies have included a verbal-only condition. Tentatively, one might conclude that the addiction of vocal cues to verbal ones increases the transparency of lies to observers. Although this difference is far from significant, the direction of the effect is in keeping with all of the evidence reviewed earlier which suggests that tone of voice can sometimes betray a person's true feelings.

One result which is quite clear is that people are substantially more successful at detecting deception when they have access to words (either alone or in combination with other vocal and/or visual cues) than when they must make their judgments solely on the basis of nonverbal cues (see Table 7). But how does verbal content signal deception to decoders? One possibility is that the contents of deceptive messages contain expressions of a "nonimmediate" or indirect nature (Wagner & Pease, 1976; Wiener & Mehrabian, 1968). For example, to dissimulate liking, a person might say "I like John's company" rather than "I like John." Wagner and Pease (1976) showed that deceptive statements were more nonimmediate than truthful statements and their data suggest that receivers may be more likely to believe the content of immediate statements than that of nonimmediate statements.

The triumph of verbal messages over wordless ones might be especially disappointing to those who believe that nonverbal cues put on their best show in interpersonal interactions characterized by subtlety

TABLE 7
Estimates of Accuracy of Detecting Deception
in Various Channels (Medians)

	Channel	Number of Studies	Median d
Verbal Cues	Audiovisual	8	.64
Present	Audio	4	.98
	Verbal	2	.78
	Mean		.80[a]
	Tone of Voice	2	.32
Only Nonverbal	Face	9	.25
Cues Present	Body	3	.15
	Mean		.24[a]

a. t (4) for the difference between these means = 5.08, p < .008.

and intrigue, as deceptive transactions must be. To the duly disillu-
sioned, we offer three lines of consolation.

First, although noverbal cues are in general much less revealing of
deception than are verbal ones, the impact of nonverbal cues is also
strikingly more variable than the impact of verbal cues, $F(13, 13)$ for the
difference in homogeneity = 6.16, $p = .0025$. The three biggest effect sizes
and all five of the negative effect sizes are all from samples of judges who
observed purely nonverbal cues. What makes this consolation a prize is
the fact that nonverbal cues—though generally less useful than verbal
cues in pointing to deceit, and occasionally downright disastrous—will
sometimes serve as the royal road to truth. Clearly, the task of future
research is to determine when nonverbal cues lie about lies and when
they tell the truth.

Second, almost all of the detectability effects reported in Tables 1 to 6
were based on judgments of the degree of deceptiveness, rather than on
judgments of affects. Thus, they are relevant primarily to issues of
deception rather than of leakage. It cannot be assumed that detection
effects will be comparable for leakage and for deception. Both DePaulo
and Rosenthal (1979b) and Feldman (1976) have found that people are
much more accurate at discerning when lying is occurring than they are
at identifying a sender's true underlying feelings. The present data
support that suggestion. Two of the five negative detection effects
(which indicate inaccurate judgments), but only two of the 22 positive

effects, were from studies in which the observers made judgments about particular affects rather than about the presence or degree of deception. With respect to the issue at hand, the relative revealingness of verbal versus nonverbal cues may not be the same for leakage as it is for deception. Supportive of this suggestion is evidence from a study by DePaulo et al. (Note 1) in which verbal and nonverbal revealingness was measured separately for leakage and for deception. In keeping with previous findings, verbal cues were more informative overall than were nonverbal cues, and deception was much more accurately recognized than was leakage; however, the purely nonverbal channels were relatively more revealing of leakage than of deception, while modalities that included verbal cues were relatively more revealing of deception. Thus, although lie-detectors are still much better off having access to verbal cues than to nonverbal ones, the verbal advantage is not nearly so pronounced when the judgments are about a sender's true, but concealed feelings. In a *relative* sense, verbal cues are cues to deception while nonverbal cues are cues to leakage.

This analysis leads to one further inference, namely, that nonverbal cues will be relatively more revealing when the deception concerns affect (e.g., when the senders pretend to like someone they actually dislike) than when it concerns an opinion (e.g., when the senders give false information about a particular event); verbal messages may show the reverse pattern. The rationale for this prediction is that when senders dissimulate affect, nonverbal cues may indicate stress (thus serving as deception cues). However, when the sender dissimulates an opinion, there is less affect to be leaked and consequently nonverbal cues lose one of their main functions. On the other hand, because an opinion includes detailed information that must make sense, its verbal content is as likely or more likely to reveal deception than the verbal content of expressed affect. The conclusions of this analysis are straightforward: The relative utility of different channels for detecting deception may depend not only on the nature of the particular channel but also on the nature of the lie that is to be detected.

Finally, the evidence we have presented regarding modality effects was gleaned solely from situations involving dissimulation. However, the relative revealingness of verbal versus nonverbal modalities is not necessarily the same for feigned affects as it is for "pure" or nondeceptive ones. That brings us back to one of our initial motivating assumptions, namely, that the study of modality effects in the detection of deception is especially interesting precisely because the modalities might line up differently when the message being communicated is a deceptive one compared to when it is a nondeceptive one. In a study which compared the relative effectiveness of verbal and nonverbal modalities in conveying deceptive and nondeceptive messages (DePaulo et al., Note 1), the predicted interaction was in fact found. Although modalities involving verbal cues were much more informative overall than were modalities involving only nonverbal cues, and although pure messages were more readily recognized than were deceptive messages, verbal superiority was not nearly so striking in communications involving deception as it was in communications involving no deceptive intents (e.g., expressions of pure liking or of pure disliking).

METHODOLOGICAL ISSUES WITH THEORETICAL IMPLICATIONS

In most (though not all) of the studies we have reviewed, senders were videotaped while telling lies and these videotapes were then shown in whole or in part (e.g., audio-only) to a group of judges. The revealingness of a given modality, then, was defined by the degree to which judges could detect deception when given access to only that modality. This, of course, does not indicate how much information or what kind of information people typically pick up from a given modality when information from that modality is made available simultaneously with information from other modalities, as is usually the case in real life. This particular question is difficult to study naturalistically, especially when the sender is expressing a "pure," consistent, and nondeceptive message in which, presumably, the same affect is being communicated by all modalities. When judges indicate the affect that they believe is being expressed, how are we to specify the particular modalities upon which their judgment was based?

Experimentally, there are several ways to approach this problem. First, one could look at the differences between the judgments made when the modality in question is present compared to when it is absent. Thus, for example, to study the revealingness of tone-of-voice cues, one might look at the difference between judgments of an audiotape (which contains words and tone of voice cues) and judgments of a verbal transcript made from that audiotape. Still, one cannot be absolutely certain that the difference in information gleaned from an audiotape as compared to a transcript really does indicate the amount of information that is usually abstracted from tone-of-voice cues when other cues are available, too. That is, the amount of information that is abstracted when voice and words are combined may not be equal to the sum of the information that is abstracted from each separately. Cue sources may modify or add to each other, such that more information can be obtained from several taken together than from any one alone, or it may happen that less information is abstracted from the whole than from the sum of the parts, as might be the case if subjects exposed to one input alone pay more attention to that input and abstract more information from it than they do when that input is part of a more complicated stimulus array.

A second approach to this question is to experimentally manipulate the affects that are communicated by different modalities presented simultaneously. Thus, for example, a negative tone of voice can be paired with a positive face. If judges rate this voice-face combination as especially positive, then they are relying relatively more on the visual than on the auditory information (cf. DePaulo et al., 1978). This methodology does indicate the relative reliance on a given modality when other modalities are present, too; however, it is limited to the study of discrepant messages, and there is evidence to suggest that the relative reliance on different modalities is not the same for discrepant as for nondiscrepant communications (DePaulo et al., 1978; Zuckerman et al., 1980).

A third possibility is to correlate the judgments of a communication made by subjects given full audiovisual access to that communication with the same judgments made by subjects given more restricted access to it, for example, audio-only, verbal-only, visual-only. Those modalities that correlate most strongly with the full audiovisual modality may be the ones that subjects rely on most when making judgments based a wealth of verbal and nonverbal cues.

A variation on the modalities issue we have been addressing is 'the question, "What information does a judge abstract from a given modality when instructed to attend especially to that modality?" If, for instance, tone-of-voice cues really are more revealing of deception than are face or body cues, then subjects instructed to attend especially to tone of voice (compared to those instructed to pay particular attention to the visual cues) should be relatively more accurate at detecting deception. This is a somewhat more naturalistic way of studying modality-revealingness than is the method of presenting modalities in isolation, since in this approach subjects are given full access to all available modalities (e.g., words, facial expressions, and tone of voice). One such study (DePaulo et al., Note 3)—in which judges were told to pay particular attention either to the tone of voice, the words, or to the visual cues, or were given no particular attentional set—provides evidence consistent with the data presented in Tables 1 to 6 above. Compared to the control group, subjects were most successful at detecting lies when told to pay particular attention to the tone, and least successful when told to pay special attention to visual cues.

Still another approach to the study of modality effects in the detection of deception is to manipulate the degree of deception that subjects are led to expect and then examine their relative reliance on different modalities as a function of these induced expectations. This kind of approach tells not so much about the actual informativeness of different modalities as about people's lay theories (not necessarily conscious ones) about modalities. This methodology was used by Zuckerman et al. (Note 4), who found that subjects who expected more deception (compared to those who expected less) were relatively more influenced by tone-of-voice cues than by facial cues. If tone-of-voice cues are in fact "leakier" than facial cues, then this strategy (of switching to audio cues as messages become more deceptive) is an appropriate one, as it should facilitate success at detecting dissimulation. Converging evidence for the use of this strategy comes from studies in which nothing specific was said about deception, but subjects were presented with messages that varied in degree of discrepancy. In these studies, subjects were relatively more influenced by audio than by visual cues as messages became more discrepant, and presumably more deceptive (cf. DePaulo & Rosenthal, 1979a; DePaulo et al., 1978), an effect which appears to increase with age (Zuckerman et al., 1980). In another study in which there was no mention of deception (Mehrabian & Wiener, 1967), this one involving verbal and vocal cues, subjects were again more influenced by the vocal than by the verbal cues when these two sources of cues communicated discrepant information.

Most of the approaches to the study of modality effects described above have been designed from the perspective of the decoder or judge; for each of these, there is an analogous encoder methodology. For example, the encoder analogue of the approach in which judges are instructed to attend preferentially to a particular modality is a methodology in which senders are instructed to communicate through a particular modality. Although there is one study in the literature in which senders were explicitly instructed to express themselves facially (Zuckerman et al., 1979), there are no published studies which varied the modality through which senders were instructed to communicate. This kind of study is important for its relevance to the issue of modality "controllability." If a given modality "leaks" deceptive information, it may do so either because senders are not able effectively to control that modality or because senders either do not think to control it or do not try to control it. Using the paradigm just described, the results might show that judges are less successful in detecting deception from tone of voice when senders are instructed to lie with it, than when senders are not instructed to communicate through any particular channel. More important, to the extent that the decrease in detection accuracy from the voice under "lie with your voice" instructions is comparable to the decrease in detection accuracy from the face under "lie with your face" instructions, it may be inferred that tone of voice is a channel that *can* be controlled, but perhaps it is not ordinarily controlled, either because senders do not think to control it or because the bulk of their communicational effort is concentrated in other modalities.

There are still other, perhaps more interesting, ways of making a particular modality salient to a sender than that of explicitly instructing the sender to communicate through that modality. One approach especially likely to be effective in this regard is to vary the kind of access that the judge has to the sender's communications. An exemplary study along these lines was conducted by Krauss et al. (Note 2), who arranged for senders to communicate to other people either in a face-to-face interaction or over an intercom. Videotapes made of the senders during both kinds of interactions were then shown to a new panel of judges. These new judges were most accurate at detecting deception when they had access only to the facial expressions of those senders who were communicating over an intercom. The intercom senders probably tried most diligently to control the auditory aspects of their communications; their visual displays, which they were led to believe would not be monitored, thereby left uncontrolled and hence were highly legible and "leaky" to the new observers. We believe that this factor of modality salience is one of the most important moderators of modality effects in verbal and nonverbal communications. In short, the postulate that we are forwarding is the following: The degree to which a sender attempts to "control" a given modality increases with the degree to which the salience of that modality to the receiver is made salient to the sender.

The extent to which this attempted control will actually be effective will be determined by other variables such as the sender's skill at dissimulation, the ease with which the particular modality which is being controlled can be understood by the receivers (this is both a modality characteristic, since some modalities are more readily read than others, and a receiver characteristic, since some receivers are more skillful judges of that modality than others), and the extent to which the modality in question is amenable to willful control. A corollary of this postulate is that when an actor attempts to control one particular channel, other channels may leak more information than they do under ordinary circumstances. The rationale is that a sender who pays more attention to, say, his or her voice, is less capable of monitoring and blocking deception and/or leakage cues from his or her face. The model is, of course, hydraulic: By making one channel less leaky, the sender inadvertently increases the leakiness of another.

FURTHER MODERATORS OF MODALITY EFFECTS

So far we have suggested that modality effects might be moderated by the kinds of cues the receiver is trying to detect (e.g., deception cues versus leakage cues), the receivers' relative attentiveness to different modalities (which may in turn be a function of suspiciousness or expectations for deception), and the sender's awareness of the receiver's differential access to different modalities. In this section, we will describe other factors that we believe to serve as moderators of modality effects. Our list is intended to be a suggestive, rather than an exhaustive one.

One encoder variable that is likely to moderate the relative revealingness of different modalities is the degree to which the lie is carefully planned and rehearsed rather than fabricated extemporaneously (cf. DePaulo et al., Note 5). In the case of off-handed, unpremeditated lies, many of the cues to deception may be verbal indicators of uncertainty. If, on the other hand, the liar has his or her verbal act down pat, he or she might then put more effort into the control of the more subtle nonverbal modalities.

From the perspective of the encoder and the decoder, factors such as their degree of arousal, their involvement in the deception, and the consequentiality to them of the success of the deception may all moderate modality effects. The decoder who is highly motivated to detect lies may scrupulously scrutinize every available source of information. Ironically, this hyperattentiveness may render the aroused decoder less successful at detecting lies than a more apathetic decoder who perhaps is often not even bothering to visually monitor the sender. Apathetic decoders thereby overlook many of the visual cues that might only have misled them anyway.

The encoder who is aroused may try especially hard to control those modalities that are being monitored by the observer. If the relevant modality is one that is readily controlled (facial expressions, perhaps) then arousal might argument the sender's success at deception; if, on the other hand, the relevant modality is not easily controlled (tone of voice, perhaps), then arousal might impair the sender's ability to perpetrate lies. Consistent with this suggestion are the Streeter et al. (1977) findings that (1) the tendency for fundamental frequency to be higher for deceptive than for truthful answers was especially characteristic of aroused senders and (2) aroused senders communicating by intercom are less successful liars than unaroused senders, whereas the reverse is true for senders communicating face to face.

Also relevant to modality effects is the particular content of the lie. A recent review article (DePaulo & Rosenthal, 1979a) has summarized evidence which suggests that particular modalities may be "specialized" to communicate particular affects. Specifically, facial cues appear to be especially effective in conveying variations in positivity, whereas tone-of-voice cues seem to be relatively more effective in communicating variations in dominance. Thus, whether a particular modality will be more or less "leaky" than another modality may depend on the particular affect that the sender is attempting to feign or to hide.

The relative revealingness of different modalities might also vary with the demographic characteristics of both the liars and the lie-detectors. In the DePaulo et al. (Note 3) study, for example, it was shown that the tendency for vocal attentiveness to facilitate lie detection success was especially characteristic of opposite-sex encoder-decoder pairs. This result is particularly intriguing since it suggests that sex differences in modality revealingness are not a simple function of differences in the ways that males and females express themselves, and they are not a simple function of differences in what males and females perceive. The DePaulo et al. (Note 3) study highlights the fact that both encoders and decoders determine the outcome of the communication process. In fact, the findings reviewed in this article do not differentiate between the encoders' and decoders' nonverbal skills. Thus, a channel may leak information because encoders cannot control it and/or because receivers do well at decoding it. Stated differently, the studies that were reviewed are based on a sending-receiving paradigm in which the senders' skill at communicating is defined by the receivers' skill at understanding. Consequently, we do not know whether differences among various modalities should be attributed to senders or receivers. Investigators can measure, of course, "objective" aspects of nonverbal cues such as frequency of smiling during deception or fundamental pitch (Ekman et al., 1976; Streeter et al., 1977; Krauss et al., Note 2). However, while this approach does examine the encoding process only, it does not allow a comparison among modalities (frequency of smiles cannot be compared to fundamental pitch) and, therefore, is not reviewed in this article.

Other individual difference characteristics in addition to sex (e.g., age, self-monitoring, machiavellianism) have been shown to mediate verbal and nonverbal skills and strategies for expressing and detecting deception (see DePaulo et al., 1980, for a review). However, for the most part the individual differences research has not yet been extended to the study of sending and receiving through different modalities. Along with individual difference considerations, the effects of setting characteristics and role relationships on modality revealingness also need to be acknowledged and examined. Future research efforts should consider not only the effects of single factors—for example, characteristics of liars and lie-detectors, types of lies, and social settings—but their interactions as well (cf. DePaulo & Rosenthal, 1979b). A multidimensional approach to lies may reveal interaction effects that otherwise would remain hidden in simpler research designs.

THE LEAP FROM MEDIATED TO LIVE COMMUNICATIONS

Most of the modalities studies up until this time have been noninteractive (senders are videotaped while telling lies and those videotapes are subsequently observed by a group of judges); however, when we do move to interactive studies of deception, we may find that liars (senders) often have the edge over the lie-detectors. Liars are on the offensive: They know what they are trying to achieve (success at deception), and they can use the reactions of the person they are trying to deceive to adjust and readjust their strategy whenever they sense suspiciousness. Receivers, too, can use aspects of the live interaction to their advantage (for instance, they can initiate probes to test their suspicions); however, perhaps their biggest impediment to success is that they must first come to suspect that deception is taking place before they can most effectively utilize their deception-detection probes. The deceiver, on the other hand, knows what the game is all along. When the deceiver suspects that the detector is becoming suspicious, he or she may put more effort into controlling the ordinarily less controlled modalities; analogously, when the receiver suspects deception, he or she may attend more and more to the ordinarily less controlled modalities. The timing of deceiver and receiver suspiciousness, then, may further moderate modality revealingness.

When modalities are added or subtracted within an interactive paradigm, much more changes than simply the amount of information that is available to the receiver. In interactive paradigms, the audiovisual modality is operationalized as a face-to-face interaction, the audio modality often involves a telephone conversation or an intercom link, and the verbal modality might be operationalized as a conversation maintained via a teletypewriter. In an extensive review comparing face-to-face with other "mediated" communications (e.g., telephone, teletypewriter), Williams (1977) suggested that the latter are in many ways less pleasant. For instance, he noted that audio-only conversations are more depersonalized, more argumentative, and narrower in focus than face-to-face conversations. Audio-only conversants perceive each other as less friendly, and sometimes seem to treat each other more as objects than as fellow human beings.

One implication of this might be that people are both more likely to try to deceive each other and more likely to suspect each other of deceit in audio than in face-to-face interactions. Whether this tenor of manipulativeness and distrust in the auditory modality might affect the liar's skill at telling lies or the receiver's skill at detecting them cannot be answered definitively at this point; however, in the one deception study that did involve a face-to-face and an intercom condition (Krauss et al., Note 2), intercom listeners were substantially more accurate at detecting lies than were face-to-face interactants.

In keeping with this suggestion that, when more and more evidence is gathered, audio-only communications may turn out to be the most revealing of the truth, perhaps we should close this section by noting, as Maier and Thurber did more than a decade ago (1968), that "the symbol of justice stands with a sword in her right hand, a pair of balance scales in her left, and a blindfold over eyes—she can only hear!" (p. 30).

SUMMARY AND CONCLUSIONS

Initially, we set out to review differences among various nonverbal channels in the extent to which they "leak" senders' true affects or reveal that deception is occurring. Although the evidence that has accumulated so far does not yet compellingly document the differences that we expected to find, the direction of the available data is at least consistent with the suggestion that facial cues are faking cues (they are not especially informative to the human lie-detector and may even be downright misleading), while auditory cues are more likely to leak the truth.

The special role of tone-of-voice cues (sometimes in combination with words) in the detection of deception was suggested by several converging lines of evidence: (1) a review of the available evidence on the detection of deception showed a trend for lies to be more accurately detected when judges had access only to auditory cues (tone plus words) than when they had access to audiovisual cues (tone plus words plus face), only verbal cues, only tone-of-voice cues (content-filtered speech), or only visual cues (see Tables 1 to 6); (2) subjects given full audiovisual access to communications, but told to pay particular attention to tone-of-voice cues, tended to be more accurate at detecting deception than subjects told to attend especially to the words or the visual cues, and they were significantly more accurate than subjects given no attentional instructions at all (DePaulo et al., Note 3); and (3) subjects shown discrepant tone-of-voice and facial communications relied relatively more on the voice as they became more and more suspicious of deception (Zuckerman et al., Note 4) and as the messages became more discrepant (DePaulo et al., 1979; DePaulo & Rosenthal, 1979a). This evidence, which suggests that tone of voice is especially likely to leak the truth, is consistent with evidence from studies not involving deception, in which tone of voice seemed to reveal people's true—though not always recognized—attitudes toward themselves and other people.

Since we believed at the outset that verbal cues would be the most easily controlled (and hence the most readily faked) of all of the communications we reviewed, we were surprised to find that they were so useful to judges attempting to detect deception. In fact, the clearest pattern to emerge from all of the evidence we reviewed was the one that showed that communications involving words were much more accurately identified as truthful or deceptive than were purely nonverbal communications (see Table 7).

Though there may be a general tendency for certain modalities to be more revealing overall than certain other modalities, we believe that this revealingness pecking order can be systematically modified by certain situational, personal, and contextual conditions. These include the liar's awareness of the salience to the lie-detector of particular channels; the liar's arousal and involvement in the lie; the suspiciousness, attentiveness, and involvement of the lie-detector; the content of the lie; and the degree to which the lie is planned or rehearsed. The factors that figured most prominently in the original formulation of the leakage model (i.e., sending capacity, internal feedback, and external feedback) are probably extremely important, too; ironically, however, empirical research aimed at substantiating the role of these factors in the mediation of modality effects is still scant.

NOTE

1. Ekman and Friesen (1969) did note, however, that one particular form of facial expression, the split-second microexpression, may also give away the deceiver's true feelings but is likely to be missed by naive observers.

REFERENCE NOTES

1. DePaulo, B. M., Rosenthal, R., Green, C. R., & Rosenkrantz, J. *Verbal and nonverbal revealingness in deceptive and nondeceptive communications.* Manuscript submitted for publication, University of Virginia, 1980.

2. Krauss, R. M., Geller, V., & Olson, C. *Modalities and cues in the detection of deception.* Presented at the meeting of the American Psychological Association, Washington, D.C., September 1976.

3. DePaulo, B. M., Lassiter, G. D., & Stone, J. I. *Attentional determinants of success at detecting deception.* Manuscript submitted for publication, 1980.

4. Zuckerman, M., Spiegel, N. H., DePaulo, B. M., & Rosenthal, R. *Nonverbal strategies for decoding deception.* Manuscript submitted for publication, 1980.

5. DePaulo, B. M., Davis, T., & Lanier, K. *Planning lies: The effects of spontaneity and arousal on success at deception.* Presented at the Eastern Psychological Association, Hartford, Conn., April 1980.

REFERENCES

Adair, J. G. & Epstein, J. S. Verbal cues in the mediation of experimenter bias. *Psychological Reports*, 1968, *22*, 1045-1053.

Argyle, M. & Cook, M. *Gaze and mutual gaze*. Cambridge, England: Cambridge University Press, 1976.

Bell, P. A., Fisher, J. D., & Loomis, R. J. *Environmental psychology*. Philadelphia: Saunders, 1978.

Bugental, D. B., Henker, B., & Whalen, C. K. Attributional antecendents of verbal and vocal assertiveness. *Journal of Personality and Social Psychology*, 1976, *34*, 405-411.

Bugental, D. E. & Love, L. Nonassertive expression of parental approval and disapproval and its relationship to child disturbance. *Child Development*, 1975, *46*, 747-752.

Cohen, J. *Statistical power analysis for the behavioral sciences*. New York: Academic Press, 1977.

DePaulo, B. M. & Rosenthal, R. Age changes in nonverbal decoding a function of increasing amounts of information. *Journal of Experimental Child Psychology*, 1978, *26*, 280-287.

DePaulo, B. M. & Rosenthal, R. Ambivalence, discrepancy, and deception in nonverbal communication. In R. Rosenthal (ed.), *Skill in nonverbal communication*. Cambridge, Mass.: Oelgeschlager, Gunn, & Hain, 1979. (a)

DePaulo, B. M. & Rosenthal, R. Telling lies. *Journal of Personality and Social Psychology*, 1979, *37*, 1713-1722. (b)

DePaulo, B. M., Rosenthal, R., Eisenstat, R. A., Rogers, P. L., & Finkelstein, S. Decoding discrepant nonverbal cues. *Journal of Personality and Social Psychology*, 1978, *36*, 313-323.

DePaulo, B. M., Zuckerman, M., & Rosenthal, R. Humans as lie-detectors. *Journal of Communication*, 1980, *30*, 129-139.

Duncan, S. & Rosenthal, R. Vocal emphases in experimenter's instruction reading as unintended determinants of subjects' response. *Language and Speech*, 1968, *11*, 20-26.

Ekman, P. & Friesen, W. V. Nonverbal leakage and clues to deception. *Psychiatry*, 1969, *32*, 88-106.

Ekman, P. & Friesen, W. V. Detecting deception from the body or face. *Journal of Personality and Social Psychology*, 1974, *29*, 288-298.

Ekman, P., Friesen, W. V., & Scherer, K. R. Body movement and voice pitch in deceptive interaction. *Semiotica*, 1976, *16*, 23-27.

Fay, P. J., & Middleton, W. C. The ability to judge truth-telling or lying from the voice as transmitted over a public address system. *Journal of General Psychology*, 1941, *24*, 211-215.

Feldman, R. S. Nonverbal disclosure of teacher deception and interpersonal affect. *Journal of Educational Psychology*, 1976, *68*, 807-816.

Feldman, R. S. Nonverbal disclosure of deception in urban Korean adults and children. *Journal of Cross-Cultural Psychology*, 1979, *10*, 73-83.

Feldman, R. S., Devin-Sheehan, L., & Allen, V. L. Nonverbal cues as indicators of verbal dissembling. *American Educational Research Journal*, 1978, *15*, 217-231.

Feldman, R. S., Jenkins, L., & Popoola, O. Detection of deception in adults and children via facial expressions. *Child Development*, 1979, *50*, 350-355.

Geizer, R. S., Rarick, D. L., & Soldow, G. F. Deception and judgmental accuracy: A study in person perception. *Personality and Social Psychology Bulletin*, 1977, *3*, 446-449.

Harrison, A. A., Hwalek, M., Raney, D. F., & Fritz, J. G. Cues to deception in an interview situation. *Social Psychology*, 1978, *41*, 156-161.

Holzman, P. S. & Rousey, C. The voice as a percept. *Journal of Personality and Social Psychology*, 1966, *4*, 78-86.

Kraut, R. E. Verbal and nonverbal cues in the perception of lying. *Journal of Personality and Social Psychology*, 1978, *36*, 380-391.

Littlepage, G. & Pineault, T. Verbal, facial, and paralinguistic cues to the detection of truth and lying. *Personality and Social Psychology Bulletin*, 1978, *4*, 461-464.

Littlepage, G. E. & Pineault, M. A. Detection of deceptive factual statements from the body and the face. *Personality and Social Psychology Bulletin*, 1979, *5*, 325-328.

Maier, N.R.F. Sensitivity to attempts at deception in an interview situation. *Personnel Psychology*, 1966, *19*, 55-65.

Maier, N.R.F. & Janzen, J. C. The reliability of reasons used in judgments of honesty and dishonesty. *Perceptual and Motor Skills*, 1967, *25*, 141-151.

Maier, N.R.F. & Thurber, J. A. Accuracy of judgments of deception when an interview is watched, heard, and read. *Personnel Psychology*, 1968, *21*, 23-30.

Matarazzo, J., Wiens, A., Jackson, R., & Manaugh, T. Interviewer speech behavior under conditions of endogenously present and exogenously induced motivational states. *Journal of Clinical Psychology*, 1970, *26*, 141-148.

Mehrabian, A. & Wiener, M. Decoding of inconsistent communication. *Journal of Personality and Social Psychology*, 1967, *6*, 108-114.

Milmoe, S., Novey, M. S., Kagan, J., & Rosenthal, R. The mother's voice: Postdictor of aspects of her baby's behavior. In S. Weitz (ed.), *Nonverbal communication*. New York: Oxford University Press, 1974.

Milmoe, S., Rosenthal, R., Blane, H. T., Chafetz, M. E., & Wolf, I. The doctor's voice: Postdictor of successful referral of alcoholic patients. *Journal of Abnormal Psychology*, 1967, *72*, 78-84.

Rosenthal, R. *Experimenter effects in behavioral research*. Englewood Cliffs, N.J.: Prentice-Hall, 1966.

Rosenthal, R. Interpersonal expectations: Effects of the experimenter's hypothesis. In R. Rosenthal and R. L. Rosnow (eds.), *Artifact in behavioral research*. New York: Academic Press, 1969.

Rosenthal, R. & DePaulo, B. M. Sex differences in eavesdropping on nonverbal cues. *Journal of Personality and Social Psychology*, 1979, *37*, 273-285. (a)

Rosenthal, R. & DePaulo, B. M. Sex differences in accommodation in nonverbal communication. In R. Rosenthal (ed.), *Skill in nonverbal communication*. Cambridge, Mass.: Oelgeschlager, Gunn, & Hain, 1979. (b)

Rosenthal, R., Hall, J. A., DiMatteo, M. R., Rogers, P. L., & Archer, D. *Sensitivity to nonverbal communication: The PONS Test*. Baltimore: Johns Hopkins University Press, 1979.

Scherer, K. R. Nonlinguistic vocal indicators of emotion and psychopathology. In C. E. Izard (ed.), *Emotions in personality and psychopathology*. New York: Plenum, 1979.

Schneider, D. J., Hastorf, A. H., & Ellsworth, P. C. *Person perception*. Reading, Mass.: Addison-Wesley, 1978.

Snyder, M., Tanke, E. D., & Berscheid, E. Social perception and interpersonal behavior: On the self-fulfilling nature of social stereotypes. *Journal of Personality and Social Psychology*, 1977, *35*, 656-666.

Streeter, L. A, Krauss, R. M., Geller, V., Olson, C., & Apple, W. Pitch changes during attempted deception. *Journal of Personality and Social Psychology*, 1977, *35*, 345-350.

Wagner, H. & Pease, K. The verbal communication of inconsistency between attitudes held and attitudes expressed. *Journal of Personality*, 1976, *44*, 1-16.

Weitz, S. Attitude, voice and behavior: A repressed affect model of interracial interaction. *Journal of Personality and Social Psychology*, 1972, *24*, 14-21.

Wiener, M. & Mehrabian, A. *Language within language*. Englewood Cliffs, N.J.: Prentice-Hall, 1968.

Williams, E. Experimental comparisons of face-to-face and mediated communication: A review. *Psychological Bulletin*, 1977, *84*, 963-976.

Zuckerman, M., Blanck, P. D., DePaulo, B. M., & Rosenthal, R. Developmental changes in decoding discrepant and nondiscrepant nonverbal cues. *Developmental Psychology*, 1980, *16*, 220-228.

Zuckerman, M., DeFrank, R. S., Hall, J. A., Larrance, D. T., & Rosenthal, R. Facial and vocal cues of deception and truth. *Journal of Experimental Social Psychology*, 1979, *15*, 378-396.

6

Sex Stereotypes
Through the Life Cycle

FRANCES K. DEL BOCA
RICHARD D. ASHMORE

Frances K. Del Boca is a Ph.D. candidate in the Social Psychology program at Rutgers—
The State Unviersity. Her principal research interest is intergroup relations, especially
female-male and black-white relations. She is coauthor of "Psychological Approaches to
Understanding Intergroup Conflict" (1976) and "Sex Stereotypes and Implicit Personality
Theory: Toward a Cognitive-Social Psychological Conceptualization" (1979).
Richard D. Ashmore is Associate Professor of Psychology at Livingston College,
Rutgers—The State University, where he is Co-Ordinator of the Social Psychology Area.
His major areas of interest are social problems (coauthor, with John B. McConahay, of
Psychology and America's Urban Dilemmas) and intergroup relations, especially female-
male relations, and adults' perception of children.

O ver the past decade there has been a dramatic rise in concern with
the general area of female-male relations and the more specific topic of
sex stereotypes (cf. Ashmore & Del Boca, in press). This is evident in
books and articles aimed at the general public, in analyses by and for
"practitioners" (e.g., doctors and teachers), and in research conducted
by social scientists from a wide variety of disciplines. The majority of sex
stereotype studies have focused on content and can be roughly grouped
into two categories. A large number of investigations—most often
conducted by psychologists—have been aimed at demonstrating that
the members of a particular group of perceivers (usually college students) agree that some set of personality traits is differentially characteristic of women and men. Even more research—often, though not

AUTHORS' NOTE: Preparation of this article was facilitated by National Institute of
Mental Health grant MH 27737 (Margaret K. Bacon and Richard D. Ashmore, Co-
Principal Investigators). We wish to thank John C. Brigham, Richard J. Butsch, Dolores
Gold, Geoffrey M. White, John E. Williams, and especially Carolyn W. Sherif for their
helpful comments on an earlier draft of this article. We also thank Robin M. Uili for help
in gathering bibliographic materials and Audrey Puskas for typing assistance.

exclusively, by sociologists—has been concerned with stereotypic images of the sexes portrayed in the mass media and in other facets of the cultural environment. Relatively little work has been done on the acquisition of sex stereotypes by children. Even less attention has been given to how stereotypic conceptions of the sexes are maintained in adulthood or how beliefs about women and men might be influenced by the various "adaptive tasks" or "stages" in the life cycle after childhood.

While "sex stereotype researchers" have been concerned primarily with the content of beliefs about and depictions of women and men, others—particularly developmental psychologists—have been studying sex roles. Even though sex stereotypes figure prominently in two major theories of sex-role acquisition (i.e., Kagan, 1964; Kohlberg, 1966), the bulk of research with children has dealt with "preferences for and adoption of sex-appropriate roles (and) little attention has been devoted to children's cognitions with respect to the content of these sex roles" (Kuhn et al., 1978, p. 445). Recently there have been suggestions that a life-span approach be taken to studying sex-role socialization (e.g., Katz, 1979), but again the focus has been on preferences and role-appropriateness of behavior at various points in adulthood rather than on how beliefs about the sexes might vary as individuals move through the life cycle.

This article has two interrelated goals: to stimulate a life-span approach to investigating sex stereotypes and to illustrate how several currently isolated research literatures might contribute to such an approach. We begin by considering the meaning of the term *sex stereotype* and other other related constructs. The next section is devoted to a selective review of different bodies of literature relevant to sex stereotypes at various points in the life cycle. The final three sections of the article raise issues that are important to the development of research and theory on sex stereotypes through the life course. First, three general orientations to the study of stereotypes are presented. Next, several models of individual development are discussed in terms of their implications for the acquisition and alteration of stereotypic conceptions of the sexes. The concluding section of the article discusses more general implications of a life-span approach to sex stereotypes.

SEX STEREOTYPES AND RELATED CONSTRUCTS

An unfortunate, though perhaps unavoidable, by-product of the wide-ranging interest in female-male relations is that the same term is often given different meanings (conceptually as well as operationally) and different terms are used to describe the same phenomenon (cf. Beere, 1979, p. 14). It is beyond the scope of this article to comprehensively and critically address the existing terminological confusion. We can, however, avoid contributing to the disorder by explicitly defining the construct, sex stereotype, and by differentiating our usage of the term from related concepts.[1] On the basis of a survey of the sex stereotype literature and a consideration of the meaning of the word *stereotype* as applied to other social groups, sex stereotypes are defined as "*the structured sets of beliefs about the personal attributes of women and of men*" (Ashmore & Del Boca, 1979, p. 222). The general phrase *personal attributes* is used because we believe that the content of stereotypes includes not only personality traits (used most often in sex stereotype measures) but also physical and other properties that "define" category membership (e.g., facial hair), as well as behaviors and behavior sequences expected of, and feelings aroused by, members of a particular social category. Further, we reserve the term *sex stereotypes* for the sets of beliefs regarding women and men held by an individual and use *cultural sex stereotypes* to describe shared or consensual sets of beliefs about the sexes. (See Ashmore & Del Boca, 1979, for rationale.)

At times both the terms *sex role* and *sex-role attitude* have been defined in a way similar to *sex stereotype* or have been used interchangeably with this concept. These terms do refer to interrelated phenomena, and beliefs about women and men cannot be understood without reference to sex-linked roles or evaluations of the sexes. (In fact, we will draw on the sex-role development literature to illuminate the process of sex stereotype acquisition.) Progress in understanding female-male relations is hampered, however, if the differences in meaning of these terms as scientific constructs are not made explicit. *Sex role* is here used to denote the characteristics (e.g., interests and traits) and behaviors normatively prescribed for the social categories female and male. In short, sex roles are *rules* about what females and males *should be like* and how they *should behave*. Just as *role* will be reserved for a set of "shoulds" associated with a particular social category, *attitude* will be used to refer to an evaluative (good-bad) orientation. A number of self-report techniques for measuring sex-role attitudes are currently available (e.g., the Attitude Toward Women Scale of Spence & Helmreich, 1972). These instruments assess an individual's evaluation of particular roles for women and for men (generally, evaluative orientation toward "traditional" or "conservative" versus "modern" or "liberal" roles). There are also methods for indexing prejudice against women (e.g., Goldberg, 1968) and attitudes toward specific groups of women (e.g., the Women as Managers Scale of Peters et al., 1974). While the attitude object varies (sex roles, women as a group, women managers), all of these techniques assess evaluative orientations relevant to female-male relations; such orientations will be distinguished from beliefs about the personal attributes of females and males.

RESEARCH RELEVANT TO SEX STEREOTYPES THROUGH THE LIFE CYCLE

While most studies explicitly concerned with sex stereotypes have involved self-reports of college students or content analyses of media and other cultural portrayals, there is considerable research that is relevant to the basic question, how do beliefs about the sexes vary through the life cycle? Before reviewing this research it is important to note that we are primarily concerned with the different views of women and men *held by* persons at different points in the life course. We will touch on, but not treat in any depth, the related issue of stereotypic *beliefs about* women and men of different ages (e.g., "dirty old man").

Following Williams et al. (1975), we distinguish six basic types of "learning about sex": ability to identify others' sex, ability to identify own sex (including labelling of self as "girl" or "boy," and gender constancy, the belief that one's sex is immutable), sex-role identity, perception of one's parents (including both their behavior and their characteristics), ability to recognize child play and adult work activities as sex-linked, and beliefs about the personality trait characteristics of the sexes (including beliefs about boys and girls as well as about women and men). While all of these "learnings" are relevant to the acquisition of sex stereotypes, space restrictions make it impossible in this section to discuss the considerable amount of work concerned with sex-role identity.

It is interesting, though not surprising, that research on the various "learnings about sex" has varied with the age of the subject sample. Studies of young children (from birth to about age four) have concentrated on ability to identify the sex of others and to label self as a girl or boy. According to Kohlberg (1966), identification of others' sex develops between the ages two and three and consistent self-labelling between three and four. Lewis and Weinraub (1979) argue that children have knowledge about own and others' gender at a much earlier age. While they acknowledge that the "form of this knowledge" is not clear and that it is not "fixed," they believe that knowledge about gender is developing during the first year of life and is clearly present by 18 months of age. The Lewis and Weinraub (1979) position is consistent with Donaldson's (1976, especially pp. 283-284) suggestion that infants less than eight months of age have incipient person categories and with Moerk's (1977, pp. 83-89) contention that children begin to learn "the differentiation of $\pm$ female" at about seven months of age. The challenge for those concerned with "sex learnings" is to identify how these incipient gender categories are formed, how they are represented in memory, and "what conditions interfere with the use and accessibility of those capacities the young child does possess" (Gelman, 1979, p. 904). It is important to remember that these categories and capacities are ones that the child has developed in social interaction (with particular others in particular situations) and that they are the child's constructions and not just the child's understanding of adults' categorizations (Moerk, 1977).

While the bulk of research on "sex learnings" with children over the age of four has been concerned with sex-role identity (cf. Kuhn et al., 1978, p. 445), considerable attention has been devoted to children's perceptions of parents. This research is pertinent to the acquisition of sex stereotypes since mother and father are among the most salient women and men in the child's life, especially prior to school attendance.[2] According to Kohlberg (1966), the literature indicates that (1) preschoolers see fathers as high in Potency (i.e., dominating and strong) and as competent, while mothers are regarded as friendly and supportive and (2) these perceptions are not based primarily on actual parent behavior since they persist across variations in social class, race, and father absence. Our reading of the accumulated studies, both pre- and post-1966, suggests that the first conclusion must be modified and the second regarded as uncertain. While the mother-as-accepting and father-as-potent views seem well documented, the father-as-competent notion is not clearly demonstrated.

Do children's views of parents vary with demographic factors? There is simply not enough evidence regarding social class and race to answer this question. While perceptions of parents have seldom been directly assessed in studies of father absence, there is evidence that the "sex learnings" of both boys and girls are influenced, though in different ways, by father absence (cf. Lamb, 1979). That father absence does seem to affect sex-role development (cf. Biller, 1976) suggests it may also

influence children's views of parents. The picture regarding the effect of
maternal employment is clearer. Hoffman's (1974, pp. 206-208) review
of the literature led her to conclude that children with employed mothers
see mothers and fathers as more similar than do children of nonworking
mothers. This conclusion has been supported by subsequent research
(e.g., Gold & Andres, 1978). Recent studies also indicate that children
whose mothers are employed outside the home are also lower in sex
stereotyping, that is, they attribute similar personality attributes to
women and men (e.g., Marantz & Mansfield, 1977). Thus, it appears
that maternal employment has a significant influence on how mothers
and fathers, and the sexes more generally, are perceived.

Many studies have assessed the knowledge children have about play
and work activities associated with females or males. All of these studies
begin by having adults judge the sex appropriateness of various activities; children's choices are then compared with this standard. Using a
modified form of the It Scale for Children (Brown, 1956), preschool
children score about 75% correct and six-year-old boys score 100% (cf.
Horance, 1977). Using specially developed measures, Thompson (1975)
and Kuhn et al. (1978) found that children as young as two years old had
considerable knowledge about sex-linked activities. For example,
Thompson found that subjects 24 months of age scored 61% correct in
linking toys, tools, appliances, and so on with boy/man pictures or
girl/woman pictures and that this value increased to 78% and 86% at 30
and 36 months of age. The accumulated evidence suggests that children
very early link certain activities and objects to one sex or the other and
that by the time they enter school, most children score at or near an adult
criterion.

Several questions remain, however. First, how early does this process
begin? We suspect that children are learning quite a bit in the first year,
but this remains to be demonstrated. Second, what exactly is the child
learning? Most studies have simply computed a single "knowledge"
score. It would be useful to break this down into components (e.g., adult
male work activities and boy play activities) and assess when each
component is learned. Third, how are the various components learned?
It may be, for example, that typical boy-girl activities are learned quite
early and that the way parents "structure" the child's environment is
central to this process. This conjecture is based on the consistent finding
that parents dress their children differently and buy them different types
of toys (Maccoby & Jacklin, 1974). Fourth, what is the meaning of
preschool children's high knowledge scores? There is reason to suspect

that these scores do not mean that preschoolers are simply "miniature adults." For example, young children often explain their choices by saying, "I like to play with it," while older children will say, "most boys do _____."
Thus, it may be that young children know less about boys and girls than about what they themselves do and do not do (see Kohlberg, 1966). Distinguishing between actual knowledge and high knowledge scores by preschoolers due to egocentric responding is a priority task for this type of research. And finally, what are the other beliefs children have about the behaviors of boys/men and girls/women? To date, only behaviors consistent with adult notions of sex roles have been considered. What, from the child's perspective, are the activities in which the sexes engage?

The final type of "sex learning," beliefs about the personality characteristics of the sexes, is the most similar to the bulk of work done with adults. This area of research has a long history (see Smith, 1939, for a very ambitious early study) and there is currently quite a bit of activity. With few exceptions (e.g., Kuhn et al., 1978; Flerx et al., 1976), most studies have involved school-age children. The most concerted attempt to track the development of children's beliefs about the sexes has been made by Williams and his colleagues. They began by developing a picture-story measure, the Sex Stereotype Measure, "to assess children's knowledge of adult-defined, conventional, sex-trait stereotypes" (Williams et al., Note 1, p. 1).

Only the highlights of research with the Sex Stereotype Measure (SSM) can be presented here. First, five-year-old children have considerable knowledge of conventional adult sex stereotypes, that is, they score above chance on both female and male items. Second, for white children there is a steep increase in knowledge from ages 5 to 9 to 11 and a gradual increase from 11 to 15, with 15-year-olds scoring slightly below college students. Third, from 5 to 13 years of age, children score higher on knowledge of the male stereotype than of the female stereotype. And, it is the Potency component of the male stereotype that children acquire earliest. At age 5, the trait on which children score "best" (in terms of adults' standards) is "strong," with over 90% linking this to males. The next highest knowledge is for "aggressive-assertive" (94% male in one study and 78% male in a second). It is important to note that the frequently discussed male-as-competent stereotype is not very salient for children. For example, "logical-rational" is linked to males by 67% of 5-year-old boys, 66% of 8-year-old boys, and 54% of 11-year-old boys.

Research with the SSM has also suggested sex differences in knowledge of cultural sex stereotypes.[3] While the scores of female and male

subjects correlate quite well at 8 (.76) and 11 (.75), the correlation is only
.40 at age 5. Silvern (1977), using fourth- and sixth-grade subjects, also
found marked differences between the sex stereotypic conceptions of
boys and girls. In fact, there was agreement on only 8 of 26 items (boys
were seen as "mean," "rough," "adventurous," "fights," and "brave";
girls were viewed as "weak" and "neat"). These findings suggest that
careful attention should be paid to sex differences in children's beliefs
about the sexes.

Much of the research on recognition of play/work activities as sex-
linked and beliefs about the personality traits of the sexes has been
implicitly guided by the assumptions of the sociocultural approach (see
below). Children are given activities (e.g., ironing) or personality traits
(e.g., "aggressive") *that adults (usually college students) agree are sex-
linked* and are asked to indicate whether the activities or traits are more
characteristic of boys/men or girls/women. To the degree that the
children agree with the adults' responses, they are said to have knowledge of cultural sex stereotypes. While this is a useful strategy, it should
not be the only approach to assessing what children believe about the
sexes. We suggest that greater attention be given to children's own
language for describing (and, presumably, thinking about) people and
to assessing the cognitive structures used by children to organize their
beliefs about boys/men and girls/women. Building on an implicit personality theory conceptualization of sex stereotypes (cf. Ashmore & Del
Boca, 1979), Champagne (Note 2) used a three-step procedure to
uncover children's cognitive structures associated with sex of person
perceived. First, a children's vocabulary was derived by identifying
words and phrases frequently used by children in open-ended descriptions of a variety of target persons. Second, an independent sample of
children used this vocabulary to describe people they knew. This provided an index of psychological similarity between all possible pairs of
personality descriptors. Finally, the distance measures were subjected to
multidimensional scaling analysis. For all the subject samples (boys and
girls in the 6th, 9th, and 12th grades), there was a clear sex of target
dimension with females more often described in terms of "soft" qualities
(e.g., "lovable") and males associated with "hard" personality characteristics (e.g., "strong"). This pattern is consistent both with the "sex
learnings" discussed above and with research with adults on sex as a
factor in implicit personality theory (cf. Ashmore, in press). Most sex
stereotype assessment studies have employed college student samples.
Broverman and her colleagues (Broverman et al., 1972) report one of the

few investigations of sex stereotypes across various age groups in adult-hood. They compared the responses to the Sex Role Stereotype Ques-tionnaire of three age groups (i.e., 17-24 years, 25-44 years, and 45-56 years) and found a great deal of agreement across the groups. While this research does demonstrate "consensus" across age, we do not regard the possibility of important changes in sex stereotypes in adulthood as foreclosed. This is a possibility deserving more research attention and we suggest that such research should seek to relate stereotypic concep-tions of the sexes not just to chronological age but also to significant "stages" in the life course.

One purpose of this section was to raise questions that might guide research on sex stereotypes through the life cycle. We close by suggest-ing that such work be undertaken with more attention to psychometric and methodological considerations than has been the case to date. The reliability and validity of measuring devices are seldom tested (cf. Beere, 1979, pp. 164-167). Further, there has been an almost exclusive reliance on self-report measures with very little concern with how conscious and nonconscious factors may distort subjects' responses. While distortions such as social desirability responding seem an obvious consideration in work with adults, we believe that children may be quite able to discern the purpose of many instruments in current use and also able to regulate their responses in order to present a particular view of themselves. If so, investigators concerned with sex stereotypes at all points in the life course (not just adulthood) will have to develop less reactive measures.

ORIENTATIONS TO THE STUDY OF STEREOTYPES

Elsewhere (Ashmore & Del Boca, in press) we have identified three basic approaches to the study of stereotypes: sociocultural, psychody-namic, and cognitive. In this section, each of these orientations will be discussed in terms of its implications for sex stereotype acquisition and change. It is important to note at the outset that these are not "theories"; rather, they are perspectives or frames of reference that guide, often quite implicitly, the conduct of research.

The Sociocultural Orientation

For those adopting the sociocultural orientation, stereotypes (here, cultural stereotypes or widely shared beliefs regarding the characteris-tics of social groups) are viewed as part of a society's nonmaterial culture. According to this perspective, individuals are socialized into a particular culture and, through social rewards and punishments, led to accept (i.e., act in accordance with and internalize) prevailing norms and values. Beliefs about social groups are acquired as part of the socialization process.

The recent upswing in sex stereotype research involves an almost total (though frequently implicit) commitment to the sociocultural orientation: Sex stereotypes are assumed to be part of the same cultural pattern that specifies sex roles and sex-role standards. Two points illustrate this commitment. First, most definitions of the term *sex stereotype* that appear in the literature include the notion of consensus (cf. Ashmore & Del Boca, 1979, pp. 221-223). And second, most sex stereotype research to data has been solely or primarily concerned with documenting the pervasiveness of stereotypic conceptions of females and males in American culture.

Two kinds of research have dominated the sex stereotype literature. The aim of the first type has generally been to assess the extent of agreement regarding sex differences in personality within a particular group of perceivers. Participants in such studies are usually required to describe "women" and "men" or the typical adult versions of each (e.g., the "typical adult male") using an adjective checklist (e.g., Williams & Bennett, 1975) or rating scale format (e.g., Rosenkrantz et al., 1968). While a wide variety of perceiver groups have been employed in sex stereotype assessment research, college students are clearly the most often studied and mental health professionals (e.g., psychotherapists and counselors) probably the next most popular population (see Whitley, 1979, for a review). Often implicit in this first type of research is the assumption that there is a single set of sex stereotypes in American culture and that the chief task of the investigator is to ascertain the degree to which different segments of the population endorse this cultural standard. Certainly cultural patterns of belief regarding the sexes exist and are potent factors in shaping the course of female-male relations. However, the rise of conflict theories in sociology (cf. Ashmore & Del Boca, in press) and cognitive approaches in anthropology (cf. Burton & Kirk, Note 3) suggests that even in those disciplines most concerned with a cultural level of analysis, there is growing recognition of the diversity within cultures and the need to systematically explore such variation. Thus, it seems likely that current approaches to sex stereotype assessment may overlook important subcultural differences in beliefs regarding females and males.

The second popular line of sex stereotype research involves content analysis of various aspects of the cultural environment (e.g., school materials and mass media). Although literally hundreds of investigations of this type have been conducted, a disproportionate number are concerned with media portrayals of the sexes (cf. Gordon & Verna, 1978). Within this domain, a wide variety of materials have been analyzed, ranging from Sunday comic strips (Brabant, 1976) to television commercials (e.g., McArthur & Resko, 1975). The most consistent finding to emerge from these studies is that, relative to men, women are underrepresented numerically. When they do appear in the media, women tend to occupy traditional roles. In contrast to males who are presented as powerful and rational, females tend to be portrayed as attractive, warm, happy, and as victims of aggression. Not all studies, however, obtain such results. Analyses of daytime television serials, for example, tend to find the sexes on more equal terms (see Liebert & Schwartzberg, 1977).

As the preceding overview suggests, the sociocultural orientation has stimulated a large volume of research dealing with sex stereotypes. Very little attention, however, has been devoted to the mechanisms which underlie the cultural transmission of sex stereotypes. On the one hand, there is an abundance of research focusing on the "causes" of stereotypes (e.g., content analyses of the media) and, on the other, a large quantity of research dealing with "effects" (e.g., sex stereotype assessment studies). However, just how cultural portrayals of the sexes become translated into the beliefs that individual perceivers hold regarding women and men is presently unclear.

It seems likely that sex stereotype acquisition and change involve a complex interplay of intra- and interpersonal processes. Existing research points to a wide variety of materials (e.g., textbooks, movies, and television commercials) that are potentially important sources of information regarding women and men. Although generally neglected by sex stereotype researchers, agents of socialization other than the mass media—family, peers, and teachers—undoubtedly play a significant role in the transmission of sex stereotypes.[4] A life-span developmental perspective suggests that various channels of socialization may be differentially influential at different stages of development. It is likely that parents are most important early on, that peers and schools are particularly significant during childhood and adolescence, and that the mass media exerts a continuing influence throughout the life course.

Although the manner in which these different aspects of the sociocultural environment shape perceptions of the sexes has not been addressed directly, several lines of investigation are potentially relevant. For example, it seems clear that any adequate explanation of the role of the mass media in sex stereotype development and change will have to consider the cognitive mechanisms that direct attention to, and interpretation of, gender-relevant information in media portrayals. There is a large literature in cognitive psychology on text comprehension (cf. Paris, 1975) and a small but growing body of findings on the processing of audiovisual narratives (e.g., Collins et al., 1978) that might be applied to the question of how children acquire beliefs about females and males from the print and film media, respectively. With regard to the potential role of parents in "teaching" sex stereotypes, there is also suggestive research. For example, several writers (cf. Matteson, 1975, pp. 63-70) have proposed that children, particularly girls, learn to behave appropriately vis-à-vis the opposite sex through interaction with the opposite-sex parent. This raises the intriguing possibility that children may acquire some significant part of the "sexual" component of the stereotype of the opposite sex directly from one parent. This possibility remains to be tested.

In addition to highlighting the socialization process, the sociocultural perspective points to groups and intergroup relations as important factors for understanding sex stereotypes through the life cycle. First, females and males constitute significant social categories and these categories are accorded differential status. Thus, the analysis of sex stereotypes cannot ignore either the individual-level (e.g., sex-role attitudes and prejudice against women) or societal-level (e.g., institutional arrangements that discriminate on the basis of sex) concomitants of this status differential. Second, individuals interact with one another in the context of groups (e.g., family, peer group, classroom group, and work group) and the nature and significance of different groups varies through the life course. For example, preschool children's earliest play groups are generally not segregated by sex while those of grade-school children are; and, boys in middle childhood tend to play in larger groups than girls and to form more stable status hierarchies (cf. Maccoby & Jacklin, 1974, pp. 210, 256-257). A sizable literature in social psychology concerns the effects of group size and heterogeneity, norms and status characteristics, as well as intergroup factors such as cooperation and competition, on how groups and individual members of groups are perceived (cf. Austin & Worchel, 1979). One promising avenue of investigation is the application of these research findings and related conceptualizations to understanding how the structural aspects of social groups and intergroup relations shape the nature of individual and collective beliefs about the sexes.

The Psychodynamic Orientation

The central tenet of the psychodynamic orientation is that beliefs regarding social categories derive from and function in the service of deep-rooted personality needs. Historically, psychodynamic writers have been more interested in the underlying sources of hostility directed against various groups than in the content of beliefs about these groups. In the area of ethnic prejudice, derogatory stereotypic beliefs have most often been regarded as justifications for antipathy toward a particular group (cf. Ashmore & Del Boca, in press). The issue of female devaluation has generated two quite different interpretations. The classic Freudian viewpoint traces negative views of women to their anatomical deficiency (i.e., they have no penises). However, a number of psychodynamically oriented writers have rejected what they term the "phallocentric" argument in favor of alternative explanations. While several somewhat different theories have been advanced, these explanations tend to share a common theme: Actual and perceived differences between the sexes are significantly colored by the dominant role played by women in child care. (See Stockard & Johnson, 1979, for a review.)

Perhaps the most popular current variation on this theme is presented by Dinnerstein (1976). According to this author, the child's earliest experience of female is with the mother, a being who is perceived not as a separate human but, given present sexual arrangements, as a monolithic, omnipotent source of distress as well as pleasure. One consequence of this early experience is that women come to be regarded as not quite human. In Dinnerstein's words, "femaleness comes to be the name for, the embodiment of, these global and inchoate and all-embracing qualities, qualities very hard indeed to reconcile with personness" (p. 93). Lerner (1974) has specified in some detail the implications that the child's early experience with an all-powerful mother has for subsequent beliefs regarding women and men. Essentially, sex stereotypes are thought to reflect a *defensive reversal* of the early dependency relationship with the mother: "the desirable 'feminine' woman is one who embodies all aspects of the good mother (e.g., cleaning, feeding, providing emotional understanding, comfort, softness, warmth), but who possesses no elements of power, dominance, and control that are also factors within the imago of the omnipotent, envied mother" (p. 543).

While such explanations for perceptions of the sexes are provocative, they are, like other psychodynamic formulations, difficult to test empirically since they seldom lead to unambiguous predictions. Thus, there is at present little directly relevant evidence by which to evaluate them. Despite this drawback, however, the psychodynamic perspective highlights two facets of human experience that are relatively neglected by the sociocultural and cognitive approaches: affect and motivation. To date most sex stereotype research (and stereotype research more generally) has focused solely on the individual's cold cognitions (e.g., beliefs regarding traits or interests) with respect to social categories. As noted above, we believe that the feelings characteristically associated with particular groups should be regarded as elements of stereotypes. Here we will simply add that significant social groups arouse affect, that this affect is differentiated (not just positive-negative but also "joy," "interest," and so on plus "fear," "disgust," and so on) and that such differentiated affect is likely to have some bearing on the development and change of beliefs regarding the characteristics of such groups.

Stereotypes are also likely to be influenced by motivational factors. The potential importance of sexual motivation has been strongly emphasized in psychoanalytic theory. Humans are sexual beings and it seems to us that sexuality and sex stereotypes are related phenomena. (While this seems an obvious observation, the literatures on these two topics seldom make contact with one another.) Biologically based sources of motivation, however, are not the only ones recognized by psychodynamic writers. Erikson, Sullivan, and others have stressed the social nature of (wo)man. For us, the psychodynamic emphasis on motivation raises the question of how the immediate and long-range goals and purposes of the individual shape the number and content of gender-related social categorizations at various points in the life cycle. For example, the school-age boy is likely to have a simple and undifferentiated view of females (at least of his own age-mates) as a group of outsiders that is "not much fun to be around." The typical male college student, on the other hand, probably has a very different, more elaborated view of his female peers and welcomes opportunities for mixed-sex interaction.

The Cognitive Orientation

A major assumption underlying the cognitive orientation to the study of stereotypes is that beliefs regarding social groups are similar to the cognitions individuals hold about nonsocial objects. Thus, stereotypes are viewed as "normal" (albeit not necessarily desirable) rather than aberrant psychological phenomena. In recent years this perspective has attracted an increasing number of proponents, and it has stimulated a growing body of research in social psychology dealing with the effects of cognitive schemata (like stereotypes) on social information processing. Many studies have demonstrated the effects of what are assumed to be cognitively represented social categories on the encoding and retrieval of information about exemplars of such categories (cf. Hamilton, in press). Little of this research has dealt directly with sex stereotypes (see, however, Borgida et al., in press).

Developmental psychologists who adopt a cognitive orientation have, however, been concerned with sex stereotypes. Two different lines of inquiry can be distinguished. First, the concept of sex stereotypes has been central to cognitive-developmental theories of sex-role acquisition (i.e., Kagan, 1964; Kohlberg, 1966). As noted earlier, even though sex stereotypes figure prominently in such theories, little empirical work on stereotypes has been generated by these models. Second, there is an accumulating body of research using children as subjects that parallels the work currently being done by cognitive social psychologists with adults. Such studies examine the effects of traditional sex stereotypes on attention and recall. Because this line of research is still in its infancy, conclusions must be stated tentatively. The evidence that is available suggests that children do not selectively attend to same-sex models (Bryan & Luria, 1978). They do, however, appear to show better recall for depictions of actors performing sex-appropriate, as opposed to sex-inappropriate, behavior, and this tendency is more pronounced for male targets (e.g., Liben & Signorella, 1980).

Most of the empirical work on stereotypes that has been guided by the cognitive perspective has been process-oriented. This emphasis on process redresses a shortcoming of stereotype research that has persisted through the decades (cf. Ashmore & Del Boca, in press). Researchers adopting a cognitive orientation have focused on explicating the nature of cognitive biases that *result from* holding stereotypes (cf. Hamilton, 1979, pp. 64-76). (In most studies, the existence of stereotypes, or similar cognitive structures, has simply been assumed.) While this research helps us to understand how stereotypes are maintained, particularly in the face of stereotype-discrepant information, the question of how the developing child acquires a set of beliefs about the sexes remains to be addressed. (There is, however research with college students that demonstrates the existence of cognitive biases that might be implicated in the formation of stereotypes, cf. Hamilton, 1979, pp. 55-64.)

The cognitive orientation also raises an important question regarding the content of stereotypes: How are beliefs about social categories (including the sexes) cognitively organized? Extensive research in cognitive psychology indicates that there are three characteristics of a category concept: "(1) its central tendency or prototype; (2) the dimensions along which its members differ; and (3) the degree of variability among the category members" (Glass et al., 1979, p. 344). The sex stereotype assessment procedures generated by the sociocultural orientation focus on one of these characteristics. In describing typical instances of categories such as "the typical adult male" (e.g., Rosenkrantz et al., 1968) or "the typical female college student" (e.g., Spence et al., 1974), respondents provide information about category prototypes. However, the notion of dimensions along which category members differ raises the possibility that perceivers may perceptually distinguish different "types" of women (e.g., "liberated woman") and men (e.g., "male chauvinist pig"). It suggests further that gender-relevant classifications in such a typological schema are organized in terms of Sex X Dimension subcategories. The question of variablity implies that there may be individual differences in the "compactness" of stereotypic conceptions of the sexes. It is likely that developmental changes occur in terms of all three category characteristics and future research efforts should explore this possibility.

A life-span perspective suggests that age is one important dimension along with females and males are perceived to vary. That is, it seems probable that perceivers partition the social environment into Sex x Age subcategories (e.g., "little old lady in tennis shoes" and "dirty old man"). To date, research has focused either on stereotypes regarding women and men or on beliefs about various age groups, particularly the elderly (cf. McTavish, 1971). A more complete understanding of how beliefs regarding females and males are cognitively organized requires that age and sex be considered concurrently.

Dimensions other than age are also likely to interact with sex to "define" types of women and men. We would predict that the salience of these dimensions will be related to the individual's goals and purposes and that such goals and purposes vary through the life cycle. For example, young adults are likely to differentiate the social categories female and male in terms of dimensions relevant to heterosexual intimacy, dimensions such as career and family plans (e.g., "career woman" and "confirmed bachelor"), physical attractiveness (e.g., "fox" and "hunk"), and sexual activity (e.g., "loose woman" and "skirt chaser").

SEX STEREOTYPES AND MODELS OF
INDIVIDUAL DEVELOPMENT

The basic assumption of this section is that social scientific understand-ing of sex stereotypes would benefit from a consideration of individual development through the life cycle. Since extant knowledge regarding sex stereotype acquisition and change is limited, the intent is to suggest questions for research rather than to delineate a life-span developmental theory of sex stereotypes. In so doing, we will draw primarily on the models of individual development presented in Table 1.[5]

Sex Stereotypes: A Life-Span Perspective

In recent years the use of life-span developmental frameworks in the analysis of human experience has proliferated. Most such formulations describe the nature of changes that occur as individuals pass through various age categories and identify transition points, often referred to as "crises" or "conflicts," that require some degree of psychological adap-tation for resolution. While the demarcations proposed by various writers are neither standard nor validated empirically, there is wide consensus that significant changes in personality and behavior are not restricted to childhood and adolescence, that developmental change occurs throughout the life course. It is our contention that such change is likely to have significant implications for perceptions of the sexes.

The first step in developing a life-span approach to the study of sex stereotypes is to identify those points in the life cycle where changes occur that might logically be related to sex stereotype acquisition and change. Table 1 includes two different developmental frameworks that take the individual from the cradle to old age: Erikson's (1959) stage theory of personality development and Katz's (1979) model of female sex-role development. Erikson delineates the major, near-universal, psychosocial crises of life, while Katz deals with a more delimited domain and gives greater emphasis to specific biological and role changes that women and men encounter through the life course. The intent in presenting these two models is to illustrate the variety and nature of life experiences that might influence how the sexes are per-ceived. Consideration of other life-span developmental conceptualiza-tions will be necessary for complete understanding of sex stereotypes through the life cycle.

In formulating a framework to guide research on the development and change of beliefs regarding females and males, it is not sufficient to

(text continued on p. 183)

TABLE 1
Toward a Life-Cycle Framework for Sex Stereotypes

Life Stage (Approximate Chronological Age)	Psychoanalytic Perspective[a] Psychosocial Crisis (Stage)	Cognitive Developmental Perspective[b] Kohlberg	Ullian	Female Sex-Role Development[c] Level of Sex Role	Central Acquisition Tasks	Development of Person Perception[d]
Infancy (0-2 years)	Trust vs. mistrust			Level I: Learning of appropriate child sex roles	Discrimination of males and females / Correct categorization of self	
		Acquiring gender identity: learn own gender label (2-3 years)				
	Autonomy vs. shame and doubt					
Preschool (2-6 years)	Initiative vs. guilt	Gender labeling of others: label gender by general physical criteria (3-4 years)			Learning content of sex roles / Acquiring gender constancy	
		Acquiring sex-role stereotypes: male = "Power and prestige," "aggression and exposure to danger;" female = "Nurturance and child care" (p. 99). (5-6 years)				

Table 1 (Continued)

Life Stage (Approximate Chronological Age)	Psychoanalytic Perspective[a] Psychosocial Crisis (Stage)	Cognitive Developmental Perspective[b] Kohlberg	Female Sex-Role Development[c]			Development of Person Perception[d]
			Ullian	Level of Sex Role	Central Acquisition Tasks	
Grade School (6-12 years)	Industry vs. Inferiority	Moralizing sex-role stereotypes (5-8 years)	Biological orientation (1) M-F traits based on bodily differences (6 years) (2) M-F traits independent of bodily features (8 years) Societal orientation (3) M-F traits inherent in social roles and are immutable (10 years)		Elaboration of child sex-role content Development of strong same-sex friendships	Absolute invariance: Egocentrism, inability to decentre, syncretic thought Intermediate stage: Describes target in terms of multiple features of behavior, uses more extended time frame, and makes less reference to concrete factors (8-12 years)
Early Adolescence (12-15 years)	Identity vs. role confusion		(4) M-F traits due to arbitrary historical and social forces (12 years)	Level II: Preparation for adult sex roles	Adjustment to puberty and sexuality (e.g., body changes, sexual feelings); concern with physical attractiveness	Integrated invariance: Behavior is seen as "lawful"

Table 1 (Continued)

Life Stage (Approximate Chronological Age)	Psychoanalytic Perspective[a] Psychosocial Crisis (Stage)	Cognitive Developmental Perspective[b]		Female Sex-Role Development[c]		Development of Person Perception[d]
		Kohlberg	Ullian	Level of Sex Role	Central Acquisition Tasks	
Late Adolescence (15-19 years)			Psychological orientation (5) M-F traits based on psychological identity (14-16 years) (6) M-F independent of traditional roles (18 years)		Concern with sexual behavior, intimacy, and role conflicts (e.g., combining vocation with marriage); decreased academic interest	
Young Adulthood (20-35 years)	Intimacy vs. isolation			Level III: Development of adult sex roles	Concern with occupation, marriage, and possibly pregnancy and child care	
Middle Adulthood (35-50 years)	Generativity vs. stagnation				Adjustment to changes in marriage and/or child care responsibilities; adjustment to feelings of loss of youth; possibly developing vocation	
Late Adulthood	Ego integrity vs. despair				Adjustment to physical and other late-life changes (e.g., retirement)	

a. Adapted from Erikson (1959).
b. Derived from Kohlberg (1966) and Ullian (1976).
c. Adapted from Katz (1979, pp. 162-163).
d. Derived from Livesley and Bromley (1973).

identify points of transition and their associated changes in terms of sex stereotype content and organization. Such a framework will also have to consider what actually accounts for developmental change, that is, the factors that combine to instigate crises and restore equilibrium. Quite likely, different factors have differential impact at various phases in the life cycle. Biological change—maturation and, later, debilitation—is a significant factor at the two "ends" of the life continuum. Social norms relating to age and gender probably play their strongest role during interim periods. In addition, situational constraints also influence the timing of life events that shape perceptions of the sexes.

In considering the effects of life events on sex stereotypes, two points should be noted. First, there is considerable variability among individuals in terms of the ages at which various adaptive tasks are confronted. Further, the sequencing of such adaptations is not invariant and not all individuals experience the same set of life events. Thus, chronological age is probably not a totally adequate index for transition points in the life cycle. (A number of aspects of development are, however, closely tied to chronological age. For example, most children in American society attend school between the ages of 6 and 16.) Second, individuals do not simply react to life events. Rather, they actively participate in creating their own experience. Marriage, for example, is not something that simply "happens" to people and requires them to react. Instead, individuals choose if, when, and who they will marry. Thus, the life course of an individual is marked by considerable continuity as well as by significant discontinuities and this consistency is very much a result of the individual's own purposes and goals. Future research efforts might be directed at investigating developmental change and individual continuity, as well as the important personal concerns of individuals, that condition the processes of assimilation and accommodation through the life cycle.

Sex Stereotypes and Sex-Role Development

Although very little attention has been devoted to the topic of sex stereotype acquisition and change, a number of models of sex-role development have been proposed. These formulations represent a variety of perspectives; in fact, each of the three orientations discussed above is associated with its own general theory of sex-role learning (cf. Frieze et al., 1978). Because stereotypes are here conceptualized as cognitive structures, we have chosen to focus on frameworks developed by proponents of the cognitive orientation. The two models of sex-role acquisition presented in Table 1 are based on Piagetian theory. Kohlberg (1966) focuses on early development, while Ullian (1976) deals with childhood and adolescence. According to Kohlberg, children's earliest conceptions of females and males derive, in large part, from perceived sex differences in physical size and strength. Ullian (1976) proposes that at a later age (approximately 10 years) the child's sex-role concepts shift away from a biologically based view of the sexes to a "social orientation" where sex differences are understood to be a product of differing role requirements. Still later (between the ages of 14 and 18), individuals may transcend their earlier conceptions: Behavioral sex differences are acknowledged but they are not regarded as optimal.

Cognitive-developmental theories of sex-role learning underscore three aspects of development which are central to understanding sex stereotype acquisition. First, such formulations suggest that the manner in which the child cognitively structures information about females and males will be constrained by the cognitive capabilities that exist at various stages of development. One would not expect, for example, to find the same conceptions of the sexes in the preoperational and the concrete operational child. From a Piagetian perspective, differences across cognitive stages in beliefs about the sexes would be less likely in terms of content (though such differences are not precluded) than in the organization of the content and the reasoning used by the child to arrive at the beliefs.[6] This suggests that the direct self-report methods most often used in sex stereotype research may underestimate developmental changes by not tapping cognitive organization or underlying reasoning processes.

Second, these models direct attention to the potential importance of physical cues in the early development of stereotypes. In particular, Kohlberg has hypothesized that, from the preoperational child's perspective, size differentials between the sexes connote differences in power which become translated into beliefs regarding sex differences in personality. Since this hypothesis is consistent with findings that the social categories female and male covary with the Potency dimension in implicit personality theory research (see Ashmore, in press), we feel that it warrants an empirical test.

Third, cognitive-developmental theorists concerned with sex-role development agree that beliefs regarding the characteristics of the sexes are closely related to gender identity. Very little research, however, has been directed at explicating the nature of the relationship between these constructs. Most theoretical (e.g., Kohlberg, 1966) and empirical (e.g., Storms, 1979) work has focused on the effect of cultural sex stereotypes on the self-concept. We would argue further that self-conceptions shape beliefs about the sexes through the life span. Some cognitive social psychologists have begun to study the influence of self-schemata on social information processing in adult perceivers (e.g., Markus, 1977). The nature of the interplay involved in forming concepts about self and significant social categories in the developing child, however, has yet to be investigated.

Although we have focused here on cognitive-developmental theories of sex-role acquisition, it should be noted that there is growing awareness that adequate models of human development require the inclusion of mechanisms derived from differing perspectives. (Constantinople, 1979, presents an excellent example of such a formulation in an analysis of sex-role development that includes both cognitive and social learning mechanisms.) Further, we view sex-role development as a lifelong process. While this is not evident in the Kohlberg and Ullian formulations, it is central to the model of gender identity proposed by Katz (see Table 1).

Sex Stereotypes and Person Perception

While the overwhelming majority of person perception studies involve college student subjects, there is a growing body of research relevant to what Livesley and Bromley (1973) term the "developmental psychology of person perception." (See Chandler, 1976, especially pp. 100-107, and Livesley & Bromley, 1973, especially chapter 4, for reviews.) The most common procedure in such research is to ask children to describe individuals (e.g., "a girl [you] know very well and like") and then content analyze these descriptions. The results of these studies are consistent in indicating that with increasing age, children's descriptions—and presumably also their "perceptions"[7]—of others become less egocentric (younger more often than older children describe how the target behaves toward them) and more inferential (younger children seldom, while older children often, describe the target's traits and other psychological qualities) as well as more organized and differentiated. The following are two examples from Livesley and Bromley (1973): "Max sits next to me, his eyes are hazel and he is tall. He hasn't got a very big head, and he's got a big pointed nose" (a girl aged 7 years 6 months; p. 213); "She is very kind and friendly. She is always very sensible and willing to help people. Sometimes she gets a bit cross but that doesn't last long and soon she is her normal self" (a girl aged 14 years 4 months; p. 222).

While the research that has been done is often couched in terms of the developmental theories of Piaget and Werner, no formal model of the development of person perception has been proposed. However, Livesley and Bromley (1973, especially chapter 11) have sketched a "proto-theory" in which they identify three steps in children's development of thinking about persons. These are listed in the far right-hand column of Table 1. As can be seen, the steps proposed are *roughly* tied to Piagetian stages of cognitive development: "absolute invariance" with preoperational, the "intermediate stage" with concrete operational, and "integrated invariance" with formal operations. A critical task for researchers concerned with "developmental person perception" is the explicit relating of thinking about persons to more general theories of development. Another important task is suggested by inspection of Table 1. The Livesley and Bromley (1973) "proto-theory" only covers the age range from 7 to 15, which is roughly the age range involved in most research on this topic. A life-span developmental psychology of person perception will require attention to preschool children and adults beyond college age (see Bromley, 1978, on the latter point).

What are the implications of work on the development of person perception for understanding stereotype acquisition and change? We believe they are considerable and pose the following questions as examples: Does the egocentrism of the early school-age child influence his or her beliefs about the sexes as well as reflect itself in descriptions of specific others? (Perhaps "women" and "men" and also "boys" and "girls" are viewed by the young child largely in terms of whether they help or hinder the child.) Are social groups described (and thought about) in the same way as individuals and do the age trends obtained with descriptions of individuals apply also to social groups? (Livesley and Bromley, 1973, found that males were described by children more extensively than females and that this difference increased with age.)

CONCLUDING REMARKS

We conclude with one cautionary note and a brief discussion of two implications of the present life-span developmental approach to sex stereotypes. The caution: Developmental change must be separated from generational change (see also Emmerich, 1973, regarding sex-role development and historical change and Baltes et al., 1977, for a more general discussion of this point). There is reason to suspect that important secular changes are occurring in beliefs about the sexes. One obvious factor in such change is the Women's Liberation Movement. A somewhat less obvious, but possibly quite significant, factor is the alteration in the life circumstances of women and men. These change are apparent with regard to the high and increasing levels of female employment outside the home. Recent trends in the employment of mothers of young children is particularly striking. In 1979, 40.9% of mothers with children under age three were employed (cf. Fosburg, Note 4). This figure is up from 28% in 1971 and is put into perspective by noting that in 1950 only 20% of mothers with children under the age of *18* had jobs outside the home. The present and future trends in women's employment are likely to directly influence how the sexes are perceived. Further, they may indirectly shape sex stereotypes by transforming the family (see Hoffman, 1974), child-care arrangements (see Fosburg, Note 4), and the workplace itself.

While cross-sectional research predominates, developmental psychologists concerned with changes over the life-span have devised a number of designs and methods of analysis more suitable to partitioning developmental from historical or generational change. These sequential reearch methodologies (Baltes et al., 1977) would be helpful in the study of sex stereotypes through the life course. In addition, the recent advances in methods for extracting causal evidence from correlational data may be fruitfully applied to the question of why and how beliefs about the sexes vary throughout the life cycle. (Though not concerned with sex stereotypes or life-span development, Bentler and Speckart's, 1979, study is an example of such research.)

A life-span approach to sex stereotypes raises the broader question, what is the proper domain of social psychology? To date most sex stereotype researchers, social psychologists included, have investigated stereotypic conceptions held by perceivers of a single age group (generally 18 to 22 years old). Here we have implied that social psychologists should study how beliefs about the sexes are acquired, maintained, and altered as the individual moves through the life cycle. In so doing we have also implied a change in the definition of "social psychology." We close by making this point explicit: Social psychology is the study of the thoughts, feelings, and behavior of the individual in a social context *and of the development of the individual as a social being.* This does not entail the annexation of the field of "developmental psychology." Rather, it is suggested that we seriously reconsider the vision held by

Gardner and Lois Murphy in the 1930s: "Social psychology overlaps both child psychology and psychology of personality. Social psychology is the study of the way in which the individual becomes a member of, and functions in, a social group" (Murphy et al., 1937, p. 16).

NOTES

1. In this article we will use both "sex"and "gender" to refer to the socially defined categories female and male. See Unger (1979) for suggested distinctions regarding these terms.

2. It is not necessarily the case, however, that children so categorize their parents. Children may have a very speical one-person category, "my mother," and another, "my father," and these may transcend other possible categorizations of their parents (e.g., "adult" and "female/male"). Thus, perceptions of parents may not always be closely tied to beliefs about the sexes.

3. Williams et al. (Note 1) also have evidence of differences between white and Black children. Thus, Black children may be learning a somewhat different set of beliefs about the sexes than majority-group children and this raises the question of subcultural variation in sex stereotype content.

4. Studies which have examined the practices of parents and other socializing agents have been concerned with the socialization of behavioral sex differences and sex-role learning rather than with the teaching of sex stereotypes.

5. Table 1 should also include a column depicting the development of sex-role attitudes. Although no such formulation is presently available, Katz's (1976) description of racial attitude acquisition provides an example of the type of model we have in mind.

6. Unfortunately for those concerned with life-span development, Piaget's theory fails to consider the possibility of significant cognitive shifts subsequent to the acquisition of formal operations in early adolescence. However, Riegel (1973) has proposed a fifth stage of cognitive development, termed "dialectical operations."

7. This presumption is, of course, problematic. The use of verbal self-report descriptions as the sole measure of "perceptions of persons" confounds such perceptions with verbal skill (cf. Chandler, 1976, especially p. 102) and with various self-presentation strategies (e.g., social desirability responding).

REFERENCE NOTES

1. Williams, J. E., Best, D. L., & Davis, S. W. *Sex stereotype measure II (SSM II) technical report.* Wake Forest University, 1977.

2. Champagne, B. M. *Sex as a factor in adolescents' perceptions of others.* Unpublished master's thesis, Rutgers—The State University, 1977.

3. Burton, M. L. & Kirk, L. *Sex differences in Maasai cognition of personality and social identity.* Unpublished manuscript, no date.

4. Fosburg, S. *Family day care: The role of the surrogate mother.* Presented at the conference, "The Family as a Learning Environment," Educational Testing Service, Princeton, N.J., November 1979.

REFERENCES

Ashmore, R. D. Sex stereotypes and implicit personality theory. In D. L. Hamilton (ed.), *Cognitive processes in stereotyping and intergroup behavior.* Hillsdale, N.J.: Erlbaum, in press.

Ashmore, R. D. & Del Boca, F. K. Sex stereotypes and implicit personality theory: Toward a cognitive-social psychological conceptualization. *Sex Roles,* 1979, *5,* 219-248.

Ashmore, R. D. & Del Boca, F. K. Conceptual approaches to stereotypes and stereotyping. In D. L. Hamilton (ed.), *Cognitive processes in stereotyping and intergroup behavior.* Hillsdale, N.J.: Erlbaum, in press.

Austin, W. G. & Worchel, S. (eds.) *The social psychology of intergroup relations.* Belmont, Calif.: Wadsworth, 1979.

Baltes, P. B., Reese, H. W., & Nesselroade, J. R. *Life-span developmental psychology: Introduction to research methods.* Belmont, Calif.: Wadsworth, 1977.

Beere, C. A. *Women and women's issues: A handbook of tests and measures.* San Francisco, Calif.: Jossey-Bass, 1979.

Bentler, P. M. & Speckart, G. Models of attitude-behavior relations. *Psychological Review,* 1979, *86,* 452-465.

Biller, H. B. The father and personality development: Paternal deprivation and sex-role development. In M. E. Lamb (ed.), *The role of the father in child development.* New York: Wiley, 1976.

Borgida, E., Locksley, A., & Brekke, N. Social stereotypes and social judgment. In N. Cantor & J. Kihlstrom (eds.), *Cognition, social interaction, and personality.* Hillsdale, N.J.: Erlbaum, in press.

Brabant, S. Sex-role stereotyping in the Sunday comics. *Sex Roles,* 1976, *2,* 331-338.

Bromley, D. B. Approaches to the study of personality changes in adult life and old age. In A. D. Isaacs & F. Post (eds.), *Studies in geriatric psychiatry.* London, Wiley, 1978.

Broverman, I. K, Vogel, S. R., Broverman, D. M., Clarkson, F. E., & Rosenkrantz, P. S. Sex-role stereotypes: A current appraisal. *Journal of Social Issues,* 1972, *28,* 59-78.

Brown, D. G. Sex-role preference in young children. *Psychological Monograph,* 1956, *70,* No. 421, 1-19.

Bryan, J. W. & Luria, Z. Sex-role learning: A test of the selective attention hypothesis. *Child Development,* 1978, *49,* 13-23.

Chandler, M. J. Social cognition: A selective review of current research. In W. Overton & J. Gallagher (eds.), *Knowledge and development* (Vol. 1). New York: Plenum, 1976.

Collins, W. A., Wellman, H., & Keniston, A. H. Age-related aspects of comprehension and inference from a televised dramatic narrative. *Child Development,* 1978, *49,* 389-399.

Constantinople, A. Sex-role acquisition: In search of the elephant. *Sex Roles,* 1979, *5,* 121-133.

Dinnerstein, D. *The mermaid and the minotaur: Sexual arrangements and human malaise.* New York: Harper & Row, 1976.

Donaldson, M. Development of conceptualization. In V. Hamilton & M. D. Vernon (eds.), *The development of cognitive processes.* New York: Academic Press, 1976.

Emmerich, W. Socialization and sex-role development. In P. B. Baltes & K. W. Schaie (eds.), *Life-span developmental psychology: Personality and socialization.* New York: Academic Press, 1973.

Erikson, E. H. Identity and the life cycle (Selected papers). *Psychological Issues,* 1959, *1* (Monograph No. 1).

Flerx, V. C., Fidler, D. S., & Rogers, R. W. Sex role stereotypes: Developmental aspects and early intervention. *Child Development,* 1976, *47,* 998-1007.

Frieze, I. H., Parsons, J. E., Johnson, P. B., Ruble, D. N., & Zellman, G. L. *Women and sex roles: A social psychological perspective.* New York: Norton, 1978.

Gelman, R. Preschool thought. *American Psychologist,* 1979, *34,* 900-905.

Glass, A. L., Holyoak, K. J., & Santa, J. L. *Cognition.* Reading, Mass.: Addison-Wesley, 1979.

Gold, D. & Andres, D. Developmental comparisons between 10-year-old children with employed and unemployed mothers. *Child Development,* 1978, *49,* 75-84.

Goldberg, P. A. Are women prejudiced against women? *Transaction,* April 1968, 28-30.

Gordon, T. F. & Verna, M. E. *Mass communication effects and processes: A comprehensive bibliography 1950-1975.* Beverly Hills, Calif: Sage, 1978.

Hamilton, D. L. A cognitive-attributional analysis of stereotyping. In L. Berkowitz (ed.), *Advances in experimental social psychology* (Vol. 12). New York: Academic Press, 1979.

Hamilton, D. L. (ed.) *Cognitive processes in stereotyping and intergroup behavior.* Hillsdale, N.J.: Erlbaum, in press.

Hoffman, L. W. Effects of maternal employment on the child—A review of the research. *Developmental Psychology,* 1974, *10,* 204-208.

Horance, S. P. *Awareness of sex-role stereotypes in young boys.* Unpublished doctoral dissertation, Rutgers—The State University, 1977.

Kagan, J. Acquisition and significance of sex-typing and sex-role identity. In M. L. Hoffman & L. W. Hoffman (eds.), *Review of child development research* (Vol. 1). New York: Russell Sage, 1964.

Katz, P. A. The acquisition of racial attitudes in children. In P. A. Katz (ed.), *Towards the elimination of racism.* New York: Pergamon, 1976.

Katz, P. A. The development of female identity. *Sex Roles,* 1979, *5,* 155-178.

Kohlberg, L. A. A cognitive-developmental analysis of children's sex-role concepts and attitudes. In E. E. Maccoby (ed.), *The development of sex differences.* Stanford, Calif.: Stanford University Press, 1966.

Kuhn, D., Nash, S. C., & Brucken, L. Sex role concepts of two- and three-year olds. *Child Development,* 1978, *49,* 445-451.

Lamb, M. E. Paternal influences and the father's role: A personal perspective. *American Psychologist,* 1979, *34,* 938-943.

Lerner, H. E. Early origins of envy and devaluation of women. *Bulletin of the Menninger Clinic,* 1974, *38,* 538-553.

Lewis, M. & Weinraub, M. Origins of early sex-role development, *Sex Roles,* 1979, 5, 135-154.

Liben, L. S. & Signorella, M. L. Gender-related schemata and constructive memory in children. *Child Development,* 1980.

Liebert, R. M. & Schwartzberg, N. S. Effects of mass media. In M. R. Rosenweig & L. W. Porter (eds.), *Annual Review of Psychology,* 1977, *28,* 141-173.

Livesley, W. J. & Bromley, D. B. *Person perception in childhood and adolescence.* New York: Wiley, 1973.

Maccoby, E. E. & Jacklin, C. N. *The psychology of sex differences.* Stanford, Calif.: Stanford University Press, 1974.

Marantz, S. A. & Mansfield, A. F. Maternal employment and the development of sex role stereotyping in five- to eleven-year-old girls. *Child Development,* 1977, *48,* 668-673.

Markus, H. Self-schemata and processing information about the self. *Journal of Personality and Social Psychology,* 1977, *35,* 63-78.

Matteson, D. R. *Adolescence today: Sex roles and the search for identity.* Homewood, Ill.: Dorsey Press, 1975.

McArthur, L. Z. & Resko, B. G. The portrayal of men and women in American television commercials. *Journal of Social Psychology,* 1975, *97,* 209-220.

McTavish, D. G. Perceptions of old people: A review of research methodologies and findings. *Gerontologist,* 1971, *2,* 90-101.

Moerk, E. L. *Pragmatic and semantic aspects of early language development.* Baltimore: University Park Press, 1977.

Murphy, G., Murphy, L. B. & Newcomb, T. M. *Experimental social psychology.* New York: Harper & Row, 1937.

Paris, S. Integration and inference in children's comprehension and memory. In F. Restle et al., (eds.), *Cognitive theory* (Vol. 1). Hillsdale, N.J.: Erlbaum, 1975.

Peters, L. H., Terborg, J. R., & Taynor, J. Women as managers scale (WAMS): A measure of attitudes toward women in management positions. *JSAS Catalogue of Selected Documents in Psychology,* 1974, *4,* 27. (Ms. No. 585).

Riegel, K. F. Dialectical operations: The final period of cognitive development. *Human Development,* 1973 *16,* 346-370.

Rosenkrantz, P. S., Vogel, S. R., Bee, H., Broverman, I. K., & Broverman, D. M. Sex-role stereotypes and self-concepts in college students. *Journal of Consulting and Clinical Psychology,* 1968, *32,* 287-295.

Silvern, L. E. Children's sex-role preferences: Stronger among girls than boys. *Sex Roles,* 1977, *3,* 159-170.

Smith, S. Age and sex differences in children's opinions concerning sex differences. *Journal of Genetic Psychology,* 1939, *54,* 17-25.

Spence, J. T. & Helmreich, R. The attitudes toward women scale: An objective instrument to measure attitudes toward the rights and roles of women in contemporary society. *JSAS Catalogue of Selected Documents in Psychology,* 1972, *2,* 66. (Ms. No. 153).

Spence, J. T., Helmreich, R., & Stapp, J. The personal attributes questionnaire: A measure of sex role stereotypes and masculinity-feminity. *JSAS Catalogue of Selected Documents in Psychology,* 1974, *4,* 127. (Ms. No. 617).

Stockard, J. & Johnson, M. M. The social origins of male dominance. *Sex Roles,* 1979, *5,* 199-218.

Storms, M. D. Sex role identity and its relationship to sex role attributes and sex role stereotypes. *Journal of Personality and Social Psychology,* 1979, *37,* 1779-1789.

Thompson, S. K. Gender labels and early sex role development. *Child Development,* 1975, *46,* 339-347.

Ullian, D. Z. The development of conceptions of masculinity and femininity. In B. Lloyd & J. Archer (eds.), *Exploring sex differences.* London: Academic Press, 1976.

Unger, R. K. Toward a redefinition of sex and gender. *American Psychologist,* 1979, *34,* 1085-1094.

Whitley, B. E., Jr. Sex roles and psychotherapy: A current appraisal. *Psychological Bulletin,* 1979, *86,* 1309-1321.

Williams, J. E. & Bennett, S. M. The definition of sex stereotypes via the Adjective Check List. *Sex Roles,* 1975, *1,* 327-337.

Williams, J. E., Bennett, S. M., & Best, D. L. Awareness and expression of sex stereotypes in young children. *Developmental Psychology,* 1975, *11,* 635-642.

Subselves

THE INTERNAL REPRESENTATION OF SITUATIONAL AND PERSONAL DISPOSITIONS

COLIN MARTINDALE

Colin Martindale is Professor of Psychology at the University of Maine. He is the author of *Romantic Progression: The Psychology of Literary History* (Washington, D.C.: Hemisphere, 1975), *Cognition and Consciousness* (Homewood, Ill.: Dorsey, forthcoming), and of over 50 articles on various topics in psychology. He is currently editor of the *Empirical Studies of the Arts*.

Controversy about the unity or consistency of personality has gone on for centuries. One example of this controversy can be seen in theories about the self. Here, the question has been whether a person has one dominant and enduring self or many subselves that compete for the control of behavior.[1] In the early nineteenth century the dominant viewpoint, exemplified by theorists as diverse as Kant and Bain, was that there is a unitary self or transcendental ego. By the end of the century, the theoretical consensus was just the opposite. Among many others, Ribot (1895), Prince (1929), and Sidis and Goodhart (1904) explicitly denied the existence of a superordinate self and postulated the existence of multiple selves. A widely held view was that in the normal personality these different selves are elicited by different situations, while in the abnormal personality one or more of them may attain an unwonted autonomy.

By the mid-twentieth century, the consensus of theoretical opinion had swung back toward the view that the self is unitary. Allport (1937), Rogers (1961), and Maslow (1962) spoke of the self in the singular. Although they were willing to admit that a person may exhibit subsidiary social selves or roles, these were seen as being somehow less "real," "central," or "authentic." The notion that there is a "real" self which can in some sense be imprisoned by a "social" self goes back at least to Rousseau and is advocated in modern times most explicitly by Laing (1961). Another variant of the theory of a unitary self is the view that people are possessed of multiple subselves or subpersonalities but that these are or can be connected to or integrated with a deeper-level unitary self. This view goes back at least to Myers (1961) and is explicitly espoused by Jung (1956), Assagioli (1976), and Vargiu (1974). While there were some early dissenters to the doctrine of a unitary self (e.g., Gergen, 1968; Murray, 1940; Smith, 1968), it is only quite recently that the view has reemerged that personality may be composed of subselves (Klinger, 1971; Mair, 1977; Watkins & Watkins, 1979).

Current theory and research in cognitive psychology provide a framework for dealing with the question of the self in psychology. After briefly outlining a cognitive model, I will attempt to show what cognitive psychology can contribute to self theory. The basic argument of the cognitive theory to be proposed is that personality is best conceived of as being ultimately composed of a set of subselves. A subself is defined as a cognitive unit that receives input from a number of sources (e.g., information concerning the situation one is in, one's self-concept, and one's emotional state) and sends output to a number of cognitive units coding dispositions for action. In the normal course of affairs, most of the inputs to subself units may remain fairly constant. In this case, changes in the situation will tend to be the prime determinant of which subself becomes regnant. Thus, the theory offers one explanation of how and why behavior tends to be rather inconsistent across situations (Mischel, 1968). More interesting are instances of "dissociation" where the elicitation of different subselves cannot simply be attributed to differing situations. Examples of such dissociations include multiple personality, sudden personality change, the hidden observer phenomenon in hypnosis, and creative inspiration. The theory provides a ready explanation of such phenomena.

A COGNITIVE MODEL

The cognitive model presented below is developed in detail elsewhere (Martindale, Note 1). It is based upon an earlier theory presented by Konorski (1967). In general, both Konorski's model and my revision of it are consistent with current thinking in cognitive theory (e.g., Shiffrin & Schneider, 1977; Wickelgren, 1979b). Our major divergence is in the emphasis placed upon the concept of lateral inhibition, but this concept is far from alien to current cognitive theories (e.g., Crowder, 1978; Deutsch, 1969; Walley & Weiden, 1973). Because of space limitations, only a schematic outline of the cognitive model can be presented. For details and supporting evidence, the reader is referred to Martindale (Note 1) and Konorski (1967).

Konorski hypothesizes that perception, recognition, and understanding of stimuli are carried out by hierarchically arranged cortical "analyzers." These analyzers are feature-detection systems of the sort postulated by Selfridge (1959) and Hubel and Wiesel (1965). Each analyzer is devoted to the processing of a specific type of information. All analyzers are composed of from four to six layers. On each layer are a number of cognitive units.[2] Each unit codes some specific aspect or feature of a stimulus. Lateral connections among units on the same layer are inhibitory. Thus, any one layer works in the same way that the retina works (Ratliff, 1965). On the other hand, vertical connections among units on different layers tend to be excitatory. Each analyzer is thus a latticelike network composed of units and connections among these units. This gives rise to several effects. Masking and interference effects arise from lateral inhibition: Activating one unit inhibits or masks surrounding units. Expectation or context effects arise from vertical facilitation: Previously activated units prime other units with which they are vertically associated. Each unit is assumed to have a threshold: A given amount of input is necessary before the unit can be activated or turned on. Units also differ in strength—that is, how activated they can become once they are turned on. Repeated stimulation of a unit leads to adaptation effects. The unit is fatigued and ceases to be active. As a consequence, surrounding units may be disinhibited. Cognitive units are also hypothetically connected to units outside the analyzer in which they reside. Some or all of them are connected to the arousal system. These connections serve to "amplify" activation of a unit and are important—as will be explained below—in focusing attention. Some units are connected to the emotional system. These units can be referred to as motives. Perception and recognition of a given object are equivalent to "bottom-up" activation of the set of units coding that object by an external stimulus. Imagery and thought are "top-down" activation of units by other cognitive units. Finally, consciousness or short-term memory is the set of currently activated units in an analyzer. Attention refers to the one or two most activated of these conscious elements.

Konorski deals with two types of analyzers. There is a sensory analyzer for each of the senses (e.g., vision, hearing, and taste). These analyzers process the raw sensory signals specific to the sense in question. Their output goes to gnostic or perceptual analyzers. There are gnostic analyzers for each of the major types of percept we deal with. Among others, Konorski postulates separate gnostic analyzers for speech, printed words, faces, and music. In my revision of Konorski's model, I postulate three additional types of analyzers: a semantic analyzer which codes the meaning of percepts, an episodic analyzer which codes episodic information (such as time-tagged memories), and an action system which initiates both mental and motoric acts. Figure 1 illustrates the general model.

As an example of how the system works, consider what hypothetically occurs when someone hears the sentence JOHN HANDED THE PENCIL TO MARY. Auditory input goes first to the acoustic sensory analyzer. There, physical features of the input activate cognitive units coding these features. These units, in turn, activate units in the speech analyzer. At the lowest level of the speech analyzer are units sensitive to distinctive features (Jakobson et al., 1963). These are the acoustic cues that characterize speech sounds. About 8 to 10 distinctive features characterize the 30 or so phonemes in any language. At the next higher level are units coding these phonemes (elementary speech sounds). Any one phoneme-unit is activated when all of the distinctive features defining it are activated. At the next higher level are probably syllable units. There is one such unit for each of the possible syllables in a language. At the highest level of the speech analyzer are morpheme units. There is one of these for each morpheme (sound pattern of a "word") in a language. Hearing the spoken word PENCIL consists of simultaneous activation of the morpheme, syllable, phoneme, and distinctive feature units coding this word. Hearing the whole sentence consists of momentary activation of the units coding each of the component words. Thus, perception *is* activation of preexisting units in long-term memory (the speech analyzer in this case).

The morpheme units are connected to units at the highest level of the semantic analyzer (see Figure 1). These units code concepts. They receive input not only from the speech analyzer but also from units at the highest levels of other analyzers, such as those coding the visual "image" of a pencil or the tactual feel of a pencil. At deeper levels of the semantic system are units coding the meaning of concepts. In other words, the semantic system contains a network of interconnected units or nodes similar to that proposed by Collins and Loftus (1975) and others. For example, the PENCIL unit would be connected by "labelled" associations to other units so as to convey information about a pencil such as PENCIL → WRITING IMPLEMENT, PENCIL → LEAD, and so on. Hypothetically, the deeper the level in the semantic system, the more abstract or general the features of meaning that the units on the level code. Some units (e.g., HONOR, LOVE) in semantic memory are hypothetically connected to the emotional system. Following McDougall (1932), these units or the concepts they code might be called sentiments.

Presumably, person-concepts as well as the self-concept are also stored in semantic memory (see Cantor & Mischel, 1979). For example, JOHN may be coded as JOHN → PARTY-GOING-TYPE → EXTRAVERT. MARY may be coded as MARY → FLIRTATIOUS TYPE → FEMME FATALE. Hypothetically, many people will be classified as PARTY-GOING-TYPES. To the extent that John is highly typical of such a type, the bond between JOHN and PARTY-GOING-TYPE will be stronger (cf. Cantor & Mischel, 1979; Rosch & Mervis, 1975). It makes sense to argue that Jungian archetypes are deep-level person-prototypes in semantic memory that are strongly connected to the emotional system. For most males, the femme fatale prototype would be archetypical while the extravert prototype would not.

Of course, to understand our sample statement, syntactic analysis must also be performed. We must not only understand what PENCIL, HAND, MARY, and JOHN mean but also who is supposed to hand what to whom. This is presumably done by translating the sentence into a proposition (Fillmore, 1968). A proposition describes an action or event in terms of action, agent, object, recipient, and other cases. For example, our sample sentence could be expressed in propositional form as HAND (JOHN, PENCIL, MARY, PAST). Propositions can be expressed or realized as sentences, pictures, mental images, thoughts, or overt actions. Hypothetically, the proposition is the basic unit on the highest level of the episodic system. Thus, the episodic system may aid in decoding the sentence and also preserve an episodic memory of it. As shown in Figure 1, there are deeper levels of the episodic system. The second level from the top hypothetically codes what Propp (1968) called functions. A function is a class of propositions—for example, agent gives recipient a present. Hypothetically, all narratives are composed from a quite limited (about 30) lexicon of functions. Meta-functions are general classes of functions. At the bottom level of the episodic analyzer are narrative-units. Hypothetically, these code whole "narratives" such as personal memory episodes, plans for action, plots of stories one has heard or fantasies one has had, and so on.

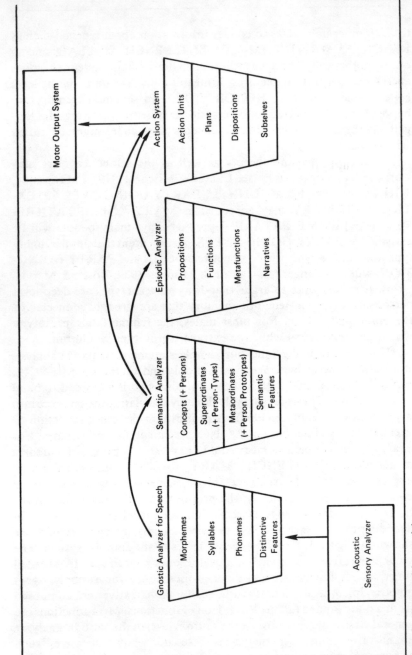

Figure 1: The cognitive model.

THE ACTION SYSTEM

How did John give the pencil to Mary in the first place? Shallice (1972, 1978) has postulated the existence of an action system. According to Shallice, the action system consists of a large number of action units. He argues that there is at least one action unit for every transitive verb. These units code actions such as EATING, WALKING, THROWING, HANDING, and so on. Shallice postulates that action units exist in a lateral inhibitory field. Activation of any one of them laterally inhibits surrounding action units. Such lateral inhibition is functional in preventing the simultaneous execution of mutually exclusive acts, such as swallowing and talking. Output from action units goes to motor systems that take care of the "details" of the action. According to Shallice, the system follows a principle of "executive ignorance." We may be conscious of the activation of action units. However, we are not conscious of the lower-level motor movements brought about by activation of action units.

Input to action units comes from two sources. First, there are inputs from gnostic, semantic, and episodic systems. These inputs correspond to the stimuli that elicit an action. Action units code habits. That is, they are chunking units (Wickelgren, 1979a) that link stimuli with motor responses. Presumably, any one stimulus is connected to many action units. The strength of these connections may be presumed to vary. The set of action units connected to any one stimulus unit would be what Hull (1943) called a habit family hierarchy. Second, action units also receive inputs from deeper levels of the action system. Activation via such units may be accompanied by a subjective sense of volition, intention, or will. At any given moment, the action unit that is most activated will inhibit other action units and will in turn activate the motor plans it controls. Relatively automatic actions are hypothetically controlled by action units that need only input from stimulus units in order to become fully activated. Other action units will require input from both stimuli and from deeper levels of the system in order to become fully activated.

Action units must have access to certain types of sensory information so that they can receive feedback about the success or failure of the act they control. Consider riding a bicycle. The action units involved would need access to visual, tactual, and possibly auditory information. However, they would have no need for, say, gustatory information. In general, it seems likely that many action units must be "anesthetic" with regard to certain senses. By the same token, action units must control "conceptual" motor areas. An action unit dealing with bicycle riding may send commands to a hand or a foot and receive sensory information about them, but it has no "knowledge" or "interest" in the ultimate neural or motor control of hands or feet. Anthropomorphically, an action unit wants information about a hand in the everyday sense of the term. It does not care that tactual sensory receiving areas do not coincide with the everyday sense of the term *hand.* To continue with the anthropomorphic analogy, a hysterical glove anesthesia would make perfect sense to an action unit. A hysterical paralysis would also make perfect sense. Our hypothetical bicycle-riding unit has access to or control of only some motor systems. It would, for example, presumably have no access to the speech apparatus.

In my adaptation of Shallice's action system, I postulate several deeper strata in the action system. Immediately below the level of action units are inputs that code plans or scripts in the sense that Schank and Abelson (1977) use these terms. These units code behavioral sequences such as "going to a restaurant" or "going to work." When such a plan unit is activated, it in turn activates a series of shallower-level action units in the correct serial order. Estes (1972) presents a plausible model explaining how lateral inhibition can be employed to activate a set of units in the correct serial order. Some plan units (e.g., opening a combination lock) are affectively neutral, while others (e.g., going to a restaurant) are connected to the emotional system. Following McDougall (1932) again, we might refer to plan units connected to the emotional system as tastes. Klinger (1977) would argue that virtually any plan or script unit can become at least temporarily a "current concern" and operate as what McDougall called a taste.

At the next lower level of the action system we may envision units coding dispositions. These collate large numbers of plan units. These units would typically be called motives to the extent that they are strongly connected to the emotional system. Murray's (1938) list of needs can be viewed as an enumeration of the more common of these units. For example, a unit coding n Achievement would be strongly connected to a number of plans involving achievement (e.g., building a piece of furniture), less strongly connected to plans that less focally involve achievement (e.g., bowling), and not connected to plans that do not involve achievement at least in a given individual's mind (e.g., going to a movie). It should be made explicit that the postulated motive units are not identical with Murray's needs. A disposition simply collates (i.e., is connected to) a set of plans, and plans are internal representations of quite specific actions. While Murray's (1938, p. 124) needs are held to "organize perception, apperception, intellection, conation and action," the motives in the action system are held to organize only intellection (covert action) and action. I do not deny that they are *connected to* units in gnostic and semantic systems that organize perception and apperception, but I agree with McDougall (1932) that much confusion is avoided if we clearly distinguish preferences for objects from preferences for actions.

At the bottom level of the action system are subself units. Each of these is vertically connected to a set of motive or dispositional units. Subselves are rather like what Murray called complexes. While Murray listed only five complexes, I would argue that this is only an enumeration of a few of the possible subselves. To use the example of Murray's needs, a given subself might be strongly connected to n Achievement, n Power, and n Exhibition. Another might be connected strongly to n Exhibition and n Abasement but not at all to n Power or to n Achievement. Note that the same motive may be connected to several subself units. Via the motive or disposition units, any one subself would ultimately have access to a set of plans and actions. Presumably, however, any one subself would not have access to all of the dispositions, plans, and actions in the person's repertoire. There would seem to be no reason to postulate an even deeper level of the action system with one single self-unit collating all of the subself units. Such a unit would be completely superfluous. We may have a unitary self-concept, but it seems unlikely that we have a single self. Hypothetically, the subjective sense of "I-ness" accompanies activation of any of the subself units.

Metaphorically, we might see the action system as a hierarchical "bureaucracy" for the control of behavior. The regnant subself determines general policy. That is, it selects which dispositions or motives will be given high priority. It does this by priming (partially activating) them. Its "term of office" will generally be fairly long. That is, once a subself unit becomes regnant, its activation decays very slowly. Which of the primed dispositions will actually be fully activated will to a large extent depend upon the "day-to-day" stimulus configuration. The primed dispositions will in turn prime some plan units. Which plans are actually brought into play will depend upon the "hour-to-hour" stimulus configuration. Which actions are emitted will depend upon the "minute-to-minute" stimulus configuration. As for the "second-to-second" business of behavior, this is hypothetically delegated to lower-level sensory and motor systems. The action system has no knowledge of or interest in exactly where its information ultimately comes from or exactly how its orders are ultimately executed.

While there are differences in detail, it should be pointed out that this model of the action system is quite close to Murray's (1938) theory of personality. Murray is explicit in postulating actones (cf. action units), needs (cf. motives), and complexes (cf. subselves) arranged in a hierarchical system. A close reading of Murray—especially his comments on themas (press-actone-need networks)—makes clear that he anticipated Shallice's concept of the action system. Prince (1929), although in a less precise way, also anticipated many of the notions presented in this section.

NEED FOR THE CONCEPT OF AN ACTION SYSTEM

There are several theoretical gaps that are filled by the model of the action system presented here. The theoretical necessity of action units is most apparent. Action units are essentially the internal representations of habits. Behaviorists did not want to talk about internal representations, but times have changed. Cognitive psychologists view internal representations as the whole subject matter of psychology. If there are habits (S-R bonds), then they must have some internal representation. Otherwise the organism would not "remember" what its habits were. Even if this be granted, it might be asserted that action units are completely superfluous. If one wants to postulate that cognitive units coding stimuli are connected to other cognitive units coding motor responses, why interpose action units rather than merely postulating direct connections? One reason is that even a rat in a maze learns an abstract action (getting to the goal box) rather than a specific set of motor responses (Restle, 1957; Tolman, 1932). Wickelgren (1979a) has dealt with this question in compelling detail from another perspective. He argues that virtually all S-R connections in humans and other higher animals are probably mediated by intermediate chunking units (such as action units). Consider compound conditioning: An organism must make a response given the simultaneous presence of two stimuli (say, a red light and a green light) but not in the presence of only one or the other stimulus. If there were only direct S-R connections, we could hypothesize a connection from a red-detecting unit to the response unit and a connection from a green-detecting unit to the response unit. An organism "wired" in this way would give the response to red, green, or both. However, it could not possibly withhold the response if only one or the other color were present. On the other hand, this task would be very easy (as it is for humans) if connections ran from the red-detector and the green-detector to a chunking unit, the output of which went to the response unit. In this case, the chunking unit serves as an AND-gate: It is activated if and only if both of its inputs are activated. Virtually all human action involves such compound stimuli. For example, if someone asks, "how's the water," you are supposed to say "fine" *if* there is some water around *and* it really is fine. Chunking units are necessary to account for how this sort of knowledge is represented. Shallice (1978) discusses a number of other reasons for the postulation of action units.

As for plans, there is no question that people can execute integrated series of actions in the correct order. Examples range from playing a piano concerto to driving to work. Lashley (1951) has shown that the execution of such a series of actions cannot be explained by simple chaining of responses where each response elicits the next one. (In our model this would correspond to hooking the action units together into an excitatory chain.) On the other hand, a hierarchical control system can explain such serial behaviors quite easily. The plan units correspond to the necessary deeper-level control units in such a system. Theorists from James (1890) to Murray (1938) have discussed the necessity for the concepts of motive and disposition. There is no need to reiterate their arguments here.

However, there is need to justify the theoretical necessity of the concept of subself. If one accepts Wickelgren's (1979a) argument that cognitive units are always connected via intermediate chunking units, then the concept of subself might be seen as a logical necessity. A subself is simply a chunking unit that connects sets of units in other analyzers with a set of response units (i.e., a group of disposition units in the action system). There is a good deal of evidence that different situations elicit different behavioral dispositions in the same person (Mischel, 1968). A subself may be seen as a mediating unit connecting units in semantic memory that code the meaning of the situation with the disposition units that the situation elicits. By the same token, the same person may behave quite differently in the same situation as a function of feeling different emotions. In this case, a subself may be seen as a mediating unit connecting units in the emotional system with dispositional units. In general, then, a subself is a mediating or chunking unit that allows the connection of units in other analyzers to dispositional units. Just as stimulus units cannot be directly connected to response units but must be linked to them via mediating action units, so deeper-level units in other analyzers cannot be directly connected to dispositional units but must be linked to them via mediating subself units.

EVIDENCE FOR THE EXISTENCE OF SUBSELVES

Unless one assumes a cognitive perspective (everything must have an internal representation) and accepts the contention that all internal representation can be connected only via intermediate chunking units, the foregoing arguments prove nothing at all about subselves. We need evidence of a more direct sort.

Self-Reports

One obvious line of inquiry is simply to ask people if they have subselves. Assagioli (1976) and Vargiu (1974) briefly explained their concept of "subpersonality" to patients in psychotherapy and students in training. Both report that the concept was readily accepted. Vargiu (1974) reports that patients will readily describe and even name their subselves. Some of the names that he elicited were the Hag, the Claw, the Pillar of Strength, the Religious Fanatic, the Sensitive Listener, and the Bitch Goddess.

Of course, self-report evidence of this sort is subject to obvious demand characteristics, since in all cases the subjects have been told the rudiments of the theory. Somewhat more compelling are spontaneous self-reports in autobiographical writings. James (1902) cites a number of these. One of the more striking bears requoting:

> The first time that I perceived that I was two was at the death of my brother Henri, when my father cried out so dramatically, "He is dead, he is dead." While my first self wept, my second self thought, "How truly given was that cry, how fine it would be at the theatre." I was then fourteen years old.
>
> This horrible duality has often given me matter for reflection. Oh, this terrible second me, always seated whilst the other in on foot, acting, living, suffering, bestirring itself. The second me that I have never been able to intoxicate, to make shed tears, or to put to sleep. And how it sees into things, and how it mocks [A. Daudet, quoted by James, 1902, p. 144].

Hypnosis

Hilgard (1977) has recently reported the existence of what he calls "hidden observers." Deeply hypnotizable subjects were rendered anesthetic and then subjected to painful stimulation. They claimed to feel no pain. However, when asked to raise a finger if "some part" of the hypnotized person was feeling the pain, a large percentage of subjects did so. Analogous findings have emerged with hypnotically induced deafness. The hidden observer apparently remains completely aware of everything that happens during the hypnotic session. Watkins and Watkins (1979) have found that subjects often have more than one hidden observer. Once a hidden observer has been contacted, subjects were asked if any other part had been aware. In many cases, subjects responded positively. Watkins and Watkins also report preliminary results suggesting that the hidden observer phenomenon is not due to demand characteristics: Unhypnotized subjects instructed to feign the hypnotic state never report hidden observers.

Although Hilgard argues that hidden observers are not enduring subselves, a different interpretation is given by Watkins and Watkins (1979). They argue that hypnotic hidden observers are in fact enduring subselves (though they prefer Federn's, 1952, term "ego state"). Watkins (1978) has developed hypoanalytic ego-state therapy. In this procedure, an attempt is made to perform a sort of family therapy with the ego-states comprising a person. These ego states reportedly tend to give themselves names related to their function in the personality (e.g., The Machine, Love, Medusa, The Evil One). Each experiences itself as "I" and refers to other subselves as "he," "she," or "it." They differ in their memories and can often state when they were "born." In an important experiment, Watkins and Watkins (1979) hypnotized five patients previously treated with hypnoanalytic ego-state therapy in order to test for the hidden observer effect. Of 10 hidden observers emerging, 8 identified themselves as subselves that had previously emerged during therapy. These results strongly support the Watkins' contention that hypnotic hidden observers are in fact enduring subselves.

Multiple Personality

The existence of case of multiple personality constitutes the firmest evidence for the existence of subselves. Prince's (1929) case of Miss Beauchamp is fairly typical. She exhibited three distinct personalities. The Saint was serious, idealistic, religious, conscientious, and generally prim. The Realist, as the name implies, was a more practical and realistic person. Sally was opposite to both of the other personalities. She was fun-loving, carefree, and detested religion. Whereas the Saint loved to read and could speak French, Sally hated reading and had no knowledge of French. Sally alternated with the Saint but was also co-conscious (i.e., she was aware of the Saint's thoughts but not vice versa). Sally also exhibited specific sensory defects. She had no sense of pain or temperature, and she never felt hungry or thirsty. On the other hand, vision and audition were normal. Each of the personalities felt only some emotions. Sally, for example, could not feel fear or disgust but could feel anger. Precisely the reverse was the case with the Saint. Finally, with regard to episodic memory, the Saint had no access to Sally's episodic memories, while Sally had access to both sets of memories.

Dissociative States

A variety of phenomena that received intensive study until around the turn of the century are supportive of the notion of subselves. These include motor automatisms such as automatic writing, trance utterances, and use of of the planchette. In all of these cases meaningful or quasi-meaningful messages are produced, supposedly without the subject's conscious intention to do so. Sensory automatisms, such as crystal visions, can also be interpreted in the same light. Myers (1961) reviews some of this early evidence. Watkins (1976) also touches upon it as well as describing current work on mental imagery that derives from it. Of course, these techniques are all susceptible to the criticism that the results are merely the result of demand characteristics.

Conversion Reactions

A variety of hysterical conversion reactions make sense in terms of the action system. As mentioned above, action units hypothetically control conceptually defined rather than neurologically defined sensory receptive fields and motor regions. Conversion hysteria is in this view a disease of at least the shallower levels of the action system. Multiple personality and dissociative reactions may be seen as involving an abnormal dominance of one subself at the expense of others. However, these do tend to involve sensory and motor symptoms as well. It may be that conversion reactions are due to the same cause—that is, inhibition of a subself—but that the sensory or motor symptoms are simply more noticeable (cf. Janet, 1901).

Creativity

There is a surprising unanimity with which the self-reports of highly creative people stress the spontaneous nature of creative inspiration. For example, Thackeray (quoted by Harding, 1940) remarked that "I have been surprised at the observations made by some of my characters. It seems as if an occult power was moving the pen. The personage does or says something, and I ask, how the dickins did he come to think of that?" Robert Louis Stevenson claimed that his stories were created by "Little People" or "Brownies," while Dickens held that his characters "spoke" to him (Myers, 1961). Harding (1940) and Ghiselin (1964) have collected a number of self-reports of creative people which show that the above quotations are not isolated examples. One way of accounting for such phenomena would be to attribute them to the activity of subselves. That is, the "dictation" creative writers so often describe comes from an autonomous subself. The muse, Graves (1966) observes, is not a rhetorical device but a real psychic entity.

Sudden Personality Conversion

Personality exhibits a good deal of stability across time (Block, 1971). However, it is undeniable that personality change is sometimes extremely sudden. An everyday example of this is falling in love "at first sight." In terms of subself theory this can be seen as occurring when a person of the opposite sex matches very well with a deep-level person-prototype (Jung, 1956, would call this an anima or animus figure) in semantic memory. This person-prototype is strongly connected to a subself unit. The match produces a "short circuit" which evokes the subself. The resulting symptoms are well enough known. The affected person changes in many ways. It is not merely that he or she feels a certain set of emotions. All sorts of other behaviors, interests, and sentiments change as well. One loses many old interests and dispositions and gains new ones. These losses and gains are often not directly attributable to the state of being in love. Such coherent changes do make sense in terms of subself theory. The subself evoked by being in love has at least some interests and dispositions that are not directly relevant to being in love. Being in love involves evocation of a "coherent" self rather than being merely a special emotional state.

Religious conversion is another example of personality change that is often almost instantaneous. The change is not confined purely to a change in religious attitudes but involves changes that are much more general. One coherent personality is replaced by another that is often its mirror opposite. James (1902) quotes a number of case histories of such conversions. Identity crises of adolescence offer another example of fairly rapid and radical personality changes (Erikson, 1950).

ORGANIZATION AND DYNAMICS OF THE SUBSELF FIELD

Hypothetically, any subself has a number of connections with other cognitive units. These connections are illustrated in Figure 2.

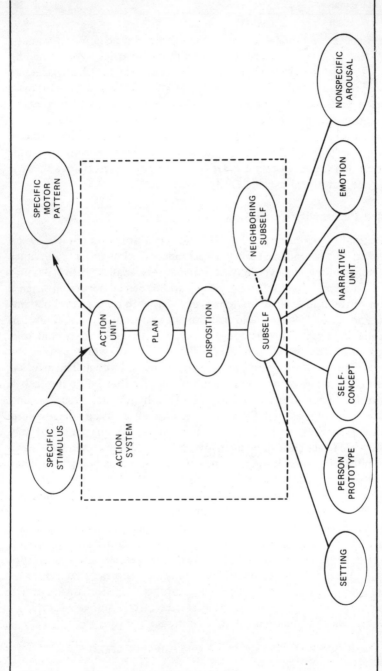

Figure 2: Direct and indirect connections of subself units to other cognitive units.

Vertical Excitatory Connections

Subselves are vertically connected with motive or disposition units. The upshot of this is that activation of a motive unit will tend to activate subself units with which it is connected. Conversely, activation of a subself unit will tend to activate all of the motive units with which it is connected. If a given subself is activated, it will vertically activate or prime a "column" of disposition, plan, and action units. This priming will have several possible effects. It will make it easier for relevant stimuli to activate fully the disposition, plan, and action units because they are already primed or partially activated. The result will be overt behavior. In the absence of relevant stimuli, the priming may be sufficient to make the primed units enter consciousness. That is, the person will think about the plans and actions.

Depending upon the idiographic details of exactly what dispositions, plans, and action units a subself is connected to, it is perfectly plausible that subselves could exhibit all sorts of agnosias, anesthesias, and paralyses. For example, a subself with no connections to action units receiving information from pain centers would have no sense of pain; a subself with no connections to action units receiving visual information would be "blind." Because we often realize quite different motives in fantasy than in overt action, it seems reasonable to ask whether the "I" of fantasies and dreams is the same as the "I" of overt action. That is, may it not be that different subselves are involved? Recall Bachelard's (1960) statement that it is the *anima*—as opposed to the self in the usual sense—that dreams in us. To the extent that a person's overt and covert actions are different, the person may develop an implicit personality theory that differentiates the "real" self (i.e., the regnant subself of covert actions) from the "inauthentic" or "social" self (i.e., the regnant subself of overt actions).

Lateral Inhibitory Connections

Subself units are hypothetically connected with one another in a lateral inhibitory network. Activation of a subself will inhibit neighboring subselves. Given the vertical connections of subselves, this lateral inhibition will result in an inhibited "fringe" of disposition, plan, and action units around the activated "column" described in the previous section. The principle of organization of the subself field would allow a more or less complete suppression of subselves inappropriate to a given situation. The situation elicits an appropriate subself and this subself inhibits opposite subselves which would be inappropriate for the situation. An example would be the fun-loving extravert on a solemn occasion. The somber subself inhibits the typically stronger extraverted subself. This inhibition may not be complete. The extraverted subself may be inhibited to a degree that it cannot drive action units so that they would be activated enough to unleash motoric behavior. However, it may produce enough activation to unleash "inner speech." It may then carry on a running commentary concerning its reactions to the regnant subself's actions. By the same token, we often "hear ourselves saying" things that we wish we were not saying.

Connections to Other Analyzers

Subself units are hypothetically connected with units in several other analyzers. First, let us consider connections with semantic memory. It would seem reasonable to postulate several types of connections. Each subself must be connected with the self-concept.[3] Presumably, these connections differ in strength. That is, some subselves are strongly connected to the self-concept while others are quite weakly connected. Hypothetically, the strength of this connection would be a function of how consistent the subself is with the self-concept. Thus, some of the things we do feel more typical, natural, or congruent than do others. In other cases, we can hardly believe what we are doing. These would be cases where a subself very weakly connected to the self-concept becomes activated.[4] Second, there must be connections to units in semantic memory coding the meaning of situations. For purposes of simplicity, let us assume that a situation consists of a setting and another person. Hypothetically, subselves are connected to units fairly deep in the semantic system—that is, to units coding prototypical people and prototypical settings. A given situation (setting plus person) will tend to activate the subself most strongly connected to it. Just as with self-concept connections, person and setting connections with subselves hypothetically vary in strength. Some connections must be quite strong, so that a given situation would virtually assure elicitation of a given subself. Other connections must be quite weak. In this case, the situation would have little chance of eliciting its "appropriate" subself.

Subselves are also hypothetically either directly or indirectly connected to units in episodic memory. Thus, each subself has its own store of episodic memories. When a given subself is activated, these memories can be easily accessed. When it is not activated, these memories will be more difficult—if not impossible—to access. Each subself may be amnesic in regard to the memories of other subselves. Evidence for this assertion comes from cases of multiple personality. However, there is some evidence for the "state-boundness" of memories in normal subjects (Fischer & Landon, 1972).

Subselves must also be connected to the emotional system. Each should have its own characteristic set of emotions. It would be idle to speculate whether these connections to the emotional system are direct or indirect (via the motive units). Nemiah and Sifneos (1970) have coined the term *alexithymia* to refer to an inability to recognize one's own emotions. Evidence from multiple personalities suggests that each subself has access to information about only some emotions and is alexithymic in regard to other emotions. Finally, subself units must receive nonspecific input from the arousal system. As explained below, the amount of such input can be seen as determining amount of self-consciousness or attention to the self.

Selection of the Regnant Subself

At any moment in time the most strongly activated subself will become regnant. This means that it will control behavior and inhibit neighboring subselves. Which subself will be most strongly activated? This will depend upon several factors. First, subselves that are stronger and/or have lower thresholds will be more likely to be activated. In simple terms, the most practiced or characteristic subself will have an advantage. Leaving this aside, the subself receiving the most input from other cognitive units will be most activated and will, hence, become dominant. The relevant sources of input are self-concept, person, and setting units in semantic memory, units in the emotional system, and units in episodic memory. Hypothetically, each subself accumulates a "count" (cf. Morton, 1969) of its inputs. The subself with the highest count seizes control. Walley and Weiden (1973) discuss how this could be done in another context. A plausible explanation is that the nonspecific inputs from the arousal system *multiply* with the counts so as to exacerbate differences in activation (compare Hull, 1943). The result is that one subself becomes activated enough to inhibit others.

Which subself will become regnant clearly depends upon a large number of factors. Beyond those mentioned, we must not forget the strengths and thresholds of units contributing to the "counts" of each subself. Beyond that, of course, are the strengths and prototypicalities of environmental stimuli. Evocation of alien or unusual subselves seems often to be accomplished by very strong and archetypal stimuli. Consider the case of love at first sight: Another person who matches the "victim's" archetypal person-prototype (anima or animus) inexorably evokes a subself. The stimulus is so strong that it overrides inputs from other sources. Recall how immune to the usual situational determinants of behavior lovers often are. They walk in the rain, make love in public places, and talk to strangers, among other things. Religious conversion (James, 1902) and behavior in crowds (Le Bon, 1896) are similar—not in regard to walking in the rain and all that, but in regard to strong environmental stimuli evoking an alien or unusual subself.

Cognitive units can in general be adapted or fatigued, so it makes sense to ask whether this may not occur with subselves as well. Consider a person with a "good" subself and a "bad" subself. All may go well until the good subself is stimulated too long (e.g., the person has to care for an ailing parent day and night). We might expect fatiguing of the good subself and a consequent disinhibition of the bad subself. Just the reverse seems to happen in religious conversion. In general, sudden personality change seems to occur in high-arousal situations. One consequence of high arousal is that the regnant subself will be more activated and, hence, will be more quickly fatigued. Perhaps the reason that societies have invented such things as eight-hour work days, holidays, and so on is that in the absence of such rest periods, occupational or "work" subselves would fatigue. The old psychiatric prescription of a vacation to cure a neurosis may not have been quite so ridiculous as has long been thought.

Individual Differences

There are a variety of ways in which people could differ in terms of the model that has been presented. One obvious way would be in the number and type of subselves they possess. Another dimension of possible individual differences would concern the relative strength of different types of inputs to subself units. We know that some people are more cross-situationally consistent than others (Bem & Allen, 1974). One possible explanation would be this: Consistent people tend to have stronger connections from self-concept units to subself units, while inconsistent people tend to have stronger connections from situation (setting and person) units to subself units. Thus, in consistent people the self-concept can generally "outvote" the situation, while the reverse is the case with inconsistent people.

Another relevant dimension concerns degree of dissociation. In Figure 3 are pictured two hypothetical action systems. For purposes of

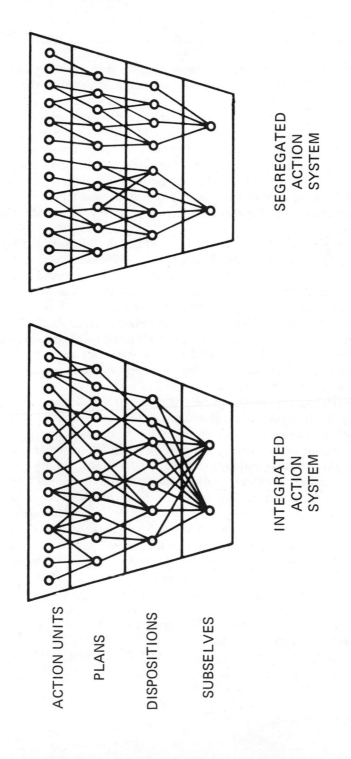

Figure 3: Examples of integrated (left) and segregated (right) action systems.

simplicity, only a few units are shown on each level. In the action system on the left, both of the subself units are connected to all of the disposition units. In a person for whom this were the case, subself theory would be completely irrelevant. No matter which subself were in control, behavior would be the same. On the right side of Figure 2 is an action system exhibiting complete segregation. The two subselves share no disposition, plan, or action units. Presumably this diagrams the condition found in multiple personality. Hypothetically, normal personalities range between these two extremes. To the extent that they are nearer the segregated end of the continuum, they will be prone to dissociative states.

Self-attention (e.g., Carver, 1979; Duval & Wicklund, 1972) and self-control (e.g., Bandura, 1978; Mischel, 1979) have recently received a good deal of attention, but in both cases the focus has tended to be upon the self-concept (the *me*) rather than upon the self-as-actor (the *I*). Self-attention is held to facilitate comparison of one's behavior with internal standards. Self-control is held in large part to involve deciding upon rewards for one's behavior. Both of these involve operations in the semantic system. I do not deny that these operations occur, but I would like to suggest that a quite different sort of self-attention and self-control occurs in the action system.

In the cognitive model presented in this article, attention is seen as being due to inputs from the arousal system. Attention to "I" or to a subself is equivalent to augmenting its activation via nonspecific inputs from the arousal system. The result of this will be increased vertical facilitation of disposition, plan, and action units. At any moment, action units receive this sort of vertical input as well as input from units in other analyzers coding environmental stimuli. The greater the amount of vertical input, the greater will be the chance that action units will be activated by ascending inputs from the action system rather than by environmental stimuli. It seems reasonable to hypothesize that people differ in the amount of ascending vertical facilitation that they tend to exhibit. The subjective aspect of ascending vertical facilitation in the action system is nothing other than will or volition. In short, people can exert self-control by means of will (as well as by establishing contingencies for ourselves) and people differ in the amount of willpower that they possess. This personality dimension is probably related to the dissociative dimension, since it has long been held that dissociative personalities suffer from abulia, or lack of will (Janet, 1901).

Smith (Note 2) points out that the degree of dissociation to be found in the general population may vary across historical time. Trilling

(1972), basing his argument on the differential usage of terms such as "sincerity" and "authenticity" during different historical periods, makes a related point. If this is the case, then it may be that shifts in the theoretical consensus concerning the viability of concepts such as sub-selves, will, and dissociation reflect not so much swings in scientific fashion or advances in scientific knowledge but actual changes in the extent to which the underlying phenomena are observable in the general population.

NOTES

1. By the term *self* or *subself* I refer to what James (1890) called the *I* or the self as actor rather than to the *me* or self-concept.

2. Konorski identifies the analyzers with specific areas of cortex. The layers of each analyzer are held to correspond to the layers of cortex; cognitive units are held to correspond to neurons (although many neurons compose any one cognitive unit). It is immaterial to the validity of the theory whether it is "neurologized" in this fashion.

3. I assume for the sake of simplicity that there is one unitary self-concept rather than many subself-concepts in semantic memory. It seems rather likely, however, that there must be some equivalent of the subself in semantic memory (see James, 1902).

4. Note that subselves control actions (which can be described by verbs) while most of the "traits" associated with the self-concept are probably best described by adjectives or adverbs. Thus, it is not a straightforward matter for a person—or for a psychologist studying personality—to decide if acts and "traits" are consistent.

REFERENCE NOTES

1. Martindale, C. *Cognition and consciousness.* Manuscript in preparation, 1980.
2. Smith, M. B. Personal communication, 1979.

REFERENCES

Allport, G. W. *Pattern and growth in personality.* New York: Holt, Rinehart & Winston, 1937.

Assagioli, R. *Psychosynthesis.* Harmondsworth, England: Penguin, 1976.

Bachelard, G. *La poétique de la reverie.* Paris: Presses Universitaires de France, 1960.

Bandura, A. The self system in reciprocal determinism. *American Psychologist,* 1978, *33,* 344-358.

Bem, D. J. & Allen, A. On predicting some of the people some of the time: The search for cross-situational consistencies in behavior. *Psychological Review,* 1974, *81,* 506-520.

Block, J. *Lives through time.* Berkeley, Calif.: Bancroft, 1971.

Cantor, N. & Mischel, W. Prototypicality and personality: Effects on free recall and personality impressions. *Journal of Research in Personality,* 1979, *13,* 187-205.

Carver, C. S. A cybernetic model of self-attention processes. *Journal of Personality and Social Psychology,* 1979, *37,* 1251-1281.

Collins, A. & Loftus, E. A spreading activation theory of semantic processing. *Psychological Review,* 1975, *82,* 407-429.

Crowder, R. G. Mechanisms of auditory backward masking in the stimulus suffix effect. *Psychological Review,* 1978, *85,* 502-524.

Deutsch, D. Music recognition. *Psychological Review,* 1969, *76,* 300-307.

Duval, S. & Wicklund, R. A. *A theory of objective self-awareness.* New York: Academic Press, 1972.

Erikson, E. *Childhood and society.* New York: Norton, 1950.

Estes, W. K. An associative basis for coding and organization in memory. In A. W. Melton & E. Martin (eds.), *Coding processes in human memory.* Washington, D.C.: Winston, 1972.

Federn, P. *Ego psychology and the psychoses.* New York: Basic Books, 1952.

Fillmore, C. J. The case for case. In E. Bach & R. T. Harms (eds.), *Universals in linguistic theory.* New York: Holt, Rinehart & Winston, 1968.

Fischer, R. & Landon, G. On the arousal state-dependent recall of sub-conscious experience: Stateboundness. *British Journal of Psychiatry,* 1972, *150,* 159-172.

Gergen, K. J. Personal consistency and the presentation of self. In C. Gordon & K. J. Gergen (eds.), *The self in social interaction.* New York: Wiley, 1968.

Ghiselin, B. *The creative process.* New York: Mentor, 1964. (Originally published, 1952.)

Graves, R. *The white goddess: A historical grammar of poetic myth.* New York: Farrar, Straus and Giroux, 1966.

Harding, R. *An anatomy of inspiration.* London: Frank Cass, 1940.

Hilgard, E. R. *Divided consciousness: Multiple controls in human thought and action.* New York: Wiley, 1977.

Hubel, D. H. & Weisel, T. N. Receptive fields and functional architecture in two nonstriate visual areas (18 and 19) of the cat. *Journal of Neurophysiology,* 1965, *28,* 229-289.

Hull, C. L. *Principles of behavior.* Englewood Cliffs, N.J.: Prentice-Hall, 1943.

Jakobson, R., Fant, G., & Halle, M. *Preliminaries to speech analysis.* Cambridge, Mass.: MIT Press, 1963.

James, W. *Principles of psychology.* New York: Holt, Rinehart & Winston, 1890.

James, W. *The varieties of religious experience.* New York: Longmans, Green, 1902.

Janet, P. *The mental state of hystericals.* New York: G. P. Putnam, 1901. (Originally published, 1892.)

Jung, C. G. *Two essays on analytical psychology.* Cleveland: Meridian, 1956.

Klinger, E. *Structure and functions of fantasy.* New York: Wiley, 1971.

Klinger, E. *Meaning and void: Inner experience and the incentives in people's lives.* Minneapolis: University of Minnesota Press, 1977.

Konorski, J. *Integrative activity of the brain.* Chicago: University of Chicago Press, 1967.

Laing, R. D. *The divided self.* Harmondsworth, England: Penguin, 1961.

Lashley, K. The problem of serial order in behavior. In L. A. Jeffress (ed.), *Cerebral mechanisms in behavior.* New York: Wiley, 1951.

Le Bon, G. *The crowd.* London: T. Fisher Unwin, 1896.

Mair, J.M.M. The community of self. In D. Bannister (ed.), *New perspectives in personal construct theory.* London: Academic Press, 1977.

Maslow, A. *Toward a psychology of being*. New York: Van Nostrand, 1962.

McDougall, W. *The energies of man: A study of the fundamentals of dynamic psychology*. New York: Scribner's, 1932.

Mischel, W. *Personality and assessment*. New York: Wiley, 1968.

Mischel, W. Toward a cognitive social learning reconceptualization of personality. *Psychological Review*, 1973, *80*, 252-283.

Mischel, W. On the interface of cognition and personality: Beyond the person-situation debate. *American Psychologist*, 1979, 740-754.

Morton, J. Interaction of information in word recognition. *Psychological Review*, 1969, *76*, 165-178.

Murray, H. A. *Explorations in personality*. New York: Oxford University Press, 1938.

Murray, H. What should psychologists do about psychoanalysis? *Journal of Abnormal and Social Psychology*, 1940, *35*, 150-175.

Myers, F.W.H. *Human personality and its survival of bodily death*. New York: Arno, 1961. (Originally published, 1903.)

Nemiah, J. C. & Sifneos, P. E. Psychosomatic illness: A problem in communication: *Psychotherapy and Psychosomatics*, 1970, *18*, 154-160.

Prince, M. *Clinical and experimental studies in personality*. Cambridge, Mass.: Sci-Art, 1929.

Propp, V. *Morphology of the folktale*. Austin: University of Texas Press, 1968. (Originally published, 1923.)

Ratliff, F. *Mach bands: Quantitative studies on neural networks in the retina*. San Francisco: Holden-Day, 1965.

Restle, F. Discrimination of cues in mazes: A resolution of the "place-vs.-response" question. *Psychological Review*, 1957, *64*, 217-228.

Ribot, T. *The diseases of personality*. Chicago: Open Court, 1895.

Rogers, C. *On becoming a person*. Boston: Houghton-Mifflin, 1961.

Rosch, E. & Mervis, C. Family resemblances: Studies in the internal structure of categories. *Cognitive Psychology*, 1975, *7*, 573-605.

Schank, R. & Abelson, R. *Scripts, plans, goals and understanding*. Hillsdale, N.J.: Erlbaum, 1977.

Selfridge, O. G. Pandemonium: A paradigm for learning. In *Symposium on the mechanization of thought processes*. London: Her Majesty's Stationery Office, 1959.

Shallice, T. Dual functions of consciousness. *Psychological Review*, 1972, *79*, 383-393.

Shallice, T. The dominant action system: An information-processing approach to consciousness. In K. S. Pope & J. L. Singer (eds.), *The stream of consciousness: Scientific investigations into the flow of human experience*. New York: Plenum, 1978.

Shiffrin, R. M. & Schneider, W. Controlled and automatic human information processing: II Perceptual learning, automatic attending, and a general theory. *Psychological Review*, 1977, *84*, 127-190.

Sidis, B. & Goodhart, S. P. *Multiple personality: An experimental investigation into the nature of human individuality*. Englewood Cliffs, N.J.: Prentice-Hall, 1904.

Smith, M. B. The self and cognitive consistency. In R. P. Abelson et al. (eds.), *Theories of cognitive consistency*. Chicago: Rand-McNally, 1968.

Tolman, E. C. *Purposive behavior in animals and men*. Englewood Cliffs, N.J.: Prentice-Hall, 1932.

Trilling, L. *Sincerity and authenticity*. Cambridge, Mass.: Harvard University Press, 1972.

Vargiu, J. Subpersonalities. *Synthesis*, 1974, *1*, 51-90.

Walley, R. E. & Weiden, T. D. Lateral inhibition and cognitive masking: A neurological theory of attention. *Psychological Review,* 1973, *80,* 284-302.

Watkins, J. G. *The therapeutic self.* New York: Human Sciences Press, 1978.

Watkins, J. G. & Watkins, H. H. Ego states and hidden observers. *Journal of Altered States of Consciousness,* 1979, *5,* 3-18.

Watkins, M. *Waking dreams.* New York: Gordon and Breach, 1976.

Wickelgren, W. A. Chunking and consolidation: A theoretical synthesis of semantic networks, configuring in conditioning, S-R versus cognitive learning, normal forgetting, the amnesic syndrome, and the hippocampal arousal system. *Psychological Review,* 1979, *86,* 44-60. (a)

Wickelgren, W. A. *Cognitive psychology.* Englewood Cliffs, N.J.: Prentice-Hall, 1979. (b)

Equity Theory, Social Identity, and Intergroup Relations

8

BRIAN CADDICK

Brian Caddick is a Lecturer in the School of Applied Social Studies, Bristol University, Bristol, England. After a short time in industry following the completion of his first degree, he returned to full-time study, taking an M.A. in Psychology at Simon Fraser University, Vancouver, and a Ph.D. in Social Psychology at Bristol University. His research interests include the social psychology of intergroup relations and small group behavior.

INTRODUCTION

Of the many different concepts, formulations, and sets of proposals which contribute to the theoretical repertoire of present-day social psychology, equity theory would probably be ranked as one of the more important. The idea that equal relative outcomes in the social transactions between people can act as a powerful social value affecting the nature and course of those transactions has exercised a significant influence on the study and theoretical analysis of social interaction. The extent of this influence is reflected in recent suggestions that equity theory may just provide "the glimmerings of the general theory that social psychologists so badly need" (Berkowitz and Walster, 1976, p. xi).

The appeal of equity theory is due, in part, to its being conceptually succinct—a characteristic it shares with other social psychological arguments stemming from the "economic rationality" view of man. Walster et al.'s (1973) definitive formulation consists of just four propositions (reproduced in Table 1), yet the ground covered by these four is considerable by any measure. To begin with, a philosophical

AUTHOR'S NOTE: I would like to thank Howard Giles, Henri Tajfel, Otto Klineberg, Marilynn Brewer, and Harry Reis for their comments on earlier drafts of the article.

position on the nature of man is adopted (Proposition I) and from this certain views about the nature of society and social life follow. The essence of these views is that, for their continued existence, social groups need to devise ways of controlling the disruptive struggle between members whose primary interest is to maximize their own individual outcomes. This, it is suggested, is accomplished by the working out of social standards embodying the principle of equal relative outcomes (for details see Proposition IIA, Table 1) and the creation of conditions which encourage equitable interaction in these terms and discourage behavior which goes against the basic principle. Here the argument is qualified and extended with the acknowledgment that while equitable relationships thus come to be seen as "good," the specifics of equity—that is to say, the outcomes and inputs as defined in Table 1—may be evaluated differently by the different parties. This, of course, raises the possibility that individuals will experience and become aware of inequity in their relationships, a result which is held to cause distress (Proposition III), and, subsequently, to lead to action aimed at reducing distress by restoring equity (Proposition IV). Further refinements of affective, conative, and cognitive detail are also introduced so that distress, for example, is linked to guilt in the case of the inequitably advantaged and to anger in the case of the inequitably disadvantaged. Additionally, equity restoration is seen to occur either by way of the actual alteration of one's own or another's outcomes and/or inputs or by their psychological alteration (i.e., cognitive distortion). The whole is thus a comprehensive, yet elegantly concise theoretical statement which successfully combines breadth of scope with a specificity which permits the analysis of social relationships in some depth.

Social psychologists have been quick to capitalize on these virtues. There is now a sizable research literature (see Adams & Freedman, 1976, for an annotated bibliographical listing) which provides considerable empirical support for the basic notions contained in the Walster et al. outline. For instance, where subjects have been given the opportunity to allocate rewards to themselves and/or others after the performance of some task, or where task performance has followed an assessment of ability or an agreement on a payment schedule, it is frequently observed that the rewards given or the effort expended are in line with the previous inputs or agreed outcomes. Where, on the other hand, conditions have been arranged so that subjects are placed in an inequitable relationship or are scrutineers of an inequitable relationship involving other parties, then moves to restore equity have usually been apparent. On the theoretical/conceptual side, equity theory has proved

TABLE 1
The Basic Propositions of Equity Theory as Formulated by
Walster, Berscheid and Walster (1973)

Proposition I: Individuals will try to maximize their outcomes.

Proposition IIA: Groups can maximize collective reward by evolving accepted systems of "equitably" apportioning rewards and costs among members.

In formal terms, equity—or equal relative outcomes—is said to exist when the ratio (outcomes-inputs)/inputs for participant A equals the ratio (outcomes-inputs)/inputs for participant B. As used here, "outcomes" refers to the consequences which follow from a relationship and "inputs" to the participants' contributions to the exchange.[a]

Proposition IIB: Groups will generally reward members who treat others equitably and generally punish (increase the costs for) members who treat others inequitably.

Proposition III: When individuals find themselves participating in inequitable relationships they become distressed. The more inequitable the relationship, the more distress individuals feel.

Proposition IV: Individuals who discover that they are in an inequitable relationship attempt to eliminate their distress by restoring equity. The greater the inequity that exists, the more distress they feel, and the harder they try to restore equity.

a. Negative inputs require a modification to this basic formula, details of which are provided by Walster et al. (1976).

congenial to integration with a number of other social psychological formulations. Among those with which links of one sort or another have been forged are dissonance theory, exchange theory, social comparison theory, and the concepts of distributive justice and relative deprivation (Adams, 1963, 1965; Walster et al., 1973), status imbalance (Anderson et al., 1969), the frustration-aggression hypothesis (Brown & Herrnstein, 1975) and justice theory (Lerner, 1975, 1977). Theoretical connectiveness and strong empirical support, along with the theory's applicability to a variety of social settings or events, contribute substantially to the idea mooted by Berkowitz and Walster (1976) that equity theory might point the way toward a general theory of social interaction.

It is not as though the promise of equity theory has been seen in relation to academic interests alone, however. Adams and Freedman (1976) have argued that while equity theory is not yet fully developed, it has great relevance to "economic, legal, interpersonal and intergroup relationships" (p. 55) and also that "it is not foolishly optimistic to believe that a public understanding of inequity would make a difference in ameliorating conflicted relationships" (p. 55). Were these comments to hold true in the area of intergroup relations, then it is clear that a result of wide significance would have been achieved. It is of some interest, then, to consider what the prospects are for the application of equity theory to intergroup behavior and it is with this and certain related topics that the present article will be concerned.

Two different but not entirely unrelated problems make a discussion of equity theory in relation to intergroup behavior a less than straightforward task. The first of these is a dearth of pertinent research. The Adams and Freedman bibliography, for instance, contains no references to work directly concerned with the application of equity concepts to intergroup relations, and there is now serious doubt about the wisdom of attempting to account for intergroup events by extrapolation from research whose focus is essentially interpersonal (Tajfel, 1978; Turner, 1975; Billig, 1976; Tajfel, Note 1). Still, a certain amount of relevant material does exist as part of a body of research associated with some fairly recent attempts to develop a more comprehensive social psychology of intergroup behavior and this will be the primary source of data for our discussion here. There are two reasons for this. First, the studies to which we will refer raise some interesting questions about equity theory's significance with regard to intergroup relations. Second, as these studies are concerned with what has been called social identity theory (Tajfel, 1975, 1978; Turner, 1975; Tajfel & Turner, 1979; Brewer, 1979; Tajfel, Note 1), they afford an opportunity for considering how the processes outlined in equity theory and the social identity approach to intergroup relations compare and interrelate.

The second of the two problems referred to above has to do with a limitation in equity theory itself. A careful reading of the Walster et al. proposals shows that, despite Adams and Freedman's comments about the relevance of equity theory to intergroup relations, these proposals are essentially *intra*group in their orientation. That is to say, the argument is built on the idea that it is in the interests of a group to develop an equity outlook *among its members* and to create conditions *within its own boundaries* which help to promote equitable behavior. So long as we restrict ourselves to intergroup relations between subgroups of a single cultural unit, then we remain within the compass of this argument. If, however, we turn our attention to relations between groups with different cultural backgrounds, then, strictly speaking, we go beyond the argument as stated and it can legitimately be asked whether the proposals, as they stand, are still meant to apply. Lerner's (1977) discussion and categorization of the different forms of justice implies that the answer to this question is no: He associates the justice of equity with unit (i.e., intragroup) relations but *not* with nonunit (i.e., intergroup) ones. Lerner's is not the last word, of course, and there are at least two options open to those who would continue to argue equity theory's relevance to the whole range of intergroup possibilities. One would involve a direct rephrasing of intragroup equity in intergroup terms, giving rise to the proposal that different cultural groupings, in order to control conflicts between themselves, generate common views about the need for equitable relations and create accordingly the conditions which foster equitable interaction and discourage actions of a self-serving, inequitable kind. It is not hard to think of examples which seem to fit such an analysis; the problem is that the number of conceivable exceptions is unquestionably greater, making the basic argument a difficult one to sustain. The second option would be to assume that intragroup notions of equity simply generalize to inter-group contexts of all kinds. That is to say, the equity influences which act on and concern me in my transactions with X, who happens to be a member of my group, are, in principle, no different from those which act on and concern me in my transactions with Y, who happens to be a member of another, culturally different group. Once again, however, while examples can be suggested, exceptions abound (Sumner, 1906; Sumner et al., 1927; Brewer, 1968). In short, neither approach provides a wholly satisfactory resolution.

The problem of how to align intragroup equity theory, as conceived by Walster et al., with interactions between groups with different cultural backgrounds is one we will not pursue any further here. The discussion which follows side-steps the issue, in fact, by focusing on data derived from symbolic or actual encounters between groups whose members are, to all intents and purposes, culturally homogeneous. In the long run, however, it may prove necessary either to alter or qualify the Walster et al. proposals in some way or to assume that the social process to which Propositions IIA and IIB refer has yet to be completed at the level or in the context in question, and that assessments of the theory's relevance are in those circumstances premature. Meanwhile it is important to note that, in proceeding with the proposals as they stand, we are limiting ourselves to what we might call intracultural intergroup phenomena and that our use of the terms *group* and *intergroup*, and our findings, need to be interpreted accordingly.

EQUITY AND INTERGROUP BEHAVIOR

As has been said, the central thesis of equity theory is that social groups encourage their members to behave in an equitable manner and to restore equity when inequitable relationships are experienced or encountered. The two parts of the thesis—behaving equitably and equity restoration—will be considered separately beginning, in this section, with the former.

A number of different experimental designs have been employed to investigate whether subjects are disposed toward behaving in an equitable manner. Many can be grouped into one broad category of experimentation which takes as the dependent variable to be studied the subject's performance on some task after having first been appraised of the rate(s) of pay for the task and/or his or her ability (vis-à-vis others) to perform it. Perhaps because "performance" has numerous dimensions (e.g., quality, quantity, novelty, consistency, endurance, withheld or suspended, and so on) the findings have not always been unambiguous. Nevertheless, there are data which show that subjects will alter their behavioral inputs so as to insure that a balance between the outcomes and inputs of the different participants accrues (Adams & Rosenbaum, 1962; Adams, 1963; Goodman & Friedman, 1968; Wiener, 1970; Pritchard et al., 1972). A second broad category of experimentation—the reverse of the first—is concerned with the way in which the subject allocates rewards, usually money, after some task has already been performed. Of these allocation studies, two general types can be distinguished: one is where the subject is him/herself one of the recipients (self-other allocations), and the other is where he/she is merely an arbiter making decisions about the rewards to go to others (other-other allocations). The latter is less common, but the evidence is clear in suggesting that the aim of most subjects is to insure an equitable distribution of rewards among the eligible recipients (Leventhal et al., 1972, 1973). The results for self-other allocations show a similar trend toward equitable distribution modified, to a greater or lesser extent, by self-interest or by the tendency, in some female subjects, to sacrifice equitable advantage and opt instead for parity or near parity disbursements (Leventhal & Michaels, 1969; Leventhal & Anderson, 1970; Leventhal & Lane, 1970; Benton, 1971; Lane & Messé, 1971; Lane et al., 1972). The contexts for which all of these allocations are required are typically of an interpersonal or intragroup nature; certainly there are no intimations that those eligible to receive rewards belong to different groups. It is interesting, therefore, that the intergroup literature includes two studies which, though concerned with other issues, are almost exact parallels of the basic equity reward allocation design.[1]

The first of these is an experiment by Tajfel et al. (1971). Tajfel et al. asked 14- to 15-year-old male subjects (all from the same class in a

British state school) to engage in the simple task of distributing rewards to pairs of their fellow subjects—the method of distribution being the choice, for each pair, of a number or reward couplet from matrix arrays similar to the one displayed in Figure 1. There were, as can be seen from Figure 1, certain special features associated with the request. Most significantly, the recipients were identified only by a code number and a group designation, the latter being the same as or different from the reward allocator's. The origin of the group classification was, to the subjects, quite straightforward. Earlier, and apparently as part of a different study, they had been shown pairs of paintings and asked to express their preference "between paintings of two foreign modern painters, Klee and Kandinsky." Their supposed individual preferences—supposed because, in fact, classification was random—were then communicated to them privately and were used, said the experimenter, in the subsequent reward allocation study only because it permitted administrative efficiency when the rewards were eventually disbursed.

An important feature of the matrices themselves was that they presented the allocators with several different reward choice strategies. For instance, for the matrix displayed in Figure 1 (which we will call version 1), allocators could choose so as to maximize the joint payoff of the two recipients (MJP, extreme right-hand box), or the ingrouper's payment (MIP, same box) or, at a cost, the difference in favor of the ingrouper (MD, extreme left-hand box). Equal reward, which under the circumstances was also the most equitable, could be allocated by choosing the middle box. Other matrices, identical to the one in Figure 1 but with the order of the recipients reversed (Kandinsky/Klee instead of Klee/Kandinsky), combined MJP, MIP, and MD choices in the extreme right-hand box (version 2). By comparing subjects' responses on each of the two versions, it could be determined whether an overall ingroup-outgroup strategy was employed. For instance, choice of the same box for each version of the matrix would indicate an effort to balance or equalize ingroup and outgroup payment overall (again, under the circumstances, an equitable choice). Choice, in version 1, of a box to the left of the one chosen in version 2, would indicate that maximizing the difference in favor of the ingroup was the primary overall interest.

In summary then, the boys were asked to allocate rewards to classmates, pair by pair, but under the constraint that nothing about the recipients was known except whether their membership in an essentially trivial group matched that of the allocator himself. Different reward choice strategies, including equity, were available and allocators knew—this was stressed—that in no case would they be distributing rewards to themselves. In other words, decisions of the other-other variety were required with the added dimension that the pairs for which decisions were to be made were comprised of an ingroup and an outgroup member.

The results, confirmed since by similar experiments in Britain and elsewhere (Doise et al., 1972; Billig & Tajfel, 1973; Turner, 1975), showed that out of the several strategies available to the subjects, it was the creation of an ingroup-favoring differential that attracted them most. In short, equity was not the prevailing response and the subjects were even willing to sacrifice ingroupers' rewards (i.e., movement to the left in version 1) in order to insure an ingroup-favoring outcome.

There are two points to be considered in relation to these findings. First, instrumental self-interest was not involved in the choices. Indeed, it was the specific intention of Tajfel and his colleagues to demonstrate that, even in the absence of all the usual explanations for discriminatory intergroup bias—frustration, instrumental self-interest, a history of hostile relations—a significant level of ingroup favoritism would still be observed. Later studies also showed that neither similarity/attraction effects (Billig & Tajfel, 1973) nor experimenter effects (Billig, 1973) or factors arising out of affiliative needs in unfamiliar surroundings (Tajfel & Billig, 1974) could account for the initial results. In other words, the bias that was observed was—theoretically speaking—unusual, apparently gratuitous, and therefore quite striking.

Second, though ingroup-favoring bias was the predominant finding, it was nevertheless clear that other factors exerted an important influence on the responses given. As Tajfel et al. emphasized, any discussion of their findings "would not be complete without stressing the importance in the determination of choices of the variable of fairness (F). . . . All the choices in the experiment could be conceived as tending to achieve a compromise between F and other variables" (1971, p. 173). To put it another way, the responses may have been inequitable but not thoroughly so. Evidently, the equity ideal (or something very much like it) did exercise an influence, but more in a moderating than in a governing fashion.

There is, then, evidence in the Tajfel et al. study for an equity effect in intergroup settings but evidence, too, for more pressing interests motivating the subjects in the direction of ingroup-favoring inequity. Tajfel (1978, Note 1) has since developed a view of intergroup behavior

Booklet for group preferring Kandinsky

Direction: The numbers in the boxes below represent rewards which can be given to the persons listed. Study the boxes carefully and then choose *one* box which shows the rewards you wish to give. The upper number in the box will be given to the person listed first and the lower number to the person listed underneath. Work carefully but quickly.

Member no. 74 of Klee group	1	3	5	7	9	11	13	15	17	19	21	23	25
Member no. 44 of Kandinsky group	7	8	9	10	11	12	13	14	15	16	17	18	19

Fill in below details of the box you have just chosen:

Amount

Reward for member no. 74 of Klee group   _____

Reward for member no. 44 of Kandinsky group   _____

Figure 1: Sample matrix format for reward allocations (after Tajfel et al., 1971, Experiment 2).

227

which attempts to explain trends of the latter sort and it is useful, before
we continue any further, to outline some of the main features of his
theory. In essence, his argument is a detailed treatment of some of the
processes to which Proposition I merely refers.

The starting point is with some of the psychological underpinnings of
intergroup behavior. Tajfel begins by pointing out that intergroup
behavior is impossible unless, for the individuals involved, the social
environment can be segmented into entities which permit the definition
of "we" and "they." A necessary cognitive operation, therefore, is social
categorization or the ordering of the social environment in terms of
groupings of persons in a manner which makes sense to the subject.
Though this is an obvious requirement, it is fair to say that the
implications of defining a we-group by social categorization have not
generally been fully appreciated by most investigators. For his part,
Tajfel argues that one especially significant aspect of social categorization lies in its provision of a social identity for the individual—an
outcome which then opens up the possibility of certain further
consequences. These consequences follow from the formal definition of
social identity as that part of a person's self-concept which derives from
his or her knowledge of membership in a social group (or groups)
together with the value and emotional significance attached to that
membership, and the assumption that a fundamental need of most
individuals is to have a satisfactory self-concept. Together they lead to
the notion that, in intergroup settings, at least one concern of those
persons involved may be with whether theirs is a positively valued social
identity. But positivity, of course, is relative and largely determined by
the making of comparisons—social comparisons—between one's own
group and suitable others along dimensions felt at the time to be salient.
(Tajfel's version of social comparison is thus more inclusive than
Festinger's, 1954, initial treatment, especially in its recognition of both
the importance of intergroup comparisons and the diversity of comparative dimensions.) What the individual looks for is an indication
that, on some valued dimension(s), in- and outgroups are located in
relation to one another in such a way that the ingroup's position—and
thus the individual's own social identity—can be interpreted as a
favorable one.

What then follows depends upon the outcome of this social
categorization—social identity—social comparison process. According
to Tajfel, if the group is seen to provide for the individual a positive
social identity, then he or she will tend to remain a member and, if
necessary, take steps to maintain that positivity against threat. On the

other hand, social comparison may reveal that the group is not making a satisfactory contribution to social social identity—perhaps because the situation is so badly defined that it is impossible to ascertain the place of one's group within the existing circumstances; or because similarity with another group prevents a distinctively positive social identity from being defined; or because one's group is seen as occupying a favorable (superior) or unfavorable (inferior) position relative to a comparison group but in circumstances where it is possible to visualize a reversal in this status. Tajfel suggests two different classes of response to these sorts of experiences. Where it is both possible and desirable to leave the group and join another, the individual may do just this. Where it is not, then any action undertaken needs to be in group terms—that is to say, it needs to have as its aim maintaining or improving the comparative standing of the group in order to create a more favorable social identity and hence a more favorable self-concept.

According to the theory, action in group terms may take a number of forms. Differences in favor of the ingroup may be created either psychologically or through actual behavior; they may result from a reinterpretation or a revaluation of existing "negative" differences, or a vigorous emphasis or re-emphasis of existing "positive" differences. At its simplest level, one is likely to observe what appears to be gratuitous pro-ingroup bias along whatever dimensions are available and salient. Thus, Tajfel's explanation for the bias in the Klee/Kandinsky data is that the boys used the reward allocation task to create a positively valued differentiation between their own and the other group, thereby defining for themselves—in otherwise uncertain circumstances—a satisfactory social identity. At a more complex level, social identity strivings may be bound up with, and reveal themselves in, such things as the perception and use of language (Giles et al., 1977), the creation of new or the bolstering of old ideological systems (Billig, 1976), the structure or conduct of social relations (Mason, 1970, quoted in Tajfel, Note 1), and so on.

Certain additional features of Tajfel's argument will be introduced later on in our discussion. For the moment, however, the outline above is sufficient to enable us to make sense of the bias expressed in the Tajfel et al. experiment and to see the results as demonstrating both the presence of, and a conflict between, social identity interests and equity motivations. Seen in this way, it may appear that our initial classification of the study as being within the "other-other" tradition of reward allocation experiments is inappropriate. The point will not be debated here. Instead, we will briefly review a second intergroup experiment where "self-other" allocations were explicitly required of the subjects. This second experiment was conducted by Turner (1975) and his findings neatly illustrate the complexity of, on the one hand, interactions between self, social identity, and equity motivations, and, on the other, the individual's perceptions of the setting as an intergroup or an interpersonal one. Turner repeated the original Klee/Kandinsky study but, in connection with the reward matrices, introduced two modifications of particular interest here. In addition to the usual ingroup-outgroup (O-O) allocations, he also asked his subjects to make self-other (S-O) awards, the other being, in some cases, a member of the ingroup, and, in others, a member of the outgroup. Second, he required half of his subjects to make their S-O allocations first (S-O/O-O), and the other half to make theirs in the reverse order (O-O/S-O). Turner reasoned that the self-other allocations of the O-O/S-O subjects would be influenced by their earlier commitment to a group identity in their initial O-O choices. Thus he expected that any bias in favor of self in these subjects' S-O choices would be less marked when the other was an ingrouper than when the person was an outgrouper. As for the S-O/O-O subjects, since they had experienced no initial group membership "set," it was anticipated that ingroup and outgroup others would be discriminated against in favor of self equally. (The expectation of self-favoring bias in *all* subjects' S-O responses derived from Tajfel's basic assumption that individuals seek to establish a positive self-concept and will do so by S-O, rather than by group differentiations if that is an available option.) The results confirmed Turner's predictions in every respect. The self-other choices of all the subjects did show bias in favor of self— but the bias was equal in extent for ingroup and outgroup others in the case of the S-O/O-O subjects and showed a differentiation between the two in the manner predicted for the O-O/S-O subjects.

Again there are points to be noted. Self-favoring choices, as with the ingroup-favoring choices of the Tajfel et al. study, were more strongly influenced by MD type interests than by anything else. That is, subjects leaned toward creating favorable differences between themselves and others even if this required a sacrifice in the absolute value of their own reward. Second, though Turner did not concern himself with the "fairness" issue, his data could also be adequately characterized by the phrase Tajfel and his co-workers used to describe theirs: That is, his subjects' responses could be seen as the outcome of attempts to "achieve a compromise between F and other variables." Where the context was perceived as an intergroup one, this compromise was not so vigorously sought for outgroupers as it was for ingroupers. Nevertheless, full-scale bias was avoided by the subjects and the data are consistent with the idea that the effects predicted by equity theory were operating, even if differentially.

The conclusion to be drawn from the Tajfel et al. and Turner findings is that behaving equitably is a consideration which acts upon and influences the participants in intergroup events, at least when it comes to the allocation of small rewards. At the same time, it must be acknowledged that that influence is a moderating, and not a governing, one and that ingroup rather than outgroup others are more likely to benefit from its operation if ingroup membership is salient. Of greater impact, it seems, are needs to establish a positive social identity—these motivating in the direction of ingroup-favoring inequity. It is interesting to note that, for the examples cited, these social identity needs have expressed themselves in connection with groups of a trivial kind. This raises the question as to whether behaving equitably, as a value in intergroup settings, carries much weight if it can be prevailed against by motivations arising out of such transient and inconsequential memberships. This question will receive something of an answer in the next section, where we consider research relating to equity restoration and make reference to material concerned with groups of a more ego-involving nature.

INEQUITY AND INTERGROUP BEHAVIOR

Equity theory holds that participation in an inequitable relationship is distressing for the individual and leads to attempts to reduce distress by restoring equity. Equity restoration may take place in various ways, its form depending on whether one is concerned with the "harm-doer" or the "victim" and whether the conditions are such as to favor the actual alteration of the participants' outcomes, inputs, rewards or costs, or their modification by some kind of psychological distortion. Walster et al. (1973) propose, and cite a certain amount of formal and anecdotal evidence for, each of the following:

1. Harm-doers may attempt to restore equity by:
   a. compensating their victims (actual)
   b. reducing their own relative outcomes to the victim's level (actual)
   c. maintaining that the victim deserves the inequitable treatment (psychological)
   d. minimizing the victim's suffering (psychological)
   e. denying responsibility for the inequitable act (psychological).

2. Victims may attempt to restore equity by:
   a. demanding and receiving compensation (actual)
   b. increasing the costs for harm-doers by retaliation (actual)
   c. forgiving the harm-doer (actual or psychological)
   d. justifying the inequity (psychological).

As for the conditions which lead to equity restoration by actual or psychological means, Walster et al. suggest that:

1. Harm-doers are:
   a. less likely to employ compensation if the resources for doing so are not adequate
   b. more likely to employ some form of psychological justification if it requires little distortion of reality, or if contact with the victim (or the victim's sympathizers) is minimal.
2. Victims, on the other hand:
   a. will normally seek redress through compensation or retaliation, but
   b. where they are too weak to do either and the admission of weakness is itself distressing, they may seek to justify their inequitable disadvantage.

A common format for the investigation of the idea that individuals, as victims or beneficiaries, will seek to redress an inequity has been to offer subjects the opportunity to reallocate rewards, normally money, after inequitable disbursements have first been made. In general, reallocations in the direction of equity have been observed, at least in those cases where the original inequitable disbursement is seen to be intentional, and where the inequity is not so extreme as to motivate the subjects to leave the field (Leventhal, Allen, & Kemelgor, 1969; Leventhal, Weiss, & Long, 1969; Kahn, 1972; Schmitt & Marwell, 1972; Garrett & Libby, 1973). As before, the subjects' symbolic or actual transactions with others are typically of an interpersonal or intragroup kind, but once again—and this time not entirely fortuitously—the experimental intergroup literature provides some more-or-less comparable designs.

A particular case in point is a recent investigation by Commins and Lockwood (1979). This was an explicit attempt to study reactions to inequitable reward in an intergroup setting in which social identity interests were also expected to be aroused. Subjects were ostensibly divided into two groups—overestimators and underestimators—on the basis of their performance in estimating the numbers of dots in several rapidly presented and briefly exposed dot clusters. They were then led to believe either that the groups were equal in estimating accuracy or that one was better than the other. Following this, they were asked to complete reward choice matrices roughly similar to those employed in the Tajfel et al. experiment but, just before doing so, some of the subjects were advised privately that the two groups began with a 25-point differential (equal to a small sum of money) between them. In some cases, the ingroup was said to have been given this advantage; in others, it was the outgroup which began in the more favorable position. Taken together with the original performance similarities or differences between the groups, this prematrix point manipulation resulted in instances of equitable advantage, equitable disadvantage, inequitable advantage, and inequitable disadvantage. The subsequent matrix responses therefore permitted an examination of the extent to which differentiation for social identity purposes was added to or reduced by attempts, in conditions of inequity, to restore an equitable state of affairs.

Overall, the subjects' matrix response trends consistent with the idea that equity restoration is an important issue which can interact with social identity interests and influence accordingly the extent to which identity-enhancing reward differentiations are made. This effect seemed strongest in the case of inequitable disadvantage: The greatest shift, in the direction of increased ingroup bias, was observed in cases where the prematrix award was out of line with the relatively better performance of the ingroup. Where the group members' experience was one of inequitable advantage, a somewhat smaller shift, generally in the direction of a reduction in ingroup bias, was observed. Though smaller, this shift nevertheless gives rise to an interesting result. When Commins and Lockwood combined the data for all instances of inequitable advantage which the various conditions of their experiment defined, they found that, overall, the tendency to differentiate in favor of the ingroup disappeared (statistically speaking). In other words, when these subjects' matrix disbursements for the two groups were totalled and the prematrix differences added in, the result was a final disbursement which, on average, was not significantly different from the point of equal reward. This would seem to indicate that the beneficiaries of the inequitable treatment of one group over another may in some cases be moved to restore at least some measure of equity to their comparative relationship. It also seems to suggest—though Commins and Lockwood do not say so—that equity considerations may occasionally overpower the tendency to establish or maintain a positively valued differentiation in favor of the ingroup.

Commins and Lockwood's study is a rare—and therefore valuable— extension of equity theory into intergroup contexts, but its overall relevance in these contexts is limited in two ways. First, responsibility for the inequity in the experiment lay not with some of the participants but with a third party—the experimenter; second, in intergroup settings outside the laboratory, inequitable advantage or disadvantage is normally the condition of the superior or inferior status group, respectively, not the other way around. There are other data available which, to a greater or lesser extent, meet these objections. However, as these derive from experimental evaluations of certain aspects of Tajfel's theory which have not yet been presented, we need to supply this additional information before proceeding any further.

Tajfel's ideas about social identity-motivated intergroup behavior have been developed mainly in connection with intergroup settings characterized by status differentials between the groups. According to the theory, when the members of groups linked in a superior/inferior status relationship become aware that alternatives to this relationship are possible, then it is likely that those who belong to the high-status group will take steps to maintain their group's position while those belonging to the low-status group will attempt to define a new status arrangement which is more favorable to them. Tajfel mentions two conditions in which an awareness of alternative status arrangements may develop: one is where there are indications to those involved that the differential which presently exists between the groups is an unstable one; the other is where, for one reason or another, this differential is perceived to be illegitimate. Because of its overlap with perceived inequity, it is the latter which is of interest here. In connection with group members' perceptions that the status relationship is illegitimate, Tajfel (1978) makes the following predictions:

(1) Members of illegitimately superior groups will attempt to find justifications for the maintenance of the status quo, either by creating (actually or psychologically) new forms of positively valued distinctiveness or by enhancing those among the old ones which are still serviceable.

(2) Members of illegitimately inferior groups will attempt to change the status quo, either by reinterpreting or revaluing the existing "inferior" characteristics or by creating (actually or psychologically) new group characteristics, so that a positively valued distinctiveness from the other group is established.

A comparison of these proposals with those made by Walster et al. about equity restoration reveals some general similarities and one important difference. The difference is that, in Tajfel's view, the aim is to establish or maintain a differential, not eliminate an inequity. Thus, Tajfel does not entertain the possibility that superior group members may respond to illegitimacy by acting so as to actually diminish their advantage vis-à-vis the other group. This, if true, has obvious implications for the resolution of injustice and conflict although, as the next study shows, it may be an overly pessimistic view.

The study in question is by Turner and Brown (1978). These investigators set out to produce and then monitor the effect on intergroup behavior of variations in both the legitimacy and the stability of relations between two groups. Their intention was to test out Tajfel's predictions regarding unstable and illegitimate status relations but only the latter will concern us here. There are—as will be seen—certain peculiarities associated with the Turner and Brown study and therefore we need to outline the experimental procedure in some detail.

The subjects were college students, recruited to work as members of three-person groups in what was purported to be a study of reasoning skills. The ostensible task of these groups, which were tested one at a time, was to discuss an issue with social/philosophical overtones and then to prepare and tape record the group's views on this issue and the reasons for holding these views. Supposedly, the taped remarks were to be used as the data to be analyzed later for reasoning skills.

Before entering into their discussions, group members were also given some additional information which served to define the conditions of the experiment. It was first pointed out, in connection with the fact that the group's members were either all Arts or all Science students, that while reasoning skills were important for all students, research suggested that there were known performance differences between the two faculty groups. This defined a status differentiation which, for half of the subjects, was favorable and, for the other half, unfavorable. Following on from this the experimenter commented that the difference was either unfair and unreasonable or fair and to be expected. Unfairness was said to derive from an inbuilt test bias not well-recognized by psychologists and undoubtedly to blame for discriminatory outcomes when such tests were used in personnel selection and assessment. Subjects receiving the fair message also heard about the testing bias, but this time it was described as legitimate, well-known, and taken into account and corrected for in practice. Finally, subjects were informed either that the normal findings relating to reasoning skills differences were almost certain to obtain in the present circumstances or were, in fact, open to the possibility of change.

Three measures were taken to trace the effects of the manipulations. First, the groups were asked to give ratings of their taped arguments and those of another group (provided by a standard tape identified as being prepared by a group from the other faculty). Ratings were given using the matrix format, suitably modified for the purpose. Then, subjects were asked to suggest—if they wished—other methods by which reasoning skills might be assessed, and factors other than reasoning skills which needed to be taken into account in assessing overall intellectual ability.

Drawing from Tajfel's proposals, Turner and Brown predicted that their illegitimate superiors would seek to justify and maintain their advantage and would show this by heightened ingroup bias in their ratings of the tapes, and by using the opportunity provided by the "methods" and "factors" questions to suggest new and alternative dimensions of comparison. Illegitimate inferiors, it was expected, would also use the methods and factors questions to suggest other dimensions of comparison. Their findings, though complex, were taken to give a measure of support to Tajfel's proposals. Yet, notwithstanding the authors' intentions and interpretations, there is a methodological problem in relation to the responses of the illegitimate superiors which calls this conclusion into question and opens the way for a markedly different view.

The methodological problem is straightforward enough. Tajfel states that justification by the members of illegitimately superior groups will manifest itself as an enhancement of differences on those comparative dimensions which are still serviceable, and/or by the creation of ingroup-favoring differences on newly created dimensions of comparison open to such use. For neither possibility, however, did the experimenters provide a response format suitable for the expression of these kinds of behaviors. The tape ratings were inappropriate since they referred to a dimension of comparison already identified by the experimenter as unfair and unreasonable. The methods and factors suggestions were similarly inappropriate since, if the subjects had been listening to the experimenter's comments, they could only have concluded that what were needed were new methods and new factors to help restore justice and fairness to the whole process of assessment. The fact, then, that the illegitimate superiors—like the illegitimate inferiors—seemed willing to suggest new methods and new factors implies that they were seeking to redress an unjust imbalance from which in-groupers might unfairly benefit. As for the tape ratings, the illegitimate superior data are unfortunately too variable (one apparently high in-group bias, one low) to permit any satisfactory conclusions. Indeed, the variation underscores a second methodological fault: with so few groups (n = 2) in each cell of the experimental design, and with no independent ratings of in- and outgroup performance, it is impossible to say whether the ingroup-favoring ratings that were observed do or do not demon-strate bias.

Both the Commins and Lockwood and the Turner and Brown studies give evidence for actual equity restoration in intergroup settings. The latter, of course, comes closer to the reality of ex-laboratory intergroup settings in associating inequitable advantage and disadvantage with high and low status, respectively. The two are similar, however, in linking responsibility for the inequity to the actions of some third party. This naturally raises the question as to whether the members of illegitimately or inequitably advantaged groups would behave in a similar manner were they more directly responsible for the advantage enjoyed. A study by Caddick (1978)—the last to be cited—provides us with data that touch on this issue.

As in the previous investigation, Caddick's interests were in tracing the effects of perceived illegitimacy and perceived instability on intergroup behavior. Once again, however, we will limit our attention to the first of these.

The subjects in the study were 13- to 14-year-old schoolboys attending British state schools at the third form level. In their school setting they were randomly formed into three- or four-person groups and, in the crucial second session of the experiment, were tested in a two-group context, paired groups being balanced in terms of member numbers. The boys were led to believe that they were participating in a study aimed at determining how well pupils might accomplish school work if they were permitted to work together with others.

Groups came to the second sessions having each completed two tasks in an earlier session in which all of the groups were present. One of the tasks was to draw a map of their schoolground showing where a gang of robbers might have most effectively hidden some stolen money. The second was a spot-the-ball (SB) task in which members of the group viewed a set of action football photographs and recorded their collective views as to which, if either, of two paper discs affixed to each photo covered the ball. In the second session, false feedback on their performance on this latter task was conveyed to the two groups present so that a differentiation between the groups was created. At this point, a new SB task was administered, the answers "marked," and again feedback was given to the effect that there was still a performance difference between the groups, albeit a smaller one. Following on from this the subjects gave ratings of their own and the other group. They also evaluated each other's previously drawn maps and, finally, they distributed rewards using matrices similar to those employed in other intergroup studies.

The following points are relevant to our interest. "Control" groups were defined by leading certain high and low performance groups to see the difference in performance between themselves and the other group as being legitimate. Illegitimate superiors and inferiors, on the other hand, experienced certain procedural changes designed to make the members of both groups perceive the performance difference as unfair. The earlier low scoring group was first required to perform the new SB task under a handicap which was made to appear to be the consequences of the other group's action (a vote—the outcome of which was "fixed" by the experimenter). Specifically, these subjects were required by the vote's outcome to make their second SB decisions using a photo set with three (rather than two) discs on each photo, arranged in a closely clustered array. The task was clearly harder and, as the SB trials were closely timed, the handicapped group had obvious difficulty keeping up. The other group, meanwhile, having "voted" itself the two-disc set, maintained the pace easily.

The crucial manipulation came after the performance feedback. Commenting on the difference between the group's scores the experimenter made no mention of the handicap the members of the three-disc group had suffered. This, of course, occasioned their protests, but the experimenter stated that, as he had never tested with the three-disc set before, he could not say whether their comments were justified. For the time being, then, the difference must stand. This was unfair treatment and it was expected that an impression of illegitimate differentiation would be created in which, to some extent, the members of the superior group would also be implicated by virtue of their previous vote. A posttest questionnaire check showed that the low scorers did feel themselves to have been dealt with unfairly.

Some of the findings are presented in Table 2. Those denoted as "matrix" are the results calculated from responses given to the two versions of the matrix described in connection with Figure 1. The numbers tabled are the mean values of what are generally termed "pull" scores; that is, they show the pull exerted by MD (maximizing a

TABLE 2
Matrix and Map Evaluation Scores for High and Low
Performance Groups under Conditions of Legitimate and
Illegitimate Intergroup Differentiation

Measure	Legitimate (Control)	Illegitimate	tD^a
Matrix			
High Performance	0.19	2.89	2.84***
Low Performance	0.07	3.77	3.89***
Map			
High Performance	9.57	27.45	2.06*
Low Performance	2.18	21.30	2.20**

*p < .06; **p < .05; ***p < .01

a. As noted in the text, the overall experiment included other conditions and therefore other planned comparisons. To control against the Type I error of multiple t-testing, Dunnett's test (1-tailed) was used.

difference in favor of the ingroup) against other strategies of reward. Scores above 0 indicate that maximizing the difference in favor of the ingroup is the prevailing interest (maximum MD score = 12); a score of 0 indicates an overall balance between ingroup and outgroup award. The results labelled "map" are the mean differences in evaluations given to the ingroup and outgroup maps constructed in the first session. Clearly, the results for both groups in the illegitimacy condition show motivation to favor the ingroup, even—as is the case for the map ratings—where the object of assessment is unrelated to the spot-the-ball outcome and procedure. The responses on all of the other dependent measures (in- and outgroup ratings, other matrix types) showed trends in a similar direction.

From a social identity perspective, these results are straightforward: While the illegitimate inferiors sought to establish new differentiations in their favor, the illegitimate superiors attempted to bolster up and maintain the status quo. An equity theory explanation is rather more complicated. Certainly the responses of the unfairly treated group can be seen as an attempt to obtain direct (the matrices) and indirect (the map evaluations) recognition for its efforts. Furthermore, it is clear that the members of the advantaged group had no interest in giving the other group its due. Indeed, what could be said to be indicated by their inflated matrix claims (inflated by comparison to the "controls") is that they were somehow able to minimize the obvious difficulties experienced by the other group and to see their own efforts as much more deserving of reward. Their ratings of the two groups' efforts on the unrelated map task, seen as a "halo effect" carryover, is further evidence for the existence of some kind of psychological distortion. Arguably, then, these subjects' responses are an example of psychological equity restoration and, as such, stand in contrast to the findings of the two previous studies where actual equity restoration by the inequitably advantaged group was the indicated tendency. Of course, whether the social identity or the equity theory explanation is the more appropriate is impossible to determine.

Several points emerge from the material presented in this section. All of the studies cited could be said to provide evidence that members of groups experiencing inequitable disadvantage or unfair treatment are likely to seek some form of redress. There are also data which appear to show that members of equitably advantaged groups may endeavor to restore equity or justice—although "psychological," rather than "actual," methods may be employed. It is of interest that maintaining an ingroup-favoring differential for social identity purposes seemed unimportant to the inequitably advantaged groups in the Commins and Lockwood and Turner and Brown studies. This is a rather different picture of the relative strengths of social identity and fairness needs from that which emerged from the previous section. On the other hand, it seems probable that complete third-party responsibility for the inequity substantially reduced these subjects' interest in maintaining a relationship that others had defined. It is worth noting here that, in those conditions of their experiment where Commins and Lockwood made equitable payment to the groups, significant ingroup bias was still observed in the subjects' matrix awards. Evidently, then, it would be wrong to suppose that equity interests might easily be made to prevail over needs to maintain or establish a satisfactory social identity by discriminatory bias.

THE NEED FOR RESEARCH

In the preceding sections of this article, we have explored the applicability of equity theory concepts and ideas to intergroup relations by considering in some detail the results of a small number of experimental studies. What we have seen is that fairness considerations have an important, if not necessarily predominant, influence in at least some kinds of intergroup settings. There are also indications that equity theory may provide a plausible explanation for response trends in cases of inequitable relations between groups. As for the significance to be attached to these findings, it is clear that a cautious view is warranted. While the conditions of laboratory experimentation are likely to encourage equitable behavior and discourage the expression of selfish motives—we are thinking here of such features as close interpersonal contact, explicit or implicit scrutiny of responses by a powerful figure, minimal rewards for acting self-interestedly, vulnerability to retaliation or esteem-damaging accusations—they are unlikely to characterize many intergroup settings in the "real world." Perhaps the message to be taken from this is that, while it is doubtful that intergroup equity is little more than an experimental artifact, equity effects will be seen to be strongest where the opportunities for communication, scrutiny, and influence are maximal. Clearly, more research is needed.

The first priority should be the creation of an adequate empirical base. Turner's (1975) experiment, discussed earlier, shows that subtle but important differences in behavior result when the perception of events switches from an interpersonal to an intergroup one. What is needed, therefore, is research which is explicitly intergroup in its orientation. Many of the existing equity research designs are amenable to the introduction of an intergroup dimension, making the generation of some basic data a fairly straightforward task. Modifications which would enhance the value of such material would include the greater use of real, as against ad hoc, groups, and the employment of tasks and the definition of inequities of a more compelling kind (except for the third-party involvement, the Turner and Brown experiment provides a good example of the latter). More field research would be a definite asset, in the sense of providing an evaluation of intergroup equity effects in more testing conditions. Overall, of course, the aim should not be just to demonstrate equity effects but also to discover the conditions which strengthen these against the tendency to maximize ingroup outcomes for social identity purposes and the other selfish interests to which the first proposition of equity theory refers.

Attention needs also to be given to equity restoration and, in particular, to the problem of psychological equity restoration. There are two issues here. First, discovering the factors which heighten the need to be fair and equitable in one's dealings with the members of another group will be of little use if inequities are then "eliminated" in a psychological manner. Thus the investigation and analysis of the conditions which encourage actual as against psychological equity restoration is of some importance. As noted earlier, Walster et al. make suggestions about the kinds of factors which can influence the nature of the advantaged person's responses in cases of inequity. These include the adequacy of the compensation which he/she can offer the victim, the extent to which credibility is affected by the distortion, and the extent to which the harm-doer is able to isolate him/herself from the victim's distress. Each of these has meaning in intergroup terms and is worth pursuing for the light that may be shed on how psychological equity restoration is encouraged and/or maintained.

The second issue is more of a theoretical one and somewhat more complex. As our discussion of Caddick's findings indicates, it may well be a difficult matter to ascertain whether it is psychological equity restoration or an attempt to maintain a satisfactory social identity that underlies some responses. Since the aims are fundamentally different—dealing with distress on the one hand and maintaining an advantage on the other—the problem is rather crucial. It is obviously important to know whether motivational arousal is in the direction of equity restoration or, in fact, the reverse.

An experimental differentiation between the two may be possible. For example, for subjects who have already given responses thought to be either psychological equity restoration or social identity differentiation, a further choice might be offered: between actual equity restoration on the one hand and increased ingroup-favoring bias on the other. Presumably, those most influenced by inequity distress would opt for the former and avoid the latter, while those whose interests were social identity based would do the reverse. Similar methods might also be used to ascertain whether the responses of the members of disadvantaged groups are aimed at restoring equity or at creating a difference which favors their group over the other.

There are, then, some interesting research problems to pursue, ranging from the creation of an adequate data base to the investigation of certain theoretical overlaps and the conflict between different motivational tendencies. The value in doing so has been succinctly put by Adams and Freedman:

> As society grows, its social components become increasingly differentiated, the number of relationships among components increases, and potential conflict between persons, groups, organizations, and institutions rises. In the circumstances, a consequential opportunity to provide understanding is placed before equity theorists [1976, p. 56].

If, as seems to be suggested by the material we have considered here, there are aspects of human motivation which push in the direction of fairness and equity, then equity theorists may indeed have something to offer. In the area of intergroup relations, however, there is much research yet to be done.

NOTE

1. The emphasis throughout most of this article will be on intergroup studies in which outcomes (rewards or "points") rather than inputs are the dependent variables. This emphasis mirrors that of the experimental intergroup literature itself and is not meant to imply that input variation is irrelevant or unimportant.

REFERENCE NOTE

1. Tajfel, H. Intergroup behaviour, social comparison and social change. Katz-Newcomb Lectures, University of Michigan, Ann Arbor, 1974.

REFERENCES

Adams, J. S. Toward an understanding of inequity. *Journal of Abnormal and Social Psychology,* 1963, *67,* 422-436.

Adams, J. S. Inequity in social exchange. In L. Berkowitz (ed.), *Advances in Experimental Social Psychology* (Vol. 2). New York: Academic Press, 1965.

Adams, J. S. & Freedman, S. Equity theory revisited. In L. Berkowitz and E. Walster (eds.), *Advances in experimental social psychology* (Vol. 9). New York: Academic Press, 1976.

Adams, J. S. & Rosenbaum, W. E. The relationship of worker productivity to cognitive dissonance about wage inequity. *Journal of Applied Psychology,* 1962, *46,* 161-164.

Anderson, B., Berger, J., Zelditch, M., & Cohen, B. P. Reactions to inequity. *Acta Sociologica,* 1969, *12,* 1-12.

Benton, A. A. Productivity, distributive justice, and bargaining among children. *Journal of Personality and Social Psychology,* 1971, *18,* 68-78.

Berkowitz, L. & Walster, E. (eds.). *Advances in experimental social psychology* (Vol. 9). New York: Academic Press, 1976.

Billig, M. Normative communication in a minimal intergroup situation. *European Journal of Social Psychology,* 1973, *3,* 339-344.

Billig, M. *Social psychology and intergroup relations.* London: Academic Press, 1976.

Billig, M. & Tajfel, H. Social categorization and similarity in intergroup behaviour. *European Journal of Social Psychology,* 1973, *3,* 27-52.

Brewer, M. B. Determinants of social distance among East African tribal groups. *Journal of Personality and Social Psychology,* 1968, *10,* 279-289.

Brewer, M. B. Ingroup bias in the minimal intergroup situation: a cognitive-motivational analysis. *Psychological Bulletin,* 1979, *86,* 307-324.

Brown, R. & Herrnstein, R. J. *Psychology.* London: Methuen, 1975.

Caddick, B.F.J. Status, legitimacy and the social identity concept in intergroup relations. Unpublished doctoral dissertation, University of Bristol, 1978.

Commins, B. & Lockwood, J. The effects of status differences, favoured treatment and equity on intergroup comparisons. *European Journal of Social Psychology,* 1979, *9,* 281-289.

Doise, W., Csepeli, G., Dann, H-D., Gouge, G. C., Larsen, K., & Ostell, A. An experimental investigation into the formation of intergroup representations. *European Journal of Social Psychology,* 1972, *2,* 202-204.

Festinger, L. A theory of social comparison processes. *Human Relations,* 1954, *7,* 117-140.

Garrett, J. B. & Libby, W. L., Jr. Role of intentionality in mediating responses to inequity in the dyad. *Journal of Personality and Social Psychology,* 1973, *28,* 21-27.

Giles, H., Bourhis, R. Y., & Taylor, D. M. Towards a theory of language in ethnic group relations. In H. Giles (ed.), *Language, ethnicity and intergroup relations.* London: Academic Press, 1977.

Goodman, P. & Friedman, A. An examination of the effect of wage inequity in the hourly condition. *Organizational Behavior and Human Performance,* 1968, *3,* 340-352.

Kahn, A. Reactions to generosity or stinginess from an intelligent or stupid work partner: A test of equity theory in a direct exchange relationship. *Journal of Personality and Social Psychology,* 1972, *21,* 116-123.

Lane, I. M. & Messé, L. A. Equity and the distribution of rewards. *Journal of Personality and Social Psychology,* 1971, *21,* 1-17.

Lane, I. M., Messé, L. A., & Phillips, J. L. Differential inputs as a determinant in the selection of a distribution of rewards. *Psychonomic Science,* 1971, *22,* 228-229.

Lerner, M. J. The justice motive in social behaviour. *Journal of Social Issues,* 1975, *31,* (3), 1-19.

Leventhal, G. S., Allen, J., & Kemelgor, B. Reducing inequity by reallocating rewards. *Psychonomic Science,* 1969, *14,* 295-296.

Leventhal, G. S. & Anderson, D. Self-interest and the maintenance of equity. *Journal of Personality and Social Psychology,* 1970, *15,* 57-62.

Leventhal, G. S. & Lane, D. W. Sex, age, and equity behaviour. *Journal of Personality and Social Psychology,* 1970, *15,* 312-316.

Leventhal, G. S. & Michaels, J. W. Extending the equity model: Perception of inputs and allocation of reward as a function of duration and quantity of performance. *Journal of Personality and Social Psychology,* 1969, *12,* 303-309.

Leventhal, G. S., Michaels, J. W., & Sanford, C. Inequity and interpersonal conflict: Reward allocation and secrecy about reward as methods of preventing conflict. *Journal of Personality and Social Psychology,* 1972, *23,* 88-102.

Leventhal, G. S., Popp, A. L., & Sawyer, L. Equity or equality in children's allocation of reward to other persons? *Child Development,* 1973, *44,* 753-763.

Leventhal, G. S., Weiss, T., & Long, G. Equity, reciprocity and reallocating rewards in the dyad. *Journal of Personality and Social Psychology,* 1969, *13,* 300-305.

Mason, P. *Race relations.* London: Oxford University Press, 1970.

Pritchard, R. D., Dunnette, M. D., & Jorgenson, D. O. Effects of perceptions of equity and inequity on worker performance and satisfaction. *Journal of Applied Psychology Monograph,* 1972, *56,* 75-94.

Schmitt, D. R. & Marwell, G. Withdrawal and reward allocation as responses to inequity. *Journal of Experimental Social Psychology,* 1972, *8,* 207-221.

Sumner, W. G. *Folkways.* Boston: Ginn, 1906.

Sumner, W. G., Keller, A. G., & Davie, M. R. *The science of society.* New Haven, Conn.: Yale University Press, 1927.

Tajfel, H. The exit of social mobility and the voice of social change: Notes on the social psychology of intergroup relations. *Social Science Information,* 1975, *14*(2), 101-118.

Tajfel, H. (ed.). *Differentiation between social groups: studies in the social psychology of intergroup relations.* London: Academic Press, 1978.

Tajfel, H. & Billig, M. Familiarity and categorization in intergroup behaviour. *Journal of Experimental Social Psychology,* 1974, *10,* 159-170.

Tajfel, H., Flament, C., Billig, & Bundy, R. P. Social categorization and intergroup behaviour. *European Journal of Social Psychology,* 1971, *1,* 149-177.

Tajfel, H. & Turner, J. C. An integrative theory of intergroup conflict. In W. G. Austin and S. Worchel (eds.), *The social psychology of intergroup relations.* Belmont, Calif.: Wadsworth.

Turner, J. C. Social comparison and social identity: some prospects for intergroup behaviour. *European Journal of Social Psychology,* 1975, *5,* 5-34.

Turner, J. C. & Brown, R. J. Social status, cognitive alternatives and intergroup relations. In H. Tajfel (ed.), *Differentiation between social groups: Studies in the social psychology of intergroup relations.* London: Academic Press, 1978.

Walster, E., Berscheid, E., & Walster, G. W. New directions in equity research. *Journal of Personality and Social Psychology,* 1973, *25,* 151-176. Reprinted in L. Berkowitz and E. Walster (eds.), *Advances in experimental social psychology* (Vol. 9). New York: Academic Press, 1976.

Wiener, Y. The effects of "task- and ego-oriented" performance of two kinds of overcompensation inequity. *Organizational Behaviour and Human Performance,* 1970, *5,* 191-208.

Constructing a Science of Jury Behavior

9

RONALD C. DILLEHAY
MICHAEL T. NIETZEL

Ronald C. Dillehay is Professor of Psychology and Behavioral Science at the University of Kentucky, where he chaired the Department of Psychology from 1973 to 1980. He combines basic research and theory (authoritarianism, social cognition) with consultation on attorney training, psycholegal training, jury selection, and case preparation and presentation. He received a James McKeen Cattell Fund Award for 1980-1981 to pursue applications of psychology to law.
Michael T. Nietzel is Associate Professor of Psychology and Director of Clinical Training at the University of Kentucky. A clinical psychologist by training, Nietzel's research interests are concentrated on evaluations of social learning theory treatments, applications of psychology to community problems, bail reform, jury selection, and consultation on courtroom dynamics.

Psychologists' interest in jury behavior dates to the early part of this century, when personality and social psychology in their infancy were not yet noted for an experimental research emphasis. Munsterberg (1914), with an interest in applications of psychology and a background in the German "new experimentalism," conducted research on what he considered to be jury processes. His experiments, with his own classes, examined the influence of group discussions on the accuracy of judgments. As we shall see, Munsterberg's experiments are noteworthy because they tested a feature of juror behavior in a laboratorylike setting using materials that have nothing to do with the subject matter of jury or juror tasks.

In the last decade we have seen a dramatic increase in experimental research described as jury simulation or jury analogue research. This literature is the focus of our discussion, but ours is not an inclusive review. We deal instead with issues of method and theory using repre-

AUTHORS' NOTE: Our thanks to Lawrence Wrightsman and Miron Zuckerman for their constructive evaluations of an earlier version of this article.

sentative research. Recent reviews appear in Davis et al. (1977), Gerbasi et al. (1977), Brooks and Doob (1975), and Elwork et al. (in press). Tapp (1976) provides perspective on the place of juror/jury research in the arena of law and psychology generally. Wrightsman (1978) discusses provocatively the relationship between assumptions of the jury trial and theory and research from psychology. Saks and Hastie (1978) review jury research in their treatment of psychology and the courtroom.

Our overall aim in this article is to assess the contributions of mock juror/jury research to an understanding of the behavior of real juries. This assessment requires an evaluation incorporating two perspectives: that of the scientist concerned with discovering general principles of behavior and that of the practitioner viewing the utility of behavioral knowledge. Because we are concerned with the research literature, our discussion deals first with the major issues of internal and external validity raised by the use of hypothetical trials or cases. We then examine two investigations of experimental jurors exposed to actual trials in courts of law. Our attention turns next to issues for psychologists bent on applying behavioral knowledge to jurors or juries. Finally, we offer some suggestions for a science of jury behavior.

ESSENTIAL FEATURES OF MOCK JURY RESEARCH

Essential features of the mock juror/jury literature are that experimental subjects, frequently students, make judgments of a defendant in a hypothetical trial. The subjects typically provide individual judgments of guilt before deliberation, after deliberation, or both. Sometimes additional judgments by individual subjects are obtained, such as recommended punishment for the alleged crime. In some of the research, group or jury verdicts are obtained in addition to individual responses. The typical independent variables are defendant characteristics, victim characteristics, subject variables, social and demographic indices, amount and timing of information, limitations on the kind of judgment to be made, and the like. Settings for the research are the laboratory, university or college classroom, and sometimes a law school courtroom or an available real courtroom secured for the research. A cataloguing of various features of 72 juror/jury experiments conducted over the past 20 years is available in Bray and Kerr (in press).

Researchers emphasize the application of their experiments to courtroom processes. The issues to be treated in the experiment are justified frequently in terms of their relevance for the trial, the materials and conditions of the experiment are developed in these terms, and the discussion covers the applicability of the findings to the courtroom. In addition, it is commonplace for researchers to note limitations on applying the results to trial events. The investigators frequently identify among these limitations the hypothetical nature of the "case," its brevity, the artificiality of its presentation, and the lack of any consequences for the "defendant" being judged. With few exceptions, however, a reader is left with the impression that even given these animadversions, the findings still apply. Dillehay and Nietzel (in press) provide a more extensive discussion of the qualifications of the research and the limitations on conclusions which are acknowledged by many investigators. The importance of this question of applicability prompts us to turn first to some requisite considerations of it.

METHODOLOGICAL CONSIDERATIONS

External Validity Is Not Applied Explanatory Power

The practical utility of experimental jury research is typically regarded as a question of external validity. A matter of interactions between treatments and persons, settings, and history (Cook & Campbell, 1979), external validity directs one to ask if a proposition generated by the research is true for other persons in other settings and at other times. However important external validity may be as a scientific issue, it does not go far enough when one is concerned with the usefulness of the results of an experiment in understanding variations of behavior in a given social setting. The failure to acknowledge this fact has resulted in confusion about the purpose and accomplishments of the experimental juror/jury literature. To differentiate the external validity of an empirically generated proposition from its applied importance, we will use the concept of *applied explanatory power*.

The crux of the matter is this: An empirically derived proposition may be true in contexts other than the one in which it is demonstrated and still have little or no explanatory power in these other contexts. What is statistically significant and theoretically valid for a given situation may yet be of little or no practical value because the relationship described accounts for so little of the variance in the focal outcome variable. In other words, what is of importance to a practitioner is the amount of variation in the behavior he/she confronts that is accounted for by the relationship specified in the proposition. This distinction between theoretical and practical significance has seldom been identified in the discussions of the generality of results from experimental psycholegal research.

A related distinction appears in Elwork et al. (in press) who recognize that an effect obtained in experimental research may attain statistical significance, and therefore be of theoretical value, while falling short of practical significance. Their corrective is for researchers "to discuss the size of the effects found in their research to a much greater extent than has been done in the past" (p. 78). Large effects in the laboratory, however, could still typically account for relatively small amounts of variance. Moreover, a large effect in experimental data may still account for little variation of practical significance because of the triviality in the applied setting of the causal or independent variable. Applied explanatory power requires not only the influential presence of the causal variable in the applied setting but also substantial effects of that variable on outcomes of interest.

With the difference between scientific concerns and applied necessity obscured, the literature lacks clarity on what we are learning about trial jury behavior. How has this state of affairs arisen? The answer seems to be twofold: First, juror/jury research has for the most part proceeded as experimental personality or social psychology *sui generis*. Second, this research enterprise does not include a means suitable for evaluating its social significance because research in the laboratory cannot assess or determine the importance of factors operating in the natural setting.

Regarding experimental research, the model demonstrated early on by Triplett (1897) and practiced by Lewin in his early experimental research is uncommon today among experimental social and personality psychologists. With a few exceptions, this model is rare in juror/jury research. Triplett's analysis of a natural setting led to a transposition (Lewin, 1951, pp. 163-164) of the observed phenomena so as to experimentally test a social psychological proposition. Transposition requires the careful diagnosis of the naturally occurring phenomena of interest to identify the social or psychological processes at work, and then creation of experimental conditions that capture the essential cause-effect relationships operating there. A successful transposition requires that the "essential structural characteristics" of the phenomena to be studied be preserved in the laboratory. "Experiments become artificial if merely one or another factor is realized, but not the essential pattern" (Lewin, 1951, p. 164). Our understanding of transposition aimed at practical explanation is that in the experiment one does more than demonstrate the plausibility of a causal relationship; the research must also maintain a conceptual fidelity to the natural setting.

Instead of patterning research on this model, experimenters typically proceed by examining the literature of their discipline and effortfully teasing out and clarifying relationships among variables. Some will protest that, to the contrary, they are following Lewin's account of transposition; but we think a careful appraisal of most work will disclose that the important missing element is the identification of fundamental social and psychological constellations in natural settings. Rather, what happens is that the researcher designs a set of circumstances in which to demonstrate some effect. This effort entails considerable honing of the independent variables until manipulation checks verify their presence clearly, after which the relationship of interest can be assessed. The problem for investigation typically comes from the personality or social literature and the focus of concern is on internal validity and statistical conclusion validity, with little research effort on external and construct validity (see Cook & Campbell, 1979).

Do the mock juror/jury researchers really mean to contribute to a scientific understanding of courtroom juries? Apparently a number of them do, though confusion on this matter arises in several forms. We have already noted many investigators' reservations about application of their findings. However, these same investigators often proceed to overcome their reservations by argument (e.g., we cannot study real juries, good experimental research *has* external validity) or they leave the reader to assess the experiment's relevance. Another form of confusion about the experimenter's intention is the casual treatment of the real jury's circumstances. What is the place of the independent varible under investigation among the phenomena of the trial? Does it have any status beyond its influence when "other things are equal?" In short, is the claim being made that the variable matters in jury outcomes? This claim and its burden are rightly a weight for researchers with applied pretentions; the disciplinary researcher may disregard it. But why talk of juror or jury behavior in experimental research if it is not a science of jury behavior in which we are interested?

Is Mock Juror/Jury Research Equivalent to Role Playing?

In the experimental research on jurors/juries, subjects are sometimes asked to behave "as if" they were real jurors. This is role playing research. As a method it has generated a share of debate (e.g., Freedman, 1969; Greenberg, 1967) and generally appears to be inadequate to the task of understanding real juries. Some researchers, on the other hand, claim that subjects in juror/jury research are providing their own views, as nonjurors, of triallike issues (e.g., guilt and punishment). What is unclear in the latter instance is whether subjects are behaving in accord with their dispositions at the moment or whether they are predicting what they would do if they were actual jurors. When triallike language is used in an experiment, the question "How do you find the defendant—guilty or not guilty?" may inevitably become "How would you find such a defendant if you were a juror in a court of law?", in effect requiring the experimental subject to predict his or her own behavior.

The significance of these distinctions is manifest when one notes their effects in other social psychological research on judgments about or actions against another person. Lerner (1971) discovered that predictions about what a person would do when confronted with a suffering other were widely discrepant from and much more flattering than was the actual behavior of subjects like themselves in the judgment situation. Milgram's (1965) finding of a similar difference between behavior that subjects predict for others and the behavior of actual subjects provides another reliable example. People seem unable to predict how they or others will behave when it comes to passing judgments on others or taking harmful actions against them. This research is not reassuring where a generalization from role playing research (or a likeness of it) to courtroom decisions against another person is concerned.

Simulations, Models, and Analogies

Some investigators describe the experimental juror/jury research as simulation of juror or jury behavior. At times "simulation" merely signals the use of imitation jurors and trials. Modifiers like "mock" or "analogue" would do as well in this usage. Another use of "simulation" is that the research should be differentiated from typical psychology experiments because it serves as a representation in another context of the real processes at work in the courtroom. According to Runkel and McGrath (1972) an experimental simulation "tries to emulate a behavioral system that might actually be found in reality to the extent that the actuality is well enough known to be imitated thus, the simulation must to some degree be a particular case. The laboratory experiment, on the other hand, typically tries to represent an entire class of settings by reproducing only those characteristics that are common to the "populations" of settings; thus, the experiment must to some degree partake of a *universal* setting" (p. 82).

Mock juror/jury experimental research does not have the features of person or social group simulations discussed by Abelson (1968) or those conforming to the difference between the laboratory experiment and the experimental simulation identified by Runkel and McGrath (1972, pp. 96-99). The typical factorial mock juror/jury experiment lacks the form of "a flexible imitation of processes and outcomes for the purpose of clarifying or explaining the underlying mechanisms involved. The feat of imitation per se is not the important feature of simulations, but rather that successful imitation may publicly reveal the essence of the object being simulated" (Abelson, 1968, p. 275). The differences between experimental jury research and bona fide simulations are further clarified by comparing actual juror or jury simulations (e.g., see Penrod & Hastie, 1979) with the typical mock juror/jury experiment.

One occasionally encounters a defense of the juror/jury experiment based on its inferred similarity to biological research in which animal species are used as "models" for humans to test the effects of drugs, physiological or neurological damage or deficit, and the like. A close examination of this analogue reveals significant differences from the experimental juror/jury research. A main difference concerns the inducing agent or treatment variable. In drug research using animal models the drug of interest, not a substitute or facsimile, is used as the inducing agent. In experimental juror/jury research typically there is low fidelity to the events of the trial that are targeted for research.

Sometimes research using simulations of gravity-free environments is invoked as a parallel to, and therefore a justification of, mock jury research. But the courtroom environment is not reproducible in the laboratory under current levels of conceptualization (what is the analogue to weightlessness?) or standards of research ethics. Other ways to view the difference is to consider that what behavioral scientists doing research on jurors and juries in the laboratory are trying to get subjects to do is the equivalent of *imagining* that they are in a gravity-free environment, or attempting to mimic visual or proprioceptive effects of weightlessness without actually producing it. A great deal would have to be known about the organism in a weightless environment to be able to produce psychological equivalence in the laboratory. In parallel fashion, a considerable knowledge about the juror and the jury in the courtroom trial would have to be known to faithfully create a satisfactory mock-up jury in the laboratory. It is precisely that science of juror and jury behavior that we lack at present and are trying to fill in large measure by looking in the laboratory rather than in the courtroom.

Research in the Laboratory Cannot Determine the External Validity or the Applied Explanatory Power of Mock Juror/Jury Research

Some investigators contend that the issue of applicability to the courtroom is a matter for empirical resolution. Thus, Kerr et al. (1979) sought to examine the potential effects of the lack of real consequences from mock jury decisions by the use of student subjects in two conditions. In the "actual" jury condition they told students that they were trying a case from a neighboring campus where student juries were under consideration as a way of dealing with student discipline. In the other condition, which was intended to create a sense that the subjects' were merely in an experiment dealing with a hypothetical instance, subjects were asked to imagine that they were jurors deciding the case. The students in this condition believed that their judgment would have no effect on the person supposedly being tried. The analyses showed that data from the two conditions were not significantly different; these null results were taken to mean that verdicts rendered by experimental subjects, in which there will be no consequences for the defendant, can be used to understand verdicts produced in the courtroom. We do not believe, however, that a condition employing this type of deception is a proper analogue for a court's jury.

Laboratory research comparing members of a community who are eligible for jury duty with student subjects finds that under various conditions the two groups do not differ (Bray et al., 1978) or the difference between them accounts for little variance (Feild & Barnett, 1978). What this research tells us is that in the laboratory, students and community residents produce comparable results. The chasm between the laboratory and the courtroom is still there; marching up and down on one side of it will neither make it go away nor substitute for a bridge.

We are skeptical that the prototypical jury analogue is capable of capturing the complex socialization processes which are produced by jury experience. The psychological impact of a trial is mediated by events such as prolonged exposure to the court environment, frustration attending the incompleteness and discrepancies of the evidence, impatience generated by the leisurely pace of some courts, drama-tinged exchanges occasionally required by adversarial relationships, and opportunities to form evaluations of the principal trial characters based on many nonevidential cues. To our knowledge, analogue research which attempts to simulate this range of influences is not available.

A study of the determinants of recommendations for bail by actual judges illustrates the pitfalls with research using hypothetical cases isolated from the natural setting. Ebbeson and Konecni (1975) provide information on both the actual bail-setting behaviors of real judges and judges' responses to hypothetical cases submitted to them in a commonplace experimental fashion. In response to the hypothetical cases, the judges were influenced by the prior record of the accused, his or her local ties to the community, and the district attorney's recommendations. In the actual court cases, however, the only significant determinant was the district attorney's recommendations. Psychotherapy outcome research has learned the lessons of analogue research (see Dillehay & Nietzel, in press); comparable investigations on sexual bias among psychotherapists are producing a similar skepticism (e.g., Stricker, 1977).

Method Variance Within the Laboratory

Variations in the mode of presentation of case material have been demonstrated to have an important effect on verdicts rendered by experimental subjects. Juhnke et al. (1979) presented subjects with trial information in one of four modes: black and white videotape, the audio portion alone, a transcript of the audio portion, or a written summary. The frequency of guilty verdicts from individual subjects, without deliberation, varied significantly across conditions, with the videotape version yielding significantly more votes for conviction than any of the other conditions. The literature already contains expressions of concern about other methods factors—such as the special nature of case materials used and continuous scales to measure guilt—that plausibly limit applied explanatory power.

PREDELIBERATION OPINIONS, FIRST-BALLOT VOTES, AND GROUP DECISIONS

Considerable research attention has been given to the relationship between the initial distribution of individual opinion and final group judgments of mock juries. Several models have been examined (e.g., DICE, Penrod & Hastie, 1979) for their ability to predict experimental data, and in one instance (Gelfand & Solomon, 1975) for the fit with some important first-ballot data from Kalven and Zeisel (1971). In their landmark research, Kalven and Zeisel (1971, pp. 487-489) reported the relationship between first-ballot votes and final jury verdicts for a sample of 225 cases. The first-ballot votes were determined by interviewing jurors after their service on these criminal cases. The investigators construed their results as indicating that in roughly 90% of the cases in which there was an initial majority, that majority vote predicted the final verdict. These results are used in key ways in the research literature.

In their examination of the consequences of voir dire on jury verdicts, Zeisel and Diamond (1978) estimated the verdict that would have been returned by the first 12 jurors called in each trial. This would have been the impanelled jury if the attorneys had exercised no peremptory challenges. Zeisel and Diamond used the findings by Kalven and Zeisel to estimate the jury verdict for the reconstructed "juries without challenges." To get this verdict they used the predeliberation votes of the peremptorily removed jurors, who were among the first 12 persons called from the venire. These votes, obtained from all experimental jurors prior to any deliberation, were combined with the estimated first-ballot votes of those jurors who remained on the court's jury throughout the trial, thereby comprising the first-ballot votes for the reconstructed "juries without challenges." Using these derived first-ballot votes, Zeisel and Diamond predicted final verdicts of the reconstructed "juries without challenges" by using the relationships between first-ballot votes and final verdicts reported by Kalven and Zeisel.[1]

For reasons of both theory and method, it may be important to note that the predeliberation votes of individual mock jurors probably are not equivalent psychologically to the first-ballot votes of real juries. This distinction is due to the likelihood that the typical first ballot of the real jury occurs after some actual discussion of the case. Its significance is that the curve fitting of the modelers may produce a decision rule (e.g., a two-thirds majority decides the verdict, otherwise hung) that does not accord with the same two data points in a real jury. Is this an important matter, or a trivial conceptual difference? Would DICE or the other models reviewed by Penrod and Hatie fit as well the actual relationship between individual votes of real jurors at the time they enter the jury room, before they converse at all on the case, and the jury verdict after deliberation?

The only simulation we are aware of that models the first-ballot/final-verdict relationship of real juries is by Gelfand and Solomon (1975). Gelfand and Solomon use the data from Kalven and Zeisel in their simulation. They produced a distribution of verdicts that closely approximates the Kalven and Zeisel results. These data suggest the difference between predeliberation votes and first-ballot votes may not matter. But we are wary of this conclusion. With interview data from real jurors we should be able to determine if there is a greater change from predeliberation opinions to jury verdicts than from other first ballots to verdicts. The early portion of the deliberation may be significant for a segment of the jury.

EXPERIMENTAL RESEARCH IN THE COURTROOM

A limited body of research employs methods appropriate to the study of procedurally complete trials conducted in their natural settings. This research is important for our present concerns because it intends to develop an applicable knowledge of juror/jury behavior.

Two experiments conducted on actual courtroom trials indicate differences between the verdicts of experimental juries and courts' juries. In the study by Zeisel and Diamond (1978), after the real jury had been impaneled the judge asked the remaining persons in the venire, including those who had been peremptorily excused, to participate in the research. Nearly 90% consented. From these volunteers, Zeisel and Diamond formed two "shadow" juries: one consisting of peremptorily excused jurors and one composed of members of the venire who had not been questioned during voir dire. There were 12 experimental juries made up of peremptorily excused jurors. These juries ranged in size from 4 to 12. The 11 juries consisting of persons not questioned during the voir dire, dubbed "English" juries, contained 6 to 12 members (it was not possible to get an English jury for one of the cases). These shadow juries were treated by the court as though they were real juries on the case.

The finding of interest to us at this juncture is that on individual juror ballots taken as a first vote, 80% of the English jurors and 66% of the peremptorily excused jurors voted for guilt; by contrast, 61% of the court's jurors so voted.

Zeisel and Diamond combine the data for the peremptorily excused jurors and the real jurors (combined n = 223) and reported a significant difference between these jurors and the English jurors. They reasoned (p. 511) from previously observed relationships between first-ballot individual juror decisions and jury verdicts (from Kalven and Zeisel, 1971) that the English juries would have convicted in each of the trials. The real juries in fact acquitted on 5 of the 11 trials and hung on a sixth.

The English juries differed from the other two juries "in two important respects: None of the English jurors underwent the full voir dire questioning and none of them engaged in the jury deliberations that

actually would lead to conviction or acquittal of the defendant" (p. 512).
The investigators minimize the possibility that the difference is due to
the absence of real consequences of the decision of the English juries,
pointing out that the challenged jurors' verdict was not consequential
either and concluding that not participating in voir dire leaves the
English jurors more conviction-prone.

In our own research we have examined the behavior of experimental
juries, called *alternative juries,* in the courts of Fayette County, Kentucky (see Nietzel et al., 1976). With the cooperation of the local judges[2]
we took our alternative juries into criminal trials and provided them an
experience as close to that of the real juries as possible: They heard a
recording of the remarks that the judges give to a newly assembled
venire, sat through the entire voir dire but did not undergo questioning,
and occupied the front rows of the courtroom during the trial. They
were admonished to follow the judge's directions regarding out-of-court
behavior during recesses, and they received their copy of the judge's
instructions prior to starting deliberations in their own jury room.
Alternative juries had access to all exhibits introduced as evidence.
Except for the fact that they were recruited on the campus and in some
cases received class credit for their participation, alternative juries were
like the English juries of Zeisel and Diamond (1978). Juries varied in size
from 8 to 12. The cases were all criminal cases and ranged in seriousness
from lesser felonies to charges carrying penalties of 20 years to life
imprisonment. Several defendants faced multiple charges. Cases were
excluded that in the prior judgment of the judge or one of the participating attorneys were likely to extend beyond one day's duration. Like
Zeisel and Diamond (1978), we observed no significant difference
between the deliberation times of alternative (M = 1 hour 20 minutes)
and actual (M = 1 hour 31 minutes) juries.

Our alternative juries found the defendant guilty on 18% of 'the
charges, hung on 35% of the charges, and acquitted on the remaining
47%. If the data are examined according to case, and a defendant is
considered guilty whenever a guilty verdict is returned on any of several
charges, the alternative juries convicted on 30% of the cases, acquitted
on 30% and hung on the remaining 40%. For the real juries, the figures
were 50% guilty, 30% not guilty, and 20% hung.

An important point to learn from these jury verdicts is that the
English juries and alternative juries differed from their corresponding
real juries but in different directions. From Zeisel and Diamond's data
one would expect that experimental juries (without voir dire) would be

significantly *more* likely to convict than the real jury. Our data would not support this conclusion. Our alternative juries tended to be more lenient than the court's juries, but this difference was not significant. In three trials the court's jury convicted, and our jurors either acquitted or hung. In one instance, an alternative jury voted to convict when the real jury voted for acquittal.

The possible reasons for these differences between our alternative juries and Zeisel and Diamond's English juries are (1) differences between student and community subjects, (2) the difference in federal district court practice and state court practice, and (3) the fact that the verdicts of our alternative juries were reached after complete deliberations while verdicts for English jurors were extrapolated from first-ballot votes. There are a number of components to each of these, but space allows us to mention only a few.

Our student jurors were relatively young and were participating in the courtroom as research volunteers. The psychological characteristics implied by these factors—being relatively more liberal on social and economic issues, being more optimistic regarding human nature, and requiring a higher standard of proof—might well make them less con-viction-prone initially than the court's jurors in our study. We would guess that Zeisel and Diamond's shadow jurors were more like the real jurors in our study and in theirs than like our alternative jurors.

Judicial practice differs in the federal court system in which Zeisel and Diamond conducted their study and the state criminal court in which we worked. Voir dire in federal practice is conducted largely by the judge. By contrast, and with wide judicial discretion, attorneys conduct much of the voir dire in Kentucky criminal courts. The psychological difference is substantial. While the judicial purposes of the voir dire are to determine if potential jurors are statutorily qualified to serve, other purposes are possible when the attorneys are allowed to conduct the questioning. Attorney questioning promotes the development of rapport between the attorneys and the jurors and can elicit tacit commitments to certain courses of action. Attorneys skilled in voir dire use such techniques, and they might affect onlooking experimental jurors in ways that the federal practice of voir dire would not allow.

Another obvious difference is the length of the trials that were studied. While we do not know the precise length of Zeisel and Diamond's trials, we judge that their average trial duration may have been longer than ours, and this difference invites speculation. On other matters, like the kind of cases tried, the trials seem similar in spite of the fact that theirs was a federal court setting and ours a state court.

Finally, we are not convinced that jury deliberation is a minor influence on verdicts. Until the distinction between first-ballot and predeliberation ballots is examined more completely, researchers should be cautious about assuming that first-ballot votes always precede all of a jury's deliberations.

Employing the ultimate in procedural fidelity, these two experiments show substantial differences in judgment between experimental juries and real juries that carry both theoretical and practical importance. One message may be that many of the multiple variations in natural courtroom settings make a difference in jury behavior. However, to recommend from that possibility that the path to increased understanding of the juries is through the experimental laboratory seems misguided. Among the good reasons for doing laboratory research is surely not the belief that the natural setting is so complex as to defy its explication. If that were the case, then no amount of laboratory-derived knowledge would provide practical, useful information for policy or practice in living institutions.

THE SEVERAL SIDES IN THE RESEARCH
AND RELEVANCE CONTROVERSIES

Psycholegal experimental research has been criticized and defended in ways that obscure some important considerations. Aspects of the controversy are reminiscent of the early days of psychology's interest in the courtroom (e.g., see Elwork et al., in press): Experimental psychologists claim an understanding or a relevance that practitioners dispute or challenge. But the debate is not solely between practitioner and disciplinary researcher, and what is being defended and what attacked is often unclear. For example, defenses of laboratory research encountered in psychology journals seem directed at researchers who claim that the research we do should be done closer to the courtroom and the juryroom, conceptually if not contextually. Those defending the laboratory as the path to sure scientific knowledge seem to assume that the best way to provide *useful* knowledge is through the demonstration of causal relationships. Behavioral scientists recognizing the distinction between disciplinary and policy-action research would certainly demur (e.g., Cook, 1962; Ford, 1977). But this demurrer is not typically an indictment of *all* laboratory research, only that with pretentions to direct relevance. Is the objective of the experimental jury research to obtain knowledge that would be useful for an understanding of real juries? This aspiration seems manifest in many experimental efforts. And furthermore, astute participants and analyzers (e.g., Davis et al., 1977; Wrightsman, 1978), while recognizing problems, seem generally ready to embrace the experimental research as policy laden in its meaning.

We have suggested elsewhere (Dillehay & Nietzel, in press) three strategies for research that should help clarify the issues. These strategies are not new but they lack clear focus in today's literature. They are (1) the direct study of the phenomena of interest, (2) the pursuit of generic psychological and social research, and (3) an experimental, theoretical attack on important social and psychological issues diagnosed in the legal arena.

On the first point we argue for the use of archival data, observation in the courtroom, jury interviews, and the like. All are available and some have been used (e.g,, Ebbesen & Konecni, 1975; Broeder, 1965; Zeisel & Diamond, 1976).

The second suggestion arises from the conclusion that too much of the experimental work is neither good science nor useful in practice or policy in the courtroom. There is little or no general theory anchoring much of this work.[3] Although legal terms may abound in it, procedural infidelity is typical. As a consequence the research results cannot be used for either advancing scientific understanding or informing social policy or practice. Psychologists and any of their various potential audiences, including colleagues, would be markedly better off if the experiments were conducted as generic psychology with the scientist's vigilance for internal and external validity regarding method and sophistication and clarity regarding theory. The justification for such work is not its practical usefulness in understanding juror/jury behavior. Any such interpretation requires extrapolation by argument, including a weighing of the various influences potentially at work in the practical setting. In fact, to avoid the appearance of gratuitous claims, researchers in this mode should not raise the banner of relevance.

The third suggestion is that experimental research be done on issues that have been assessed to be important in the functioning of actual juries. An essential element of this strategy is the *careful diagnosis* of the social and psychological factors operating in the courtroom so that they might be transposed (Lewin, 1951; see our discussion above) for examination in experimental settings. This strategy requires that someone actually go into the courtroom with the purpose of assessing the factors there that determine juror and jury behavior. The methods appropriate to the direct study of the behavior of jurors and others in the setting are of signal importance to the first step in this approach. It is only after the searching assessment of the phenomena of interest that the enterprise is removed to the experimental setting, taken there because of the issues of control and precision so widely recognized as laboratory strengths, or because one cannot do in the jury system itself experiments on alternatives to the system.

Guidance on the application of social psychological knowledge and the conduct of applied social psychological research is available in the literature of social psychology. Lewin, for example, in his post-1940 emphasis on action research, seems more cited than read. In fact, an interesting exercise is to try to locate a complete reference to Lewin's statement that there is nothing so practical as a good theory. Frequently referred to in print, the statement is virtually never referenced, and is typically used as a justification by theorists to applied scientists and practitioners for the social relevance of laboratory research. The more complete passage has a message for the experimentalist, too:

> [Close cooperation between theoretical and applied psychology] can be accomplished in psychology, as it has been accomplished in physics, if the theorist does not look toward applied problems with highbrow aversion or with a fear of social problems, and if the applied psychologist realizes that there is nothing so practical as a good theory [Lewin, 1951, p. 169].

It is well to note, also, that Lewin's early research which was experimental laboratory work conducted in a manner fitting his prescription for transposition (e.g., see discussion in Marrow, 1977, pp. 27-28, 105) should be distinguished from his later work that came to be called action research, and whose characteristics might have led Lewin to avoid the laboratory on any policy or practice issue surrounding the jury. Students and colleagues of Lewin, or others concerned with practical knowledge, have long recommended that the laboratory not be used or be used late in pursuit of solutions for significant social problems. For example, Cook (1962) would counsel laboratory research only after considerable other research on the problem has produced significant knowledge. Sanford (1970) would avoid the laboratory altogether.

An exemplar for this strategy is research by Thibaut, Walker, and their students (e.g., Thibaut & Walker, 1975). An interdisciplinary effort including social psychologists and lawyers, the research has been experimental in method and focused on procedural aspects of the legal system. Doing many of the things criticized in other experimental research (e.g., using college students and law students as subjects, presenting materials to subjects in ways never permitted in a courtroom, asking subjects to make judgments that jurors would not be asked to make), these investigators avoid or blunt any such criticism by having taken a procedural feature of the legal system, abstracted it in such a way that it applied to the resolution of disputes in general, and pursued it with attention to its effects on the ability to withstand intrusions of various kinds that might frustrate efforts for justice. A major theme has been the difference between the adversary system and the inquisitorial system, and a major conclusion of the work is the adversary system is superior in reaching just outcomes. Their research is not jury research or juror research so much as it deals with decision makers generally, including but not limited to jurors as triers of fact.

The three types of research we have identified are compatible with one another. In fact, the application of both kinds of experimental research requires a careful prior appraisal of the life of real juries. However, our present vantage point shows us that we should not misidentify these research types. Misidentification confuses the basis of the use of knowledge derived from experimental research by claiming that it is research on juries or done under circumstances that shortcircuit the usual extrapolation to natural events from experimental settings. A mature science of jury behavior will surely incorporate data and theory properly used from all three categories of investigation.

NOTES

1. Some assumptions and logic are required in constructing the individual juror votes for the real juries and for some of the shadow jurors (see Zeisel & Diamond, 1978, pp. 502-503).

2. We wish to acknowledge the cooperation and support of Judges Park, Mead, Angelucci, Barker, Tackett, and Grant, without whose participation this research would not have been possible. We also thank Mr. Donald Taylor, Administrator of the Fayette County Circuit Court, for his valuable help.

3. There are exceptions in which a program of research has been built around psychological theory, so that should it be stripped of its relevance for the courtroom the research remains a contribution to a general understanding of behavior. Examples are the research programs by Davis (see Davis et al., 1977) on group decision schemes and Kaplan (e.g., Kaplan & Kemmerick, 1974) on information integration.

REFERENCES

Abelson, R. P. Simulation of social behavior. In G. Lindzey & E. Aronson (eds.), *The handbook of social psychology* (Vol. 2). Reading, Mass.: Addison-Wesley, 1968.

Bray, R. M. & Kerr, N. L. Use of the simulation method in the study of jury behavior: Some methodological considerations. *Law and Human Behavior,* in press.

Bray, R. M., Struckman-Johnson, C., Osborne, M. D., McFarlane, J. B., & Scott, J. The effects of defendant status on decisions of student and community juries. *Social Psychology,* 1978, *41,* 256-260.

Broeder, D. Occupational expertise and bias affecting juror behavior: A preliminary look. *New York University Law Review,* 1965, *40,* 1079-1100.

Brooks, W. N. & Doob, A. N. Justice and the jury. *Journal of Social Issues,* 1975, *31*(3), 171-182.

Cook, S. W. The systematic analysis of socially significant events: A strategy for social research. *Journal of Social Issues,* 1962, *18*(2), 66-84.

Cook, T. D. & Campbell, D. T. *Quasi-experimentation: Design and analysis issues for field settings.* Chicago, Ill.: Rand McNally, 1979.

Davis, J. H., Bray, R. M., & Holt, R. W. The empirical study of decision processes in juries. In J. L. Tapp & F. J. Levine (eds.), *Law, justice, and the individual in society: Psychological and legal issues.* New York: Holt, Rinehart & Winston, 1977.

Dillehay, R. C. & Nietzel, M. T. Conceptualizing mock jury/juror research: Critique and illustrations. In K. S. Larsen (ed.), *Psychology and ideology.* Monmouth, Oregon: Institute for Theoretical History, in press.

Ebbesen, E. B. & Konecni, V. J. Decision making and information integration in the courts: The setting of bail. *Journal of Personality and Social Psychology,* 1975, *32,* 805-821.

Elwork, A., Sales, B. D., & Suggs, D. The trial: A research review. In B. D. Sales (ed.), *Perspectives in law and psychology* (Vol. 2). New York: Plenum, in press.

Feild, H. S. & Barnett, N. J. Simulated jury trials: Students vs. "real" people as jurors. *Journal of Social Psychology,* 1978, *104,* 287-293.

Ford, T. R. The production of social knowledge for public use. *Social Forces,* 1977, *56,* 504-518.

Freedman, J. L. Role playing: Psychology by consensus. *Journal of Personality and Social Psychology,* 1969, *13,* 107-114.

Gelfand, A. E. & Solomon, H. Analyzing the decision-making process of the American jury. *Journal of the American Statistical Association,* 1975, *70,* 305-310.

Gerbasi, K. C., Zuckerman, M., & Reis, H. T. Justice needs a new blindfold: A review of mock jury research. *Psychological Bulletin,* 1977, *84,* 323-345.

Greenberg, M. S. Role playing: An alternative to deception? *Journal of Personality and Social Psychology,* 1967, *7,* 152-157.

Juhnke, R., Vought, C., Pyszczynski, T. A., Dane, F. C., Losure, B. D., & Wrightsman, L. S. Effects of presentation mode upon mock jurors' reactions to a trial. *Personality Social Psychology Bulletin,* 1979, *5,* 36-39.

Kalven, H., Jr. & Zeisel, H. *The American Jury.* Chicago: University of Chicago Press, 1971. (Originally published, 1966.)

Kaplan, M. F. & Kemmerick, G. D. Juror judgment as information integration: Combining evidential and nonevidential information. *Journal of Personality and Social Psychology,* 1974, *30,* 493-499.

Kerr, N. L., Nerenz, D., & Herrick, D. Role playing and the study of jury behavior. *Sociological Methods and Research,* 1979, *7,* 337-355.

Lerner, M. J. Observer's evaluation of a victim: Justice, guilt, and veridical perception. *Journal of Personality and Social Psychology,* 1971, *20,* 127-135.

Lewin, K. Action research and minority problems. *Journal of Social Issues,* 1946, *2*(4), 34-46.

Lewin, K. Problems of research in social psychology. In D. Cartwright (ed.), *Field theory in social science.* New York: Harper & Row, 1951. (Reprinted from *Journal of Social Psychology,* 1943, *17,* and *University of Iowa Studies in Child Welfare,* 1944, *20.*)

Marrow, A. J. *The practical theorist.* New York: Teachers College Press, Columbia University, 1977. (Originally published, 1969.)

Milgram, S. Liberating effects of group pressure. *Journal of Personality and Social Psychology,* 1965, *1,* 127-134.

Munsterberg, H. *Psychology and social sanity.* Garden City, N.Y.: Doubleday, 1914.

Nietzel, M. T., Dillehay, R. C., & Rogers, G. *Method innovation in jury research: Alternative juries and archival data.* Presented at the meeting of the American Psychological Association, Washington, D.C., September 1976.

Penrod, S. & Hastie, R. Models of jury decision making: A critical review. *Psychological Bulletin,* 1979, *86,* 462-492.

Runkel, P. J. & McGrath, J. E. *Research on human behavior.* New York: Holt, Rinehart & Winston, 1972.

Saks, M. J. & Hastie, R. *Social psychology in court.* New York: Van Nostrand Reinhold, 1978.

Sanford, N. Whatever happened to action research? *Journal of Social Issues,* 1970, *26*(4), 3-23.

Stricker, G. Implications of research for psychotherapeutic treatment of women. *American Psychologist,* 1977, *32,* 14-22.

Tapp, J. L. Psychology and the law: An overture. *Annual Review of Psychology,* 1976, *27,* 359-404.

Thibaut, J. & Walker, L. *Procedural justice: A psychological analysis.* Hillsdale, N.J.: Erlbaum, 1975.

Triplett, N. The dynamogenic factors in pacemaking and competition. *American Journal of Psychology,* 1897, *9,* 507-533.

Wrightsman, L. S. The American trial jury on trial: Empirical evidence and procedural modifications. *Journal of Social Issues,* 1978, *34*(4), 137-164.

Zeisel, H. & Diamond, S. S. The jury selection in the Mitchell-Stans conspiracy trial. *American Bar Foundation Research Journal,* 1976, *1,* 151-174.

Zeisel, H. & Diamond, S. S. The effect of peremptory challenges on jury and verdict: An experiment in a federal district court. *Stanford Law Review,* 1978, *30,* 491-531.

10

Circumplex Models of Interpersonal Behavior

JERRY S. WIGGINS

Jerry S. Wiggins is Professor of Psychology at the University of British Columbia, where he is coordinator of the graduate program in personality. His major interests are in personality theory and assessment. He is a former editor of the *Journal of Research in Personality* and is currently a consulting editor for the *Journal of Consulting and Clinical Psychology* and the *Psychological Review*. He is currently President-Elect of the Society of Multivariate Experimental Psychology.

The study of interpersonal behavior encompasses a variety of research paradigms for the investigation of social transactions in diverse populations of subjects, at different levels of analysis, from a variety of theoretical perspectives (Swenson, 1973). The present exposition is focused, rather narrowly, on the topic of providing a structural representation of the ordinary language used to describe interpersonal transactions. Although the topic is a specialized one, it is nevertheless central to many approaches to the study of interpersonal behavior.

When descriptions of interpersonal transactions are properly scaled, the interrelationships among the variables form a circular pattern, an ordering without beginning or end. This empirical fact has been known for many years, and conceptual rationales for its occurrence, of varying degrees of plausibility, may be traced back to second century Greek medicine. Periodically, over the last quarter of a

AUTHOR'S NOTE: This work was supported by Social Sciences and Humanities Research Council of Canada Grant 410-79-0148. I am grateful to Robert C. Carson, Charles G. McClintock, Dale T. Miller, Walter Mischel, and James A. Russell for their helpful comments on an earlier version of this article.

century, many writers have emphasized the advantages of a circular model for representing interpersonal behavior in general, and disordered interpersonal behavior in particular (Adams, 1964; Benjamin, 1974; Carson, 1969, 1979; Foa, 1961; Foa & Foa, 1974; Freedman et al., 1951; Leary, 1957; McLemore & Benjamin, 1979; Schaefer, 1959, 1961; Wiggins, 1968, 1979). Yet, the potential of the circumplex as an integrative conceptual model for research in personality and social psychology does not appear to be widely recognized. This chapter is meant to illustrate that potential.

On a more general level, this chapter can be viewed as a plea for the use of explicit structural models in research in personality and social psychology (Loevinger, 1957; Messick & Ross, 1962). In that sense, the circumplex model to be discussed is only one of a large number of structural representations that might bring conceptual coherence to contemporary research on interpersonal transactions. It is not my purpose to compare the circumplex model with other structural representations (e.g., the factor-analytic model). Instead, I will illustrate applications of the circumplex model to a few selected areas of research that have a sufficient empirical base to benefit from such application. Although several other areas of research could have been discussed, the ones I have chosen are social cognition, social exchange, and dimensions of personality.

Space limitations precluded a detailed consideration of psychometric procedures for evaluating circumplexity in empirical data (see Wiggins et al., Note 1). The essential properties of a circulant correlation matrix are evident in the representation of the intercorrelations among eight variables given in Table 1. The correlation of a variable with itself is assumed to be unity, so that ones appear along the principal diagonal of the matrix. Note that the correlations along the first off-diagonal and the correlation in the lower left corner all have the same value (r_1). This means that "adjacent" variables (1 and 2, 2 and 3, . . . 8 and 1) are related equally to one another. The same is true of variables that are "separated" from one another by one (r_2), two (r_3), or three (r_4) variables. In real data, the values within each minor diagonal are seldom exactly equal to each other. The departure of a given empirical correlation matrix from the matrix of estimated population correlation coefficients represented above provides a statistical test of the hypothesis that the empirical correlations are a sample of a population correlation matrix with circulant properties (MacDonald, 1975).

When principal components are extracted from correlation matrices of the kind illustrated above, two "circumplex components" (Wiggins

TABLE 1
Intercorrelations among Eight Variables

Variables	1	2	3	4	5	6	7	8
1.	1							
2.	r_1	1			where $r_1 > r_2 > r_3 > r_4$			
3.	r_2	r_1	1					
4.	r_3	r_2	r_1	1				
5.	r_4	r_3	r_2	r_1	1			
6.	r_3	r_4	r_3	r_2	r_1	1		
7.	r_2	r_3	r_4	r_3	r_2	r_1	1	
8.	r_1	r_2	r_3	r_4	r_3	r_2	r_1	1

et al., Note 1) will serve as coordinates for the circular ordering of variables illustrated in Figure 1. The area of the circle is determined by the proportion of variance accounted for by the two circumplex components and the extent to which the variables are "equally spaced" around the circle reflects the extent to which the empirical variables satisfy the condition that correlations in the same minor diagonals are equal to each other.

The variable labels given in Figure 1 are from my earlier taxonomy of trait descriptive adjectives in the interpersonal domain (Wiggins, 1979). This system of classification is a modification of successively refined systems suggested by Leary (1957), Foa (1961), and Rinn (1965). It is not meant to apply to other domains of human characteristics (e.g., cognitive, temperamental, physical), although the study of inter-domain relationships is an important priority. In the material that follows, I will be suggesting that some type of system, similar to the one in Figure 1, may be useful in bringing order to diverse realms of personality and social psychology. My own bias, of course, is that such a system should be very much like the one illustrated in Figure 1.

SOCIAL COGNITION

The recent and highly active area of investigation concerned with "social cognition" reflects an ever-increasing emphasis, in studies of impression formation and person perception, upon the cognitive mechanisms and processes whereby stimulus information about persons is encoded, stored, and retrieved (e.g., Carroll & Payne, 1976;

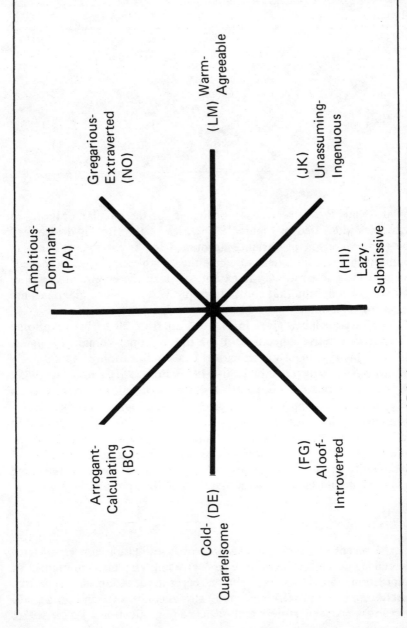

Figure 1: Circumplex Model of Interpersonal Behavior.

Ambitious-
Dominant
(PA)

Gregarious-
Extraverted
(NO)

(LM) Warm-
Agreeable

Arrogant-
Calculating
(BC)

(JK)
Unassuming-
Ingenuous

Cold- (DE)
Quarrelsome

(HI)
Lazy-
Submissive

(FG)
Aloof-
Introverted

Hastie et al., in press; Higgins et al., in press; Nisbett & Ross, 1980). In this context, there has been a renewed interest in cognitive *categories* of person perception and their similarity to categories employed in the classification of other objects of the natural environment (e.g., Fiske & Cox, 1979). Although Heider (1958) originally emphasized the continuities between person and object perception, it remained for Cantor and Mischel (1979a) to integrate these two literatures by subsuming the former under the conceptual scheme employed by Rosch and her associates in their pioneering studies of human categorization of natural objects. In this section I wish to emphasize the potential fruitfulness of the methodologies employed by Cantor and Mischel (1979a) and to suggest that their approach may benefit from the conceptual precision introduced by the use of a specific circumplex model. I will do so with reference to several concepts of Rosch that seem particularly applicable to categories of interpersonal perception.

Analog versus Digital Processing

The traditional view of the nature of the categories of human thought has been that such categories are "well-defined" in the sense that category membership is an all-or-none (digital) affair, in which all members fit neatly into one or another discrete category on the basis of possessing *all* of a small set of critical criterial features, thus rendering all category members functionally equivalent. On the basis of extensive empirical research on human categorization, Rosch (1973) has argued that categories do not have well-defined boundaries and that they possess an internal structure organized around clear cases or exemplars and surrounded by other category members of decreasing similarity to these clear cases. Thus, some reds are "redder" than other reds, and some birds are more "birdlike" than others. Our use of "linguistic hedges" (Lakoff, 1972) such as "almost" and "virtually" reflects the varying degrees of membership that may exist within a given category (Rosch, 1975). Within this (analog) representation of categorization, natural categories are viewed as "fuzzy sets," that is, categories without sharp boundaries whose membership is probabilistic rather than discrete (Hersh & Caramazza, 1976; Labov, 1973; Zadeh, 1965).

The circumplex model appears to be particularly well-suited for representing the fuzzy boundaries and continuous (as opposed to discrete) class membership of adjectives describing interpersonal (Wiggins, 1979) and affective (Russell, in press) qualities. In this representation, the elements of a given domain, such as the interpersonal, are distributed continuously around the perimeter of a circle, with each fuzzy category merging into its neighboring categories. Elements from other domains (e.g., physical appearance) would be expected to fall toward the center of the circle, although not necessarily at the center, as the overall taxonomy whereby different domains are distinguished is itself likely to be fuzzy (Cantor & Mischel, 1979a; Kintsch, 1974). The meaning of interpersonal adjectives has been investigated by a variety of scaling procedures that all tend to give the same result; rather than clustering in discrete categories, the adjectives are spread more-or-less evenly around the perimenter of a circumplex (e.g., Conte, 1975; McCormick & Kavanagh, in press). The same is true for adjectives describing affective qualities (Russell, in press). Examination of the similarity matrices from these multidimensional scaling studies provides clear support for the notion of fuzzy sets distributed as a circumplex.

Family Resemblances and Prototypes

According to Rosch and Mervis (1975), the similarities among category members are best construed in terms of Wittgenstein's (1953) notion of "family resemblances." Rather than all possessing a small set of critical features, members of a category resemble each other in overlapping and criss-crossing ways that vary in kind and number. And just as there is a "family look," there is a prototype or exemplar of a category which serves as a cognitive reference point or focal stimulus (Rosch, 1975) for all members of that category. It is now rather firmly established that human subjects utilize prototype schemas in learning and classification tasks (Posner, 1973) and that the prototypicality of members of a category can be reliably rated by judges (Rosch, 1973). It is only quite recently, however, that the importance of the concept of prototype has been recognized in social cognition.

Cantor and Mischel (1979a) review a number of recent studies that demonstrate the utility of the prototype concept in social cognition research. The prototypicality of a target person is related to the ease with which information about that person can be recognized, recalled, and categorized (Cantor and Mischel, 1977, 1979a, 1979b). The concept of prototype has been fruitfully applied to information processing with reference to a "self" prototype (Markus, 1977; Rogers et al., 1977), and to the field of stereotype research (Hamilton, 1979). It has also been demonstrated convincingly that subjects can reliably rate the prototypicality of persons with reference to type categories (Cantor &

Mischel, 1979a), as well as the prototypicality of behaviors with reference to trait categories (Buss & Craik, in press).

Within a circumplex model of interpersonal behavior, the concept of prototype is represented geometrically as the center of a wedge-shaped segment chosen, somewhat arbitrarily, to portray a category of a given width. Although prototypes should, in general, be located near the perimeter of the circle, their location is also affected by the amount of common variance a particular category shares with all other categories in the system (communality). It is the case empirically (although not conceptually) that "weaker" categories of interpersonal behavior (docility, modesty, trust) tend to contribute less variance to circumplex solutions and, hence, prototypes of these behaviors may fall closer to the center of the circle than do prototypes of behaviors such as extraversion, ambition, and dominance.

Psychometrically, the cue validity (Rosch et al., 1976) or category resemblance (Tversky, 1977) of prototypes may be assessed in terms of a function that adjusts the multiple correlation of the prototype with its own category members, in terms of its correlations with related *and* opposite categories. Although studies of object categorization have not typically employed polar-opposite contrast categories, such contrasts (e.g., extravert versus introvert) are required for person categories (Cantor and Mischel, 1979a). Perhaps the greatest contribution of a circumplex model to the study of interpersonal prototypes is its precise specification of related, orthogonal, and opposite contrasts for each category under investigation.

A study of prototypes of interpersonal behaviors, by Buss and Craik (in press), may be used to illustrate the conceptual advantages of a circumplex model. Students and expert judges were required to rate the prototypicality of 100 descriptions of dominant actions, according to instructions adapted from Rosch and Mervis (1975). The major finding of the Buss and Craik study was a very substantial increase in the ability of conventional personality trait scales of dominance to predict self-reported prototypical dominant actions over their ability to predict less-prototypical dominant actions. This finding is perhaps the best news that the field of personality assessment has had in recent years, and the importance of the concept of prototype for assessment research is now highly evident.

An equally interesting finding emerged when sex differences in the prototypicality ratings of men and women were examined (Buss, Note 2). Males tended to rate self-centered, Machiavellian, and destructive actions as prototypically dominant, whereas females tended to rate gregarious and extraverted actions as prototypically dominant. Within a circumplex model of interpersonal behavior (Wiggins, 1979), it is clear that males' concepts of dominance extend counterclockwise to the adjacent category of arrogant-calculating and even to the next category of cold-quarrelsome. Females, in contrast, extend the concept of dominance clockwise to the adjacent category of gregarious-extraverted. Add to this the finding that arrogant-calculating and cold-quarrelsome categories are *male* sex-role stereotypes, while the gregarious-extraverted category is a *female* sex-role stereotype (Wiggins & Holzmuller, 1978, in press), and these results become more meaningful. Such a pattern would not be evident in the absence of an explicit structural model.

Basic Level Categories

Rosch (1978) conceives of category systems as having both a vertical and a horizontal dimension. The vertical dimension is one of inclusiveness or abstractness, as would be found in the ordered categories of kitchen chair, chair, furniture, inanimate object. The horizontal dimension divides categories of different content that are at the same level of inclusiveness, as would be true, for example, of the categories of chair, dog, cat, bus, and so on. As will be discussed below, Cantor and Mischel (1979a) have presented evidence that taxonomies of *person types* are structured within this two-dimensional framework, as well. Before considering the work of Cantor and Mischel, however, I would like to call attention to the structural similarities of Rosch's two-dimensional framework to Guttman's (1954) radex model.

According to Guttman (1954), psychological tests may be construed as differing along the two dimensions of complexity and kind. The first dimension, called a *simplex,* orders tests in terms of increasing complexity, as would be found in tests of addition, subtraction, multiplication, and division. Thus, abilities at a higher order of complexity (e.g., division) presuppose or include abilities at a lower order of complexity (addition, subtraction, multiplication). The simplex model is perhaps most familiar in the context of attitude measurement in which the so-called Guttman scale has the property that agreement with an item of a given level of intensity entails agreement with all items of a lower intensity. Conceptually, this would seem to be equivalent to Rosch's vertical dimension of inclusiveness. Guttman's second dimension is called a *circumplex* and it describes the circular ordering that exists among tests of different content that are at the same level of complexity, such as tests of verbal ability, numerical ability, and so on. This dimension corresponds to Rosch's horizontal dimension that divides categories of different content (chair, dog, cat) at the same level of inclusiveness. The circumplex model is, of course, much more specific about the empirical relationships expected among categories at a given level of inclusiveness.

The referents of the Rosch and Guttman models are obviously different, since the former is concerned with the internal structure of perceptual and semantic categories and the latter is concerned with the interrelationships among mental test scores. Nevertheless, the fidelity with which the circumplex model has captured the structure of perceptual judgments in a variety of stimulus domains (Shepard, 1978) suggests that the extension of the model to the domain of categorization is not without strong precedent.

An important implication of Rosch's two dimensional system of categorization is that different levels of abstraction are not equally useful from the standpoint of cognitive economics. In fact, there is extensive empirical evidence supporting the notion of a *basic level* of categorization at which categories carry the most information, possess the highest cue validity, and are most differentiated from one another (Rosch et al., 1976). Categories that are subordinate to this basic level may be richer in detail, but they are less clearly differentiated from one another. Superordinate categories may be more differentiated, but they are less rich in detail. The concept of basic level may have important implications for person perception research, as well, as indicated by the work of Cantor and Mischel (1979a).

As a preliminary step in the investigation of person taxonomies, Cantor and Mischel focused on four of five factors that have emerged consistently in peer-rating studies (Norman, 1963). The categories of. (1) emotionally unstable person, (2) committed (to a belief or cause) person, (3) cultured person, and (4) extraverted person were hypothesized to represent a superordinate level of abstraction. Within each of these four categories, two categories were hypothesized to represent the next (basic) level of abstraction (e.g., emotionally unstable person was more narrowly specified as phobic and as criminal madman). At a level hypothesized to be subordinate to the middle or basic level, still finer specification was made (e.g., phobic was specified as claustrophobic, acrophobic, and hydrophobic). A hierarchical clustering analysis of judges' card sorts of the above stimuli confirmed the hypothesized three-level taxonomy. Further studies employing the attribute-listing technique of Rosch and her colleagues (1976) provided support for the basic level concept with respect to the richness, distinctiveness, and vividness of attributes associated with categories at differing levels of abstractness.

Within the domain of interpersonal taxonomies, the radex model provides an even more explicit representation of categorization schemas than does the two-dimensional model of Rosch. At each level of abstraction along the vertical dimension, the circumplex model specifies the degree of differentiation expected between a given category and other categories that are adjacent, opposite, or orthogonal to it on the circle. It is important to note, however, that this circular relationship is expected to hold only *within* the interpersonal domain, and that the inclusion of stimulus materials from other domains is likely to introduce factors in addition to the two that serve as coordinates for the circumplex (Foa, 1965). Thus, in Cantor and Mischel's (1979a) taxonomy, the domains of *psychopathology* (emotionally unstable), *beliefs* (committed to a belief or cause), *social role* (culture), and *interpersonal* (extraverted) may represent a mixture of domains that are likely to be factorially complex. In terms of research strategy, it may be more efficient to identify the structure of person perception categories within specific domains before investigating "mixed" taxonomies.

The vertical dimension of abstraction or inclusiveness has been implicit in the writings of interpersonal theorists (e.g., Leary, 1957; Sullivan, 1947) and has been made more explicit by Foa and Foa (1974) who have specified the elements of a hierarchical facet structure underlying the categories of social perception. Similarly, the concept of a basic level of categorization has been implicit in the writings of interpersonal theorists and in the specific taxonomies proposed by assessment psychologists. For example, Leary (1957) distinguished 16 finely tuned categories of interpersonal behavior, but for most purposes of assessment employed a more abstract system based on 8 categories. Thus, while it may be possible to distinguish the narrow categories of "gregarious" and "extraverted" behaviors, the more inclusive category of "gregarious-extraverted" behavior is more readily distinguished from other more inclusive categories such as "ambitious-dominant" and "warm-agreeable" (Wiggins, 1979). The number of categories employed for one purpose or another has ranged from 4 (Carson, 1969) to 36 (Benjamin, 1974), although the majority of investigators have used between 8 and 15 (e.g., Becker & Krug, 1964; Foa and Foa, 1974; Leary, 1957; Lorr & McNair, 1965; Schaefer, 1959; Wiggins, 1979).

The basic level of categorization for interpersonal schemas has not yet been established empirically, although the preliminary work of Cantor and Mischel (1979a) suggests that the attribute-listing techniques of Rosch and her associates (1976) could effectively shed light on that important issue. On the limited evidence available, it would appear that 8 category systems are close to a basic level, and that systems requiring as many as 16 categories, although information rich, possess many overlapping attributes (Wiggins, 1979). Although superordinate categories of interpersonal behavior have not been investigated, as such, the nature of such categories may be anticipated from work in other contexts. The interpersonal resources of *love* and *status* appear to be superordinate categories in interpersonal schemas (Carson, 1969; Foa & Foa, 1974), and these categories, in turn, are closely related to the evaluation and dynamism dimensions of affective meaning (Osgood et al., 1957), as well as to the pleasure and arousal components of affect terms themselves (Russell, in press). Thus, the most superordinate categories of interpersonal perception may lack denotative significance, not only because of their inclusiveness but also because they refer more to affective reactions of the observer than to qualities of the person observed.

As Rosch et al. (1976, pp. 430–432) note, different amounts of knowledge about objects can result in different classification schemes among subjects. They cite, as an example, a former airplane mechanic whose list of attributes common to the stimulus word *airplane* far exceded that produced by other subjects. A subject matter expert would thus be expected to have, in addition to a basic level of categorization shared with laypersons, another basic level shared with other experts. Since clinicians and personologists are presumably "person specialists" (Little, 1972), one would expect that their basic level of categorization, in their professional role, would differ from that of other persons. Thus, whereas the average person might employ an 8-category system for classifying interpersonal behavior, a clinician might employ 16. The fine distinction between "aloof" and "withdrawn," for example, may have little utility in everyday transactions, but may be essential for clinical practice. The same may be true of the extremely fine distinctions that Benjamin (1974) makes among 36 categories of interpersonal behavior. Whether clinicians do, in fact, make these distinctions is an interesting empirical question and the methods for conducting such investigations are now available.

SOCIAL EXCHANGE

The personality theory of Harry Stack Sullivan, which inspired circumplex models of interpersonal behavior (Leary, 1957; Carson, 1969), stressed the importance of cost/benefit considerations in the exchange of interpersonal resources in informal social transactions and, indeed, Carson (1979) has recently characterized Sullivan as "an early exchange theorist" (p. 248). Although Sullivan may have anticipated, to some extent, the formulations of more contemporary social exchange theorists (e.g., Homans, 1961; Thibaut & Kelley, 1969), his writings are probably largely unknown to the many social psychologists who have studied social exchange within the paradigm of experimental games. Contemporary interpersonal theorists, on the other hand, have attempted to incorporate the concepts of social exchange theory within a circumplex model of interpersonal behavior (Carson, 1969, 1979; Foa & Foa, 1974).

The principal difference between the Sullivanian tradition and the social exchange tradition of social psychology would seem to lie in the nature of the *resources* exchanged in two types of interpersonal transaction. Whereas subjects in experimental games typically exchange money, persons in informal social transactions are thought to exchange *love* and *status* (Foa & Foa, 1974). Carson (1979) views the exchange of love and status as largely symbolic in character; such exchange serves as a "metacommunication" defining the nature of a relationship (Watzlawick et al., 1967).

In this section, I will examine some of the communalities and differences between research generated from structural models of interpersonal behavior and research conducted within the experimental games paradigm, and I will conclude that each tradition would benefit from more awareness of the other. In particular, I will argue that although the situational constraints, and particularly the resources exchanged, differ in experimental games and informal social transactions, there are sufficient similarities between the two situations to permit the application of interpersonal theory to experimental games and the application of experimental game methodology to the study of interpersonal transactions.

The prototype of laboratory research on the nature of social exchange is found in the Prisoner's Dilemma Game (PDG). In this experimental paradigm, the outcomes (payoffs) of two or more players are dependent upon their mutual choices of moves. The "dilemma," in versions of the PDG, stems from the fact that the choices which would be independently most beneficial to the players are jointly harmful to both. Such a situation would seem to be a potentially fruitful one for studying the influence of motivational orientations upon social interactional patterns of exchange.

Although social psychologists have tended to focus on relatively limited situations, such as "cooperation" and "competition" in experimental games, there have nevertheless been a number of studies that have found interesting relationships between personality characteristics and gaming behavior (e.g., Bem & Lord, 1979; Bennett & Carbonari, 1976; Terhune, 1968; Wrightsman, 1966). The work of Kelley and Stahelski (1970) is especially interesting in this respect, because it illuminates the subtle manner in which personal dispositions to be "cooperative" or "competitive" in a PDG situation determine the information one receives from social interaction and hence influence one's beliefs or expectations regarding the probable behaviors of others in future interactions. Thus, the "competitive" person tends to view life as a jungle because his competitive opening moves (in PDG-like situations) have forced others, including cooperators, to behave in a competitive fashion. The "cooperative" person has a more differentiated world view because his cooperative opening moves have been met sometimes by cooperation and sometimes by competition. Carson (1979) has incorporated the Kelley and Stahelski (1970) formulation within his fourfold circumplex taxonomy in which hostile-dominance is equated with "competition" and affiliative-dominance with "cooperation." Carson (1979) has also extended this attributional analysis to include hostile-submissive and affiliative-submissive persons as well (see also Golding, 1977).

A relatively complete taxonomy of both games and motivational orientations is required to untangle the complex interactions of game format, motivational orientation of players, and perception of partner's behavior in the PDG situation. An impressive beginning in this respect has been made by McClintock, Messick, and their associates at Santa Barbara. These investigators are less interested in testing prescriptive economic theories of choice behavior and more interested in assessing the *motivational orientations* of subjects who participate in experimental games (Messick & McClintock, 1968). As a consequence, they have developed "decomposed games" as alternatives to the standard PDG situation in order to separate the motivational from the strategic aspects of gaming behavior. In a decomposed game, the subject's choice on each trial determines both his own payoff and that of his partner, this information being displayed to the subject in the form of a simple 2 × 2 payoff matrix. Interdependence is maintained by informing both subjects that their payoffs will be the cumulative results of both of their choices. Strategies are avoided by keeping each player ignorant of the other's choices. This paradigm permits the study of a player's motivational orientation to maximize his own payoff, his partner's payoff, and the relative difference between the two, the latter having been established earlier as an important motivational orientation (McClintock & McNeel, 1966; Messick & Thorngate, 1967). Thus, one can characterize motivational orientations as "individualistic" (maximizing own gain), "cooperative" (maximizing joint gain), or "competitive" (maximizing own relative gain).

Griesinger and Livingston (1973) have devised a geometric model to represent motivational orientations in the decomposed games of McClintock, Messick and their colleagues. As can be seen from Figure 2, the coordinates of this two-dimensional representation are: (A) other's payoff and (B) own payoff.[1] Each choice (X and Y) in a decomposed game involves a pair of values (a, b) corresponding to the payoffs for Player A (other) and Player B (own). Thus, the coordinates A and B provide a plane within which choices X and Y can be represented as *choice vectors* passing through the payoff points (a_x, b_x) and (a_y, b_y), respectively. The utility of a given choice for a given player is assumed to be a linear combination of the payoffs to A and B, weighted by the motivational orientations of the player:

$$U(a_i, b_i) = m_A a_i + m_B b_i.$$

The *motivational vector* of a player may be thought of as a vector passing through those points (m_A, m_B) which satisfy that player's motives with respect to other payoff, own payoff, and the relative difference between the two. The orientation of this vector may be expressed with reference to the angle it forms with the A axis. Thus, in Figure 2, pure "altruism" would be represented by a motivational vector that was coextensive with the other's payoff coordinate (A), "cooperation" would be represented by a vector of 45°, and "individualism" by a vector of 90°. In Figure 2, in which the choice vectors for X and Y are of equal length, it would be predicted that Y would be chosen, because it is oriented more nearly in the θ_m direction (i.e., has the greater projection on M).

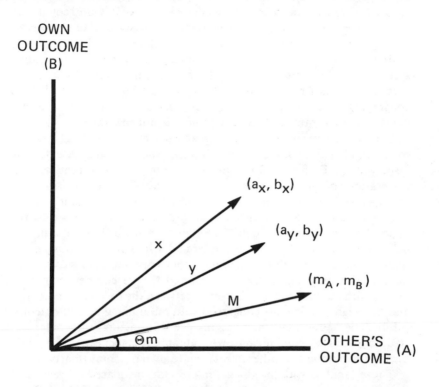

Figure 2: Geometric representation of choice vectors (X and Y) and a motivational vector (M) in a decomposed game (after Griesinger & Livingston, 1973).

Within the geometric model of Griesinger and Livingston, it is possible to assess a subject's motivational orientation with a high degree of precision. On the assumption that a subject will choose the payoff vector oriented most nearly in the direction of his motivational orientation (θ_m), the results of a series of choices between equal-length payoff vectors can be used to estimate that subject's motivational orientation. Assume that a subject is presented with a choice between a cooperative payoff of 45° (X) and a payoff of −45° that tends to maximize the other's gain at the expense of his own (Y). The choice of X, under these circumstances, would narrow the region of uncertainty regarding the subject's motivational orientation to between 0° and 180°. If on the next trial, the subject chose a cooperative payoff of 45° (X) over a competitive payoff of 135° (Y), the region of uncertainty would be reduced by half: 0° to 90°. Further selected trials of this kind could then be employed to estimate the motivational orientation of the subject to the limits of his ability to discriminate differences. Griesinger and Livingston (1973) have written a computer program for an on-line system that determines a subject's motivational orientation in the manner just described. They report that the method is highly efficient, converging on an estimate of θ_m in an average of nine trials, and that deviation from transitivity of preferences is not marked.

In a recent study of the prediction and perception of social motives, Maki et al. (1979) investigated the eight motivational orientations displayed in Figure 3. In addition to the common motivational orientations of altruism, cooperation, individualism, competition, and aggression, the authors included the more "abnormal" orientations of sadomasochism, masochism, and martyrdom that are implied by the logic of the geometric model. Note that each social motive is strictly defined by the payoff matrix for other and self. Thus, for example, the individualist is relatively indifferent to other's outcome and is concerned mainly with maximizing own outcome (0,1), the competitor is concerned with maximizing the difference between the two outcomes (-1,1) and the aggressor is most concerned with minimizing other's outcome (-1,0). The "abnormal" motives involve minimizing both outcomes (sadomasochism), minimizing own outcome (masochism), and maximizing the outcome of other in relation to own outcome (martyrdom).

Those familiar with the clinical interpretations placed on vectors of the interpersonal circumplex (e.g., Carson, 1969; Leary, 1957) will have little difficulty recognizing these "abnormal" social motives and, in fact, the total circumplex implied by Figure 3 can be seen to be virtually identical to that portrayed in Figure 1. Since no mention is made of other interpersonal circumplex models in the Griesinger and Livingston (1973) article, in the Maki et al. (1979) article, or in related articles by the Santa Barbara group, it would appear that, once again, quite independent lines of investigation have converged on a common structural model (Foa, 1961). This is an especially significant "convergence," however, because the individual differences approach and the experimental games approach are associated with quite distinct methodologies that may prove especially fruitful when applied to a common subject matter.

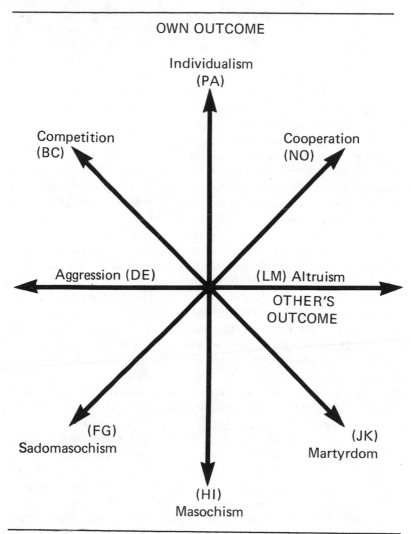

Figure 3: Motivational orientations in decomposed games (after Maki et al., 1979).

Maki et al. (1979) conducted two experiments to determine the extent to which subjects construe the gaming behavior of others in terms of the eight social motives indicated in Figure 3. Their subjects were required to observe and then predict the behavior of a "chooser" whose choices were preprogrammed to provide a consistent representation of the eight motivational orientations. In terms of percentage of correct prediction, subjects were able to detect individualism and competition quite easily and aggression, cooperation, and altruism less well. They appeared to experience the most difficulty in detecting masochism, martyrdom, and sadomasochism, the latter being at a chance level. Thus, in an experimental game situation, the motives of individualism and competition appear to be more comprehensible in others than are prosocial or self-sacrificing motives. The authors interpreted this finding from an interaction-expectancy framework: "The more popular a particular social motive is perceived to be as an interaction goal, the more likely it will be anticipated (and detected) in the behavior of others" (Maki et al., 1979, p. 218).

The above findings, and the plausible interpretation placed upon them, serve to underscore the fact that persons bring with them quite different sets of expectations to experimental games than they do to ordinary social interactions. In ordinary social interactions, the social motives of altruism (LM) and cooperation (NO) are clearly the most popular or socially desirable, and the motives of competition (BC) and of aggression (DE) are just as clearly the least popular or desirable (Wiggins, 1979, p. 407). This intuitively obvious difference between games and ordinary social interactions is perhaps not sufficiently appreciated in Kelley and Stahelski's (1970) assumption that: "The goals that subjects set for themselves when they enter the laboratory PD game reflect the orientations they generally adopt for a wide variety of their social relationships" (p. 76).

In addition to differing in implicit rules and expectations, experimental games differ from ordinary social transactions in terms of the nature of the resources being exchanged. The resource that is usually exchanged in experimental games is money or tokens of money (points). Exchanges that are uniquely "interpersonal" in nature may be thought of as involving social (status) and emotional (love) outcomes (Foa & Foa, 1974). The left-hand side of Table 2 indicates the hypothetical composition of interpersonal variables in terms of the underlying components of love and status (Wiggins, 1979, p. 397). The right-hand side displays the relative weights placed by the "chooser" on his own and other's outcomes in the experiment of Maki et al. (1979, p. 216). The payoffs for interpersonal behaviors and for moves in experimental games are not directly comparable, since two resources (love and status) are at stake in the former, and only one resource (money) in the latter. However, it is possible to calculate the mean overall payoff to self and to other in interpersonal behaviors by averaging across love and status. Thus, for example, ambitious-dominant behavior involves a payoff to *self* of +1 (love) and +1 (status), the average of which is +1. The payoff to *other* for this behavior, averaged across love and status, would be zero. Thus, it can be seen that the average overall payoff to self and other in interpersonal situations is identical to that hypothesized by Maki et al. for experimental games. The crucial difference between games and interpersonal transactions, however, resides in the nature of the resources exchanged.

Foa and Foa (1974) have presented a cognitive-developmental account of the manner in which different *categories* of resources come to be differentiated in the cognitive structures of children. Out of an initially undifferentiated matrix of "warmth, softness, food, and care," the categories of services and love are differentiated. Subsequently, services and love undergo parallel differentiations; the former into money, goods, and services, and the latter into love, status, and information. A unique feature of the Foas' account is their specification of the structure of perceived differences among these six resource classes in terms of the orthogonal coordinates of "concreteness" and "particularism." The ordering among resource classes is circular and, starting at twelve o'clock and moving counterclockwise, takes the form: love, status, information, money, goods, and services.

Within this conceptualization, love differs from money in being a more *particularistic* commodity, that is, it makes a great deal of difference *who* is involved in the exchange of love. Likewise, status is less particularistic than love, and it is expressed in more symbolic forms. Although love may be expressed in relatively concrete terms, the exchange of both love and status in informal social transactions typically serves as a metacommunication defining the interpersonal situation (Carson, 1979). Thus, although the literature of experimental games contains hints that persons' motivational orientations toward the exchange of money may be correlated with their orientations toward the exchange of love and status, there is little reason to expect that this relationship would necessarily be a strong one.

The hypothesized structure of perceived differences among resource classes has been confirmed by the results of several experiments (Foa &

TABLE 2
Outcomes for Interpersonal Behaviors and for Moves in Decomposed Games

Interpersonal Behaviors	Love		Status		Money		Motivational Orientations
	self	other	self	other	self	other	
Ambitious-Dominant (PA)	+1	+1	+1	−1	+1	0	Individualism
Arrogant-Calculating (BC)	+1	−1	+1	−1	+1	−1	Competition
Cold-Quarrelsome (DE)	−1	−1	+1	−1	0	−1	Aggression
Aloof-Introverted (FG)	−1	−1	−1	−1	−1	−1	Sadomasochism
Lazy-Submissive (HI)	−1	−1	−1	+1	−1	0	Masochism
Unassuming-Ingenuous (JK)	−1	+1	−1	+1	−1	+1	Martyrdom
Warm-Agreeable (LM)	+1	+1	−1	+1	0	+1	Altruism
Gregarious-Extraverted (NO)	+1	+1	+1	+1	+1	+1	Cooperation

Foa, 1974; Turner et al., 1971). The procedures employed in these experiments are as intriguing as the results because they suggest the possibility of studying interpersonal resource exchange in a laboratory setting. In one study, for example, a confederate "subject" delivered a series of messages to another subject through a message slot in a partition that separated them from each other's view. The messages were short statements, typed on 3×5 index cards, that represented the resource classes of love (I feel affection for you), status (you do things very well), information (here is my opinion), money (here is some money for you), goods (here is a package for you), and services (I ran that errand for you). The subject's task was to return a resource message that was most similar and a resource message that was least similar to the one received. In another study, subjects were asked to indicate the resource they would most prefer to receive (e.g., the person says that he is very fond of you) in exchange for doing something for another person (e.g., helping a person by providing certain services for them). With sufficient ingenuity, it may be possible to devise an "interpersonal decomposed game" in which players choose between alternatives that offer different payoffs to themselves and to their partners in terms of love, status, and other resource classes. Although such a game would likely be contrived and lacking in mundane realism, it may nevertheless be closer to the substance of informal social transactions than are games based solely on the exchange of money. The possiblity of validating self-report measures of interpersonal dispositions against precise measures of motivational orientations obtained from experimental games is an exciting one, as is the possibility of observing play-by-play exchanges of love and status between subjects preselected on self-report measures.

DIMENSIONS OF PERSONALITY RESEARCH

As interest in the grand theories of personality waned, academic personologists and clinicians came to focus their attention on more limited constructs that lent themselves to systematic empirical investigation. The last 25 years of personality study may be characterized as a period of construct elaboration in which a variety of single dimensions of personality (e.g., authoritarianism, achievement, aggression) have been studied in depth in experimental, correlational, and field designs. Despite the considerable advances that have been made in understanding specific dimensions of personality, there has been a notable absence of a generally accepted theoretical framework that would determine the choice of constructs to be investigated and that would specify a common nomological network in which individual constructs are embedded. In a historical survey of personality scales and inventories, Goldberg (1971) has emphasized that personality measuring devices have focused upon personality constructs arising out of applied societal pressures rather than constructs suggested by theories of personality: "the most potent source of variance in the determination of the constructs for past scales and inventories has been sheer historical accident" (p. 335).

From a historical perspective, it is also the case that the popularity and eventual fate of any given construct is better understood from the sociology of psychological research than from any theory of personality. Personality constructs seldom expire dramatically; they just fade away. The history of the study of *relationships* among indicants of single constructs is even more discouraging. Journal editors are perhaps more aware than their readership that the overwhelming majority of personality studies are "one-shot" enterprises in which Jones' X-scale is correlated with Smith's Y-scale in a sample of 100 college sophomores, and the statistically "significant" correlation of .28 is reflected upon in a theoretically muddled discussion section. The choice of which two constructs are to be related is not informed by theoretical considerations. Rather, it appears to be determined by an author's reading of the zeitgeist in terms of the *frequency* with which the names of the two constructs have appeared in the titles of journal articles during the preceding year. Thus, if it is a vintage year for "fear of success" and "field dependence," a study of "The relationship between fear of success and field dependence in student nurses" is surefire, regardless of conceptual rationale or lack of same.

Findings with respect to the principal dimensions of experimental and psychometric personality research have been summarized by, for example, Byrne (1974), Blass (1977), and, most recently, London and Exner (1978). With some exceptions, the principal structural model for organizing this literature has been "alphabetical," in the tradition of Murray (1938). London and Exner (1978) have stated this explicitly:

There obviously has been no overreaching plan or theory, implicit or explicit, guiding the selection of topics for trait researchers. Indeed the editors were forced to organize the book by means of the unsophisticated tactic of simply placing chapters in alphabetical order [p. xiv].

Many of the personality dimensions considered by London and Exner are *interpersonal* in nature and, as such, can be construed from the vantage point of the circumplex model. If nothing else, the circumplex model of interpersonal behavior is based on a systematic theoretical framework that provides a coherent rationale for expecting a definite pattern of relationships to exist among indicants of persono-logical constructs. Such a framework might postulate that some constructs (e.g. power and achievement) are so closely related con-ceptually as to be nearly interchangeable. Other constructs (e.g., Machiavellianism and interpersonal trust) are conceptual opposites that should be highly negatively related. Still other constructs (e.g., domi-nance and nurturance) would be expected to be virtually unrelated. Although the postulated relationships just stated are, in part, based on empirical observations, there are also good theoretical reasons for expecting them to obtain (e.g., Carson, 1969; Foa & Foa, 1974; Leary, 1957). The lack of such an agreed-upon theoretical framework is all the more lamentable in light of recent methodological advances that permit the precise testing of structural hypotheses related to convergent and discriminant validities of indicants of personological constructs (Schmidt, 1978).

Figure 4 is a representation of the hypothesized interrelationships among dimensions of experimental personality research, that may serve as an alternative to alphabetical models. Before commenting on the potential usefulness of such a framework, several qualifications should be made. The classification scheme depicted in Figure 4 is meant to apply to *interpersonal behavior* under an explicit definition of that domain (Wiggins, 1979). As such, it is not necessarily applicable to other domains of research such as *attitudes* (authoritarianism), *beliefs* (locus of control, dogmatism), *cognitive styles* (field dependence/independ-ence), *affects* (anxiety, depression), or *defensive styles* (need for approval, sensitization/repression). The relationship between inter-personal variables and those from other domains is, in fact, an empirical question that can be investigated rather precisely by use of circumplex methodology.

It should also be noted that the schema presented in Figure 4 is not committed to any particular number of categories as representing a *basic level* of categorization. Although 8 categories may be close to the number of categories employed in everyday social cognition, 16 categories may be meaningful to personality and social psychologists. Finally, and perhaps most important, this classification scheme is not meant to condone the procedure of equating scales that bear similar labels, or experimental studies that bear similar titles, in the absence of convincing empirical and psychometric evidence for making such assertions. Although the problem of establishing an isomorphism between personality scales from different instruments has been most extensively discussed in the factor-analytic literature, it applies with equal and perhaps greater force to scales developed by internal consistency procedures. Establishing the convergent validity of personality scales, or of experimental manipulations, is a complex procedure (construct validity) that requires more than the matching of labels. With respect to structural considerations of construct validity (Loevinger, 1957), the circumplex model provides explicit and detailed criteria of convergent and discriminant validity for evaluating putative measures of interpersonal traits.

In addition to providing a framework for comprehending the interrelationships among the diverse and mainly unrelated efforts of contemporary investigators, this scheme serves to generate specific hypotheses concerning directions for future research. Particularly, this framework makes it possible to capitalize on the analytic potential of experimental designs that incorporate genuinely orthogonal dimensions of individual differences as independent variables. The prototype of this design is Eysenck's program of research employing introversion-extraversion and neuroticism-normalcy as orthogonal factors. Eysenck's relatively simple design has served an enormously clarifying function in detecting patterns of relationship, between performance measures and individual difference measures of neuroticism and extraversion, that would simply have gone unnoticed had the two individual difference measures been employed separately. It is clear from his work that even relatively simple personological typologies (neurotic-extravert, normal-introvert, and so on) have considerable heuristic potential.

From inspection of Figure 4, it is evident that there may be other kinds of orthogonal contrasts that could provide new insights into well-established relationships between individual difference and performance measures. At the simplest level of analysis, it can be noted that each variable appearing in Figure 4 has a polar opposite variable, as well as two orthogonal bipolar contrast variables. Consider, for example, the research on Machiavellianism, which has provided a rather consistent picture of the differences between high (Machiavellianism) and low

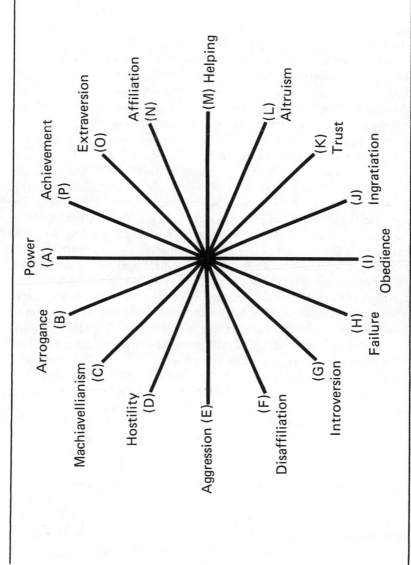

Figure 4: Hypothesized interrelationships among dimensions of experimental personality research.

(trust) scoreś on this single dimension (Christie & Geis, 1970). As summarized by Geis (1978, pp. 353-355), high Machs are cool, objective, unflustered, and in control. They attend to cognitions, resist social influence, and control groups. In contrast, low Machs are warm, empathizing, involved, and distractable. They attend to persons and accept social influence and social structure defined by others. Note, however, that the logic of the model presented in Figure 4 suggests that the dimension of high and low Machiavellianism is *orthogonal* to the dimension of introversion-extraversion. This implies a typology consisting of introverted-high Machs, extraverted-high Machs, introverted-low Machs, and extraverted-low Machs. Previous studies of this dimension have tended to emphasize the introverted nature of high Machs and the extraverted nature of low Machs. However, the present formulation suggests that, in addition to introverted-high Machs and extraverted-low Machs, there should also be extraverted-high Machs and introverted-low Machs. The implementation of this fourfold typology within an experimental design might be worth investigating.

Although both helping and aggressive behaviors have been the subjects of a great deal of research, they have seldom been considered as bipolar opposites of a single continuum. When crossed with the orthogonal dimensions of dominance-submission, a potentially useful typology is formed which consists of dominant and submissive helpers and of dominant (active) and submissive (passive) aggressors. Similarly, the logic of the interpersonal circumplex suggests that the dimension of affiliation-disaffiliation can be crossed with arrogance-ingratiation to form a typology consisting of arrogant and ingratiating affiliators and of arrogant and ingratiating disaffiliators. As a final example, when the dimension of achievement-failure is crossed with hostility-altruism, it suggests an interesting typology of hostile and altruistic achievers and of hostile and altruistic failures. All of this is, of course, totally speculative, but it does represent a framework for hypothesis generation that may lead to empirical findings that prove to be more systematic and lasting than those generated by alphabetical or "shot-gun" models.

NOTE

1. Griesinger and Livingston actually labelled the X axis as own payoff and the Y axis as other's payoff. In the present exposition, these axes have been reversed to avoid possible confusion in the discussion which follows.

REFERENCE NOTES

1. Wiggins, J. S., Steiger, J. H., & Gaelick, L. *Evaluating circumplexity in personality data.* Unpublished manuscript, University of British Columbia, 1979.
2. Buss, D. M. *Sex differences in the evaluation and manifestation of dominant acts.* Unpublished manuscript, University of California, Berkeley, 1979.

REFERENCES

Adams, H. B. "Mental illness" or interpersonal behavior? *American Psychologist,* 1964, *19,* 191-197.

Becker, W. C. & Krug, R. S. A circumplex model for social behavior in children. *Child Development,* 1964, *35,* 371-396.

Bem, D. J. & Lord, C. G. Template matching: A proposal for probing the ecological validity of experimental settings in social psychology. *Journal of Personality and Social Psychology,* 1979, *37,* 833-846.

Benjamin, L. S. Structural analysis of social behavior. *Psychological Review* 1974, *81,* 392-425.

Bennett, R. P. & Carbonari, J. P. Personality patterns related to own-, joint-, and relative-gain maximizing behaviors. *Journal of Personality and Social Psychology,* 1976, *34,* 1127-1134.

Blass, T. (ed.). *Personality variables in social behavior.* Hillsdale, N.J.: Erlbaum, 1977.

Buss, D. M. & Craik, K. H. The frequency concept of disposition: Dominance and prototypically dominant acts. *Journal of Personality,* in press.

Byrne, D. *An introduction to personality.* Englewood Cliffs, N.J.: Prentice-Hall, 1974.

Cantor, N. & Mischel, W. Traits as prototypes: Effects on recognition memory. *Journal of Personality and Social Psychology,* 1977, *35,* 38-48.

Cantor, N. & Mischel, W. Prototypes in person perception. In L. Berkowitz (ed.), *Advances in experimental social psychology* (Vol. 12). New York: Academic Press, 1979. (a)

Cantor, N. & Mischel, W. Prototypicality and personality: Effects on free recall and personality impressions. *Journal of Research in Personality,* 1979. (b)

Carroll, J. S. & Payne, J. W. (eds.). *Cognition and social behavior.* Hillsdale, N.J.: Erlbaum, 1976.

Carson, R. C. *Interaction concepts of personality.* Chicago: AVC, 1969.

Carson, R. C. Personality and exchange in developing relationships. In R. L. Burgess & T. L. Huston (eds.), *Social exchange in developing relationships.* New York: Academic Press, 1979.

Christie, R. & Geiss, F. L. *Studies in Machiavellianism.* New York: Academic Press, 1970.

Conte, H. R. A Circumplex model for personality traits (Doctoral dissertation, New York University, 1975), *Dissertation Abstracts International,* 1975 (University Microfilms No. 7601731).

Fiske, S. T. & Cox, M. G. Person concepts: The effect of target familiarity and descriptive purpose on the process of describing others. *Journal of Personality,* 1979, *47,* 137-161.

Foa, U. G. Convergences in the analysis of the structure of interpersonal behavior. *Psychological Reivew*, 1961, *68*, 341-353.

Foa, U. G. New developments in facet design and analysis. *Psychological Review*, 1965, *72*, 262-274.

Foa, U. G. & Foa, E. G. *Societal structures of the mind.* Springfield, Ill.: Charles C Thomas, 1974.

Freedman, M. B., Leary, T. F., Ossorio, A. G., & Coffey, H. S. The interpersonal dimension of personality. *Journal of Personality*, 1951, *20*, 143-161.

Geis, F. L. Machiavellianism. In H. London & J. E. Exner, Jr. (eds.), *Dimensions of personality.* New York: Wiley, 1978.

Goldberg, L. R. A historical survey of personality scales and inventories. In P. McReynolds (ed.), *Advances in psychological assessment* (Vol. 2). Palo Alto, Calif.: Science and Behavior Books, 1971.

Golding, S. L. Individual differences in the construal of interpersonal interactions. In D. Magnusson and N. S. Endler (eds.), *Personality at the cross-roads: Current issues in interactional psychology.* Hillsdale, N.J.: Erlbaum, 1977.

Griesinger, D. W. & Livingston, J. W., Jr. Toward a model of interpersonal motivation in experimental games. *Behavioral Science*, 1973, *18*, 173-188.

Guttman, L. A new approach to factor analysis: The radex. In P. A. Lazarsfeld (ed.), *Mathematical thinking in the social sciences.* New York: Macmillan, 1954.

Hamilton, D. L. A cognitive-attributional analysis of stereotyping. In L. Berkowitz (ed.), *Advances in experimental social psychology* (Vol. 12). New York: Academic Press, 1979.

Hastie, R., Ostrom, T., Ebbesen, E., Wyer, R., Hamilton, D. L., & Carlston, D. (eds.). *Person memory.* Hillsdale, N.J.: Erlbaum, in press.

Heider, F. *The psychology of interpersonal relations.* New York: Wiley, 1958.

Hersh, M. M. & Caramazza, A. A fuzzy set approach to modifiers and vagueness in natural language. *Journal of Experimental Psychology: General*, 1976, *105*, 251-276.

Higgins, E. T., Herman, C. P., & Zanna, M. P. (eds.). *Social cognition: The Ontario Symposium on Personality and Social Psychology.* Hillsdale, N.J.: Erlbaum, in press.

Homans, G. C. *Social behavior: Its elementary forms.* New York: Harcourt Brace Jovanovich, 1961.

Kelley, H. H. & Stahelski, A. J. Social interaction bias of cooperators' and competitors' beliefs about others. *Journal of Personality and Social Psychology*, 1970, *16*, 66-91.

Kintsch, W. *The representation of meaning in memory.* Hillsdale, N.J.: Erlbaum, 1974.

Labov, W. The boundaries of words and their meanings. In C. J. Bailey and R. Shuy (eds.), *New ways of analyzing variations in English.* Washington, D.C.: Georgetown University Press, 1973.

Lakoff, G. Hedges: A study in meaning criteria and the logic of fuzzy concepts. *Papers from the Eighth Regional Meeting Chicago Linguistic Society.* Chicago: University of Chicago Linguistics Department, 1972.

Leary, T. *Interpersonal diagnosis of personality.* New York: Ronald Press, 1957.

Little, B. R. Psychological man as scientist, humanist and specialist. *Journal of Experimental Research in Personality*, 1972, *6*, 95-118.

Loevinger, J. Objective tests as instruments of psychological theory. *Psychological Reports*, 1957, *3*, 635-694. (Monograph No. 9)

London, H. & Exner, J. E., Jr. (eds.). *Dimensions of personality.* New York: Wiley, 1978.

Lorr, M. & McNair, D. M. Expansion of the interpersonal behavior circle. *Journal of Personality and Social Psychology*, 1965, *2*, 823-830.

MacDonald, R. Testing pattern hypotheses for correlation matrices. *Psychometrika*, 1975, *40*, 253-255.

Maki, J. E., Thorngate, W. B., & McClintock, C. G. Prediction and perception of social motives. *Journal of Personality and Social Psychology*, 1979, *37*, 203-220.

Markus, H. Self-schemata and processing information about the self. *Journal of Personality and Social Psychology*, 1977, *35*, 63-78.

McClintock, C. G. & McNeel, S. P. Reward and score feedback as determinants of cooperative and competitive games behavior. *Journal of Personality and Social Psychology*, 1966, *4*, 606-613.

McCormick, C. C. & Kavanagh, J. A. Scaling interpersonal checklist items to the circumplex model. *Applied Psychological Measurement*, in press.

McLemore, C. W. & Benjamin, L. S. Whatever happened to interpersonal diagnosis? A psychosocial alternative to DSM-III. *American Psychologist*, 1979, *34*, 17-34.

Messick, D. M. & Thorngate, W. B. Relative gain maximization in experimental games. *Journal of Experimental Social Psychology*, 1967, *3*, 85-101.

Messick, D. M. & McClintock, C. G. Motivational bases of choice in experimental games. *Journal of Experimental Social Psychology*, 1968, *4*, 1-25.

Messick, S. & Ross, J. Introduction: Psychological structure and measurement models in personality assessment. In S. Messick and J. Ross (eds.), *Measurement in personality and cognition*. New York: Wiley, 1972.

Murray, H. A. *Explorations in personality*. New York: Oxford, 1938.

Nisbett, R. E. & Ross, L. *Human inference: Strategies and shortcomings*. Englewood Cliffs, N.J.: Prentice-Hall, 1980.

Norman, W. P. Toward an adequate taxonomy of personality attributes: Replicated factor structure in peer nomination personality ratings. *Journal of Abnormal and Social Psychology*, 1963, *66*, 574-583.

Osgood, C. E., Suci, G. J., & Tannenbaum, P. H. *The measurement of meaning*. Urbana: University of Illinois Press, 1957.

Posner, M. I. *Cognition: An introduction*. Glenview, Ill.: Scott, Foresman, 1973.

Rinn, J. L. Structure of phenomenal domains. *Psychological Review*, 1965, *72*, 445-466.

Rogers, T. B., Kuiper, N. A. & Kirker, W. S. Self-reference and the encoding of personal information. *Journal of Personality and Social Psychology*, 1977, *35*, 677-688.

Rosch, E. On the internal structure of perception and semantic categories. In T. E. Moore (ed.), *Cognitive development and the acquisition of language*. New York: Academic Press, 1973.

Rosch, E. Cognitive reference points. *Cognitive Psychology*, 1975, *7*, 532-547.

Rosch, E. Principles of categorization. In E. Rosch and D. B. Lloyd (eds.), *Cognition and categorization*. Hillsdale, N.J.: Erlbaum, 1978.

Rosch, E. and Mervis, C. B. Family resemblances: Studies in the internal structure of categories. *Cognitive Psychology*, 1975, *7*, 573-605.

Rosch, E., Mervis, C. B., Gray, W. D., Johnson, D. M., & Boyes-Braem, P. Basic objects in natural categories. *Cognitive Psychology*, 1976, *8*, 382-439.

Russell, J. A. A circumplex model of affect. *Journal of Personality and Social Psychology*, in press.

Schaefer, E. S. A circumplex model for maternal behavior. *Journal of Abnormal and Social Psychology*, 1959, *59*, 226-235.

Schaefer, E. S. Converging conceptual models for maternal behavior and child behavior. In J. C. Glidewell (ed.), *Parental attitudes and child behavior*. Springfield, Ill.: Charles C Thomas, 1961.

Schmitt, N. Path analysis of multitrait-multimethod matrices. *Applied Psychological Measurement*, 1978, *2*, 157-173.

Shepard, R. N. The circumplex and related topological manifolds in the study of perception. In S. Shye (ed.), *Theory construction and data analysis in the behavioral sciences*. San Francisco: Jossey-Bass, 1978.

Sullivan, H. S. *Conceptions of modern psychiatry*. Washington, D.C.: William Alanson White Foundation, 1947.

Swenson, C. H., Jr. *Introduction to interpersonal relations*. Glenview, Ill.: Scott, Foresman, 1973.

Terhune, K. W. Motives, situation, and interpersonal conflict within prisoner's dilemma. *Journal of Personality and Social Psychology Monograph*, 1968, *8*(3, Pt. 2).

Thibaut, J. W. & Kelley, H. H. *The social psychology of groups*. New York: Wiley, 1959.

Turner, J. L., Foa, E. B., & Foa, U. G. Interpersonal reinforcers: Classification, interrelationships, and some differential properties. *Journal of Personality and Social Psychology*, 1971, *19*, 168-180.

Tversky, A. Features of similarity. *Psychological Review*, 1977, *84*, 327-352.

Watzlawick, P., Beavin, J. H., & Jackson, D. D. *Pragmatics of human communication*. New York: Norton, 1967.

Wiggins, J. S. Personality structure. *Annual Review of Psychology*, 1968, *19*, 293-350.

Wiggins, J. S. A psychological taxonomy of trait-descriptive terms: The interpersonal domain. *Journal of Personality and Social Psychology*, 1979, *37*, 395-412.

Wiggins, J. S. & Holzmuller, A. Psychological androgyny and interpersonal behavior. *Journal of Consulting and Clinical Psychology*, 1978, *46*, 40-52.

Wiggins, J. S. & Holzmuller, A. Further evidence on androgyny and interpersonal flexibility. *Journal of Research in Personality*, in press.

Wittgenstein, L. *Philosophical investigations*. New York: Macmillan, 1953.

Wrightsman, L. S. Personality and attitudinal correlates of trusting and trustworthy behaviors in a two-person game. *Journal of Personality and Social Psychology*, 1966, *4*, 328-332.

Zadeh, L. A. Fuzzy sets. *Information and Control*, 1965, *8*, 338-353.

11

Situated Action
AN EMERGING PARADIGM

G. P. GINSBURG

G. P. Ginsburg joined the University of Nevada, Reno, in 1963 to help establish the Inter-disciplinary Ph.D. Program in Social Psychology, which he now chairs. Professor Ginsburg's current work focuses on the analysis of episodes of human action in their situational contexts, and he has written several chapters and edited a volume of original contributions on the topic.

In recent years, social psychology has experienced considerable soul searching and loss of confidence, and there have been calls for new approaches, new perspectives, and new paradigms. Although this may engender dismay and pessimism in some, I share with Cartwright (1979) a much more optimistic view about the field. Social psychology currently is in a state of intense theoretical activity with immense potential for change in both its conventional modes of explanation and its conventional strategies of investigation. It is true that this activity is taking place on ground fertilized by the "crisis" concerns of the late 1960s; but the fervor of those concerns was generated largely by doubts about the wisdom and morality of the widespread use of deception as a research technique (see Ginsburg, 1978, for a detailed review), whereas the current ferment is more creatively productive. It is challenging some of our basic presuppositions and clearly is in the process of producing new theoretical and methodological perspectives.

Thus, I see the future of social psychology as being very promising. This is due in part to a particular paradigm taking shape and emerging from the activities of the field. It is also due to the gradually growing recognition that many of the phenomena studied by psychologists, such

295

as cognitive and memory phenomena, are inherently social phenomena being studied in social settings, and that their interpretation requires a reasonable degree of social psychological sophistication. My intention in this chapter is to trace the structure and perhaps the future form of what I see as a paradigm emerging from contemporary social psychology.

The paradigm contains both substantive and metatheoretical themes, and it carries with it a commitment to a particular investigative strategy. Elsewhere (Ginsburg, in press), I have referred to the paradigm as "situated action," and to the investigative orientation as "structural analysis," and I will continue that practice here. The chapter will focus on the structural analysis of situated action as an emergent paradigm in social psychological research. It will not contain a systematic review of the relevant literature, since my purpose is to describe the paradigm rather than to evaluate it.

THE SITUATED ACTION PARADIGM

The emergence of the situated action paradigm can be better appreciated if it is placed in the context of certain recent criticisms of conventional social psychology. Specifically, after several years of collaboration, Rom Harré of Oxford University and Paul Secord, then of the University of Nevada, Reno, published *The Explanation of Social Behaviour* (Harré & Secord, 1972). The book very strongly criticized conventional social psychological research and theory and offered suggestions about how such research and theorizing should be conducted. Criticisms were directed at the positivist rhetoric and ideology of the field, excessive reliance on the laboratory experiment, conceptual naiveté of the theories, misguided attempts to emulate mistaken conceptions of the natural sciences, and denial of the human capacities of the people being studied. Although justifiably criticized for its loose ends, the challenge of the book came to be taken seriously, and its basic orientation—"ethogenics"—has become respectable in the field, even appearing (Harré, 1977) as a chapter in *Advances in Experimental Social Psychology*.

At about the same time as the Harré and Secord book appeared, Israel and Tajfel (1972) published a volume which also critically evaluated contemporary social psychology. As an edited volume it did not offer as coherent a thesis as the Harré and Secord book, but its appearance and acceptance reflected the intellectual reconsiderations of the time, especially in its emphasis on the importance of group membership and social context. Other books which were published over the next few years also reflected concern and reconsideration (Armistead, 1974; Strickland et al., 1976). Michael Argyle and his group at Oxford soon became involved in the discussions and added significantly to the development of the ideas along empirical as well as theoretical lines, although much of their work remained independent of the ethogenic approach. This intense activity has continued, and its products are contained in a number of recent volumes and articles. Examples include Peter Collett's (1977) edited volume on social rules; edited volumes by Brenner et al. (1978) and Ginsburg (1979), which deal with the contexts of social psychological research and with the research strategies that appear most compatible with the emerging perspectives; an insightful but methodologically wanting research monograph by Marsh et al. (1978) which demonstrates the rule-guided nature of violence; a concise challenge to Humean casuality by Harré and Madden (1975), who propose instead natural powers as a basis for scientific explanation (this is a technical elaboration of the 1972 Harré and Secord argument); and, most recently, an extended development of the ethogenic approach by Harré (1979), an edited volume by Brenner (in press) on the structure of action, and a book on social situations by Argyle et al. (in press).

This brief historical review traces only one line of the widespread reexamination occurring in social psychology today, and it is not the only line or necessarily the most important (see Gergen & Morawski, this volume, for a wider review). However, it is central to the particular paradigm of situated action, and it may help to set that paradigm in a historical context. On the other hand, it is unlikely that any one of the other people cited above as contributors to the development of the situated action paradigm would subscribe wholly to this articulation of it. The following formal statement of the paradigm should be seen as a personal statement, not a consensual one.

The description which follows will deal first with the substantive themes of the emerging paradigm and then with the metatheory in which it is embedded.

Substantive Themes

Many of the productively critical works cited earlier contain certain themes in common, and those themes also are central to the situated action paradigm.

1. The primary objective of social psychology is the understanding of human action. By focusing on human actions rather than on intrapsychic wellsprings of action or on mental experiences as the phenomena to be understood, attention is directed to essentially knowable phenomena as the objects of analysis.

2. Persons are the performers of human actions and are construed as active agents who are capable of making plans and pursuing objectives, of acting as well as reacting, of doing things for reasons as well as having been forced to do them by causes (Kelley, 1980, develops a similar view). Therefore, we must be prepared to use both reasons and causes in understanding human actions (see Buss, 1978). However, although persons are active agents, they also are biosocial entities and are both constrained and empowered by biological and social factors. Part of the scientific challenge to us is to discover the biological and social aspects of the nature of the person which jointly empower or constrain him to act as we discover him to do. A few examples will be helpful.

Language performance is a good example of a combined biosocial capacity. The discovery of the biological and social structures which allow—but do not necessarily cause—the acquisition and performance of linguistic communication is a major challenge. Unfortunately, that challenge generally is ignored by North American social psychologists, certainly as a focus of study. In fact, few of the major textbooks in social psychology treat the acquisition and structure of linguistic communication, despite the fact that its acquisition and effective use is a cornerstone of socialization and of interaction in general. Furthermore, if one is interested in that topic, it is better to review *Semiotica* and *Child Development* than the *Journal of Personality and Social Psychology* or the *Journal of Experimental Social Psychology*. Currently, the most important contributions in this field are being produced by neuropsychological and developmental linguistic research. An extended example of the latter will be given later in this chapter.

An example of a short-term biological *liability* is the altered emotional reactivity of a person whose level of circulating epinephrine has been increased by some event. In Western culture, that person is likely to react more emotionally until his circulating adrenalin is metabolized and returns to baseline—a matter of at least a few minutes. During those few minutes, the person may see and interpret actions toward him differently than usual, and he may embark on a sequence of activity that will commit him and others to an extended emotional episode. Following Harré and Secord (1972), the term *liability* is used here to mean susceptibility, with respect to which the person is a sufferer (Buss, 1978) rather than an active agent. However, the term is misleading since it implies a necessary disadvantage, while in fact a particular liability may well prove advantageous in some specific instance. The heightened reactivity of a person in the preceding example is part of an adaptive fight/flight reaction pattern, with obvious advantages under appropriate circumstnces. Similarly, our actions usually are guided by rules which pertain to various roles of the situation, and this rule-following tendency can be construed as a *social* liability. But it, too, is often advantageous in that it allows for smooth, relatively automatic interaction.

In general, the active agency of persons involves a complex mix of biological and social powers and liabilities. For example, people have the capacity to take on an objective, analytic set toward themselves, and this capacity has proven useful in the personal control of the intensity and duration of pain. This capacity comes into play when a person is given advance information about the sensations, their meanings, and the actions to be taken with regard to them; but the objective set cannot be produced if the pain already is under way when the information is provided (Leventhal et al., 1979). By that time, the person is in a subjective, emotional state—a liability which constrains the person's capacities and actions.

3. All human action is situated, and to understand an action it is necessary to understand the situation within which that action is known or believed to occur. One important aspect of the situation is the framework of roles and rules by which our actions are guided, but there are other features of situations that also must be identified in order to understand the situation itself and its contained actions. Argyle (1979, in press) construes situations as comprised of seven interdependent components: elements and sequences of behavior, roles, rules, skills, cognitive concepts (required by the situation), the physical setting and its props, and goals. Argyle emphasizes interdependency among the components, as opposed to linear causality, which—as will be seen later—makes his argument compatible with a structural orientation. Bem, too, has maintained a concern with the situation as the setting of action and has made an interesting recent contribution in his use of the Q-Sort to identify the personality characteristics implied by or likely to succeed in a situation (Bem & Funder, 1978; Bem & Lord, 1979). However, it is

important to note that situations are not merely settings within which actions occur, but have the capacity to generate as well as constrain those actions. Furthermore, the analysis of the situation will provide information about categories of actions, so that a performed action can be understood as being an action of a certain type; but the understanding of a situation will not necessarily allow the prediction of the concrete action of a particular person. Moreover, detailed actions usually run off relatively automatically in familiar situations, in what Langer (1978) has called a "mindless" fashion; but when an action is performed which diverges from the role/rule framework, it will pose an enigma and will constitute a condition under which attention is focused upon it, reflection occurs, and inferences and perhaps attributions are made.

The preceding comments about the situated nature of human action may appear inconsistent with the earlier discussion of active agency, but the two themes actually complement each other. Persons have the capacity to choose, create, and—as will be noted below—redefine situations; nevertheless, the understanding of a situated action requires an understanding of the situation in which it occurred. The simultaneous existence of these complementary themes constitutes an important basis for the obvious complexity of social psychology as a science. Fortunately, most situations in daily life are relatively standard and occur fairly frequently, and the actions within them usually unfold in routine fashion with a minimum of creative definition of the situation. As Harré (1979, p. 70) puts it, "Improvisation is the dominant mode of social interaction only in the opening and constructive phases of a social encounter."

A final matter of importance concerning the situated nature of action is that the component features of situations, such as goals and skills, reside in the situations, not in persons. For example, with regard to goals, situations provide the opportunity for specifiable accomplishments, so that the description of the situation requires specification of the accomplishments which it affords. The range of afforded accomplishments, or goals, is constrained by the role, rules, physical settings, and other situational features suggested by Argyle (1979, in press). Goals, from this perspective, are not a function of the personal states or traits of specific individuals, except as those individuals create, modulate, or transform a situation. It is true that situations exist only as people create and implement them, but they are emergent phenomena which can be discussed and specified independently of specific people.

The more conventional discourse in psychology and social psychology treats situational features as qualities and desires of persons. This practice reduces the concept of situation either to a setting within which action takes place, but which has no explanatory force regarding the action, or to a potential which has no force until it combines with a person to produce action. If we wish to understand an action in part on the basis of what type of action it is, that understanding can be gained in large measure from an understanding of the situation itself. The issue of specification of the situation independently of the vocabulary of the desires, qualities, states, and abilities of people has not been resolved and reflects a conceptual ambiguity within the situated action paradigm. An "affordance" approach seems straightforward and attractive, but it has yet to be developed systematically.

4. Human action is organized both sequentially and hierarchically. That is, an action occurs in the context of both the particular actions that have immediately preceded it and the larger act which it is helping to accomplish. It is important to recognize the dual organization of action because the principles by which we understand a person's entry into an act may be quite different from the principles by which we explain his rapid performance of a sequence of actions by which he accomplishes that act. For example, the principles by which we understand a person's entry into the act of asking a question are different from the principles by which we understand the rapid performance of linked actions which constitute the question act itself. The organization of action has received considerable attention from ethologists (e.g., Dawkins, 1976) and also from psychologists and social psychologists with linguistic interests (for example, see Bruner, 1975; Clarke, 1979; Kreckel, in press). Harré and Secord (1972) also give extensive consideration to the structure of action, and emphasize the relationship between an act, such as a wedding, and the constituent actions whose successful performance accomplishes that act (the utterance, "I do," at the appropriate location in the sequence would be a constituent action of both the sequence and the larger act). This relationship often is referred to as "act/action structure."

A major problem regarding the organization of action is the identification of units. Collett (in press), reviewing the work of both anthropologists and psychologists, suggests that there are no inherent units, but that unitization is imposed by the observer of the action. However, following the argument of J. J. Gibson (1963, 1966) in perception, it can be argued that units, segmentations, and other structural features of action are not imposed but rather detected by us as we become differentially sensitive to them. This view is compatible with the suggestion by Cohen and Ebbesen (1979) that an observer's goals and set influence the level of detail at which he attends and in terms of which he talks about the observed person's actions. The details are there; the observer detects them selectively.

5. Perhaps the most complicated theme in the situated action paradigm is "meaning." The meanings of actions, acts, and settings are important for the understanding of human action, but few of the contributors to the paradigm have dealt explicitly with the definition or conceptual analysis of meanings in ongoing interaction (Harré, 1979, Rommetveit, in press, and Shotter, in press, do deal explicitly with meanings). Still, a summary of the emerging view of meanings and their role in situated action can be offered.

The meaning of an action has two components, both of which are implicational in nature. The meaning is partly given by the implications of the action—that is, by the subsequent actions implied by it. This allows the performer to take the role of the other party (Mead, 1934) and modify his own action even as he produces it by covertly responding to it from the perspective of the recipient. In addition, action necessarily is the empirical manifestation of the implications of prior actions in the sequence. The meaning of an action, then, is in part the specific implication of the prior actions in the sequence which the present action makes manifest. Therefore, the meaning of an action *is* its situated action implications *and* the implication of prior actions which the focal action expresses. These implications exist within the act/action structure discussed above, of course, since the range of implications—or meaning—of a situated action is specified by the act which the action is helping to accomplish.

As implications, meanings are always changeable and negotiable; and negotiation of the meanings is a pervasive and important feature of interactional processes. In fact, a recent study (Luckenbill, 1977) of a large number of routine homicides suggests strongly that the victim participates in a process of negotiated escalation of stakes just as fully as does the killer. The process which culminates in a common murder appears to be one of joint negotiation by the killer and his victim of the meanings of their actions, containing such sequences as, "Oh yeah? What kind of person do you think I am?"

The negotiated and negotiable nature of meaning also underlines another feature: Coordinated interaction relies upon a shared framework of meanings, otherwise the implications of actions will be ambiguous and uninformative. Frequently, negotiation loops are embedded in an interaction sequence to disambiguate the implicational aspect of an action. (Rommetveit, in press, discusses this in detail.)

It is worth noting that the implicational conception of meaning does not require linguistic competence on the part of the performer and is compatible with earlier, response-based theories of meaning (e.g., Osgood, 1953). However, if linguistic competence does exist and is operative in the interaction, then the range, subtlety, and temporal extensity is vastly increased.

The issue of meaning is related to the previously noted problem of identification of units of action. Following the same argument, one can say that there are natural, perceivable, *meaningful* units of action; but since actions occur as constituents of act/action structures and derive their meanings in part from them, we should *not* expect a single unique set of such units. Instead, it should be necessary to discover those units of action which are meaningful in any particular episode, and the interactors are likely to have provided us with clues, since they must indicate to each other what is meaningful. One approach, to be discussed later, is the use of the tone unit (Kreckel, in press) or phonemic clause (Jaffe & Feldstein, 1970) as a marker of meaningful chunks in discourse.

In any case, the discovery of the meanings of actions is central to the situated action paradigm.

6. The paradigm also contains two temporal themes, already included in the previous comments, but worthy of explicit note. First, actions are acknowledged to unfold in real time and, second, at any point in the unfolding there is an anticipatory or preparedness component for what is to come. Each of these requires some elaboration.

Acknowledgment that actions unfold in real time is an important aspect of the emerging paradigm. Theories which purport to explain actions must propose generative mechanisms which are compatible with the temporal features of ordinary interaction. For example, in ordinary conversation, utterances occur in rapid succession, and speaker and listener roles are exchanged repeatedly and sometimes swiftly. There is little if any time for the reflective inference processes which seem to be required by many of the consistency and attributional models which have been popular in social psychology for the last three decades.

The second temporal theme—that at any point in the unfolding of action there is an anticipatory component for what is yet to come—is given by the combination of the implicational nature of the meanings of actions and the temporal and hierarchical organization of action. When two persons commit themselves to the joint, coordinated production of a social act, each action in the flow is produced in part on the basis of what is still to come and therefore has an anticipatory component. This appears to be true even for the organization of detailed segments of one person's utterance. That is, the utterance actually is continually constructed and organized slightly ahead of its physical production, so that each uttered word or phrase is influenced in part by that which it physically anticipates (but which is still modifiable, since it has not been performed). For example, if we are interrupted in the middle of an utterance, we frequently take up again by repeating (with less timbre) the last few words we had uttered, and then go on (in full timbre) to what we were about to say. Moreover, we then may get out only a few more words, and then say, "I forgot what I was going to say" (Yngve, 1973). Our organization of speech action anticipates at least slightly our actual performance, and probably the performances of our interacting partners.

7. Persons are capable of monitoring both their actions and the stylistic appearance of their actions. This means that the characters we display are monitored and potentially managed, and such character management is a natural and ubiquitous feature of human life. The importance of this point for the interpretation of any research involving human subjects is obvious (Ginsburg, 1978)—and it may pertain as well to other species which have some sense of character and negotiable status (see Gallup, 1979, and Meddin, 1979, regarding other high primates, such as chimpanzees and gorillas).

8. Finally, many of the purportedly intrapersonal processes of the person are social in nature. This is consistent with the arguments of Mead (1934) and includes reflective thought and similar I-Me "dialogues." For example, when we justify, excuse, or otherwise account for our actions or their consequences privately to ourselves, we are engaging in a social act with ourselves. This has ramifications for a number of contemporary mini-theories, such as dissonance, attribution, and misattribution, most of which construe the processes by which predicted outcomes are generated as asocial, intrapsychic, and always in operation. It may be that these processes occur only under certain social conditions, including that special situation we know as the experiment. Kelley (1980), too, recognizes the importance of specifying the conditions under which such processes occur. He points out that the manage-

ment of one's behavior often is not carried out self-consciously and acts of intending (i.e., deliberate acts of management) generally are rare in daily life.

Another example of the social nature of purportedly intrapersonal processes concerns information processing. The revealed processes of information integration may reflect the logic of defending our conclusions rather than some automatic, internal processes. In a study in which decisions either had to be reported to another person or did not have to be, the decision strategy followed in the "report" condition was more rational, more easily explained, and slower than in the "no report" condition (Cvetkovich, 1978). I do not cite this to imply that social settings and task demands influence experimental outcomes; obviously they do. The present point is stronger: Many of the psychological processes which we infer from experiments and which we presume to be automatic and natural processes in fact may be implicit social processes, performed silently.

In summary, the situated action perspective focuses on the explanation of human action, and construes human action as necessarily situated and embedded, as unfolding in real time, as involving active agents who know how to do things and often know what they are doing, and as rule guided but negotiable. These are the substantive themes of the paradigm, and they have important implications for the understanding and conduct of research with people and other "quasi-person" species.

In addition to the substantive themes, the situated action paradigm appears to incorporate a number of metatheoretical features that differentiate it from conventional approaches in social psychology. The metatheory—at least as I see it—is due as much to the history of the paradigm's development, traced earlier, as to its substantive content. The metatheory is outlined below.

Metatheory

Toulmin (1961) has argued that the ultimate objective of science is the generation of accurate and effective explanations, the creation of understandings. Prediction and control allow us to assess and advance our understandings; they are means to an end, but not ends in themselves. Scientific theories can be construed as extended statements of our understandings (Harré, 1976), but they must be preceded by the identification of a nonrandom pattern which requires explanation. Considerable research may be necessary to establish the existence of a nonrandom pattern and identify its form (Harré and Secord, 1972, refer to this as critical description), and then to specify some limits on the range of conditions under which the patterns holds. The next and perhaps most creative stage is the construction of a model of a mechanism which presumably generates the identified nonrandom pattern under the range of known conditions of occurrence of that pattern. The pattern may be an entity or state, or a process, or a change in any one of those, and it may occur within an organism or within a system of interacting organisms (Kendon, 1979; Ossorio, 1978).

Harré and his colleagues (Harré, 1979; Harré & Madden, 1975; Harré & Secord, 1972) have argued that the mechanisms which generate the observed pattern under the observed conditions inhere in the nature of the entity or system whose behavior or state constitutes the nonrandom pattern. For example, the entity may have certain powers which generate the phenomenon (e.g., an explosion) under the observed conditions, or it may have liabilities which make it susceptible to the specified conditions in the fashion manifested by the observed pattern (trees bowing or cracking in a high wind). This point of view constitutes a theory of "natural powers" which is incompatible with the Humean concepts of causality and explanation, including the conventional "transfer of influence" concept of causality in experimental social psychology. (The interested reader can see Harré & Madden, 1975, for a detailed development, or Harré & Secord, 1972, for a version concerned primarily with social psychology.) The creative task of the scientist is to construct a model of the entity or system whose behavior is of interest. The model should specify the nature of that entity in such a way as to describe its powers and liabilities as they relate to the focal phenomenon and the conditions of occurrence. The actual existence of the hypothesized mechanisms—the things or processes—may be established by further research and technological advances, at which point the theory no longer would be a model, but a description of the thing or process itself.

The idealized sequence of critical description, specification of limits, and construction of a model appears compatible with many of the theories in contemporary social psychology. Dissonance theory, for example, is a model of the nature of the person which identifies a generative mechanism for postdecision behavior. However, those theories generally are grounded in a transfer of influence view of causality which leads us to "external variable" experiments (Duncan & Fiske, 1977), in which outcomes are correlated with variables external to the processes leading to the outcomes. A natural powers elaboration of the idealized sequence is more compatible with structural research (Duncan & Fiske, 1977), in which we attempt to discover or verify the sequences and patterns of events and processes within a particular type of situated episode. When combined with the substantive themes of situated action, this metatheoretical perspective requires that careful attention be given to the situational features within which the action of interest occurs, the relationship of the action to the larger act which it is helping to accomplish and its location in the sequence of actions which *follow* as well as precede it. This is a different perspective from that within which most experimental work is done in social psychology, but it is not inherently incompatible with it. Instead, it can in principle incorporate conventional works, primarily by placing them in their situational and cultural contexts, with due recognition of the fact that the processes which occurred between the time of the experimental manipulation and that of the dependent measure were not recorded or analyzed.

The natural powers metatheory, with its structural orientation, argues against the use of conventional notions of causality for understanding human action. We try to identify relationships among component parts and processes—but none of the components is "caused" by the prior occurrence of another component; and even more important, none of the components "causes" the action or act of which they are components. The identity of the components is a functional identity which derives from the larger unit of which they are components, such as the act which the component actions are in the process of producing. The identity of a handshake, for example, derives in part from the wager, greeting, or farewell which it is helping to produce.

Cause-effect descriptions often are considered to be the hallmark of science; and in conventional social psychology, the search for causes is a respected and even ideal activity. However, as Peter Ossorio (1978) has argued cogently, the cause-effect formula for describing reality is not necessitated by the nature of reality. In fact, it often does a disservice to reality. Specifically, causal descriptions are given in the impersonal third person idiom, thereby reifying the observer perspective. Furthermore, the experimenter's part in the occurrences is removed from the substantive domain, the domain of facts to which the theories are applied, despite the fact that the experimenter's activities are part of that same real world and helped to produce those facts. Of course, a conventional cause-effect description does reflect our traditional scientific interest. We often are interested in the real world to the extent that we can manipulate it unilaterally—an essentially manipulative interest which is reified by our establishment of the cause-effect formula as the universal principle of scientific description. Restricting ourselves to causal descriptions means that we restrict ourselves to the observation of only the temporal successions of the real world, and especially to those processes of human action which are manipulable. But the complexity of human action cannot be captured or understood in cause-effect terms alone. Buss (1978), too, limits the applicability of causal descriptions, although his treatment deals primarily with attribution theory.

The active agency aspect of the situated action paradigm carries with it another metatheoretical position which only recently began coming into focus. My comments about it are tentative, but the issue is sufficiently important to warrant some attention. The issue, alluded to briefly in the preceding paragraph, concerns perspective. The dominant perspective in conventional social psychological theories is that of the observer. The theories are constructed from the viewpoint of a selfless observer, as noted above, and they construe the objects of interest (people) as observers of themselves. This is readily apparent in attribution theories and was recently criticized by Buss (1978).

There are two social perspectives of which a person is capable. Specifically, (1) he can be an observer, either of himself or of another person, and (2) he can have the perspective of an active agent. The issue has been developed forcefully by John Shotter (in press) and Ragnar Rommetveit (in press), and in a less-focused fashion by Shea and deCharms (1976). The active agent—the acting person—always exists in an extended moment of reality, with awareness of a fixed past in the sense of events which already have occurred, and of future potential. The present is a brief interval in which things are becoming, going on, being produced. This seems identical to William James's (1890) "specious present," which Ayer (1974) linked to a reasonable span of attention. The acting person *always* is in this brief interval of reality, a reality which is partly specified and always specifiable further. He always has an active agency perspective, even while he is observing and commenting on someone's actions.

The two observer perspectives involve not only observing the actions of a person, self, or other but also developing or offering accounts about those actions as well. It is this reflective component of the observer perspective which characterizes contemporary social psychological theories, to the relative exclusion of the continually present reality of the active agent. Ramifications of taking an active agent perspective into account are not yet clear, although it is compatible with some of the substantive themes discussed earlier (viz., active agency and meaning), and it does direct our attention to the fact that reflective, observer perspectives do not always obtain. Therefore, any social psychological theory which relies upon the observer perspective must also specify the conditions under which such a perspective occurs; it cannot simply be presumed to exist. Kelley (1980) has recognized this matter, too, and has proposed types of circumstances under which a person is likely to adopt a reflective stance.

A final metatheoretical issue concerns general laws or principles. This issue has been debated at length in the literature (Gergen, 1973, 1978, this volume; Ossorio, 1978; Rosnow, 1978; Schlenker, 1974; Triandis, 1978), and I will only summarize implications of the situated action paradigm with respect to it. Actions, including investigatory and explanatory actions, are always historically grounded. They occur at some location in time and space, and not in some other location. A statement which describes a general law is itself a historical event, and the substantive content of that statement is as well. Therefore, there is no question as to whether our scientific statements are independent of history, culture, or situations; neither they nor their contents are independent, for they are all events within the real history of the actual world. Moreover, just as the meaning of any historical event can change with the occurrence of subsequent events and the emergence of larger contexts within which it is embedded, so can the plausibility or accuracy of a "general law." The important issue is the identity of the real world structure of which the purportedly general laws are constituents. That is, a particular process may be culturally grounded or may occur across cultures; it may be historicaly limited or may prove to be transhistorical, at least to this point in the continuing history of reality. The range of applicability is an empirical issue. Therefore, we should strive to discover processes and structures which make the world intelligible, but we should be wise enough to recognize that those discoveries and our statements about them are limited by the world in which the discoveries are made—a world which includes the discoverer, his limited knowledge, his beliefs, and his technology. We should attempt to identify the range of functionally equivalent contexts within which the discovered processes and structures are constituents. And those processes and structures which we do discover should not be construed as immutable laws hidden by nature for our discovery. Instead, they are discoveries of relationships among those events which we happen to look at, see, and relate to other such events, given our knowledge and technology to date. They may not be wrong, but they surely can be superseded.

So, what I see as a situated action paradigm emerging in significant part but by no means exclusively from the Oxford people is based on a structural rather than sequentially causal model. We are challenged to propose and eventually discover generative mechanisms or generative processes by which the action of interest is produced under the known or believed conditions of occurrence. The generative mechanisms inhere in the biological and social nature of the entity whose actions we wish to explain. That entity may be construed as a person or as a system of interacting persons, depending on one's predilections, but it also must be seen as a constituent of larger, more inclusive entities.

Furthermore, the situated action paradigm explicitly recognizes the social and constructive character of science and eschews scientific explanations or laws as unique relationships hidden by nature and discoverable by us. And, as I summarized earlier, the paradigm focuses on the explanation of human action, which is seen as situated, hierarchically as well as sequentially organized, unfolding in real time, meaningful, and negotiable. Situations, in turn, are seen as having several types of interdependent features, including goals, roles, rules, behavior elements and sequences, and physical props.

This has been a rather sketchy summary of a complex paradigm, with relatively little justification of the assertions and very few examples. The following section provides some illustrations of work that is compatible with this view.

RESEARCH ILLUSTRATIONS

Structure of Action

The hierarchical and sequential structure of actions within a situation has become a major topic of research, although it has not yet been incorporated within the main stream of social psychological theory. The research efforts share an interest in revealing structure in the flow of the actions within a situation. In some cases, the investigators wish to describe a structure that exists; in others they hope to trace the emergence of a structure over time.

In the developmental area, detailed examination of film and video records of relatively short interactions between infants or babies and parents has burgeoned (see Osofsky, 1979; Scaife, 1979), especially in developmental psycholinguistics (see Bloom, 1978). Stern et al. (1978), for example, examined mother and infant vocalization as a type of "coaction," in which the two parties perform similar actions at the same time (mutual gaze and posture-sharing are other examples), and as a type of alternating action—a sort of "prespeech." They videotaped infants in their homes, at least once per week from the third to fourth months of life, and analyzed the vocalization and gaze patterns. Coactive vocalization was more common than alternating vocalization, but all dyads showed both patterns. Stern et al. suggest that coactive vocalizing, in conjunction with mutual gaze, is a bonding mechanism, especially during high, positive affect, and that alternating vocalization occurs at moderate levels of arousal. The mother usually, but not always, instigates the pattern. This coordinated vocalization often occurs during repetitive cycles of play which form a social interactional base upon which later development occurs (see below, regarding Bruner's work). There are now many studies of early coordination, and most of them involve detailed analysis of the structure of an extended segment of interaction.

One of the most interesting, longitudinal approaches to the study of the structure of action is that which Bruner and his group conducted at Oxford (Bruner, 1975; Ratner & Bruner, 1978; Scaife, 1979). Bruner used videotaping to record the linguistic development of young children. Starting with a 10-month-old child, his team would tape an hour or two of focused interaction between the baby and its mother every other week or so, for a period of at least another year. This allowed for a variety of socially developmental explorations. For example, when an interesting linguistic form emerged, such as the word *me,* its history could be traced backward in the tapes to examine its primordial origins. Or, if a new type of toy was introduced by the mother, its consequences could be traced forward in time. Probably the most exciting and far-reaching structural aspect of Bruner's recent work is his discovery

(Bruner, 1975) that the games that infants learn to play with their mothers contain an important interactional structure. In "Give and Take," for example, the baby learns to give an object to his mother and to receive an object from her; he also learns to give and receive a wide range of objects and to accept them from others besides his mother, and to given them to others also. In other words, the baby learns the organized sequence of an *Agent Acting* on an *Object* with regard to *Another Person.* The similarity to the case grammar structure of simple utterances is obvious; that is, Agent-Action-Object-Recipient is comparable to Subject-Verb-Object-Indirect Object. The baby's entry into syntactical language is not nearly so sudden and devoid of practice as the transformational linguists would have us believe, and it is through a discovery of the developmental changes in the structure of infant-mother play that this has become apparent.

Analyses of the extant structure of interactional episodes among adults are more familiar to U.S. social psychologists. Examples include the recent volume by Duncan and Fiske (1977), the detailed analysis of greetings by Kendon and Ferber (1973), and the recent analyses by Albert and Kessler (1976, 1978) of endings of social encounters. On the other hand, there are lines of structural research with which readers may be less familiar, especially those lines which pay particular attention to the meaning of utterances and the negotiation of those meanings.

Kreckel (in press a, in press b), for example, analyzes communication conditions and patterns within the framework of her general semiological theory. She uses information patterns as markers for identifying meaning units in discourse, thereby establishing meaningful chunks which can be used as a basis from which to explore the contents of the meanings and the understandings produced. Her tone unit is similar to the "phonemic clause" of Jaffee and Feldstein (1970, p. 22) and is only one among many perceivable structural features of interaction. However, it illustrates the existence of directly perceivable structural markers of meaning in ongoing action, the existence of which can be identified independently of the interpretive activities of observers. On the other hand, establishment of the substantive content of the units of meaning may require negotiation with the participants (Harré & Secord, 1972). Furthermore, Kreckel's analysis takes into account the fact that actions are embedded both in an ongoing sequence and in larger acts, and that the demarcations can be used to alter the nature of the act within which the action is occurring. Thus, by stressing one word rather than another in an utterance, the speaker can generate implications (meanings) that alter the tone of the conversation. Rommetveit (in press), too, discusses the negotiation of meanings and its central role in ordinary conversations.

The recent volume edited by Cairns (1979) on the analysis of social interactions further reflects the growing interest in the structural analysis of human action. Detailed analyses of the structure of action inevitably lead one to an appreciation of the joint nature of the action, its embeddedness in a social context, and the inadequacy of a conventionally causal, linear flow of effect (see Cairns's Introduction, especially p. 4; also see Kendon, 1979).

Judgmental Studies of Social Episodes

Conventional self-report and judgmental procedures can be used to study the structure of episodes of situated action, if it is kept in mind that the people filling out the questionnaires and checking the scales are informants about those episodes. Even if the episodes are hypothetical, even if the subject is engaging in a simulation study with written scenarios (Ginsburg, 1978), the information provided describes the values or expectations or beliefs of the informant's culture, or peer group, or family, or simply his own. In any case, the subject is an informant, and he is informing us *about* something and in some *context*. When we analyze and summarize the self-report or judgmental data of many such informants, we do not produce a representation of some structure or image in their heads (or minds); instead, we obtain a statistical summary of the information they have given us about the topics contained on the questionnaire, in the setting in which they completed the questionnaire. I stress this rather anthropological perspective concerning our subjects to emphasize the fact that we need not—and probably should not—construe the data they provide us as reflections or representations of the contents of their minds.

In that spirit, the multidimensional scaling (MDS) studies of social episodes by Forgas (1979) constitute descriptive information about different types of episodes from different categories of informants. For example, episodes ("visiting your doctor" and "attending a wedding ceremony") were categorized differently by Oxford housewives and Oxford students, reflecting differences in the meanings and implications of those episodes for the two groups (pp. 280-283). As one illustration, students reported various socializing and entertainment episodes as pleasant events in which they knew how to behave, but housewives expressed considerable lack of self-confidence.

In another MDS study, Forgas et al. (in press) examined the differences which different situated episodes made in people's descriptions of each other. We used a stable group, in which people knew each other well and across a range of settings. Specifically, we used the Oxford social psychology group of two faculty (and one visitor), four staff, three first-year graduate students, and six advanced graduate students. We rated each other in each of four familiar situations: A pub at which we usually convened after a weekly research seminar, regular morning coffee in the main concourse of the psychology building, a party at one of the faculty homes, and a closed research seminar open only to our group. The dimensions in terms of which we differentiated the members of our group from each other clearly and sensibly varied across the situations. Furthermore, the importance of the dimensions varied with who was doing the rating. For example, at the party, an ingratiation dimension was least relevant to those working hardest at performing it (new students), and most relevant for those observing and receiving it (faculty). Similarly, in the research seminar, the support dimension was most salient for the advanced students (who are most likely to present their work and therefore most sensitive to support or its absence from the audience members). Thus, the descriptions of each other given by the members of a stable group are a function of the situation in which interactions occur; and it is likely that situations can be classified, or at least analyzed, in terms of what interpersonal discriminations are made and what person descriptors are relevant. This approach is complementary to the recent Q-Sort work of Bem and his colleagues (Bem & Funder, 1978; Bem & Lord, 1979). Both approaches can be used to shed light on the goals made available by the situation, the strategies people use, and the personal skills or styles that are likely to yield success in the situation. However, both approaches provide only suggestive information about a situation, using the vocabulary of personal styles, skills, and motives. Neither approach is descriptive of any particular situation in concrete terms. Therefore, neither provides descriptive information about a particular situation as an entity independent of participants in it; and both use the vocabulary of individual psychology.

Another study which we recently conducted within the paradigm focused on rules and rule-breaking (Ginsburg et al., in press). Since an obvious type of evidence of a rule is the set of reactions to its breakage, an understanding of rule breakage (RB) would constitute an important step toward an understanding of rules and their functions within episodes of situated action. We used a written scenario format in which theoretically relevant features of RBs and their settings were systematically varied (see Argyle & Ginsburg, in press, for part of the theoretical statement). We sought to assess the impacts of those featured on the immediate impression of the incident, the affective reactions expected of others and of oneself, and the comprehensibility of various consequences for the rest of the episode. We also wished to discover the patterns of relationships among immediate reactions and the more extended consequences.

We found that the RBs were differentiated on a dimension of humorous/irritating and on a dimension of oddness. People's reported affective reactions to the RBs were captured by a single dimension of laughter versus anger. A path analysis revealed that one's own reported affective reactions are heavily influenced by the reactions of others in the situation, and only weakly by the nature of the RB itself, although others' reactions are seen as being due to the RB. We also found that people are angered by deliberate RBs and see them as rude and insulting, although this reaction is weaker if the RB was unusual. Moreover, unusual but deliberate RBs (such as deliberately regurgitating a mouthful of potatoes at a dinner party) are difficult to understand, whereas unusual but accidental RBs are readily understood.

Given the limitations of using only two hypothetical RB incidents and using a judgmental procedure, the rule-breaking study provides us with potentially valuable leads for further work. For example, in observational or manipulative studies, we will be sensitive to the difference between humorous and irritating infractions and to the rapid social influence process by which an incident becomes defined as an infraction. On the other hand, this study shares with the previous ones in this section a reliance on a vocabulary of personal reactions, rather than specification of the concrete features of the situation—in this case, the content of rules.

Structural Analysis of Episodes: Examples of Current Work

The structural examination of situated action is most profitably undertaken with complete episodes, so that the major hierarchical structure is on record. That way, the meaningful units of action can be identified in their constituent relationship to the larger acts within which they became embedded and which they helped to accomplish. This takes considerable time, energy, creativity, and commitment—and patience. It might be worthwhile to review a few current projects to provide a flavor of the deliberate implementation of the paradigm.

For example, one of our group has undertaken the analysis of teasing episodes among adults. A review of the anthropological, psychlogical, and sociological literature yielded virtually no references to teasing, per se, although a fair literature exists on jokes, humor, pratfalls, and the ritualized joking relationship. Moreover, there was no coherent conceptual treatment of teasing, despite its likely importance as a feature and modulator of interaction. Therefore, a conceptual analysis was undertaken, guided by the themes of a situated action perspective. That led to a tentative model of a tease episode, in which teaser, recipient, and audience (present or implied) participate, in which an action must be *objectively* ambiguous, and in which the tease cannot be said to have started until it is in fact well under way. Once it is well underway, then—but only then—an earlier action becomes the start of what is now the tease; and the tease must be resolved as a tease, in order for it to have occurred. This may sound strangely at variance with the linear flow of reality at first, but some reflection will make clear that the meanings of actions are always revisable—that is a state of the real world of human action and not sloppiness of thought. The basic material of the study is videotapes of spontaneous teasing episodes embedded in ordinary social events (e.g., friends having a dinner party). Current efforts are directed at clarification of the features of the teasing episode; the next stage will test the understandings experimentally.

Another member of the group argues that intentions are inherent in the structure of situated action, and need not be construed as states of mind. He is trying to identify the temporally extended structural features which episodes of social action afford to the perceiving participants and which imply the outcome or completion of the episode. The project derives from the ideas of J. J. Gibson (1966), G. H. Mead (1934), and Shaw and Bransford (1977).[1] Methodologically, the project involves videotaping carefully scripted scenarios which then will be segmented, systematically rearranged, and presented to subjects for identification of the nature of the episode (a pick-up in a disco). The objective is to identify those elements and sequences of actions which convey the "intention" of the actions.

Another situated action project that is just beginning concerns empathy. Following the general pattern of Bruner's work, mentioned above, we are videotaping the interaction between a mother and her infant on a biweekly basis, starting at age three months. The action episode includes routine segments that are likely to continue for at least a year and which allow for closely coordinated interaction. The activity segments include midmorning nursing, diaper changing, playing, and sometimes putting to bed for a nap. We are interested in the detailed structure of empathic interaction and also in its gradual emergence, which we plan to trace by going backward through the tapes once we have obtained clear instances of its occurrence (see Scaife, 1979).

ADVANTAGES AND PITFALLS

The structural analysis of situated action carries with it a number of advantages and pitfalls. A major advantage is that it directs our attention to the real world and to the behavioral events within it that are of interest, and it forces us to recognize those events as constituents of larger events. Moreover, it provides us with the opportunity to identify the constituent parts and processes of focal events. Much of this is made possible by the current state of film and video cinematography, especially the latter.

First, multiple perspectives can be captured simultaneously on videotape, using split-screen techniques. The actions as seen by each participant in a controlled scenario—including the experimenter or observer—can be subjected to repeated analyses, either alone or contingently with other perspectives. This is quite different from swinging the camera from one actor to another as the initiative moves back and forth, a procedure which Kendon (1979) inveighs against, and also quite different from the more common, single perspective of the observer.

Second, several levels and forms of constituent events and processes can be captured on videotape, presuming the use of multiple cameras and screen-splitting equipment. The overall acts of an episode can be coded (e.g., arguments, agreements, tease), and within each the constituent actions can be identified in terms of verbal and nonverbal features. Each action can be investigated similarly to reveal the fine grain structure of the coordinated activities. Even biological data can be included. For example, if psychophysiological variables are tapped on line, such as heart rate, blood pressure, or electrodermal activity, those data can be displayed on a polygraph or oscilloscope on which a camera is focused. They would appear, then, on the tape simultaneously with the video data.

Third, the relatively permanent video record allows for repeated review, in the process of which an interesting behavioral or physiological event may be identified. One can then trace the consequences of that event forward in time, or trace its antecedents and concomitants backward in time. Both Bruner's group (e.g., 1975) and Duncan and Fiske (1977) have used these techniques.

In sum, the situated action paradigm carries with it an important methodological and technological implication. Specifically, the structure of situated action is discovered in part by examination of the unfolding of the action in its situational and act/action context over time. Its emergence and modulation is observed and analyzed. Procedures which allow for relatively permanent records of the episode—film and video—will become increasingly popular, and an increasing amount of time and attention will be devoted to repeated analyses of the episodes. But this has certain attendant costs and problems, and it raises an important issue.

The first and most obvious problem is the reduction of data. This is especially the case in exploratory phases of the research, where the videotape is examined for patterns. Computer-based analyses of video data will become common in time, but at present neither the hardware nor the software is readily available.

A second problem concerns bias. We are likely to select episodes and settings that are easily taped or filmed, thus introducing a potential bias into the body of material available for analysis.

A third problem concerns what some people consider to be the hallmark of the situated action paradigm, at least as it has been expressed by Rom Harré and Paul Secord: the solicitation and analysis of accounts. The concept of accounts derives from certain analyses by philosophers of language—especially Austin (1962) and Searle (1969)—of the implications of utterances. This work was elaborated upon by Scott and Lyman (1968) and more recently by Backman (1976) into a framework by which we account for our actions—namely, by justifications, by excuses, and by "conventionalizations" in which we redefine the event so as to deny the need for an account (e.g., to call embezzling "borrowing"). The solicitation, use, and negotiation of accounts are complex issues, and one must be cautious and deliberate in making scientific use of them.

Specifically, a person's account should not be accepted as a priority explanation of his action. Instead, his accounts—and those of others—should be collected to enable the investigator to construct the meanings, rules, roles, and values within which the actions of interest can be made intelligible and warrantable. An illustration of this approach is Peter Marsh's (see Marsh et al., 1978) use of the accounts given by hooligans at soccer games in justification of their disruptive and occasionally violent behavior. Marsh analyzed the accounts and extracted the values, standards, and rules by which the disruptive activities were evaluated and made sensible by the collection of young rowdies, and he was able to demonstrate the existence of a coherent subculture with quite specific career stages, from "novice rowdy" to "town boy," and even to "nutter"—the ostensibly really crazy ones.

The use of accounts raises another problem which I see in the situated action paradigm: its excessive reliance on language, in regard to both meaning and active agency, and its unnecessarily exclusive applicability to our species alone. The implicational conception of meaning is applicable to other species, even if reciprocal role taking is presumed necessary to allow for the negotiation of those meanings (see Gallup, 1979, and Meddin, 1979, regarding highter primates). Furthermore, active agency also is applicable to other species, since its essential feature is the power to act intentionally—that is, to manipulate one's environment in order to achieve an end. Active agency is tied to teleology (not to "tautology" or other inadequate arguments; see Woodfield, 1976), in which an action is performed "in order to . . . ." Other species clearly have that capacity. It is my view that the power to manipulate the environment in order to accomplish an end is sufficient for the conceptual attribution of active agency. In fact, the end-seeking organism will have the active agent perspective, since it will discriminate and manipulate different features of the environment depending on the opportunities the environment affords relative to the organism's transitory states. Of course, linguistic competence greatly augments the powers of the active agent, but even within our species we engage in a great deal of meaningful nonverbal activity (see Morris et al., 1979, for an interesting survey of 20 basic gestures across several countries).

A fifth problem in the situated action paradigm pertains to the active agent perspective. Once an interval of "specious present" has gone beyond a given action, that action is part of the relatively fixed past and no longer is contained in the active agency perspective, even on the part of the original agent. Therefore, commentaries about that action, its situational context, and its network of meanings will be made from an *observer* perspective vis-à-vis that action. Corrective approximations can be used, such as role playing, or replays of film or videotape taken from the physical perspective of the active agent. The success of such corrective attempts has not been evaluated within this methodological context.

A final and critical problem concerns the issue of verification and the related matter of falsification. The issues can be hidden by a persuasive description or interpretation, but it must be recognized that a structural approach in itself contains no controls for the rejection of alternative explanations or even for the accuracy of the description. A danger in structural analyses is that we will accept a plausible interpretation as *the accurate* interpretation, without subjecting it to independent verification. This brings to light an important epistemological aspect of the situated action paradigm and structural research strategy.

In structural analyses, the record of a completed episode is analyzed over and over. There is no question about what will happen, since it already has happened. The investigator's perspective is analytical and retrospective, as opposed to the synthetic, predictive stance more common in experimental social psychology. After repeated observations of the videotape, the investigator is likely to develop a sense of understanding of the episode, if only through familiarity. That understanding will strike him as plausible—it will "feel good." This is especially likely to occur if the investigator has a prior belief about the episode and searches the tape within the framework of that belief (Snyder and Uranowitz, 1978, provide an experimental demonstration of this). Therefore, those of us engaged in the structural analysis of situated action must develop predictive designs to assess the adequacy of the understandings obtained from our structural studies.

The problems associated with the skeptical evaluation of our understandings and of the serious consideration of alternative interpretations are considerable and deserve extended attention in their own right. However, for the purposes of this chapter, it might suffice merely to note that traditional experimental designs can be blended quite easily with structural techniques, so that the process by which the experimental outcome was generated can be examined directly. For example, one could videotape a sample of the experimental participants in each cell of the design (or videotape all and then select a sample of tapes) and structurally analyze those tapes in an effort to discover the processes by which the experimental outcome results were generated. Duncan and Fiske (1977) also suggest a comparable approach and gently chide themselves for not having done it with their external variable study. Such a strategy would take advantage of the protections of experimental design, especially the minimization of unknowable bias through randomized assignment of treatments to subjects, and the interpretative benefits deriving from control or baseline comparisons built into the design.

It also is worth noting that there are verification checks inherent in a public science. One's explanation of a phenomenon must be compatible with the known instances of that phenomenon and must not be incompatible with contemporary knowledge. Harré (1976) refers to these features as "adequacy" and "plausibility," respectively. The acceptance and application of a theory depends largely on its plausibility, its compatibility with what is believed to be obviously real. But beliefs about reality change over time, within scientific circles and within whole cultures, so that even our most firmly established scientific laws are dependent on the metaphysics of the period (Harré, 1976, p. 39). We are not engaged in the discovery of natural laws, but in the discovery of nonrandom patterns and the construction of models which explain those patterns in a manner compatible with current fact. The communication of findings, explanations, and procedures constitutes an extremely important check on both the adequacy and plausibility of our theories in this particular public enterprise which we call science.

In final summary, this chapter is a distillation of a number of basic themes, both substantive and metatheoretical, which I see emerging in the field today. Much of this has been based on joint work with the Oxford group, but there are many other contributors as well. It is my opinion that a coherent, inclusive paradigm for the study and understanding of human action is emerging—a paradigm which I have labelled "structural analysis of situated action."

NOTE

1. The project described here received considerable stimulation from an unpublished presentation by Reuben Baron to the Society for Experimental Social Psychology at its annual meeting, Princeton University, November 1978.

REFERENCES

Albert, S. & Kessler, S. Processes for ending social encounters: The conceptual archeology of a temporal place. *Journal for the Theory of Social Behaviour*, 1976, *6*, 147-170.
Albert, S. & Kessler, S. Ending social encounters. *Journal of Experimental Social Psychology*, 1978, *14*, 541-553.
Argyle, M. Sequences in social behaviour as a function of the situation. In G. P. Ginsburg (ed.), *Emerging Strategies in Social Psychological Research*. London: Wiley, 1979. Pp. 11-38.
Argyle, M. The analysis of social situations. In M. Brenner (ed.), *The structure of action*. Oxford, England. Basil Blackwell, in press.
Argyle, M., Furnham, A., & Graham, J. *Social situations*. Cambridge, England: Cambridge University Press, in press.
Argyle, M. & Ginsburg, G. P. The rule-breaking episode. In M. Argyle et al. *Social situations*. Cambridge, England: Cambridge University Press, in press.
Armistead, N. (ed.). *Reconstructing social psychology*. Baltimore: Penguin, 1974.
Austin, J. L. *How to do things with words*. Oxford, England: Clarendon Press, 1962.
Ayer, A. J. *The origins of pragmatism*. London: Macmillan, 1974.
Backman, C. W. Explorations in psycho-ethics: The warranting of judgments. In R. Harré (ed.), *Life sentences: Aspects of the social role of language*. London: Wiley, 1976. Pp. 98-108.
Bem, D. J. & Funder, D. C. Predicting more of the people more of the time: Assessing the personality of situations. *Psychological Review*, 1978, *85*, 485-501.
Bem, D. J. & Lord, C. G. Template matching: A proposal for probing the ecological validity of experimental settings in social psychology. *Journal of Personality and Social Psychology*, 1979, *37*, 833-857.
Bloom, L. *Readings in language development*. New York: Wiley, 1978.
Brenner, M., Marsh, P., & Brenner, M. (eds.). *The social context of methods*. London: Croom-Helm, 1978.
Brenner, M. (ed.). *The structure of action*. Oxford, England: Basil Blackwell, in press.
Bruner, J. S. The ontogenesis of speech acts. *Journal of Child Language*, 1975, *2*, 1-19.

Buss, A. R. Causes and reasons in attribution theory: A conceptual critique. *Journal of Personality and Social Psychology*, 1978, *36*, 1311-1321.

Cairns, R. B. (ed.). *The analysis of social interactions*. Hillsdale, N.J.: Erlbaum, 1979.

Cartwright, D. P. Contemporary social psychology in historical perspective. *Social Psychology Quarterly*, 1979, *42*, 82-93.

Clarke, D. D. The linguistic analogy or when is a speech act like a morpheme. In G. P. Ginsburg (ed.), *Emerging strategies in social psychological research*. London: Wiley, 1979. Pp. 39-66.

Cohen, C. E. & Ebbesen, E. B. Observational goals and schema activation: A theoretical framework for behavior perception. *Journal of Experimental Social Psychology*, 1979, *15*, 305-329.

Collett, P. (ed.). *Social rules and social behaviour*. Oxford, England: Basil Blackwell, 1977.

Cvetkovich, O. Cognitive accommodation, language and social responsibility. *Social Psychology*, 1978, *41*, 149-155.

Dawkins, R. Hierarchical organisation: A candidate principle for ethology. In P.P.G. Bateson & R. A. Hinde (eds.), *Growing points in ethology*. Cambridge, England: Cambridge University Press, 1976. Pp. 7-54.

Duncan, S. D., Jr. & Fiske, D. W. *Face-to-face interaction: Research, methods and theory*. Hillsdale, N.J.: Erlbaum, 1977.

Forgas, J. P. Multidimensional scaling: A discovery method in social psychology. In G. P. Ginsburg (ed.), *Emerging strategies in social psychological research*. London: Wiley, 1979. Pp. 253-288.

Forgas, J. P., Argyle, M., & Ginsburg, G. P. Social episodes and person perception: The fluctuating structure of an academic group. *Journal of Social Psychology*, in press.

Gallup, G. G., Jr. Self-awareness in primates. *American Scientist*, 1979, *67*, 417-421.

Gergen, K. J. Social psychology as history. *Journal of Personality and Social Psychology*, 1973, *26*, 309-320.

Gergen, K. J. Toward generative theory. *Journal of Personality and Social Psychology*, 1978, *36*, 1344-1360.

Gergen, K. J. Toward intellectual audacity in social psychology. In R. Gilmour & S. Duck (eds.), *The development of social psychology*. In press.

Gibson, J. J. The useful dimensions of sensitivity. *American Psychologist*, 1963, *18*, 1-15.

Gibson, J. J. *The senses considered as perceptual systems*. Boston: Houghton-Mifflin, 1966.

Ginsburg, G. P. Role playing and role performance in social psychological research. In M. Brenner et al. (eds.), *The social context of method*. London: Croom-Helm, 1978. Pp. 91-121.

Ginsburg, G. P. (ed.). *Emerging strategies in social psychological research*. London: Wiley, 1979.

Ginsburg, G. P. Epilogue: A conception of situated action. In M. Brenner (ed.), *The structure of action*. Oxford, England: Basil Blackwell, in press.

Ginsburg, G. P., Argyle, M., Forgas, J. P., & Holtgraves, T. Reactions to rule breaking. In Argyle et al. *Social situations*. Cambridge, England: Cambridge University Press, in press.

Harré, R. The constructive role of models. In L. Collins (ed.), *The use of models in the social sciences.* London: Tavistock, 1976. Pp. 16-43.

Harré, R. The ethogenic approach: Theory and practice. In L. Berkowitz (ed.), *Advances in experimental social psychology* (Vol. 10). New York: Academic Press, 1977. Pp. 284-314.

Harré, R. *Social being.* Oxford, England: Basil Blackwell, 1979.

Harré, R. & Madden, E. H. *Causal powers: A theory of natural necessity.* Oxford, England: Basil Blackwell, 1975.

Harré, R. & Secord, P. F. *The explanation of social behavior.* Totowa, N.J.: Rowman and Littlefield, 1972.

Israel, J. & Tajfel, H. (eds.). *The context of social psychology: A critical assessment.* London: Academic Press, 1972.

Jaffe, J. & Feldstein, S. *Rhythms of dialogue.* New York: Academic Press, 1970.

James, W. *The principles of psychology.* New York: Holt, Rinehart & Winston, 1890.

Kelley, H. H. The causes of behavior: Their perception and regulation. In L. Festinger (ed.), *Retrospectives on social psychology.* New York: Oxford University Press, 1980.

Kendon, A. Some theoretical and methodological aspects of the use of film in the study of social interaction. In G. P. Ginsburg (ed.), *Emerging strategies in social psychological research.* London: Wiley, 1979. Pp. 67-85.

Kendon, A. & Ferber, A. A description of some human greetings. In R. P. Michael & J. H. Cook (eds.), *Comparative ecology and behavior of primates.* New York: Academic Press, 1973.

Kreckel, M. Communicative acts and shared knowledge: A conceptual framework and its empirical application. In M. von Cranach & R. Harré (eds.), *The organization of human action.* Cambridge, England: Cambridge University Press, in press. (a)

Kreckel, M. A framework for the analysis of natural discourse. In M. Brenner (ed.), *The structure of action.* Oxford, England: Basil Blackwell, in press. (b)

Langer, E. J. Rethinking the role of thought in social interaction. In J. H. Harvey et al. (eds.), *New directions in attribution research* (Vol. 2). Hillsdale, N.J.: Erlbaum, 1978. Pp. 36-58.

Leventhal, H., Brown, D., Shacham, S., & Engquist, G. Effects of preparatory information about sensations, threat of pain, and attention on cold pressor distress. *Journal of Personality and Social Psychology,* 1979, *37,* 688-714.

Luckinbill, D. F. Criminal homicide as a situated transaction. *Social Problems,* 1977, *25,* 176-186.

Marsh, P., Rosser, E., & Harré, R. *The rules of disorder.* London: Routledge & Kegan Paul, 1978.

Mead, G. H. *Mind, self and society.* Chicago: University of Chicago Press, 1934.

Meddin, J. Chimpanzees, symbols, and the reflective self. *Social Psychology Quarterly,* 1979, *42,* 99-109.

Morris, D., Collett, P., Marsh, P., & O'Shaughnessy, M. *Gestures: Their origins and distribution.* London: Jonathan Cape, 1979.

Newtson, D., Engquist, G., & Bois, J. The objective basis of behavior units. *Journal of Personality and Social Psychology,* 1977, *35,* 847-862.

Osgood, C. E. *Method and theory in experimental psychology.* New York: Oxford University Press, 1953.

Osofsky, J. D. (ed.). *Handbook of infant development.* New York: Wiley, 1979.

Ossorio, P. *"What actually happens": The representation of real-world phenomena.* Columbia: University of South Carolina Press, 1978.

Ratner, N. & Bruner, J. Games, social exchange, and the acquisition of language. *Journal of Child Language,* 1978, *5,* 391-401.

Rommetveit, R. On "meanings" of acts and what is meant and made known by what is said in a pluralistic social world. In M. Brenner (ed.), *The structure of action.* Oxford, England: Basil Blackwell, in press.

Rosnow, R. L. The prophetic vision of Giambattista Vico: Implications for the state of social psychological theory. *Journal of Personality and Social Psychology,* 1978, *36,* 1322-1331.

Sampson, E. E. Scientific paradigms and social values: Wanted—a scientific revolution. *Journal of Personality and Social Psychology,* 1978, *36,* 1332-1343.

Scaife, M. Observing infant social development: Theoretical perspectives, natural observation, and video recording. In G. P. Ginsburg (ed.), *Emerging strategies in social psychological research.* London: Wiley, 1979. Pp. 93-112.

Schlenker, B. R. Social psychology and science. *Journal of Personality and Social Psychology,* 1974, *29,* 1-15.

Scott, M. B. & Lyman, S. M. Accounts. *American Sociological Review,* 1968, *33,* 46-62.

Searle, J. *Speech acts.* Cambridge, England: Cambridge University Press, 1969.

Shaw, R. & Bransford, J. (eds.). *Perceiving, acting, and knowing.* Hillsdale, N.J.: Erlbaum, 1977.

Shea, E. & deCharms, R. Beyond attribution theory: The human conception of motivation and causality. In L. H. Strickland et al. (eds.), *Social psychology in transition.* New York: Plenum, 1976. Pp. 253-268.

Shotter, J. Towards a social psychology of everyday life: A standpoint "in action." In M. Brenner et al. (eds.), *The social context of method.* London: Croom-Helm, 1978. Pp. 33-43.

Shotter, J. Action, joint action, and intentionality. In M. Brenner (ed.), *The structure of action.* Oxford, England: Basil Blackwell, in press.

Snyder, M. & Uranowitz, S. W. Reconstructing the past: Some cognitive consequences of person perception. *Journal of Personality and Social Psychology,* 1978, *36,* 941-950.

Stern, D., Jaffe, J., Beebe, B., & Bennett, S. Vocalizing in unison and in alternation: Two modes of communication within the mother-infant dyaa. In L. Bloom (ed.), *Readings in language development.* New York: Wiley, 1978. Pp. 115-127.

Strickland, L. H., Aboud, F. E., & Gergen, K. L. (eds.). *Social psychology in transition.* New York: Plenum, 1976.

Toulmin, S. *Foresight and understanding.* Atlantic Highlands, N.J.: Humanities Press, 1961.

Triandis, H. Some Universals of social behavior. *Personality and Social Psychology Bulletin,* 1978, *4,* 1-16.

Woodfield, A. *Teleology.* Cambridge, England: Cambridge University Press, 1976.

Yngve, V. H. I forgot what I was going to say. Presented at the ninth regional meeting of the Chicago Linguistic Circle, 1973.

12

An Alternative Metatheory for Social Psychology

KENNETH J. GERGEN
JILL MORAWSKI

Kenneth J. Gergen is Professor of Psychology, Swarthmore College. He has just edited *Behavior Exchange: Advances in Theory and Research* (Plenum). His primary interest is in the topic of social explanation.
Jill Morawski is Assistant Professor of Psychology at Wesleyan University. With graduate studies in history and theory of psychology, her research has focused on the social and historical context of social psychological theory. These studies have indicated directions for developing a historiography of social psychology that accommodates changes in the conceptions of the science and in social reality.

Within the past decade we have witnessed the emergence of an acute sensitivity to the aims, prospects, and accomplishments of the traditional attempt in social psychology to develop and test fundamental principles of social behavior. In many instances, analysts have inquired into potentially fruitful readjustments in the dominant forms of research and theorizing. For example, arguments have favored greater ecological validity of social research, a decrease in the use of experimental deception, an increase in the observation range underlying existing theory, the inclusion of social structural variables in research designs, the revitalization of small group research, and an increase in the complexity and logical coherence of theoretical models. Such analyses are essentially *remedial,* inasmuch as they do not question the fundamental metatheory underlying most contemporary inquiry; their

AUTHORS' NOTE: Grateful appreciation is expressed to James Davis, Gerald Ginsburg, Joseph Rychlak, Edward Sampson, and John Shotter for their critical appraisals of an earlier draft of this article. The present article has benefitted greatly from their wisdom. Work for the article has also been facilitated by funds from the National Science Foundation (Grant 7809393) and a Doctoral Fellowship from the Canada Council.

326

primary aim is to alter emphases within the existing tradition. However, much of the accumulated reappraisal has been little short of an exhortation for *fundamental alteration* in the aims and methods of the field. These latter appraisals call into question the metatheoretical suppositions underlying the discipline more generally. In particular, they question longstanding empiricist assertions that social theory may be empirically falsified, that data can legitimately rule between competing hypotheses, that social description may be value-free, and that society's capacity for the prediction and control of behavior may be continuously advanced by engaging in the hypothetico-deductive process. Although a full summary of such work is not within the scope of the present review, we shall have reason to refer to several critical lines of argument in later discussion.

Many social psychologists have grown weary of the soul-searching appraisals of recent years. They are hostile to "attack without alternatives," and demand from their seeming assailants a fully developed model for an "improved science" along with compelling exemplars. Yet, although furnishing emotional sustenance, there is little to recommend this form of defense. Its parallel would be to fault criticisms of astrology because the critics' capacities for prophecy were not superior, or they failed to furnish alternative pastimes. Yet, on both pragmatic and intellectual grounds, there is manifest demand for an alternative metatheory. A fully developed rationale is required for the development and flourishing of alternative forms of social inquiry. With the elaboration of an alternative metatheory, one may begin to establish viable endpoints or functions for social investigation and to inquire more directly into forms of academic training, journal policies, and professional gatekeeping holding more substantial promise.

Although a fully elaborated alternative is not currently extant, it is our present contention that the contours of a nonempiricist metatheory are beginning to emerge within several significant lines of scholarship. At present the constituents of this "counterculture" dwell in relative independence; yet closer examination indicates substantial lines of metatheoretical agreement. It is these lines of fundamental agreement that may begin to furnish a basis for the elaboration of an alternative metatheory. Within the present review, we shall first highlight major developments within four counterculture constituencies: the hermeneutic-interpretive, the dialectic, the critical, and the ethogenic. We shall then consider the extent of agreement among these perspectives in terms of selective metatheoretic fundamentals. In our view such agreement as does exist within social psychology and related disciplines favors what may be termed a *socio-rationalist* alternative to the traditional empiricist metatheory.

THE HERMENEUTIC-INTERPRETIVE MOVEMENT

Prior to the eighteenth century, hermeneutic study was concerned with the interpretation of biblical scriptures. Hermeneutic scholarship served as the handmaiden of philosophy and historiography in their combined search for the proper or most accurate interpretation of early religious writings. By the end of the eighteenth century, however, hermeneutics began to take on for itself the more difficult philosophic and psychological tasks of accounting for the nature of interpretation itself (Palmer, 1969). In attempting to locate proper interpretations of scriptural passages, one must presumably be able to ascertain the writer's intentions, or the meanings which he or she wishes to convey. On what grounds can such a determination be made? The question indeed demands inquiry into the nature of communicative acts and the more general concept of social knowledge (cf. Gadamer, 1960, 1976; Ricoeur, 1974, 1976). Such inquiry has hardly been limited to the theological domain. Students of history, literature, and jurisprudence have been no less immersed in the complicated question of how accurate renderings can be made of the meaning of early historical accounts, literature, poetry, and judicial opinion. And, during the twentieth century, it has become increasingly clear that if a science of human behavior is to develop, it, too, must face these same difficult questions. One is ill-equipped to conduct a science in the traditional sense without the ability to properly identify or classify behavioral acts; yet such identification must seemingly depend on the complicated question of how one can with certainty assess an actor's intentions.

This latter issue becomes acute in light of a conclusion emerging with increasing but painful clarity among hermeneutic theorists themselves: the major criterion by which the validity of a given interpretation may be judged is the extent to which it accords with the prevailing rules of communication within the culture. In effect, interpretations may be rendered acceptable or unacceptable to the extent they meet currently adopted standards of intelligibility. This view has always been an unhappy one for theologians, literary critics, and historians, inasmuch as it implies a thoroughgoing social relativity in interpretation. From this standpoint, scriptures, literary masterpieces, and judicial opinions can only acquire the meaning inherent in the symbol or meaning system of the observer. The originator's intentions or meanings can be ascertained only within these terms. Such a conclusion is not a sanguine one for most behavioral scientists, as it suggests that the meaning of social actions is generally created by scientists themselves. Aggression, altruism, conformity, and the like are not "out there to be classified or studied," as the traditional empiricist view would have it, but are byproducts of the rules of intelligibility existing within the sciences. They are essentially created by the prevailing forms of interpretation within the sciences. Attempts to rescue the process of interpretation from the shoals of social relativism have yet proved less than compelling outside the behavioral sciences (cf. Mandelbaum, 1967; Hirsch, 1976; Ricoeur, 1976). It remains a question of some magnitude as to whether such a rescue effort is possible within the sciences (cf. Gergen, 1980).

This concern with the problematic character of social interpretation has acted as a catalyst for two significant lines of inquiry in the social sciences, both of which are now emerging within social psychology proper. The first line of inquiry has been into existing forms of interpretation. Such exploration proves quite consistent with the hermeneutic emphasis on socially dependent interpretations. Thus, the hermeneutically informed writings of Alfred Schutz (1962), along with the symbolic interactionist contributions of Cooley (1902), Mead (1934), Thomas (1966), Blumer (1969), and others, set the stage for contemporary observational studies of socially derived meaning systems. Perhaps the most visible of the earlier investigations were those falling under the general rubric of "labelling theory" (cf. Becker, 1953). Such investigations were particularly challenging in their argument that various forms of deviance are not essentially empirical in character, but are created through systems of socially shared labels. The deviant is thus a product of those who label.

The epistemological challenge implicit in labelling theory has become more fully articulated within the more recent writing of the ethnomethodologists. As envisioned by Harold Garfinkel (1967), ethnomethodology is essentially concerned with the methods by which people generate and sustain common sense, and render "visibly reportable" their understandings about the world. Thus, for example, it is commonly taken for granted that certain deaths are suicides while others are caused by natural occurrences. From an empiricist standpoint, one should be able, in principle, to record the number of suicides within the culture at any given time. Yet, as Garfinkel (1967) attempts to show, suicide is a product of social rules, the application of which must be continuously negotiated. For example, to commit suicide one must presumably "intend" to do so. Yet, intentions are not observable, and the rules for determining the presence and absence of intention are diffuse. In the same vein, Cicourel (1968) has demonstrated how systems of social understanding must be sustained by police, probation officers, and other officials in converting the immense complexity of an ever-shifting reality into ordered units such as "offenses," "family units," and "harmless behavior." In their extensive analysis of gender identifications, Kessler and McKenna (1978) have argued even more dramatically that gender is also a social creation. Men and women do not exist as two distinct social types. Biologists, medical practitioners, lawyers, children, transsexuals, and so on differ considerably in their views of what counts as male versus female. Given significant variations in such rules from one segment of society to another, the assumption of objective, real-world gender differences becomes unsupportable. Other investigators have inquired into the manner in which people construct such entities as "mind" (Coulter, 1979), social relations (Heyman & Shaw, 1978), the emotion of envy (Silver & Sabini, 1978), personal death (Sudnow, 1967), legal codes (Bittner, 1967), and so on (cf. Psathas, 1979).

The second major impact of hermeneutic thought on contemporary social science has occurred within the metatheoretical domain (Taylor, 1964). Although there has been little ethnomethodological inquiry into the means by which social scientists themselves generate "what there is" through their rules of meaning (cf. Mackey, 1973; Elliot, 1974), this possibility has hardly escaped scrutiny by those concerned with the potential of the social sciences (cf. Berger & Luckman, 1966; Radnitsky, 1970; Fay, 1976; Wilson, 1970). Both Giddens (1976) and Bauman (1978) have furnished extensive accounts of the hermeneutic critique of empirical sociology and outlined the bases for an interpretive form of science. As Giddens (1976) argues, sociology should not be concerned with a "pre-given universe of objects," but with one which is in a continuous state of reconstitution as the rules of social discourse are altered over time. For Bauman (1978), sociology should attempt to critically scrutinize the consensus reached in society. Within social psychology, Gergen's (1978) arguments for "generative theory" extend this analysis. To the extent that common-sense agreements delimit the range of possible actions, the social psychologist may serve as an agent for undermining such consensus. In the theoretical challenge to common sense, the scientist generates new alternatives for action. A less troublesome role for the social psychologist has been outlined by Gauld and

Shotter (1977). For them, the scientist may serve as an important arbiter for clarity where common-sense perspectives create social conflict. In each of these cases the chief concern of the scientist shifts from the observation and recording of behavior to the realm of creation and change through reinterpretation.

DIALECTICS

Within early Greek philosophy, as in later formulations, "dialectic" denoted a form of reasoning examining the relation of an idea to its opposite. As it is held, the process of relating these opposing or contradictory ideas ultimately leads to transformations in thought. The history of dialectical thinking is punctuated by Hegel's designation of these opposites (the thesis and antithesis) and their resolution (synthesis). According to Hegel, each synthesis provides a thesis for continuing the process of change, and the direction of change is toward a fully enlightened state, ironically termed the "objective mind." Thus, as a reasoning process, dialectics mirrors the continual change and instability of the mind and of the universe. Although overshadowed by the growing enchantment of scientific naturalism and positivism during the late nineteenth and early twentieth centuries, dialectical thinking was integral to the philosophies of Marx, Dewey, Mead, and Freud, among others. Recently, psychologists have begun to unearth the long history of psychological ideas that have drawn sustenance from dialectic thinking (Buss, 1979; Lawler, 1975; Rychlak, 1968, 1977).

As in the case of the hermeneutic-interpretive movement, dialectic thinking has been employed not only in the analysis of social science metatheory but as well in research on a wide range of substantive problems. Broadly conceived, a dialectic orientation may be used both as a method of understanding, and as a device for describing patterns of action across time (Buss, 1979; Hook, 1953; Kosok, 1976; Rychlak, 1968). In the case of metatheory, the work of Riegel (1973, 1976a, 1976b) and Rychlak (1968, 1975) has been perhaps most influential in its effects within psychology. Among the most prominent characteristics of dialectic metatheory is its emphasis on contradiction. Standing in opposition to the Aristotelian logic of identities, dialectic metatheory is concerned with the interdependence of being and negation, with an entity and its opposite. Thus, rather than viewing the scientist's task as that of describing social activity *as it is*, the dialectically oriented investigator might ask whether any entity (1) may not in actuality be its own opposite, (2) may not be opressing its opposite, (3) may not depend for its existence on its opposite, or (4) may be opposed by its opposite in a cross-time process that may yield transformation. In any case, the dialectic investigator is not content to accept that which seems "given" in human affairs. The concern with being, negation, and transformation also sets the stage for a second important emphasis in dialectic metatheory. From the dialectic standpoint, patterns of social action are essentially tenuous and the tension of oppositions is viewed as essential in fostering historical change. Thus, rather than engaging in the traditional empiricist search for patterns of cause and effect that repeat themselves across time, the dialectician will be far more concerned with patterns of change and possible directions implied by these patterns.

To illustrate the above, the dialectician would not be content to view sex roles (including androgyny) as the simple product of socialization. Any given sex role might first be viewed in terms of those forces with which it conflicts, and in terms of possible transitions occurring within the society. In the life of an individual, a given sex role may be viewed as but a stage in an ongoing process of transformation, with the possible endpoint a total rejection of sex-role stereotyping. A dialectician might also take a critical view of much existing sex-role theory and research, with particular attention given to (1) the way in which existing theory of sex-roles accommodates itself to the contemporary historical circumstances, (2) the traditional use of bipolar conceptions of sex roles, and (3) the underlying ideological commitments represented in the scientist's thinking about sex roles (Hefner et al., 1976; Rebecca et al., 1976).

Two additional emphases of the dialectic metatheory are also worthy of note. First, there is general acknowledgment of the scientist as a full-fledged member of the society. The separation of the role of scientist from that of citizen typically derived from empiricist metatheory is seen as illusory. The scientist affects society through his or her scientific activities and the knowledge produced by the science is in part a reflection of contemporary social circumstances. Further, it is argued, knowledge at the scientific level may evolve from "praxis," or the concerted action of the scientist in society. The value of existing knowledge may indeed by evaluated within praxis. The generation of knowledge and concerted action within society are thus seen to be closely linked (Kytle, 1977; Janousek, 1972; Cvetkovich, 1977; Rappoport, 1975; White, 1977). Finally, the traditional social psychologist within the liberal tradition tends to carry out research with an avowed aim of reducing social or personal conflict. Psychological crises and social disruptions are frequently viewed as undesirable and worthy of elimination from the psychological or social system. In contrast, the dialectical perspective holds that both for the individual and the society, conflicts are constructive and important events, where the discord created by contradictory forces may be a valuable source of further development (Riegel, 1977).

As dialectical psychology often emphasizes multiple dimensions of change (biological, social, historical) and plural methods of study (linguistic, longitudinal, historical), it does not easily fall into any single subdiscipline within contemporary psychology. However, dialectical analysis and research has gained the increasing interest of those concerned with social interaction. Much of this work has been specifically concerned with issues relating development and social activity. Thus dialecticians have examined mother-child interactions (Harris, 1975; Riegel, 1973, 1976), socially oriented revisions to Piagetian theory (Buck-Morss, 1975; Freedle, 1975; Lawler, 1975), the socio-historical context of ego development (Hogan, 1974; Van den Daele, 1975a, 1975b; Meacham, 1975a), the relation of learning and memory processes to broad cultural circumstances (Kvale, 1977; Meacham, 1975b, 1977; Reese, 1977), and changes in family structure across time (Gadlin, 1978). Closely allied with several traditional social psychological issues is dialectical research on the development of privacy (Altman, 1977), family relations (Brown, 1975; Sameroff, 1975; Ziller, 1977), interpersonal attraction (Adams, 1977), the self-concept (Chandler, 1975), social intervention research (Weeks, 1977), environmental settings (Altman & Gauvain, in press), and decision making (Mitroff & Betz, 1972). In all cases the dialectic perspective has been used as an analytic tool, a means of organizing diverse observations, or a means of elucidating patterns of cross-time change.

THE CRITICAL PERSPECTIVE

While the debunking and criticism of conventional thought has always been an important component of intellectual life, it was not until the early twentieth century in Germany that critical thinking became the foundation of an identifiable school. The "critical theory" of the Frankfurt School assimilated Marx's critique of the ideological underpinnings of current economic thought and his conception of history as a process moving toward a state of emancipation. Members of the Frankfurt School, including Adorno, Habermas, Horkheimer, and Marcuse, adopted as primary tasks (1) the explication of ideological biases through critical analysis and (2) the design of alternative perspectives for shaping future society. As a secondary aim, the critical theorist often shares with the dialectic theorist an interest in praxis. In attempting to delineate the forces which influence our knowledge, and to understand the dynamics of historical change, several members of the school shifted the focus of their critiques from political economy to psychology, from Marx to Freud. Yet, the essential tasks remained unaltered: Critical theory entails inquiry into the conditions which direct our knowledge of the social world and development of alternatives for purposes of social action.

Since the inception of the Frankfurt School in the 1920s, critical theory has been both hybridized and absorbed into various intellectual pursuits, and can no longer be associated with any single economic, political or psychological orientation (see Connerton, 1976; Freiberg, 1979; Jay, 1973; Ray, 1979; Holzkamp, 1976). At present, critical appraisals consistent with the Frankfurt writings are being made by social psychologists who have had very little (sometimes, no) contact with the corpus of German writing. Thus, social psychological analysis which may be traced to these earlier conceptions more properly warrants the designation of "critical perspective." Within this perspective the dual conception of criticism is retained. On the one hand the attempt is made to examine critically the valuational underpinnings and normative' dictates underlying existing theories. However, the attempt is also made to develop alternative conceptualizations. A general preference is expressed for theories that do not mirror commonsense conceptions but transform them. This preference implies that the aim of social science is "not only to systematize existing knowledge but to postulate entirely new concepts. It is now fully recognized that the exact sciences create new aspects of nature; social sciences must create new aspects of society" (Moscovici, 1972, p. 65). From another standpoint, it is said that through criticism and generation of new alternatives, people may be emancipated from their present interpretations of reality and may realize more fulfilling life patterns (Israel, 1972; Moscovici, 1972; Rommetveit, 1972, 1976).

Within current social psychology, many critical analyses have focused on ways in which social psychological knowledge is shaped by the broader social context (Buss, 1979). It is widely recognized that social psychological research is influenced by the organizational features of the scientific community: granting procedures (McGrath &

Altman, 1966), publication policies (Cartwright, 1973), disciplinary boundaries (Campbell, 1969), and elite systems of power and prestige (Lubek, 1976; Morawski, 1979; Strickland et al., 1976). However, a critical perspective extends beyond elucidation of the constraints imposed by the internal structure of a scientific community. It attempts to identify economic, political, ideological, and metatheoretical investments that may fashion what otherwise appears to be neutral or objective knowledge. To do so, it is necessary to examine theories in their historical context. It also is necessary to assess theories for their potential to yield understanding that can emancipate rather than bind people to existing forms of social reality.

It is in this vein that Archibald (1978) has, for example, examined assumptions in classical social psychological theories as they are related to their political, economic, and cultural origins. Sampson (1977) has critiqued concepts of androgyny, moral development, and mental health for the ideology of "self-contained individualism" hidden within their premises. As he points out, the ideology has its origins in the early history of American society, but that today it is neither a necessary nor even a preferable basis for social theory. Other analysts have isolated valuational bases of ostensibly neutral theories of human values and moral development (Smith, 1978; Hogan, 1978), prejudice (Harrison, 1974), person perception and nonverbal communication (Hogan, 1978), aggression (Lubek, 1977, 1979), dissonance theory (Israel, 1979), conflict (Apfelbaum & Lubek, 1979; Plon, 1974), equality (Sampson, 1975), locus of control (Furby, 1979), and the interactionist paradigm in social psychology (Gadlin & Rubin, 1979), as well as the character of methodology (Brenner, 1978; Rowan, 1974). In other analyses, it has been shown how empiricist metatheory dictates theoretical conceptions in social psychology (Gergen, 1979) and produces an image of human functioning that is unnecessarily damaging (Argyris, 1975; Zuniga, 1975). All such cases serve to undermine confidence in the empiricist assumption that social psychological theories are built inductively from neutral observation.

A second important line of work in the critical perspective has concentrated on historical accounts of the discipline. As discovered in the case of sociology (Gouldner, 1970; Peel, 1974; Schwendinger & Schwendinger, 1974) and general psychology (O'Donnel, 1979; Yaroshevskii, 1973), contemporary histories of social psychology generally serve to justify an empiricist epistemology (Baumgardner, 1976, 1977; Morawski, 1979a; Samelson, 1974). Allport's (1957) classic treatment of the field's history is thus seen as presentist; it marshalls historical evidence in a way that justifies the empiricist program. Empiricism itself has been shown to be an outgrowth of a particular moral and political climate (Blum, 1978; Leary, 1978; Steininger, 1979; Shields, 1975). Empiricist beliefs about proper scientific conduct cannot themselves be grounded in observation. Belief in them may thus be traced to the socio-historical climate in the same way one might trace the growth of religious movements to particular historical circumstances.

Historical research further points to various cultural factors affecting the success of a theory or the growth of the discipline. Critical reassessment of social psychology's heritage has unearthed important theoretical ideas previously ignored because of their divergence from mainstream ideological investments (Buck-Morss, 1977; Buss, 1977; Lubek, 1977). For instance, the history of aggression research suggests that such research has been particularly successful because it adopts the assumption of individual blame, and the view that aggression is a deviation from normative social standards and should thus be controlled (Lubek, 1979). Trends in the study of groups have been shown to be related to the general political climate (Steiner, 1974) and to the cultural backgrounds of the researchers (Gorman, 1979). Critical inquiry has also shown how social conditions such as unemployment (Finison, 1977, 1978), legislation, and the ethnic composition of the profession (Samelson, 1977, 1978) may have influenced patterns of professional interest and association.

Much work within the critical perspective also argues for alternative conceptions of social reality. For instance, Sampson (1977) counters the dominant thesis of self-contained individualism with that of communal "interdependence." Theories of interdependence would locate the responsibility for social actions in the larger community rather than with the individual. This emphasis on interdependence as the desired end to be served by social theory is shared by many others (cf. Rommetveit, 1976; Argyris, 1975; Gadlin & Ingle, 1975). Along similar lines, others have argued for a perspective that treats humans as active, responsible, and changing agents (Gross, 1974; Shotter, 1974, 1978). Ultimately, it may be possible to discover an integrated conception of human functioning and an underlying ideological commitment within these disparate images. However, this piece of analytic work remains to be accomplished.

THE ETHOGENIC ALTERNATIVE

With the 1972 publication of the volume, *The Explanation of Social Behavior*, British philosopher Rom Harré and American social psychologist Paul Secord outlined a rationale for an alternative form of social psychology termed "ethogenics." The volume, along with numerous others congenial to its fundamentals (cf. Shotter, 1975; Collett, 1977; Marsh & Brenner, 1978; Brenner, in press; Ginsburg, 1979; Armistead, 1974) has had a profound effect on British social psychology and has begun to generate sympathetic support within a steadily increasing number of American institutions. Ethogenics may be viewed essentially as a composite of ordinary language philosophy and structural anthropology. As a result of its former alliance, ethogenecists are highly critical of the behavioral model in psychology, with its emphasis on deterministic principles of human conduct. Most human action cannot be comprehended or identified, the ethogenecist argues, without the concept of intentionality. One cannot aggress, love, help, conform, lead, communicate, and so on unless one intends to do so. To strike someone intentionally is aggression; however, if the very same overt behavior is carried out unintentionally, we would not see it as aggressive but something else. Since intentions cannot be observed, the objective basis of the science is rendered problematic (Gergen, in press). From the ethogenic perspective human action is seen as relying on an agent's ability to evaluate his or her performance according to rules and plans. Deterministic, mental mechanisms are denigrated, as action is seen as performed by the person for specific purposes in particular situations. As the individual may also decide to alter his or her pattern of action— to disobey a rule or abandon a given plan—the prospects of a trans-historically predictive science are also rendered suspect (cf. Scheibe, 1978).

From structural anthropology, the ethogenecist comes to take seriously the actions of people in everyday life. Laboratory research from this perspective is fundamentally misleading. The laboratory can only distort common patterns of action in unknown ways. More important, individual acts are viewed by the ethogenecist as imbédded in larger structures from which they derive their meaning. From this perspective, individuals do not respond to punctate, temporally isolated stimuli, with all other factors held constant. Rather, they are typically engaged in complex sequences of action in which any individual act takes on significance only as it is related to other acts in the sequence (Gergen, 1978a). It is the scientist's task, in this case, to develop intelligible statements about the underlying structure of events. To this end, investigators have set out to describe the structure of seemingly disorderly acts of hooligans at football matches (Marsh et al., 1978),

rituals for incorporating strangers into social groups (Harré & De-
Waele, 1976), the way intonation patterns are used as markers for the
identification of meaning units in communication (Krakel, in press),
rules of social address (Kroger, 1979), and the common rules for ending
encounters (Albert, 1977). Such work also bears a close affinity with
that of socio-linguistics, ethnomethodology, and role-rule research in
sociology. Studies of turn-taking and closing sequences in ordinary
conversation (Schegloff & Sacks, 1973), rules governing pedestrian
behavior (cf. Wolff, 1973), and the manner in which people control
their environment by using various rules or roles (cf. Zurcher, 1970;
Schwartz, 1967; Gross & Stone, 1965) are all quite compatible with the
ethogenic orientation. A more complete account of the ethogenics
movement will not be undertaken in the present chapter as it would
be redundant with Ginsburg's (this volume) analysis of situated action.

METATHEORETICAL BASES FOR A UNIFIED ALTERNATIVE

Many of the arguments, concepts, and methods adopted within
the above domains are evidenced in the traditional, hypothesis-testing
sectors of social psychology. However, in such cases the arguments,
concepts, and methods usually serve an ancillary function; their full
implications are left unexplored. In each of the domains here reviewed,
a self-conscious attempt has been made to break with the empiricist
tradition. The question we must now ask is whether one may discern
broad metatheoretical agreement across these domains. If such agreements can be located, could they serve as a metatheoretical base for a
unifying alternative to the traditional empiricist account of scientific
activity? Is it possible that an alliance among these disparate domains
could foster a major evolution in the character of social psychology?
As a general surmise, there would appear to be five major assumptions
that would evoke substantial agreement within the domains thus far
described. Each of these assumptions stands in strong contrast to
pivotal suppositions within the traditional empiricist perspective.

1. Knowledge as Socially Constructed

From the empiricist standpoint, the investigator ideally operates
as a passive recording device, charting the contours of nature and
developing theories to map the world as observed. However, emerging
within the domains discussed above is an opposing view of scientific

activity. In this case, the investigator is viewed as one who creates through his or her theoretical lens what facts there are to be studied. From this standpoint, there are no social facts other than those which one's theoretical perspective allows one to perceive. This view is most fully articulated within the hermeneutic-interpretive and critical domains. In the former case, we found that in the interpretation of others' behavior, one necessarily projects meaning and intention into their actions. It is projected meaning of such actions and not to behavior itself to which one reacts. And, there appears to be no means of objectively anchoring such interpretations. Within the critical domain, stress was placed on inherent valuational underpinnings of social theory and the manner in which theory shapes social life as its meanings are absorbed by the society. Theory is not thus data driven, but fashioned by social circumstances. Within both the ethogenic and dialectic domains, one may discern some controversy over the assumption of social ontology. At times, ethogenic investigators speak as if the structure of conduct were available for public observation and the proper ethogenic investigation simply records the patterns of rule-governed behavior within society. This position would be consistent with traditional empiricism. At the same time, their analysis suggests that scientists, too, follow investigatory rules, and that the particular rules they follow will lead to certain forms of observation, while avoiding others. Thus the rules of scientific comportment at any given time will fashion the kind of knowledge that will result. Dialectic theorists, and particularly those moved by the concept of dialectic materialism, will often speak of human behavior as governed by economic structure. In doing so they take for granted a factual domain independent of the observer and join the empiricist tradition. However, other dialectic theorists have more fully adopted symbolic interactionist concepts in analyzing the social and ideological basis for various forms of behavioral knowledge (cf. Berger & Luckman, 1966; Buss, 1979). In effect, agreement with the assumption of a socially constructed world of action may be found within each of the dissident camps.

2. Social Action as Rule Governed

Within the traditional empiricist perspective, human behavior is believed to reflect principles of the natural order. Thus, social psychologists attempt to establish invariant principles of social behavior that might emulate principles of color perception in experimental psychology or impulse transmission in physiological psychology. In contrast, theorists in the above domains tend to view social action as fundamentally unprogrammed, and thus capable of a virtual infinity of variations. Social order at any given point may thus be viewed as the product of broad social agreement. Patterns of action termed aggressive, altruistic, intelligent, emotional, and so on are seen as rule, norm, or convention governed (cf. Pepitone, 1976). In effect, such activities are more adequately explained by a series of rules, rather than a body of immutable laws. This view of behavior as rule governed is most fully elaborated within the ethogenic domain. The ethogenic program is specifically dedicated to understanding social action in such terms; one product of scientific inquiry should, from this standpoint, be a description of the prevailing rules within society. This view is also quite congenial to the hermeneutic-interpretive standpoint. Here, the major concern is with culturally bounded rules of meaning. Indeed, within this domain, ontological structure is a product of rules in use. Although not explicit in the critical domain, the supposition of rule-based action is fundamental to the critical program. It is assumed by the critical theorist that such analyses have the capacity to alter common understanding, and through enhanced understanding, the individual is liberated from the constraints of previous assumptions. If patterns of behavior were fixed by laws of nature, such a program would have little hope of success. Within the dialectic school, conflict of opinion may again be discerned. For some traditionalists, dialectic processes proceed with natural force toward inevitable ends. It is this form of dialectic theory that Popper (1957) has critically addressed. However, for others, dialectic thinking is essentially an advanced heuristic, that may be employed at any time for purposes of changing self or social surrounds (cf. Basseches, in press). From this standpoint, dialectic theory is wholly congenial with the assumption of rule-governed action. Again, wide agreement may be discerned among the four domains.

3. Historical Relativity of Social Knowledge

The traditional empiricist orientation is generally committed to the view that science is cumulative and progressive. Through continuing research one may hope to discard empirically invalid theories and sustain or improve those receiving empirical support. The problematic character of these assumptions in the social sciences has been explored elsewhere (Gergen, 1973, 1976). However, we also find opposition to the traditional view inherent in each of the above domains, along with an alternative conception of scientific focus. As we have seen, within each of the domains there is widespread belief in human flexibility and a corresponding commitment to a rule-oriented understanding of human activity. Given these assumptions, it rapidly becomes apparent that social knowledge must be historically situated. Any given pattern of activity, including acts of behavioral interpretation, is subject to the vicissitudes of history. Thus, however thorough one's contemporary understanding, that understanding is precariously situated.

Although an unhappy conclusion within the empiricist framework, inquiry within each of the above domains is, in fact, spurred by the assumption of historical relativity. If social patterns are dependent on rule systems, and one may change rule systems through theoretical work, then the social theorist may have a direct impact on society. Theorists need not rely on "agents of application" in order to gain a fulcrum for change, but may use their conceptual skills directly for such purposes.

4. Research as Vivification of Theory

Consistent with a belief in cumulative science, traditional social psychological research generally attempts to test hypotheses relating social stimuli and responses. Through such tests, it is believed, one may emerge with theories containing a high degree of correspondence with existing fact. Yet, from the perspective emerging within the dissident domains, this general process of "testing hypotheses" is rendered suspect. First, if the scientist essentially creates a phenomenon through a particular interpretive stance, then virtually any intelligible hypothesis can be "verified" or "falsified." If one wishes to test the view that crowding leads to aggression, for example, one is led to select a context in which one can acquire interpretive agreement that people are "crowded" and that they subsequently "aggress." Yet, neither crowding nor aggression exists in a behavioral world; rather, they are essentially states of conception, and may thus be discerned wherever one has the conceptual capacity to "see" them. One may perceive himself to be crowded by the presence of a single person, or feel socially unencumbered in a sea of thousands. Further, from the standpoint of historical relativity, we find that the investigator is faced with an immense panoply of behavioral exemplars under continuous change. Thus, to "test" a hypothesis the investigator essentially engages in the process of searching out specific exemplars that will best serve theoretical investments. Using this procedure, support or threat may be generated for virtually any sensible hypothesis.

Such criticisms of traditional hypothesis testing do not entail an abandonment of so-called empirical work. Rather, they suggest that alternative functions be assigned to this form of exercise. It may be ventured that the principle function lying implicit in the domains under study is that of theoretical vivification. One may employ data of the traditional variety as a means of enabling others to perceive and appreciate the viability of one's theoretical standpoint. The research essentially invites and trains others to employ the terms of the theory to interpret their experience. Thus, when the ethogenecist purports to examine the structural features of a particular interaction, he or she is essentially proposing to the observer that the structural lens will elucidate the situation and, through systematic data, may furnish persuasive illustration. And, in the interpretive investigator's attempt to document the rules of meaning within a specific context, data serve not as a validating device but as a rhetorical function. Although critical theorists have been little concerned with carrying out systematic empirical studies, the critical program is quite consistent with the above reasoning. It must be supposed that some disagreement would be found among dialectic theorists concerning the function of empirical research, a disagreement that would again reflect differing views toward materialism and determinism. However, in general, we find that across the various dissident domains, empirical work retains an important role, although a role other than that traditionally assigned.

5. Valuational Foundations of Social Knowledge

Traditional empiricism assumes that scientific description may proceed without prescriptive bias. The investigator may remain a neutral observer and, with appropriate effort, both record the state of nature and analyze the relations among its entities without valuational biases. Yet, within recent years it has become increasingly difficult to sustain this pivotal argument. As we have seen, studies within the critical framework have demonstrated numerous ideological biases underlying social theory long believed to be value neutral, along with biases undergirding the historical accounts sustaining present-day theory and research.

Interpretive theorists have further demonstrated that social description does not essentially reflect the empirical world, but shapes the observer's conceptual construction of this world. Thus, theoretical description cannot in principle be data driven. Its source must lie elsewhere than in the world of experience itself. Both critical and interpretive theorists generally agree as well that theoretical accounts may enter into the common conceptual agreements of the culture, and in this way have the capacity to alter society. Thus, whether desired or not, theory influences social action, even if the reaction to such theory is boredom, misunderstanding, or scorn. In effect, the theorist has the capacity to alter social life for good or ill. Finally, as argued by the same ordinary-language philosophers who played such an instrumental role in the development of ethogenics, descriptions of human action inevitably rely on assumptions of intentionality (Anscombe, 1951). Thus, in the attempt to describe social life, one inevitably allocates intention. In assigning intention to action, one makes a silent pronouncement on matters of moral responsibility. To describe an experimental subject's actions as "aggression," for example, is automatically to establish an intentional basis for the action. In calling it aggression, then, the theorist is impugning the character of the subject. Such imputations appear virtually inescapable so long as one employs common descriptive terms within the culture.

As we see, there is broad agreement across the groups here discussed that the traditional fact-value dichotomy is woefully misleading. Values, ideologies, or visions of an improved society may legitimately enter the arena of "knowledge making." Critical theorists demonstrate the ideological bases of commonly accepted theories in an attempt to "emancipate" people from their implications. Both ethogenic and ethnomethodological investigators have used their inquiries to criticize structures of social action or agreement in order to open the way to preferred alternatives. Dialectic theory is often employed as a means of undermining those structures given normative support by the universalistic theories favored by the empiricist tradition. In effect, within the emerging metatheory, the life of the passions is reintegrated with the life of reason.

TOWARD AN INTEGRATED SOCIO-RATIONALISM

In many respects, the supporting base for the "counter-empiricist" assumptions outlined above is obscured by the present analysis. We have selected for attention only the work of four heterodox groups within social psychology. However, discontent with the empiricist model may be discerned throughout the social sciences, along with a pervasive affirmation of many of the aspects of the alternative metatheory described above (cf. Bauman, 1978; Bernstein, 1976). We have cited several sources of such support within sociology. However, similar concerns have been manifested within political science (cf. Almond & Genco, 1977; Fay, 1976; Alker, 1979; Moon, 1975), economics (Morgenstern, 1972; Leontief, 1971), anthropology (Bennett, 1976; Geertz, 1973; Douglas, 1975), and history (Zinn, 1970). And, as demonstrated elsewhere (Gergen, 1979), within other domains of psychology the past decade has witnessed the most intensive period of self-reflection since the 1930's emergence of behaviorism. Although not all such queries share the same assumptive base we have described above, the corpus of this critical literature strongly suggests a broad susceptibility to the development of an alternative metatheory.

One is tempted at this juncture to entertain the possibility that the socio-behavioral sciences are in the process of a fundamental shift in character. Based on our survey of four dissident groups within social psychology, and the metatheoretical assumptions variously linking them, it becomes increasingly clear that we are immersed in a contemporary form of the long-standing antagonism between empiricist and rationalist philosophy. Present-day experimental social psychology stands primarily on the shoulders of British empiricist philosophy. With its belief in a world of nature independent of the observer, traditional social psychology is fundamentally antagonistic to the rationalist belief in the world as essentially fashioned by the perceptual processes. This commitment to a contemporary form of rationalism within the four dissident domains is most clearly discerned in the recurring emphasis on facts as scientific creations. However, rationalist emphases are also revealed in the commitment to rules as explanatory bases of social action, a view that is deeply rooted in Kantian philosophy (cf. Mischel, 1975). Further, the potential for historical change through conceptual enlightenment has played a prominent role in the rationalist works of Hegel, Schopenhauer, and Bergson.

Yet, one may discern a fundamental separation between the rationalist flavor of the schools discussed above and traditional rational idealism. Although rationalist philosophy has usually been critical of the assumption that human knowledge can be determined by incoming sense stimuli, there has been simultaneously a widespread resistance to both solopsism and relativism. Such concepts as a priori ideas, divine provision, and the transhistorical perfectability of mind were all attempts to retain the sanctity of the concept of "human knowledge." Yet, the concept of knowledge itself becomes suspect within contemporary forms of rationalist social psychology. Knowledge is no longer sacrosanct, but "of the people"; it is no longer the gift of

God, built into the gene structure, or an exclusive possession of a scholarly elite. Within the emergent paradigm it has become democratized. Knowledge of the world is primarily a construction of individuals, not individuals acting independently, but engaged in processes of intersubjective communication. Public negotiation among people is necessary to determine "the nature of things." The emphasis on the negotiation of accounts in ethogenics, socially derived rules of facticity in ethnomethodology, and the intelligibility criterion for determining the acceptability of interpretation in the hermenutic-interpretive domain are all illustrative. In effect, there is good reason to view the emerging metatheoretical paradigm as a *socio-rationalism* (Gergen, 1979).

It is difficult to determine the future of the amalgamated views here termed socio-rationalist. Much resistance remains within the traditionalist camps. There is great comfort to be derived from following the well-trodden paths; hypothesis testing is an activity open to all; there are numerous outlets for its expression, and abundant promises of professional advancement. The dissident groups offer no "trusty techniques," few available publication outlets, and a rocky road to professional security. Indeed, the "new paradigm" is in danger of being squeezed out by economic exigency. With a generalized reduction in available academic positions, few institutions either desire or need to "take a risk" with a candidate bearing suspicious credentials.

Complicated conceptual issues also remain unsolved within the socio-rationalist camp. Among the most important of these is the degree to which the concept of socially constructed reality may be sustained. The threat of subjectivism and relativism run counter to deeply ingrained traditions in the United States and Canada. Even among the dissident camps there are many who do not wish to give up the ontological validity of economic structure, and a faith in the objective accuracy of their theoretical accounts. Some are struggling with new concepts of "reality" and objectivity which can avoid the pitfalls of both empiricist and rationalist accounts (cf. Ossorio, 1978; Sabini & Silver, in press). However, much remains to be done in this domain. In addition, a satisfactory account of natural science progress must be rendered by the socio-rationalists; the function of psychological explanation must also be evaluated; the status of rules, roles, and plans as guides for action must be closely assessed; and the extent to which values can guide theory construction without endangering the discipline must be examined.

However, it is also quite possible with the emergence of a new paradigm that the forthcoming decade will witness a level of unparal-

leled intellectual stimulation within social psychology. With a fundamental alteration in the grounding rationale for the discipline, we may
anticipate a revolution in theoretical activity, new forms of social
investigation, fresh proposals concerning what it is "to practice" social
psychology, innovative forms of advanced training, and a rejuvenated
sense of the discipline's significance.

REFERENCES

Adams, G. R. Physical attractiveness research: Toward a developmental social psychology of beauty. *Human Development,* 1977, *20,* 217-239.

Alker, H. R., Jr. Logic, dialectics, politics: Some recent controversies. Presented at the
Moscow Congress of the International Political Science Association, 1979.

Almond, G. A. & Genco, S. J. Clouds, clocks, and the study of politics. *World Politics,*
1977, *29,* 489-522.

Altman, I. Privacy regulation: Culturally universal or culturally specific. *Journal of Social
Issues,* 1977, *33,* 66-84.

Altman, I. & Gauvain, M. A cross-cultural and dialectic analysis of homes. In L. Liben
et al. (eds.), *Spatial representation and behavior across the life span: Theory and
application.* New York: Academic Press, in press.

Apfelbaum, E. & Lubek, I. Resolution versus revolution: The theory of conflicts in question. In L. H. Strickland et al. (eds.), *Social psychology in transition.* New York:
Plenum, 1976.

Archibald, W. P. *Social psychology as political economy.* Toronto: McGraw-Hill Ryer-
son, 1978.

Argyris, C. Dangers in applying results from experimental psychology. *American Psychologist,* 1975, *30,* 469-485.

Armistead, N. (ed.). *Reconstructing social psychology.* Harmondsworth, England:
Penguin, 1974.

Basseches, M. Dialectical schemata: A framework for the empirical study of the development of dialectical thinking. *Human Development,* in press.

Bauman, Z. *Hermeneutics and social science.* New York: Columbia University Press,
1978.

Baumgardner, S. R. Critical history and social psychology's crises. *Personality and Social
Psychology Bulletin,* 1976, *2,* 460-465.

Baumgardner, S. R. Critical studies in the history of social psychology. *Personality and
Social Psychology Bulletin,* 1977, *3,* 681-687.

Bennett, J. S. Anticipation, adaptation and the concept of culture in anthropology.
Science, 1976, *192,* 847.

Berger, P. L. & Luckman, T. *The social construction of reality.* New York: Doubleday, 1966.

Bittner, E. The police on skid row. *American Sociological Review,* 1967, *32,* 699-715.

Blum, A. F. Theorizing. In J. D. Douglas (ed.), *Understanding everyday life.* Chicago:
AVC, 1970.

Brenner, M. Interviewing: The social phenomenology of a research instrument. In M. Brenner et al. (eds.), *The social context of method*. London: Groom Helm, 1978.

Brown, L. K. Familial dialectics in a clinical context. *Human Development*, 1975, *18*, 223-238.

Buck-Morss, S. Socio-economics bias in Piaget's theory and its implications for cross-cultural studies. *Human Development*, 1975, *18*, 35-49.

Buck-Morss, S. The Adorno legacy. *Personality and Social Psychology Bulletin*, 1977, *3*, 707-713.

Buss, A. R. (ed.). *Psychology in social context*. New York: Irvington, 1979.

Buss, A. R. *A dialectical psychology*. New York: Wiley, 1979.

Campbell, D. T. Ethnocentrism of disciplines and the fish-scale model of omniscience. In M. Sherif & C. W. Sherif (eds.), *Inter-disciplinary relationships in the social sciences*. Chicago: AVC, 1969.

Cartwright, D. Determinants of scientific progress: The case of research on the risky shift. *American Psychologist*, 1973, *28*, 222-231.

Chandler, M. J. Relativism and the problem of epistemological loneliness. *Human Development*, 1975, *18*, 171-180.

Collett, P. (ed.). *Social rules and social behavior*. Oxford, England: Basil Blackwell, 1977.

Connerton, P. (ed.). *Critical sociology: Selected readings*. Baltimore: Penguin, 1976.

Coulter, J. *The social construction of the mind*. London: Macmillan, 1979.

Cvetkovich, G. Dialectical perspectives on empirical research. *Personality and Social Psychology Bulletin*, 1977, *30*, 688-696.

Fay, B. *Social theory and political practice*. London: Holmes & Meier, 1976.

Finison, L. J. Unemployment, politics, and the history of organized psychology. *American Psychologist*, 1976, *31*, 747-755.

Freedle, R. Dialogue & inquiring systems: The development of a social logic. *Human Development*, 1975, *18*, 97-118.

Freiberg, J. W. *Critical sociology: European perspectives*. New York: Irvington, 1979.

Gadamer, H-G., *Truth and method*. New York: Seabury Press, 1975.

Gadamer, H-G. *Philosophical hermeneutics* (D. E. Linge, trans.). Berkeley: University of California Press, 1976.

Gadlin, H. & Ingle, G. Through a one-way mirror: The limits of experimental self-reflection. *American Psychologist*, 1975, *30*, 1003-1010.

Gadlin, H. Child discipline and the pursuit of self: An historical interpretation. *Advances in child development and behavior* (Vol. 12). New York: Academic Press, 1978.

Geertz, C. *Interpretations of cultures*. New York: Basic Books, 1973.

Gergen, K. J. Social psychology as history. *Journal of Personality and Social Psychology*, 1973, *26*, 309-320.

Gergen, K. J. Social psychology, science and history. *Personality and Social Psychology Bulletin*, 1976, *2*, 373-383.

Gergen, K. J. Experimentation in social psychology: A reappraisal. *European Journal of Social Psychology*, 1978, *8*, 507-527. (a)

Gergen, K. J. Toward generative theory in social psychology. *Journal of Personality and Social Psychology*, 1978, *36*, 1344-1360. (b)

Gergen, K. J. Social psychology and the phoenix of unreality. Centennial address presented at the American Psychological Association, New York, September 1979.

Gergen, K. J. Toward theoretical audacity in social psychology. In R. Gilmour & S. Duck (eds.), *The development of social psychology.* London: Wiley, in press. (a)

Gergen, K. J. *Toward transformation in social psychology.* New York: Springer-Verlag, in press. (b)

Giddens, A. *New rules of sociological method.* New York: Basic Books, 1976.

Ginsburg, G. P. (ed.). *Emerging strategies in social psychological research.* New York: Wiley, 1979.

Gorman, M. Prewar conformity research in social psychology: The approaches of Floyd H. Allport and Muzafer Sherif. *Journal of the History of the Behavioral Sciences,* 1979.

Gouldner, A. *The coming crises of western sociology.* New York: Basic Books, 1970.

Gross, E. & Stone, G. P. Embarrassment and the analysis of role requirements. *American Journal of Sociology,* 1963, *70,* 1-15.

Gross, G. Unnatural selection. In N. Armistead (ed.), *Reconstructing social psychology.* Baltimore: Penguin, 1974.

Harré, R. & De Waele, J-P. The ritual for incorporation of a stranger. In R. Harré (ed.), *Life Sentences.* New York: Wiley, 1976. Pp. 76-86.

Harris, A. E. Social dialectics and language: Mother and child construct the discourse. *Human Development,* 1975, *18,* 80-96.

Harrison, G. A bias in the social psychology of prejudice. In N. Armistead (ed.), *Reconstructing social psychology.* Baltimore: Penguin, 1974.

Hefner, R., Rebecca, M., & Oleshansky, B. Development of sex role transcendence. *Human Development,* 1975, *18,* 143-158.

Hirsch, E. D. *The aims of interpretation.* Chicago: University of Chicago Press, 1976.

Hogan, R. Dialectic aspects of moral development. *Human Development,* 1974, *17,* 107-117.

Hogan, R. T. & Emler, N. P. The biases in contemporary social psychology. *Social Research,* 1978, *45,* 478-634.

Holzkamp, K. *Kritische psychologie.* Frankfurt, Federal Republic of Germany: Fischer Taschenbuch Verlag, 1976.

Janousek, J. On the Marxian concept of praxis. In J. Israel & H. Tajfel (eds.), *The context of social psychology: A critical assessment.* London: Academic Press, 1972.

Jay, M. *The dialectical imagination.* London: Heinemann, 1973.

Kosok, M. The systematization of dialectical logic for the study of development and change. *Human Development,* 1976, *19,* 325-350.

Kreckel, M. Communicative acts and shared knowledge: A conceptual framework and its empirical application. In M. von Cranach & R. Harré (eds.), *The organization of human action.* Cambridge, England: Cambridge University Press, in press.

Kroger, R. Role theory and ethogeny: With special reference to the rules of address. Presented at the meeting of the American Psychological Association, New York, 1979.

Kvale, S. Dialectics and research on remembering. In N. Datan & H. W. Reese (eds.), *Life-span developmental psychology: Dialectical perspectives on experimental research.* New York: Academic Press, 1977.

Kytle, J. Ideology and planned change: A critique of two popular change strategies. *Personality and Social Psychology Bulletin,* 1977, *3,* 697-706.

Lawler, J. Dialectic philosophy and developmental psychology: Hegel and Piaget on contradiction. *Human Development,* 1975, *18,* 1-17.

Leontief, I. Theoretical assumptions and nonobserved facts. *American Economic Review*, 1971, *61*, 331-346.

Lubek, I. A note on the power and structure in social psychology. *Representative Research*, 1976, *7*, 87-88.

Lubek, I. A brief social psychological analysis of research on aggression in social psychology. In A. Buss (ed.), *Psychology in social context*. New York: Irvington, 1979.

Marsh, P. & Brenner, M. *The social context of method*. London: Croom Helm, 1978.

Marsh, P., Rosser, E., & Harré, R. *The rules of disorder*. London: Routledge & Kegan Paul, 1978.

McGrath, J. E. & Altman, I. *Small group research: a synthesis and critique of the field*. New York: Holt, Rinehart & Winston, 1966.

Meacham, J. A. A transactional model of remembering. In N. Datan & H. W. Reese (eds.), *Life-span developmental psychology: Dialectical perspectives on experimental research*. New York: Academic Press, 1972.

Meacham, J. A. A dialectic approach to moral development and self-esteem. *Human Development*, 1975, *18*, 159-170. (a)

Meacham, J. A. Patterns of memory abilities in two cultures. *Developmental Psychology*, 1975, *11*, 50-53. (b)

Mead, G. H. *Mind, self and society from the standpoint of a social behaviorist*. Chicago: University of Chicago Press, 1934.

Mischel, T. Psychological explanations and their vicissitudes. In W. J. Arnold (ed.), *Nebraska symposium on motivation* (Vol. 23), Lincoln: University of Nebraska Press, 1975, 133-204.

Mitroff, J. J. & Betz, F. Dialectic decision theory: A metatheory of decision making. *Management Science*, 1972, *19*, 11-24.

Morawski, J. G. The structure of social psychological communities: A framework for examining the sociology of social psychology. In L. H. Strickland (ed.), *Soviet and Western perspectives on social psychology*. Oxford, England: Pergamon Press, 1979.

Morawski, J. G. Early views of social psychology's progress. Presented at the meeting of the American Psychological Association, New York, 1979.

Morgenstern, D. Thirteen critical points in contemporary economic theory. *Journal of economic literarture*, 1972, *10*, 1164-1165.

Moscovici, S. Society and theory in social psychology. In J. Israel & H. Tajfel (eds.), *The context of social psychology: A critical assessment*. New York: Academic Press, 1972.

O'Donnell, J. The crisis of experimentalism in the 1920's: E. G. Boring and his uses of history. *American Psychologist*, 1979, *34*, 289-295.

Ossorio, P. G. *What actually happens*. Columbia: University of South Carolina Press, 1978.

Palmer, R. E. *Hermeneutics: Interpretation theory in Schleiermacher, Dilthey, Heidegger & Gadamer*. Evanston, Ill.: Northwestern University Press, 1969.

Pepitone, A. Toward normative and comparative social psychology. *Journal of Personality and Social Psychology*, 1976, *34*, 641-653.

Plon, M. On the meaning of the notion of conflict and its study in social psychology. *European Journal of Social Psychology*, 1974, *4*, 389-436.

Popper, K. R. *The poverty of historicism*. London: Routledge & Kegan Paul, 1957.

Psathas, G. (ed.). *Everyday language: Studies in ethnomethodology.* New York: Irvington, 1979.

Radnitzsky, G. *Contemporary schools of metascience.* Goteborg, Sweden: Scandinavia University Books, 1970.

Rappoport, L. On praxis and quasirationality. *Human Development,* 1975, *18,* 194-204.

Ray, L. J. Critical theory and positivism: Popper and the Frankfurt School. *Philosophy of Social Science,* 1979, *9,* 149-173.

Rebecca, M., Hefner, R., & Oleshansky, B. A model of sex-role transcendence. *Journal of Social Issues,* 1976, *32,* 197-206.

Reese, H. W. Discriminative learning and transfer: Dialectical perspectives. In N. Datan & H. W. Reese (eds.), *Life-span developmental psychology: Dialectical perspectives on experimental research.* New York: Academic Press, 1977.

Ricoeur, P. *Freud and philosophy: An essay on interpretation* (Denis Savage, trans.). New Haven, Conn.: Yale University Press, 1970.

Ricoeur, P. *Interpretation theory: Discourse and the surplus of meaning.* Fort Worth: Texas Christian University Press, 1976.

Riegel, K. Dialectic operations: The final period of cognitive development. *Human Development,* 1973, *16,* 346-370.

Riegel, K. The dialectics of human development. *American Psychologist,* 1976, *31,* 689-700. (a)

Riegel, K. From traits to equilibrium toward developmental dialectics. *Nebraska Symposium on Motivation.* Lincoln: University of Nebraska Press, 1976. (b)

Rommetveit, R. Language games, syntactic structures and hermeneutics. In J. Israel & H. Tajfel (eds.), *The context of social psychology: A critical assessment.* New York: Academic Press, 1972.

Rommetveit, R. On "emancipatory" social psychology. In L. H. Strickland et al. (eds.), *Social psychology in transition.* New York: Plenum, 1976.

Rowan, J. Research as intervention. In N. Armistead (ed.), *Reconstructing social psychology.* Baltimore: Penguin, 1974.

Rychlak, J. F. *A philosophy of science for personality theory.* Boston: Houghton-Mifflin, 1968.

Rychlak, J. F. Psychological science as a humanist views it. In W. J. Arnold (ed.), *Nebraska symposium on motivation,* 1975, *23,* 205-280.

Rychlak, J. F. *The psychology of rigorous humanism.* New York: Wiley, 1977.

Samelson, F. History, origin, myth, and ideology: Comte's "discovery" of social psychology. *Journal for the theory of social behavior,* 1974, *4,* 217-231.

Sameroff, A. Transactional models in early social relations. *Human Development,* 1975, *18,* 65-79.

Sampson, E. E. On justice as equality. *Journal of Social Issues,* 1975, *31,* 45-64.

Sampson, E. E. Psychology and the American ideal. *Journal of Personality and Social Psychology,* 1977, *35,* 767-782.

Sampson, E. E. Scientific paradigms and social values: Wanted—a scientific revolution. *Journal of Personality and Social Psychology,* 1978, *36,* 1332-1343.

Scheibe, K. E. The psychologist's advantage and its nullifications: Limits of human predictability. *American Psychologist,* 1978, *33,* 869-881.

Schutz, A. *Collected papers* (Vol. 1). The Hague, The Netherlands: Nijhoff, 1962.

Schwartz, B. The social psychology of the gift. *American Journal of Sociology,* 1967, *73,* 1-11.

Schwendinger, H. & Schwendinger, J. R. *The sociologists of the chair: A radical analysis of the formative years of North American sociology* (1883-1922). New York: Basic Books, 1974.

Shields, S. A. Functionalism, Darwinism & the psychology of women: A study in social myth. *American Psychologist,* 1975, *30,* 739-753.

Shotter, J. *Images of man in psychological research.* London: Methuen, 1975.

Shotter, J. What is it to be human? In N. Armistead (ed.), *Reconstructing social psychology.* Baltimore: Penguin, 1974.

Shotter, J. The cultural context of communication studies: Theoretical and methodological issues. In A. Lock (ed.), *Action, gesture and symbol.* London: Academic Press, 1978.

Silver, M. & Sabini, J. The social construction of envy. *Journal for the Theory of Social Behavior,* 1978, *8,* 313-332.

Smith, M. B. Psychology and values. *Journal of Social Issues,* 1978, *34,* 181-199.

Steiner, J. D. Whatever happened to the group in social psychology? *Journal of Experimental Social Psychology,* 1974, *10,* 94-108.

Steininger, M. Objectivity and value judgments in the psychology of E. L. Thorndike and W. McDougall. *Journal of the History of the Behavioral Sciences,* 1979, *15,* 263-281.

Stocking, G. On the limits of "presentism" and "historicism" in the historiography of the behavioral sciences. *Journal of the History of the Behavioral Sciences,* 1965, *1,* 211-219.

Strickland, L. H. The "power structure" in social psychology. *Representative Research in Social Psychology,* 1976, *7,* 79-86.

Sudnow, D. *Passing on: The social organization of dying.* Englewood Cliffs, N.J.: Prentice-Hall, 1967.

Taylor, C. *The explanation of behavior.* Atlantic Highlands, N.J.: Humanities Press, 1964.

Thomas, E. J. Role conceptions, organizational size and community context. In B. J. Biddle & E. J. Thomas (eds.), *Role theory: Concepts and research.* New York: Wiley, 1966. Pp. 164-170.

Van den Daele, L. D. Ego development and preferential judgment in life-span perspective. In N. Datan & L. H. Ginsburg (eds.), *Life-span developmental psychology: Normative life crises.* New York: Academic Press, 1975. (a)

Van den Daele, L. Ego development in dialectic perspective. *Human Development,* 1975, *18,* 129-142. (b)

Weeks, G. R. Toward a dialectical approach to intervention. *Human Development,* 1977, *20,* 277-292.

White, S. H. Social proof structure: The dialectic of method and theory in the work of psychology. In N. Datan & H. W. Reese (eds.), *Life-span developmental psychology: Dialectical perspectives on experimental research.* New York: Academic Press, 1977.

Wilson, T. P. Normative and interpretive paradigms in sociology. In J. D. Douglas (ed.), *Understanding everyday life.* Chicago: AVC, 1970.

Wolff, M. Notes on the behavior of pedestrians. In A. Birenbaum & E. Sagarin (eds.), *People in places: The sociology of the familiar.* New York: Praeger, 1973. Pp. 35-48.

Yaroshevskii, M. G. Categorical analysis of the evolution of psychology as an independent body of knowledge. *Soviet Psychology,* 1973, *12,* 23-52.

Ziller, R. C. Group dialectics: The dynamics of groups over time. *Human Development,* 1977, *20,* 293-308.

Zinn, H. *The politics of history.* Boston: Beacon Press, 1970.

Zuniga, R. B. The experimenting society and radical social reform. *American Psychologist,* 1975, *30,* 99-115.

Zurcher, L. A., Jr. The "friendly" poker game: A study of an ephemeral role. In A. Birenbaum & E. Sagarin (eds.), *People in places: The sociology of the familiar.* New York: Praeger, 1973. Pp. 155-174.